A Collector's Guide to Automobilia

Edited By John A. Gunnell

Published by

 **krause
publications**

700 E. State Street • Iola, WI 54990-0001
Telephone: 715/445-2214

Library of Congress Catalog Number: 94-75301
ISBN: 0-87341-295-8
Printed in the United States of America

Contents

Introduction

Face it, the only way you like to look at the world is through rose-colored driving goggles. You're an unabashed car buff who keeps collecting interesting memorabilia at every swap meet. You buy what you like, but have little idea of its history or whether you paid too much or too little to own it.

What do you know about your collectibles? What's their value? Which items should you keep ... which should you sell to someone else? How much should you sell them for? Most important of all, what's available that you would love to own and don't?

Automobilia is aimed at automotive memorabilia collectors who need basic information and value estimates. There are five main sections in *Automobilia*, plus an "Automobilia Price Guide."

This handy reference and guide can really rev up your collecting interests. Do you like the "hard stuff" like gas globes or license plates? Do you collect "old softies" like literature and auto ads? "Pumps, plates and parts" are collectible items, too, as are "kid stuff" such as toy trucks and model cars.

Automobilia begins with a thorough compilation of updated articles from the expert writers who work for *Old Cars*. Some authors who contributed to this book (with their specialty in parenthesis) are: Henry Austin Clark, Jr. (photos); Rolland Jerry (truck sales literature); Howard and Shelby Applegate (auto literature and factory photos); Bill McBride (auto ads); Jay Katelle (postcards); Neal East (car magazines); Paul Hatmon (gas station collectibles); Keith Marvin (license plates and international ovals); Tim Howley (hood ornaments); William Pollack (shaving mugs); Bob Lemke (coins); Al Marwick (toys); Neil McElwee (toys); Dennis Doty (models); Wayne Moyer (models); and John Jacobus (Fisher Body Craftsman's Guild models).

The book's main appeal is expert knowledge about a variety of memorabilia categories. The price guide gives values for items mentioned or pictured in *Automobilia*, in the order they appear in the book.

Section 1 called *"Old Softies,"* covers hand books; auto sales literature; the auto literature business; old car photos; sales catalog artwork; posters; trading cards; factory photos; postcards; Christmas cards; comparison auto ads; full-line car ads; auto ads (several checklists); car magazine collecting; and car postage stamps.

Section 2 called *"Pumps/Plates/Parts,"* covers visible gas pumps; gas pump globes; Red Crown valve caps; license plates; international ovals (country badges attached to license plates); British license plates; license plate "tag toppers"; antique turn signals; hood ornaments; Merle Norman's hood ornament collection; badges, nameplates and radiator scripts; general collectibles like screw-on hubcaps, spark plugs, priming cups; and taillight lenses.

Section 3 called *"The Hard Stuff,"* covers car shaving mugs; car tokens, coins and commemoratives; whiskey decanters; Jim Beam bottles; porcelain ad signs; parking meters; motoring garb; music videos (checklist); and bronze sculpture.

Section 4 called *"Toy Autos,"* covers: pedal cars; kid cars (juvenile autos); a historical survey of pedal cars; pressed steel antique toys; cast iron antique toys; Sears cast iron reproductions of 1920s toys made in 1970; Buddy L trucks; a Smith-Miller by Al Marwick; Lilian Gottshalk — toy collector; Chrysler Airflow toys; 1930s Erector Set; a *Mini-history* by Neil McElwee on Smith-Miller toys; Buddy L flivvers; Doepke construction toys; and *Mini-histories* by Neil McElwee — about Sturditoy and Conway toys.

Section 5 called *"Model Cars,"* covers 1978 dealer promotional models; Matchbox models; car dealer promotional models; how AMT makes a model car; 1/43-scale metal models; early model car kits; scratch-built models; die-cast and hand-built models; and Fisher Body Craftsman's Guild styling models.

The "Automobilia Price Guide" takes up the rear of the book, providing price *estimates* for all items in the book in Good, Very Good and Excellent condition.

In addition to history and prices, *Automobilia* supplies sources of factory photos; auto ad checklists; petroliana collecting hints; a fully updated listing of international ovals for hundreds of nations; a list of music videos with old cars in them; and a historical survey of pedal cars.

Old Softies

Handy hand books are valuable

By Henry Austin Clark, Jr.

Take a look at the classified ad section of any of the publications in our field, club or non-club, and you will find that old car literature, middle-aged car literature, and even new-car literature is getting to be an item. There are people collecting catalogs, and the like, that never bothered to get an old car, and in many cases never will.

Our own fascination with early automotive printed matter started before we were old enough to see over a steering wheel. Father had once owned Locomobiles and a Lorraine-Dietrich. He still had a couple of catalogs for each. The former had hard covers and looked like a book, which is why the 1911 and 1912 Locomobile catalogs are relatively plentiful now. There was something immoral about throwing away a bound book, just as there was about burning one. However, it's perfectly okay to heave out, or burn, a soft cover pamphlet. This is one reason there are not very many 1910 Lorraine-Dietrich catalogs on the tables down at the Hershey antique car meet ... or anywhere else for that matter.

When we expressed an interest, we were given these four items by father. They are still in our library, carefully marked. Later on, when we were first starting to gather-in the actual iron, we stumbled on a cache of 1912 Ford literature, too. From then on we were hooked.

Why, a sane person might ask, would anybody want to collect catalogs? Even worse, why would any-one collect instruction books for cars that one does not own, never will own, and frequently would turn down as a gift? Well, aside from the fact that one is already a nut of some sort, these things take up less room than the cars themselves. (Speaking of storage, I know a few car enthusiasts who have the latest edition of the *Encyclopedia Britanica* parked out in the rain, while a shelf load of catalogs bask in dry comfort. They do the same with their cars, putting the Tin Lizzie in the garage, while mother's Country Sedan develops wet-rot in the driveway, covered up by snow and ice.)

Another good reason for collecting automotive literature is that you can learn a good deal about your car, the car you wish you owned, and in fact any old car from the catalogs and other publications. Back in the old days (and even occasionally today) we see blatant evidence of the accumulated ignorance on the date and other pertinent data of an old car. The ads for 1898 Sears Motor Buggies and 1900 Brush Run-abouts still turn up. We know of one large Automotive Museum, which because the owner is a good guy will remain nameless, where all the Buicks and Cadillacs are pre-dated by one or two years.

Probably the best reason of all for collecting old catalogs and the like is that they are beautiful pieces of literature, and in many cases, the pride of the printer's art. "We have four color plates from a very early Pierce-Arrow catalog framed in the room where this typewriter sits. We would never have the nerve to tear them out of the catalog, but someone did before us, and now we enjoy them all the more.

What should a car collector look for in literature today, and how does he beat the enormous prices that the good pieces now command? Obviously, you would pay more for a catalog or manual for your car than one for a car you did not own. However, even if you have a low-priced car, the literature may not be cheap. If you have a Ford, you're lucky. Reproductions are available on almost all of the important

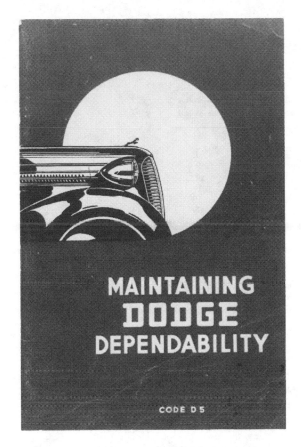

A page from the *Hand Book of Gasoline Automobiles 1904-1906* shows why these books are invaluable reference works. All the factory specifications are there, including original colors.

The 1936 Dodge owner's manual even had its own title. It was called *Maintaining Dodge Dependability*. Such manuals give information about the proper operation and mechanical care of antique autos.

pieces. Some of the one-make car clubs are also doing a good job reproducing literature on their specialties. Ones that come to mind are Chevrolet, Rolls-Royce, Pierce-Arrow and one or two others. Some put out separate reprints, and some include the reprint as part of their periodical. Either way it is great, and you can have the information for one twentieth of the cost of an original.

A few ambitious individuals, or clubs, have attempted reprinted shop manuals, in spite of their large numbers of pages. After all, when you are working on a car, there is nothing like the book the shop foreman at your friendly, neighborhood Durant agency used as his guide. A little hint for the avaricious; cultivate nice, old, retired shop foremen. Buy them an occasional boiler-maker at the local saloon. Some of them never throw anything away.

We are reminded of Bill Schellinger, shop foreman of the I.Y. Halsey Automobile Company in East Hampton, Long Island, New York. Our first meeting was back in 1946, when he helped us load a 1905 Cadillac Model F Touring on our nice new trailer. We had to take the Cadillac as part of the package with the other car, which was not in as good shape, but which we somehow wanted. The other car was a 1905 Pierce Great Arrow 28-32 horsepower touring car.

Schellinger muttered something about having a Peerless out at his place. Were we interested? Yes, we were! After some extended negotiations, we increased our offer. In fact, we doubled it to $100. That is how we came to own a rather sad 1903 Peerless two-cylinder chassis, which is no doubt one of the most difficult cars in the world to drive. Well, Bill Schellinger also had a house full of every piece of trade literature that ever came into the I.Y. Halsey Company. Eventually, some years later, we got it all.

Some of the most valuable things to the contemporary collector ... especially those who lavish loving care on the cars of the 1920s, 1930s and 1940s ... are the pages in *Chilton*, *MoToR*, and other consolidated all-make repair manuals. These books cover about four or five years of all American automobiles, telling a mechanic all he needs to know to maintain them and do ordinary repairs. In many cases, this is all the present owner needs to know. A point to remember, when you buy one for use with your 1937 Chevrolet,

Mechanically-inclined vehicle collectors will find the factory shop manual an important piece of literature. This one tells how to make repairs on the 1956 Ford trucks.

One-make car clubs and commercial dealers have reprinted shop manuals. This reprint of the *Kaiser and Frazer 1951 Models Shop Manual* included the supplements issued to cover changes in 1952 and 1953 models.

is to get a 1938 or 1939 edition. They won't be ready for you with the 1937 edition. Prices on these helpful books are still within reason today.

Another handy thing to have around is a set of hand books. What kind? Any damn kind you can get. The most famous set was introduced in 1904 by the Association of Licensed Automobile Manufacturers (ALAM). This was an august body formed of those automakers paying tribute to the infamous Selden Patent. (Not everybody belonged, the most notable exception being the Ford Motor Company.) *The Hand Book of Gasoline Automobiles* was the best buy of the automobile world, being sent out to anyone, on receipt of a three-cents stamp. With a 1904 edition now having a floor price of $75, having one was better than being in on the Teapot Dome scandal. Legal too. For some mysterious reason, the ALAM ceased to publish after the 1911 edition. Perhaps because that was the year Henry Ford won his Selden Patent lawsuit. In any case, the 1912 and 1913 editions were put out by something called the Automobile Board of Trade. From 1914 on through 1929, the National Automobile Chamber of Commerce took over, continuity being maintained by calling the 1914 issue the 11th Annual. In late 1929 something else upset the automobile world ... the depression. Stock brokers took dives out of downtown windows, and publication of the hand book ended forever. A thousand bucks is not an unreasonable price for a full mint set today. Don't hold out for all hard covers, as 1904 did not have them. Also, 1929 didn't have a soft cover edition, but those in between had both, for proletariat or executive. Our favorite has inscribed in Spencerian script: "Not to be removed from the desk of Windsor T. White." Somebody must have disregarded the edict, because it isn't there any more.

Come off it, you say, who has a thousand clams to toss around for one armful of books? Somebody must, because you never see a second advertisement. However, you don't have to. Fortunately, a number of these have been reprinted by Floyd Clymer and, more recently, by Dover Press. Another fine little book that fits in this category is *The Automobiles of 1904*, a reprint by Americana Review, which has dope on 88 cars.

The ultimate rarity in the hand book line is called *MoToR's Directory of Motor Cars*. It was published from 1906 through 1913 and perhaps earlier and later (although we have never seen such ones). It contains information about all Selden Patent licensees, plus the products of every gasoline auto maker in the United States. It also includes steam and electric cars, plus a lot of foreign vehicles. The same data is in *MoToR* magazine of the same years in somewhat spread out form. It's much easier to read in the directory.

Collecting auto sales literature is an alternative in apartment age

By Rolland Jerry

Your interests probably include automobiles, automotive engineering and, perhaps, coach building and body work. Maybe they run to such diverse areas as typography, the evolution of advertising and social and economic history.

That's quite a spread of interests, but you can satisfy all of them (and a good many more) by collecting automobile sales catalogs ... the tide of booklets, brochures and promotional material issued by dealers and agents since the dawn of the automobile.

The object of literature course was to impress, flatter, persuade, inform and cajole car buyers to make their choice. Apparently it works. Manufacturers still spend millions on "collateral material," which is advertising agency jargon for the booklets and folders intended as selling aids for the dealer force.

Many modern sales literature items are expensive today. With rising prices some cost on the order of 75 cents to $1 apiece to produce. This is high for catalog material printed by the thousands. Special purpose promotional pieces cost even more.

It's not surprising that at least one manufacturer now sells his catalogs to dealers for a nominal charge and other companies are examining the idea. There's another point in this besides economics; if dealers have to pay for the material they'll make better use of it, or so it is hoped. The collecting of sales catalogs is a specialized field of automobilia in its own right and it's an interest that's growing by leaps and bounds. Evidence of the new activity is quite apparent in the "Literature Wanted" and "Literature For Sale" columns in *Old Cars*.

I started my collection years ago ... before the war if sundry schoolboy odds and ends are included ... but not really in earnest until the early postwar years. Material was certainly much easier to come by then than it is now, but it's still around if one is willing to wait, "scratch" and search.

With car prices fast climbing out of sight, catalog collecting ... automotive philately, if you will ... is an economic and an attractive alternative to car ownership. Ownership of an old car can be a burden, at times, for reasons too numerous and familiar to relate. Then, there are collectors who have less interest in the cars themselves than in the catalogs, not an unusual characteristic among established collectors. By any standard, though, catalog collecting has a lot going for it.

All that's needed to start building a collection is a filing case and perhaps a few binders. Of course, assembling a collection takes time. It can't be done overnight (although many specimens can be purchased quickly, at stiff prices).

This brings up the investment angle in collection. Many catalogs, even fairly recent ones, fetch healthy prices these days. The high prices asked for some material are in line with the rarity, of course. Many catalogs were almost as scarce when new as they are now. Big, all-line catalogs for such makes as Mercedes, Hispano-Suiza, Isotta-Fraschini, Rolls-Royce, Cadillac and Packard, were hardly more numerous in their heyday. Usually, one had to buy the car to get the catalog.

Few were literally ever free for the asking and, of course, they were never, never generously dispensed to car-crazy, catalog-collecting schoolboys, if it could be helped.

With British and European cars, there was a sure fire way to get around this. A letter to the factory or a main London dealer, using names and addresses gleaned from *The Autocar* or *MoToR*, always produced results. Repeatedly so, if one's letters were decently spaced over proper intervals.

Catalog styles and formats haven't changed much down through the years, although there have been strides in the use of color, letter press and reproduction methods. Photography has been improved to the extent that "living" color is basic for any piece.

Actually, color photography was in use by 1914 and, perhaps, earlier. My 1914 Rolls-Royce catalog has color photographs taken by Percy Northey, a well known Rolls-Royce personality and director at the time. The artwork is described as "natural color," so presumably it was done with a photographic process, not tinting.

Pierce-Arrow made the same claim in its 1930 catalog, which was a full color job of impressive magnitude. I have seen early Ford promotional material for the Model T, perhaps 1911 or 1912, in which some of the work was executed in color. Presumably, hand-colored photographs were used that early in the catalog art.

There were essentially three styles or formats for sales material. First, there's the "proper" catalog with its gathered pages secured by binding, staples or stitching. It's still widely used. Then, there was the saver concept, a much smaller piece of literature in pamphlet or folder configuration, usually a two- or four-pager. The name is drawn from the purpose of this piece, which was to save the good catalogs for more likely sales prospects. Schoolboys and the public at large got the saver, but customers ready to sign could be persuaded with an impressive catalog. Lastly, was the costly and impressive folio presentation. This

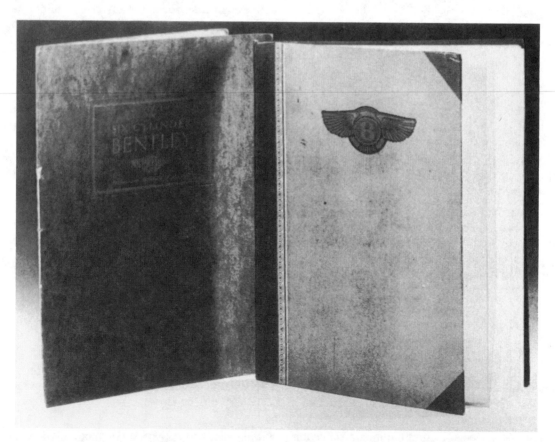

Sales catalog number 27 for the six-cylinder Bentley 6.5-litre model was printed in October 1928. It includes eight monochromatic art plates showing different body styles and a color-tinted frontispiece.

Jaguar literature is very collectible, in both prewar and postwar editions.

was a full-blown presentation with all the trappings, often including numbering and an attached card from the company president or sales manager.

In the catalog line, the most desirable item is usually the big all-liner which contains everything the manufacturer had to offer, either completely or by car range and series. Many also include a folio of tip-in mounted plates. Folios were much favored by the manufacturers of expensive cars, as well as by coach builders, to accommodate drawings and renderings of specialist coach work choices.

Many vintage folios embody decorated initials, heavy board binders (or even boxes), coupled with mounted pictures, set off in matt style by embossed margins. It's difficult to think of a quality manufacturer who didn't use the folio format at one time or another. The last American folio edition that I am aware of was the 1954 Kaiser Manhattan, a comprehensive 10-plate affair, in full color, contained in an outer box-type packet. It may have been general dealer issue. It was very elaborate and quite different from the rest of the company's rather standard literature.

Rolls-Royce offered a brochure-folio piece in 1969 for North American circulation. Rolls-Royce uses other sales material on the British home market. This is preferable, in my estimation, to the North American variety with its strong "Gee whiz, what a car" theme. The plates are contained on the last page or in the last fold of the open-out brochure.

Savers were produced in many varieties. They range from simple and cheap pamphlets to small scale facsimiles of the main all line catalog. Many were very elaborate. I have one, for the 1912 Panhard range, which is every bit as good as the larger catalog. The same applies to Renault's savers for the period; a few later Renault catalogs are less desirable, due to bad artwork.

Good quality "jumbo" catalogs are nice additions to any collection. The largest one I have is Pierce-Arrow's all-liner for 1930. It measures 10-1/4 by 16-3/4 inches or 30-odd inches across the spread. Packard's jumbo catalog for 1927 and 1928 runs a close second in size at 10 by 13-1/2 inches, with a spread in proportion.

These are big catalogs in other ways too. The Pierce-Arrow edition has 35 pages and the Packard catalog has 23 pages, plus a four-page supplement inserted into the catalog in January 1928, for later models.

It's difficult to see the reasoning behind jumbo catalogs on this scale. The largeness and unwieldiness were so apparent that creasing and tearing would have been virtually unavoidable, no matter how carefully they were handled. Nor could they have been mailed very easily (and this was a time when many catalogs were mailed). Perhaps mailing tubes were used, which seems at odds with the nature and the purpose of these extravaganzas.

Hard cover, bound books were also used for catalog presentations. Locomobile had its *Book of the Locomobile*. It is still a fairly common item. Packard went to a large format (8-3/4 by 12 inches) 39-page hard cover presentations for the Twin-Six. Mine is undated, but appears to be from around 1919 or, perhaps, earlier.

Sales literature from Swallow Sidecar, which later became Jaguar.

Certainly, one of the most impressive and costly productions in the past 40-odd years was Rolls-Royce's 44-page, 9-1/2 by 13-inch catalog for the Phantom I. My two copies were issued in 1938 and 1939, but could have been a year or so earlier. The copy is treated like an illuminated address, while all pictures are in color and mounted. Pull-out gate folds show the prospect what he was getting in a chassis (in fact, all he got from Rolls-Royce at the time). The catalog was printed on a very heavy parchment stock, the result being more of a document than a sales catalog.

Mercedes literature has been excellent for many years and, of course, still is. The separate catalogs for the 500, 540 and the Grosser Mercedes cars are exceptionally nice items with outstanding artwork and, in some instances, mounted glossy photographs. Daimler-Benz used a jumbo format in the 1920s for some of its cars. A switch to separate catalogs for each series, in the 1930s, was an improvement.

Current Mercedes sales material is well worth the effort in collecting. It's perhaps the finest work of its kind (all photographic) by any manufacturer. But, there are most assuredly other catalogs of equal merit and appeal. Cadillac's all-liner for 1970 is as nice as anything the company has ever done, although it's understandingly light on technicalities and specifications. However, as a piece of catalog art, it will be a valued item in the not too distant future.

Similarly, the massive 50-plus page jumbos, issued in recent years by Buick and Pontiac, ought to be picked up now while they are still conveniently available. Both are big format pieces, on the order of l0 x 13 inches. They are beautifully executed on high-grade stock, with artwork and reproduction to match. But again, there's an absence of technical content, which makes many of the vintage catalogs so interesting. In fact, the technical content is often the basis of their charm, besides being valuable for research.

Modern art directors equate technicalities with shop manuals. They don't feel that they belong in sales material. Actually, car manufacturers take the same stand, too. Obviously, historians in the future will have to look elsewhere for this information, when they are researching today's cars.

Catalog collecting has its own brand of disappointments. I hunted for some few years for something on the French Farman, which was a car built in very small numbers in the 1920s. Eventually, I came across a Farman saver, but only on the firm's aero engines. There was some artwork on the car, but it was so bad that the vehicle depicted could have been any car.

An Austro-Daimler catalog has escaped me so far, but not literature about the firm's vintage commercial vehicles and industrial air-cooled engines. With the nature of catalog collecting and the way collections grow, maybe the next letter will bring what I'm seeking. The fun of the treasure is in the hunt.

Literature as a restoration tool

By Howard and Shelby Applegate

Most hobbyists know that automotive sales and service literature is collected widely by a variety of enthusiasts. What is not realized, to any great extent, is the fact that the majority of people who are buying literature in today's marketplace are restorers, mechanics, owners of repair shops and individuals who make or sell reproduction parts. This contradicts the widespread belief that most automotive literature is acquired by literature collectors. To be sure, the paper collectors do buy a certain percentage of auto literature that is being sold, but these sales are minuscule compared to the purchasers of literature for restoration purposes. Although some individuals are both literature collectors and restorers, they often acquire different types of literature for each separate aspect of their hobby.

Anyone restoring a vehicle must be aware of the fact that in order to maintain, and in fact increase, the value of a collectible vehicle, it must be restored according to exact factory specifications. If a car is ever to be shown, it must be restored exactly, because show judging is very strict to the smallest detail. Even if a car or truck is not intended to be shown, but is only being restored for the owner's own amusement and amazement, it should be recognized that properly restored cars are worth more on the market than poorly restored cars. If it's worth doing, it's worth doing right.

Automotive literature is an indispensable aid to vehicle restorers. This article will outline the various types of automotive paper that restorers need for their work. There are so many types of literature available on the market, that it is often difficult for the restorer to determine priorities in the acquisition of literature to use in the restoration process. Three primary categories of automotive literature are of interest to restorers: service and repair literature; marketing and sales promotional literature; and restoration literature. Not all literature in each category is of equal importance. Yet, it is urgent that the restorer acquire literature on the basis of some priority plan.

Most restorers and mechanics seek service and repair literature first, even if their vehicle does not require immediate repair or restoration. They know that cars and trucks must be maintained properly and may require future repairs or rebuilding. Included in this category are: owner, service and repair manuals; parts books; vehicle diagrams and charts; and service bulletins and memos.

All new vehicles come equipped with an owner's manual. The purchasers of pre-owned, collector vehicles, however, might not find one in the glove compartment after their acquisition. This item's usually the first thing the restorer seeks. The owner's manual (also called owner's guide, driver's manual, operator's manual, instruction manual or handbook of information) contains basic instructions on driving controls, simple operational guidelines, comfort and convenience features, accessories, regular care and general maintenance, specifications and service information. For example, the owner's manual explains how to operate all knobs, buttons and levers on the instrument panel and dashboard. For certain years of certain makes, there may be specialized owner's manuals for such things as the radio and stereo, the convertible top or the air conditioning system.

A more advanced manual was called a reference book. This often was a combination of the basics of the owner's manual with some of the nuts and bolts instructions of the service manual. Reference books

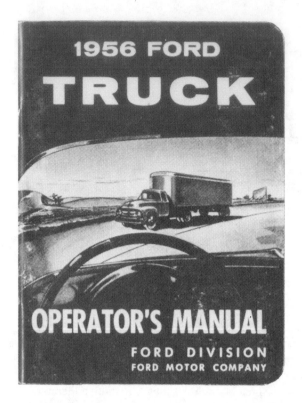

The *1956 Ford Truck Operator's Manual* covers break-in, maintenance, valve adjustments and torque specs.

AUBURN-CORD COLOR SCHEDULE
Auburn-Cord Page 1

DITZ-LAC INTERMIX SYSTEM

Auburn 1931 Models

COMBINATIONS	BODY AND FENDERS	RAISED PORTIONS	WHEELS	STRIPE
	All 8-98 Standard and Custom Body Types			
No. 10	Black	Black	Black	Gold
	8-98A (Custom) Sedan, Brougham, Coupe			
11	Homage Blue Deep (IM-1020)	Black	Black	Silver
	8-98A (Custom) Sedan, Brougham and Coupe			
12	Toga Maroon (IM-1063)	Black	Black	Gold
	8-98A (Custom) Phaeton, Sedan and Cabriolet			
13	Toga Maroon (IM-1063)	Carmine (IM-57)	Carmine	Carmine
	8-98A (Custom) Phaeton, Sedan and Cabriolet			
14	Beaver Brown (IM-957)	Black	Black	Cream

Cord 1931 Models

Sedan

Black	Black	White	
Ceylon Blue D. D. (IM-800)	Black	Black	Cream
Toga Maroon (IM-1063)	Black	Black	Gold
Cepheus Green (IM-633)	Paul Revere Green (IM-291)	Cream	Cream
Fawn (IM-956)	Beaver Brown (IM-957)	Beaver Brown	Gold
Pearl	Black	Black	Silver

Broughams

Black	Black	White	
Toga Maroon (IM-1063)	Black	Black	Gold
Cepheus Green (IM-633)	Paul Revere Green (IM-291)	Cream	Cream

Cabriolets

Gainsborough Blue (IM-342)	Blue Boy Blue (IM-948)	Blue Boy Blue	Silver
Fawn (IM-956)	Beaver Brown (IM-957)	Beaver Crown	Gold
Catseye Gray (IM-1044)	Wood Smoke Green (IM-159)	Catseye Gray	Green
Black	Black	White	

Phaeton Sedan

Venetian Sand (IM-1053)	Harding Blue (IM-63)	Harding Blue	Blue
Cepheus Green (IM-633)	Paul Revere Green (IM-291)	Cream	Cream
Black	Black	White	
Gainsborough Blue (IM-342)	Blue Boy Blue (IM-948)	Blue Boy Blue	Silver
Catseye Gray (IM-1044)	Wood Smoke Green (IM-159)	Catseye Gray	Green

1932 Auburn Colors

BODY COLOR	RAISED PORTIONS	TOP OF HOOD, COWL, ETC.	WHEELS
Gray Sequence (IM-249)	Brown Sequence (IM-425)		Light Spanish Tile
Regal Green (IM-693)	Tarragon Green (IM-525)		Cream (IM-517)
Cat's Eye Gray (IM-1044)	Wood Smoke Green (IM-215)		
Auburn Blue (IM-805)	Black	Carlton Blue (IM-825)	
Saxon Gray (IM-491)	Ravenswood Brown (IM-425)	Cedric Brown (IM-136)	
Preston Green (IM-736)	Pitch Pine Green (IM-862)		
Gun Metal Gray (IM-111)	Black	Bedford Gray (IM-587)	
Old Ivory (IM-495)	No. 4 Red (IM-536)		

1933 AUBURN COLORS
Model 8-105 Salon

COMBINATION	BODY	FENDERS	RAISED PORTIONS	WHEELS
No. 1	Black	Black	Black	White
No. 2	Saxon Gray (IM-491)	Ravenswood Brown (IM-425)	Ravenswood Brown	Cream
No. 3	Salon Blue (IM-48)	Black	Black	Cream
No. 4	Preston Green (IM-736)	Preston Green	Pitch Pine (IM-862)	Cream
No. 5	LaCrosse Beige (IM-1251)	LaCrosse Beige	Buckeye Brown (IM-71)	Buckeye Brown
No. 6	Mountain Green Light (IM-1434)	Mountain Green Light	Mountain Green (IM-1435)	Cream
No. 7	Mountain Green (IM-1435)	Mountain Green	Mountain Green Light (IM-1434)	Cream

Model 12-165 Salon

No. 8	Black	Black	Black	White
No. 9	Berwick Brown (IM-425)	Grisette Brown Dark (IM-969)	Grisette Brown Dark	Tan
No. 10	Iceland Green No. 1 (IM-1133)	Iceland Green No. 1	Iceland Green No. 4 (IM-1103)	Cream
No. 11	Salon Blue (IM-48)	Salon Blue	Black	Cream
No. 12	Desert Sand (IM-1275)	Desert Sand	Auburn Tan (IM-1267)	Casino Red
No. 13	Marine Blue Light (IM-1279)	Marine Blue Light	Marine Blue Deep (IM-1259)	Cream

This Ditz-Lac paint chart for 1931-1933 Auburns and Cords lists colors for body and fenders, moldings, wheels and stripes.

were published primarily in the 1915-1934 period, although both Ford and Chevrolet divisions have reintroduced reference books for certain vehicles. For the 1978 Mercury cars, Ford published a concise reference publication entitled *1978 Mercury Owners Maintenance and Light Repair Manual.* Cougar owners could also buy special reference tools on electrical system troubleshooting and wiring. The modern reference books are really do-it-yourself service manuals, based on the assumption that a semi-skilled person can perform certain routine, service and maintenance procedures. The owner is given 100 pages of details on lubrication, tune-up, lighting, tire and shocks, cooling, brakes and clutch, body and chrome and minor troubleshooting.

The manuals that contain much more detail for the mechanic or restorer are called service or shop manuals. These books are prepared for use of dealership service employees, garage and service station mechanics and those owners whose mechanical skills are significantly above average. A typical shop manual contains detailed information on such subjects as: lubrication, frame, body, chassis, suspension, power accessories, engine cooling, fuel and exhaust systems, transmissions, drive shaft and rear axle, electrical system, heating, venting and cooling, sheet metal and instrument panels. Usually, shop manuals are profusely illustrated, including break-down and reassembly diagnosis. In some years, the manufacturers issued separate shop manuals for the body and the chassis. Occasionally, a manufacturer did not publish a shop manual in a model year, but instead issued a supplement to the previous year's complete shop manual. For example, owners of 1964 Corvettes must purchase the *1964 Corvette Shop Manual* supplement (manual number ST-34), but this publication will not help the restorer, unless used in conjunction with the *1963 Corvette Shop Manual* (manual number ST-21).

Service manuals do not contain all the information that a mechanic or restorer might need with regard to parts, especially the part number and illustrations of original parts. The latter information is most useful if parts are missing or damaged. This data may be found in parts books which have illustrations of every major part, both chassis and body, all of which will be numbered. Price lists of parts will rarely be of any use in restoration, except perhaps as a historical footnote. Vehicle diagrams and charts are also useful in the restoration process. Of greatest value are those illustrating the wiring or electrical systems. Lubrication and tune-up charts can assist the owner with routine maintenance.

THIS NEW 1934 PLYMOUTH HAS *Everything!*

Individual Springing, Floating Power . . . Safety-Steel Body and Hydraulic Brakes

THIS YEAR—be comfortable! Ride smoothly! Ride swiftly, safely! Don't let a small-car pocketbook keep you from enjoying a "big-car" ride.

Every Plymouth model—no matter what the price—has Plymouth's new individual front wheel springing.

There's no axle to transfer shocks from one wheel to another. There's no more of the jolting, jouncing, nose-bouncing "tramp" that a rough road used to develop in a low-priced car!

And the big, husky 77-horsepower motor is cradled in Floating Power engine mountings. You get smoothness—because you have the only basic solution of engine vibration!

Then look at the body—it's of steel, reinforced with steel! Protection, at all times. Long life and quiet, too! All joints are permanently welded together.

And try hydraulic brakes just once. Smooth, sure, positive stops every time!

Brakes can never become unequalized . . . because the pressure must always be the same on all four wheels!

Longer life from your brake linings, too—because pressure *is* equal.

Yes, this new Plymouth has every-

Now—perfected ventilation—on all the De Luxe models—the whole front window drops and the windshield opens.

thing the American family wants. It has comfort. It has power. It has safety. And a glance at the picture shows it has style.

See the new Plymouth—ride in it! Any Dodge, DeSoto or Chrysler dealer stands ready, any time, to give you a complete demonstration—without the slightest cost or obligation. Get in touch *now* with the dealer nearest to you.

GOODBYE BOUNCING! Plymouth's individual Wheel Springing lets you forget the condition of the road. Each front wheel has its own individual spring. There is no front axle. That means a bumpless ride on any road.

IT'S THE *Best Engineered* CAR IN THE LOW-PRICE FIELD

This advertisement from the March 1934 issue of *Cosmopolitan* shows the "old" series 1934 Plymouth with its fully-vertical-louvers hood. This is actually a leftover 1933 model that was re-titled as a 1934.

Mechanics also find certain general service publications of use to them, including the generic category of national industry repair manuals, which are how-to-fit-it type books. Included are such publications as, *Chilton's Repair Manuals, MoToR's Repair Manuals* and similar books printed by Audels, Glenn and TAB Books. National repair manuals are usually hardbound and contain several hundred pages of repair and tune-up data of great interest to mechanics and restorers. These books generally covered a period of six or seven years for most makes manufactured during that period. A person restoring a 1941 Packard Model 110 coupe would need the manual covering 1934-1941. Chilton's and TAB now publish books on certain makes for, specified years; for example, Plymouth Barracuda 1964-1974.

Some aspects of collector vehicle repair and maintenance are not covered in service publications, especially in those books and manuals printed prior to the beginning of the specific model year. Many service and repair problems that crop up during the model year are covered in specialized articles published in periodical service bulletins or company service memos sent to dealerships. For example, the *Pontiac Craftsman Service News* for June 1963 featured a new technique for correcting tilt steering column noise and 32 other similar subjects. Buick dealer letter number 64-33 covered a new procedure for changing the engine oil Pump pressure relief valve on 1964 models.

Marketing and sales promotional literature is of great importance to the restorer, but less important to the mechanic. Included in this category are sales catalogs, accessory literature, factory photos, dealer materials, original magazine advertisements and commercial body and equipment books. In general, sales literature must be used with discretion, because illustrations and specifications are often printed before the model year begins, and any changes made thereafter, in vehicles or specifications, are usually not reflected in literature revisions.

The catalogs and folders that dealers place in showroom racks are called sales literature. They include basic vehicle specifications and detailed illustrations (sometimes photographic, but usually illustrative) for most models and series. Sometimes illustrations can be a poor guide for restorers, because creative artists sometimes take artistic license. They may draw the vehicle in a manner unlike its appearance in real life. Artists make a great effort to make the illustration look right to the eye. Length, height or width can be altered. Both exterior and interior appearance can also be modified by inadvertent changes in trim, molding, upholstery or colors. Artists might elongate a hood, exaggerate a fender sweep or widen a grille. They do all this with an eye towards making the car more attractive. By the time the artist interprets the car and paints it and the printer tries to match the printing ink to the paint, the color may be far removed from the actual factory color. Thus, the colors used in sales literature are not the paints used on the vehicles. (See reference below with regard to paint charts.) Sales literature often does have detailed illustrations of interiors, engines, accessories and options.

Sales literature is particularly useful for dating vehicles. It is very common, particularly before 1950, for a vehicle to be titled the year in which it was sold, rather than the model year. For instance, upon consulting a 1939 DeSoto catalog, the owner of a car titled in 1939 discovers that the car is not a 1939 model. In checking the 1938 catalog, the owner determines that the car is really a 1938. Authentication of the year is sometimes made difficult if the manufacturer (like Plymouth sometimes did) re-titles leftover cars as "old" series 1933 models and titles all new models as "new" series 1933 cars.

The person who buys a collector car for restoration often discovers that, during the vehicle's lifetime, a replacement grille or replacement lamps, door handles, hubcaps, trim pieces and bumpers have been installed. The previous owners may have only selected parts that happened to fit, rather than acquiring the right parts. Sales literature can aid the restorer in pinpointing such errors.

Factory photographs and original magazine ads are also useful to restorers. They illustrate what the vehicle should have looked like when it was new. Most factory photos are 8 x 10 in size and printed in black and white on glossy paper. Restorers must be sure that the factory photos are either originals or copies of original factory issues. They should check that the photos are not shots taken at antique automobile shows. Amateur photos of vehicles exhibited at antique auto shows are of limited value, especially if the car was not restored to original condition and specifications. Photos of prototypes, experimental cars, dream cars, show cars, factory mock-ups or artwork are not useful either.

Most manufacturers placed ads in major national periodicals. These original magazine advertisements are useful but the restorer must be wary of artistic change and remember not to use ads to justify paint colors. Mercury announced one special spring color, Pink Lustre. It appears on the 1964 color chart, but may not show up other places. In 1958, Dodge issued a special color chart just for spring colors.

Many manufacturers printed special literature, each model year, promoting the sale of accessories and options. This type of sales literature is most helpful to restorers, because these publications usually con-

17.31

REAR WINDOW WIPER

18.09

With the wide expanse of sloping glass in the rear windows of modern cars, a Rear Window Wiper is a practical necessity. Vacuum operated with control on the instrument panel, rain cannot obscure driver's rear vision.

VENTSHADES

Ventshades allow windows to be partially open for fresh air to circulate no matter how hard it rains or snows; prevent condensation from fogging the windshield and windows; and protect eyes from sun glare. Ventshades fit into the window frames, and blend with the car's lines. Made of stainless steel, they are highly polished on the outside and finished in soft green on the inside. They won't rust or corrode.

AIR CIRCULATOR

The wide sloping rear window may become "fogged" or frosted in rainy weather, and the driver's rear vision is obscured. The air circulator, controlled by a switch on the dash, quickly clears steam or frost from the window.

13.92

WINDSHIELD VISOR

The KF Windshield Visor is a "year 'round" accessory. In winter months the visor minimizes snow glare and helps to keep the windshield free of snow, sleet and freezing rain when car is parked. In summer, visor protects against direct rays of sun and glare, making driving more enjoyable.

HEAVY DUTY PURPOSE OIL FILTER AND ELEMENT

Not only filters the oil very efficiently, but cools it as well. Its exclusive finning arrangement draws excessive heat from the oil body, lessening oil consumption. The cartridge effectively removes dirt and carbon from the oil, thus increasing the life of the lubricant, reducing engine wear, and resulting in better performance and economy.

14.10

LUSTER-SEAL HAZE CREAM

While Haze Cream is primarily designed to use after Lustur-Seal has been applied, it is an excellent polish on any type finish. For painted, enameled or lacquered finish and for chromium or glass parts. Equally good for household refrigerators. etc.

Here's a page from a Kaiser-Frazer accessories booklet showing available extras like the rear window wiper, air circulator and windshield visor. A Kaiser salesman penciled prices for each item in the margin of the catalog.

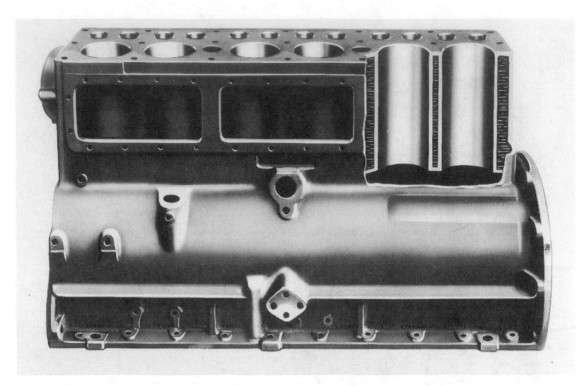

Parts catalogs contain illustrations that are helpful to vintage vehicle restorers. The cut-away view of a six-cylinder engine seen here is from the *1929 Oakland Master Parts Catalog*.

tain illustrations of accessories. Car show judges must accept accessory literature as evidence that a certain accessory could be installed or was intended to be installed on a specific vehicle. Usually, accessory catalogs were printed in limited numbers. This makes such literature both scarce and expensive. Accessory price lists have limited value, because they lack illustrations and any details of operation.

Other types of special restoration literature have proved helpful to hobbyists. Restoration guides have been published on many major makes. These books outline what needs to be done to restore a vehicle to its original condition. Interchange manuals, such as *Hollander's Interchange Manual*, provide information on what major component parts were used on various makes for a specific period of time and what substitutes can be interchanged by part, part manufacturer and vehicle manufacturer. Restoration road tests report how a restored car should do in performance testing. Club publications provide information on specific makes and bring restorers into contact with other owners. Marque registers print detailed listings of ownership records, again enabling restorers to contact other owners. The *Old Cars Price Guide*, published every other month, keeps restorers abreast of current market pricing trends. Hobby-periodicals like *Old Cars* provide automotive information on a multiplicity of levels.

It is all well and good to know what literature is helpful to mechanics and restorers, but it is another matter to find this paper. Reading *Old Cars* (Krause Publications, 700 E. State Street, Iola, WI 54990) can help in two basic ways. First, the "literature for sale" classified column identifies professional literature dealers and others who sell literature occasionally. Some dealers are specialists by type of literature (i.e. owner's manuals) or by make or company (i.e. Ford or Chevrolet), but most will be pleased to receive your list of literature wants. *Old Cars* "calendar of events" section will alert you to car shows, flea markets and swap meets where literature may be sold.

Those searching for literature are generally better off attending only the larger national or regional type flea markets. Local swap meets rarely have many vendors, much less vendors who specialize in literature. When attending flea markets, meet the various literature dealers and find out who sells what. Ask other collectors and restorers about their reputation. Most literature dealers will search out items for customers or refer them to other reputable dealers. The more you shop around, either in the pages of hobby publications or at flea markets, the better idea you will have about literature values and prices. In the field you can see literature before you buy it. It should be examined carefully for flaws and imperfections.

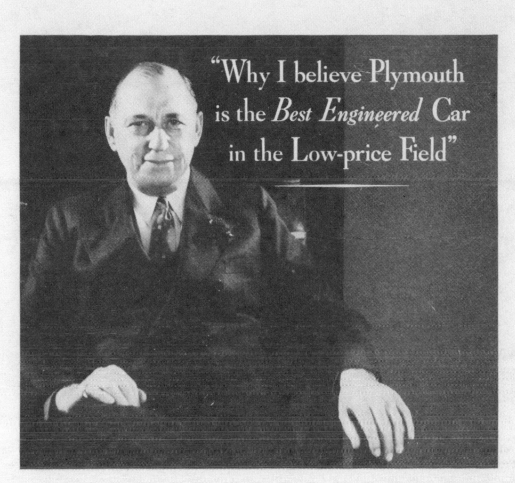

"Why I believe Plymouth is the *Best Engineered* Car in the Low-price Field"

by *Walter P. Chrysler*

"OUR BUSINESS has been very good. At this time, I believe people will be interested in knowing why. To put it as simply as I know how — our engineers have built into Plymouth the *things people want!*

"To make cars safer to drive and ride in, they developed hydraulic brakes and pioneered in the use of safety-steel bodies.

"Perhaps the biggest thing they achieved is patented Floating Power—which does away with vibration. This year, in addition, even the lowest priced Plymouth has individual wheel springing.

"These two features give you a more comfortable ride than ever.

"I've always believed that people wanted these things, not only in expensive cars but in cars workingmen could own. The public's response convinces me I was right.

"I credit our present position in the industry to these engineering achievements. I sincerely believe Plymouth is the best engineered car in the low-price field —because it is the only low-priced car that has all of them."

• • •

THE FEATURES Mr. Chrysler mentions here cannot *all* be found in any other low-priced car. Arrange to take a ride in a new Plymouth —and see how they add to your satisfaction in driving a car.

DE LUXE PLYMOUTH, America's biggest low-priced car.

Depicted in this advertisement, along with Walter P. Chrysler, is the "new" series 1934 Plymouth with vertical louvers only on the forward half of the hood side panels. The rear has horizontal vents. This is the real 1934 model.

The catalogs and folders that dealers place in showroom racks are called sales literature. They include basic vehicle specifications and detailed illustrations. This 16-page 1962 Buick booklet is worth about $12.

When buying from magazine or newspaper advertisements, insist that the literature dealer give a money-back guarantee so the item may be returned if it is not as advertised or listed.

Restorers have a variety of helpful automotive literature available to them. As with most other things today, literature is not cheap. It is important to determine priorities when purchasing literature. Buy what will be the most useful in the restoration process. If the vehicle needs major engine work, a shop manual, not a paint chart, is required. If you need to know how to operate the air conditioning, you need an air conditioning manual, not a sales catalog. If you need to know whether the engine in your car is original, consult the specifications in the sales catalog or data book. If you are still not sure what literature will help at the current stage of restoration, go to a major flea market. Have one of the professional literature dealers give you free advice. You can also get a free copy of *Old Cars* (700 East State Street, Iola, WI 54945) and write to dealers who advertise in the literature for sale section.

Literature buyer's guide

By Howard and Shelby Applegate

Double digit inflation has been a fact of life in America for the last few years. This economic phenomenon is not all that unusual, however, as more of the 205 years since the Declaration of Independence was announced in 1776 have been inflationary than either depressed or stable. Since the Great Depression of 1929-1941, Americans of even modest means have reacted to inflationary times by investing both small and large sums of money in intrinsic items; things recognized as having value in and of themselves with the hope and expectation that the items bought would increase substantially in value. Also implicit in this idea is the hope that if the buyer was caught in a financial bind, these collectibles could be sold quickly to raise cash. During the Great Depression, many families with wage earners out of work survived by selling family heirlooms to the antique dealers who went door to door through the city streets and small towns of America.

The public has always sought a popular hedge against inflation, but the scenario of the early 1990s is different from the various investment booms of the past. Now, the mass media seems obsessed with featuring various alternative hedges. Articles abut investment collectibles appear almost weekly in such business publications as *The Wall Street Journal, Business Week, Fortune, Forbes* and *Nation's Business*. Professional journals for doctors, lawyers, accountants and related occupations feature collectible investment articles and columns. National magazines, including *Time* and *Newsweek*, have followed suit. Associated Press and United Press International have made several dozen collectible investment articles available to member newspapers and the syndicated antiques columnists report that their editors and readers demand more information on what modern collectibles to buy for investment purposes. Local newspapers get into the act by printing feature stories about regional hobbyists or investors who have acquired and preserved vast quantities of one collectible or another. Even network and local television has zeroed in on collectibles as an investment. "Sixty Minutes," "The Today Show," "Good Morning America" and "The Phil Donahue Show" all have had at least one collectibles program. Who doesn't know that David Letterman collects exotic cars? Jay Leno's passion for classic cars and motorcycles is also highly publicized.

Don't buy material for investment that is about to go out of fashion. For example, interest in Model A Fords is down.

The most popular inflation hedges appear to be fine art, stamps, coins, antiques, old photographs, American Indian artifacts, jewelry, stock and bond certificates, rare books, manuscripts and pottery. In all segments of American society, the daily topic of discussion is investment collectibles as a way to cope with an out of control economy. Media and citizen concern for inflation and economic slump led, no doubt, to the defeat of President George Bush in the presidential election of 1992.

All of this has affected many of the nation's estimated 600,000 automotive hobbyists. Those with "big bucks" are trying to decide which vehicles to buy for investment potential. Many auto buffs, however, do not have big bucks and some of them are thinking about the investment prospects of automotive literature. As dealers in automotive paper, we are constantly bombarded with letters and questions at flea markets about the investment potential of automotive literature. We are asked two main questions: "Should we invest in automotive literature?" and "What automotive literature should I buy?"

It's time to slow down and rationally look at the whole idea of collecting for the sole purpose of investment, especially as it relates to the automotive hobby. Perhaps, it is time for cooler heads to prevail. What is the real investment potential in automotive literature?

The automotive literature investor, like any other investor, should start by learning all there is to know about the subject. The investor will soon find that the buying and selling of literature is not as simple as it seems. Literature investors must immerse themselves in studying this collectible and its marketplace. Of particular concern should be an analysis of all the variables that affect literature prices. The investor cannot afford the collector's luxury of buying only what they love, enjoy or need. Literature collectors sometimes luck out and build collections that later become much more valuable. This occurs when the specific literature has become more popular with a wider section of the public or when the demand has exceeded the supply. The investor misses all the collector's fun of the hunt, do to a preoccupation with deciding which literature will be worth the most two or 20 years from now. This forces the investor into becoming a gambler, as unprepared as the average layman who bets at racetracks or casinos.

Successful investors in collectibles whether it be art, metals, stamps or coins, usually have the advantage of professional advisers. Walter P. Chrysler, Jr., who built one of America's finest collections of art, employed a staff of art curators to advise him. He also retained several major dealers as acquisition consultants. Even the most modest investor in the Wall Street stock market usually listens to the advice of a stock broker. A novice literature investor should proceed cautiously, either educating himself or relying on a knowledgeable adviser. However, as with any other investment, he must be aware that there are no crystal balls that will guarantee anyone can look confidently into the future. The investor must have the luxury of extra dollars with which to gamble. Anyone who uses food, clothing or housing money to try to make money in collectibles is pursuing a risky venture.

The automotive literature investor must not only have some spare money to spend and some subject knowledge and/or good consultants, but the investor must have no emotional ties to the material and must understand when to buy and when and how to sell. The prospective money maker must realize that there is a direct relationship between the collector vehicle marketplace and the automotive literature marketplace. This is mainly because most people who buy literature today are car restorers and not literature collectors. Thus, the demands of the restorers have great importance in determining trends in the paper marketplace.

Let's use the gold market as an example. In the early 1980s, professional investors bought gold when its price was under $200 per ounce. They waited to sell until they thought that the price had nearly peaked before they took their profits and got out. Novices, attracted to gold only by the intense media hype, began to buy at $400 to $600 an ounce. Some went even higher. In the latter group of investors, some people made a few dollars per ounce, but many lost thousands of dollars because they invested at top of market, just before the commodity began to temporarily slip in price.

Veteran investors in collectibles, rather than metal commodities, make big purchases and buy at wholesale. Novices buy a piece here and an item there, usually at a price near the market value. Veterans know that fortunes are not usually made overnight. Novices buy high and they expect instant success. The experienced investor waits until just the right moment and sells his materials, at wholesale prices, to professional dealers. New investors never understand why automotive literature dealers will not pay them more than the present wholesale market price for their valuable 1955 Chevrolet catalogs or 1957 Ford retractable folders.

Remember the television news programs featuring the lines in front of the coin shops showing people selling silver coins, gold jewelry and silverware? When the price of silver was $50.25 on January 18, 1980, the coin dealer rarely paid the public more than $18 to $20 per ounce. That was the going "spot"

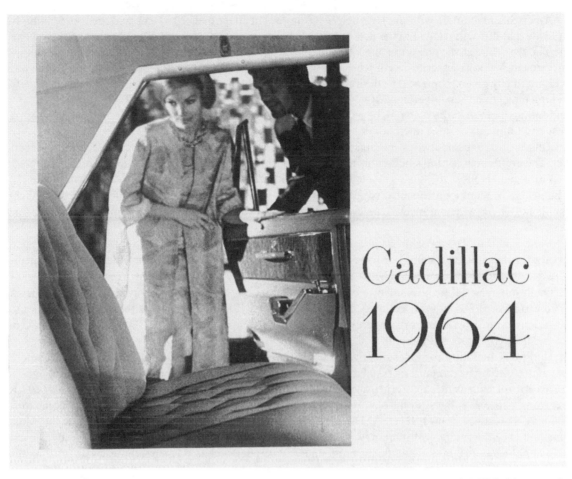

Cadillac
1964

Most dealers feel that 1960s to 1980 Cadillac sales literature has great investment potential. This 24-page sales brochure for 1964 models should continue to climb in value.

wholesale price at the time. This clearly indicates the overhead structure in the silver market. Automotive literature also has a mark-up from wholesale to retail prices, though perhaps not as rigid as in the precious metals marketplace. There are no publications that show literature values like the *Old Cars Price Guide* shows collector car values.

Literature prices seem to find their own level in the marketplace. The prices realized by the major dealers for the same item will rarely vary more than 10 percent. Literature dealers must be able to buy at wholesale prices, in order to sell at retail. They must cover their overhead and realize a profit at the same time. Dealers obviously prefer to buy literature that they can sell quickly, thus turning over their capital fast. They are reluctant to pay much for items they may have to haul to swap meets for one or two years before making a sale or material they may have to stockpile until the collectors become interested in that particular marque or model.

Active, full-time automotive hobby vendors report that their overhead costs are rising rapidly. This is especially so for those who rely on sales at swap meets and flea markets where travel is required. Costs, such as the prices of gasoline, have multiplied drastically. Overhead costs are currently about 35 percent of gross sales, excluding the cost of literature. Unless an item will move fast, most dealers simply won't buy it.

Remember, the dealer wants to buy large collections at wholesale, not pieces here and there at retail. Most established private collectors of literature probably will not be good customers of the investor, because collectors often lack the large sums of money required to acquire big quantities of literature all at once. Too often they need only a small part of the investor's hoard to add to their extensive collections. The alternative is that the investor becomes a dealer in automotive paper. While this method may result in profit taking for the investor, it will also require additional investments in overhead and time for long-range retailing.

America's love affair with the automobile has lasted for more than 100 years and there is nothing to indicate that this will change in the near future. However, the literature market ... like the collector vehicle market or the stock market or the silver market ... is fickle and quickly changeable. Your inventory investment is not necessarily worth what you originally paid. Moreover, it is only worth what someone will pay at any given moment. The desires of automotive hobbyists can and do change. This happens both in long range trends and overnight. If you love and enjoy literature, be a collector. If you enjoy the buying and selling more than the material, be a dealer. If the gambling instincts are in your blood, be an investor. Just don't mix up the three alternatives.

The shrewd investor always anticipates the marketplace instead of just reacting to changes in the market. The crafty investor buys before his acquisitions become popular. He buys low to sell high.

Professionals must use their personal expertise and remain emotionally detached from the material. This will give them a professionalism denied amateurs or dilettantes. Don't buy material for investment that is no longer widely collected, unless you expect the market trends to change drastically in the next few years.

Most astute professional literature dealers have stopped stocking up on antique automotive paper, except for the choicest catalogs or folders that can be resold instantly. This means that pre-1930s literature, except for desirable unusual items and classic paper, is now sluggish, at best.

Don't buy material for investment that is about to go out of fashion. For example, interest in Model A Ford and most 1930s V-8s is declining, except for 1932 and 1933 models, where the market continues to be "pumped-up" by a dozen or so aggressive collectors. The same is true for 1930 through 1932 Chevrolet and the early years of Plymouth.

Don't buy literature for investment when it continues to be very popular and desirable and therefore remains at the highest retail prices. Classic automotive literature continues to be expensive, although its prices are not increasing rapidly. Muscle car and high-performance car literature of the 1960s and 1970s is getting expensive, because the supply is not sufficient to meet the demand of the younger collectors. Camaro, Corvette, Firebird, GTO, AMX, Superbird, Super Bee, Barracuda, Charger, 442, Cougar, Mustang and GTX literature cost more now than ever before, but the prices may be peaking. An investment here might result in a loss, rather than a profit, unless it can be purchased at a good wholesale price and in large quantity.

Don't buy literature for investment that probably won't ever become widely popular. Included in this category might be material related to foreign family cars and trucks, possibly excepting the Japanese marques; American medium and heavy duty commercial vehicles; and American dream, show and experimental cars. Investments in this field probably will never pay off.

Don't buy literature for investment that has a very limited market. This would include areas of personal collecting interest, such as brochures describing fire apparatus, taxicabs, police cars, hearses and ambulances and flower cars. The number of buyers interested in military vehicles, motorcycles, postwar small cars (like Davis and Keller), or short-lived orphans in general, is very small. Even if this material appreciates in value, the market for selling such items is quite narrow and significantly higher value will probably take years to happen.

Remember, these are all general rules. There are always exceptions. If the material is for sale at well below wholesale prices (in other words dirt cheap) and you have the money in hand to buy it, plus the ability to hold it and store it indefinitely, it may be worth the gamble. This can happen, provided that everyone else ... especially literature dealers ... do not get the same idea. If the latter situation occurs, the marketplace will be flooded with identical material, thus keeping the price down.

There are two types of literature that investors should consider buying. Both may require long term waits before any appreciable capital gains will result. One category includes catalogs and folders on the traditional favorites like 1950s through 1970s Cadillacs, Lincolns, Imperials and other gas-guzzling, big block, V-8s.

As the world becomes geared up to using small, high-priced, fuel-sipping economy cars, collectors are moving towards buying, restoring and even driving the behemoths of the last 20 years. The literature on these cars is rising in price in direct relationship to hobbyist interest in the vehicles. Astute observers must note the trends in the current new car market. Sticker shock, the unsteady economy, and rising gas prices have increased consumer demand for used cars. The same events have stimulated people to fix-up and better maintain their existing cars.

A study of what used cars are being bought, what cars your neighborhood mechanic sees going through the shop, what 10-year old cars are still on the road in good condition, what cars the younger gen-

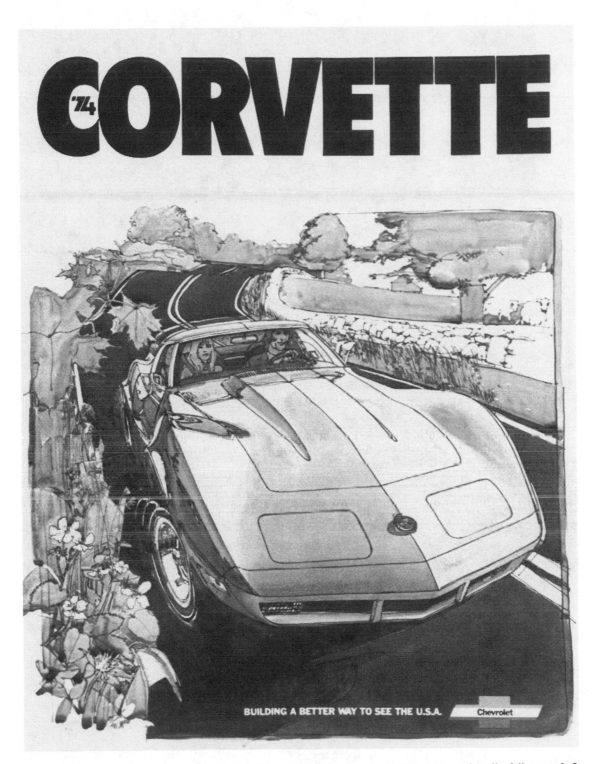

Like the Corvette itself, literature covering Chevrolet's fiberglass-bodied sports car has "cult" appeal. It seems to constantly appreciate in price, regardless of market trends.

CLASSIC 6 or V-8 · AMBASSADOR V-8 · AMERICAN

The investor willing to take some risks, should consider American Motors literature, now that the company no longer exists. This 1964 folder is getting rare and may go up in price over the next five years.

eration are buying to fix-up, will give hints to trends ahead in the collector car market and therefore the literature market.

The second type of literature investors can consider is the unexpected. This is where the skill of predicting and anticipating comes in. Many dealers think that the literature market will expand substantially for such marques as Chrysler, Pontiac, Buick, Oldsmobile, Dodge, Plymouth and Mercury. Some believe that DeSoto, Jeep, Rambler, Kaiser and light-duty items for International and GMC trucks will grow in value during the 1990s. For example, if an experienced investor expected the market for American Motors Corporation (AMC) literature to grow substantially in the next five years, he could invest in a large quantity of this material at the current, very reasonable wholesale prices. Likewise, if the investor felt that General Motors would discontinue the marketing of light-duty GMCs (following the pattern set by International Harvester Company earlier) by all means cheap and large quantities of GMC material should be acquired. Experienced investors will find such "sleepers" and make a profit. Some investors will undoubtedly make small fortunes in automotive literature, but most will not.

What impact will investors have on the automotive literature hobby? Will literature prices rise faster than at the present time? Will average collectors of paper be priced out of the literature hobby? Will vast quantities of materials be withdrawn from the marketplace, making it difficult for restorers to find what they need or want? Will investors hype the market by artificially encouraging collector interest in previously scorned items? Will investors, many of whom will not understand or appreciate the hobby, have as negative an impact on literature as they have already had on vehicles?

Our crystal ball works no better than those used by veteran investors. We don't know and neither do they. Do You?

The auto literature business

By Peter J. Winnewisser

The thirst for nostalgia, as evidenced in the vintage car boom, has been accompanied by a steadily increasing interest in hobby related collectibles such as license plates, emblems, spark plugs, tools, toys, etc. The largest of these spin-offs is the sale and collecting of old car literature. In this case, however, the collectible item is frequently put to use, since the majority of literature buyers are restorers seeking information they need about their cars.

At automotive flea markets (called swap meets), easily half the vendors sell some literature. A growing number are devoting themselves exclusively to this trade. These people, particularly those who specialize in literature, are important contributors to the old car hobby because they offer assistance to restorers who need information. They also provide help for collectors who buy paper goods related to a particular car, manufacturer or automotive era.

In general, dealers with tents and good protection feel that, short of a complete wash-out, sales are unaffected or actually helped by inclement weather.

If you are an antique auto buff, you are interested in antique auto literature, although this interest may never go further than buying a shop or owner's manual. But watch out! It's an easy step from collecting literature about your car to broadening your interest to literature for other cars. Whatever the reason, it's a good bet that sometime this year you will look over the stock of a literature dealer at some old car event or write to one in response to his advertising.

The people with whom you will do business are, for the most part, hobbyists like yourself; hobbyists whose interests have expanded into selling literature. Additionally, they tend to be people with a solid background in old cars and related paper items. The 35 dealers, from 12 states, interviewed for this article have an average of 10 years selling literature and 90 percent of them are also collectors.

For want of a better term, the merchandise sold by these dealers is referred to simply as old car literature. Exactly what this includes has never been agreed upon. Noted literature dealers and writers Shelby and Howard Applegate (who also contributed to this book) define automotive literature somewhat narrowly. They describe it as "anything that is printed by or with the authority of an automotive vehicle manufacturer or the manufacturer's agents or representatives." A broader, and perhaps more useful definition, is given to us by Tully, New York dealer Dick McKnight, who says "Literature is anything in paper goods relating to old cars."

In general, old car literature can be divided into categories such as: service publications that assist in maintaining and repairing vehicles, sales publications that helped to sell vehicles, and other books, old photos, postcards, annual reports, advertisements, paint charts and automaker's house organs, etc.

Contrary to the occasional expectations of those who patronize antique auto swap meets and flea markets, old car literature dealers are not philanthropists. They sell literature to make a profit, usually to support an old car or, as one vendor explained, "to help pay for my addiction" (in this case to Chevrolet literature).

Profit is not the only reason why a person gets involved in literature selling. "I do this," says Harry Paquin of Middletown, Rhode Island, "because I love old cars, meeting people and hearing their experiences in restoring their cars." Dan Kirchner, of Dearborn, Michigan, points out that he derives a great deal of satisfaction "from being able to help someone who needs information on his auto." Maryland vendors Grace Clark and George Ward say that, for them, the joy of literature selling is in "meeting an incredible selection of people and conversing about mutual interests.

Turned on by old cars and the people in the hobby, most literature sellers take great satisfaction in the service they offer and make every effort to maintain a good reputation. Dealers point with pride to their high rate of return business and low rate of customer complaints. They insist that they try their best to offer prices fair both to themselves and their customers. In addition, says Boonton, New Jersey vendor Howard Hoelscher, "all legitimate literature dealers will make 100 percent refund on any item not to the buyer's satisfaction. All try to condition-grade their material fairly as excellent, very good, good or fair.

Not everyone agrees. When asked why he stole literature, a thief that was caught in the act at a swap meet replied, "There's nothing wrong with stealing from people who are crooks." In addition to such hints of high prices, there are unethical practices. Several years ago, at the Antique Automobile Club of America's Eastern Division National Fall Meet at Hershey, a collector was victimized by a vendor who sold as "original" a piece of Model A Ford literature later identified as a reproduction. "There are some people who think we are taking advantage of them," explains Dan Kirchner. "They forget we are hobbyists also."

Some vendors *do* hurt the reputation of legitimate dealers by charging exorbitant prices. Of course, the buyer has some protection, in that he can refuse to pay such prices. "I see prices of some material going out of sight," says Kirchner. "At the swap meet in Carlisle, Pennsylvania, dealers were asking a fortune for a 1959 Cadillac shop manual. This prevents most restorers from obtaining the manual. We must remember that this is a hobby and try to help our fellow hobbyists."

To meet the growing demands of the hobby, literature dealers study buying trends and attempt to inventory as complete a selection of material as possible, either in all lines or in a particular area. To obtain saleable items they walk flea markets and attend auctions, estate sales and house or garage sales. They also buy and sell to/from each. Others purchase private collections, search auto industry and dealer files, buy from libraries and sell off duplicates from their own collections.

With particular needs of customers in mind, many dealers travel widely to review and buy literature. "In general," says Royal Oak, Michigan vendor Bill Bailey, " We beat the bushes."

A vending trailer offers professional literature dealers added security and weather protection. Those unable to protect their merchandise in a rain or wind storm feel that bad weather kills their business.

The size of a vendor's stock may vary from a few thousand pieces for small operations to 75,000 to 100,000 pieces (or more) for those who do a large-scale business. If the dealer buys right and keeps abreast of market trends, he can find customers for much of this material.

Although the exact number of antique auto hobbyists is unknown, the fact that they number in the hundreds of thousands is attested to by the throngs at Hershey and countless other automotive events, the growing circulation of hobby related publications such as *Old Cars Weekly* and by hundreds of local and national clubs and organizations. Whether a restorer or collector or both, each hobbyist is a potential customer for literature dealers, perhaps many times over.

John Preikschat, underlined this point when he wrote years ago, "In 21 years of collecting, my collection has grown to over 100,000 pieces of literature covering thousands of vehicles."

Extremely knowledgeable, and intensely interested in the old car hobby, Walter Miller of Syracuse, New York is a typical modern old car literature dealer. As is usually the case, Miller's interest in selling developed from his own collecting. He now works full-time at his business. Miller carries over 100,000 items in his inventory. He employs several people, answers an average 50 letters a day and logs thousands of miles per year on buying trips. He finds satisfaction in the fact that over the past four years he has had thousands of customers, but only one bad check, very few complaints or returns and 75 per cent repeat business. "I save people the trouble of finding material they want and need," Miller says. "I am helping someone and making them happy."

Miller and other dealers would agree that most buyers are fine people. "Ninety-eight percent are exceptionally nice," state Joe and Shonda Lane of Sun State Auto Literature, Orlando, Florida. "The attitude of the people with whom I do business is mostly great," says Michigan dealer Hilda Eckel. "They love their cars, are happy to find literature and enjoy talking about their cars." A mutual respect and admiration seems to characterize the relationship between dealers and hobbyists.

It's not all perfect, however. Some vendors point out that, while most customers handle merchandise carefully ("almost reverently," says Mrs. Eckel), there are always a few, at every event, who don't respect the literature and damage it. Every dealer had agonized at seeing pop, ice cream or some other sticky substance drip on his stock. All have seen a page wrinkle, tear, or soil from thoughtless handling. Then there are those who do not seem to realize that merchandise should be returned to the same envelope or box from which it came. Finally, there are a few who do not know the value of literature and insultingly suggest it should be given away for 10-cents a sheet.

One of the most important decisions that a literature vendor makes is what price to ask. This is a decision that is not as easy as it sounds. At one Hershey swap meet, years ago, a 1916 issue of *Ford Times* was priced $15 at one booth, $10 at another and $5 at a third. The condition of all three was comparable. A difference in price is not uncommon. The reason is that there are many variables that go into determining how much to charge for an item. "Price is an opinion," explains dealer Howard Hoelscher. "If the buyer and seller agree ... no problem. Buyers are not fools and sellers have to make a reasonable profit."

A number of dealers believe that there is a difference between the restorer and the collector in their attitude towards pricing. The average person, who has just one car and is seeking material just for it, frequently is not as knowledgeable as the collector. Thus, he or she is more easily appalled by the prices that some of the material commands these days. At Hershey years ago, one collector paid hundreds for a Lincoln catalog and another spent hundreds for a large deluxe catalog for a 1936 Packard Twelve. These were viewed as fair prices, but may well seem out of line to the collector or restorer debating over a 1969 AMX color sales catalog or a 1955 Thunderbird color folder costing far less.

Several factors have to be considered in determining the fair price for an item. The primary consideration is what the piece is, how rare it is, and how much demand there is for it. A second consideration is the condition. A third factor will be the price the dealer had to pay for the piece. A fourth point, and one that is frequently misunderstood, is the overhead costs for the dealer. Buyers need to recognize that a vendor's price has to include the cost he incurs in running his business and that these have risen significant in recent years. Among these expenses are, advertising; mailing; shipping; insurance; travel; phone calls; space rental packaging; equipment such as tents, tables, boxes and envelopes; paying help; deterioration from handling and weather; storage; and replacement of merchandise.

Another important factor in determining price is the dealer's right to a reasonable profit. Here, there are no agreed upon guidelines. What is reasonable to one may be out of line to another. The controlling factors will include demand, scarcity, competition and buyer resistance. The Packard catalog mentioned earlier was originally priced even higher. Buyer resistance brought the price down.

Last, but not least, the final price will depend on whether or not the buyer and seller bargain over it. This practice is followed frequently at flea markets, but not on mail orders. Dealer opinion on this flea market "tradition" is divided. Some are absolutely opposed to it. "People who want to bargain are second rate customers," maintains one vendor. "I determine when to give a discount ... not the buyer," he points out. Others have mixed feelings. "I would rather keep prices lower and offer a set discount on purchases above $20," says dealer Bruce Perry of The Yellow Dog Garage in Bradford, Pennsylvania. "But most people want to bargain. I guess, in all honesty, I want to bargain when I'm purchasing, so we'll have to live with it."

For the majority, this kind of "horse trading," as Del Bates of Romeo, Michigan, calls it, is part of the adventure and excitement that only the flea market provides. "I don't blame anyone for trying to save a few dollars," says Harry Paquin. "Nothing wrong with it," states Howard Hoelscher. "This is part of the fun. Sometimes we can bargain sometimes we can't.

Whether bargaining does save customers money is open to question. Buyers like to think it does and, undoubtedly, at times this is true. On the other hand, hobbyists must also realize that the possibility of having to negotiate the final price can cause dealers to raise their asking price. "I don't mind." writes one vendor. "I just mark up everything and let them bargain. That makes them leave real happy."

Most of the dealers surveyed do business at flea markets and by mail and find advantage and disadvantages to both. The mail order business can be carried out from the comfort of one's own home or shop and avoids many of the inconveniences of flea market selling. On the other hand, it involves advertising, postage and packaging costs, plus the time that has to be devoted to phone calls, answering mail and wrapping material. Selling by mail also means accepting the risk of personal checks (although dealers report an amazingly low incidence of bad checks) and tolerating customers who do not include an self-addressed stamped envelope (SASE). It also means tolerating the problems of the United States Post Office's mail system.

Flea market vending takes a different kind of commitment; one that begins with hours of sorting, cataloging and packing. Some dealers spend a month or more preparing for an event such as Hershey. It also entails travel, the back-breaking work of setting up and taking down a stand, long hours of manning the booth and the risk of handling and weather damage.

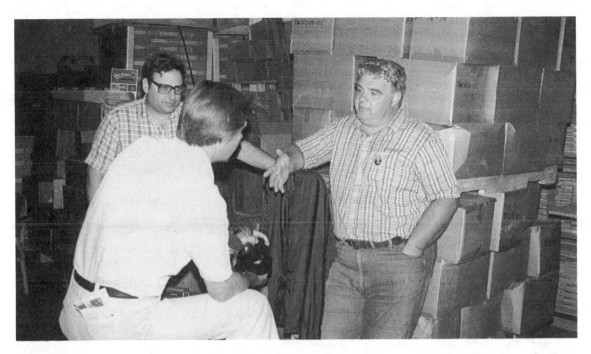

Dealers sell their merchandise to literature collectors, car restorers and automotive historians. Howard Applegate (right) was an active member of the Society of Automotive Historians (SAH) and is seen here at an SAH meeting.

Despite all this, however, most literature dealers feel that the old car flea market is where the action is. There is no other method of selling that can expose their stock more quickly to a great many potential buyers and do it with so much fun.

A major flea market liability can be the weather ... particularly rain. A windy day also brings its own sorrows. How bad is a rainy day for business? Opinions range from "a disaster" and "it can destroy us" to "it does not bother me." In general, dealers with tents and good protection feel that, short of a complete wash-out, sales are helped by reasonably inclement weather. Those with little protection for their merchandise feel it kills their business.

An added flea market risk, and one that is on the increase, is theft. Although most dealers share the opinion of Hilda Eckel that "literature collectors are fine, honest people," they are also aware that there is disturbing evidence that a certain element at flea markets is out to victimize vendors. Ten years ago, stealing was practically non-existent. Today, that has changed. "What used to be an infrequent problem," Howard Applegate points out, "has intensified in the last two or three years." Especially vulnerable are dealers with large inventories. Those who do not report stealing either run small, easily-monitored operations or do not have a good inventory system to quickly spot their losses.

Numerous cases of theft have been reported. At a National Literature Meet held in Maryland, a dealer caught a man trying to steal $500 worth of manuals, At Hershey, a customer covered an envelope of 1930s Ford literature with his brief case, picked both up, and simply walked a way. Elsewhere on the field, two thieves took advantage of one man's absence from his booth. While one thief engaged the booth-watcher in conversation, the other made off with 10-12 items. This meant a loss of $300. Two years in a row, at Hershey, another vendor had his entire bag of Corvette literature taken. Each bag was worth about $400 at the time.

Other examples of dishonesty include buying an item at a discount and then receiving a full refund from another person in the booth or claiming, in the dealer's absence, that he has promised a substantial discount on a certain item (when he hasn't). Although the total amount stolen is relatively low, (about one percent says one of the larger dealers), the fact that disturbs vendors is that the rate of stealing has increased so sharply in the last few years.

A number of suggestions have been made to help dealer's minimize loss from theft. The first step is for each vendor to be aware it could happen to him and be more alert. A second step is to provide enough help to adequately cover the booth at all times. Other suggestions are to keep the very good material close at hand and to organize vendors in the same area so that they can help each other. Perhaps the most important deterrent can be provided by honest collectors and restorers who watch for thieves and report them to vendors.

No less than any businessman, the automotive literature dealer is faced with the necessity of knowing what the market demands are for his merchandise. He finds that he can do this best if he keeps aware of trends in old car collecting, for as the cars go, so goes the literature. In recent years the focus of restoring and collecting has shifted to cars of the 1930s and 1940s, and to those of the postwar era. While the demand for Model A Ford classic literature remains fairly strong, pre-1920 and Model T Ford material has shown a marked fall-off as the interest in newer cars and their literature has strengthened. One large volume dealer reports that, four years ago, he had very little demand for literature of the 1960s. Now, about two-thirds of his business involves literature from that era.

At the present time, there is strong collector interest in postwar high-performance cars. These are muscle cars like the Pontiac GTO, Dodge Charger, Ford Mustang, Chevrolet Camaro, American Motors AMX, etc. Also showing strength are compact cars of the early 1960s, such as Rambler, Valiant, Lark, and Corvair. Light-duty truck literature covering 1946 to present models is in demand, too. Along with increased demand for certain vehicles, there is a corresponding increase in interest in their literature.

During the past 18 months, dealers have also become aware of increased interest in foreign-car literature on the part of both American and European collectors. Due perhaps to the international exchange rate fluctuations and the fact that much of the literature in Europe was destroyed during World War II, more foreign collectors seem to be turning to the American market.

Future market tendencies? According to one dealer, upcoming trends may well include increased demand for literature covering so-called "gas guzzlers," especially Imperials, Lincolns and Cadillacs.

To keep up with the trends and to avoid putting money into stock that will not sell requires a good deal of business sense on the part of the dealer. It also requires a good record keeping system, "If you want to keep up with the trends on what is selling, " offers Howard Applegate, "keep your literature records on a monthly basis."

There are a number of additional concerns shared by the literature people of the old car hobby. Shelby and Howard Applegate feel that the public needs to be educated about the value and use of automotive literature "People are often amazed at what they can learn from literature," they state. "It can save them money and prevent them from buying the wrong parts." Some vendors have expressed a desire for an auto literature club and magazine and for more articles and books on the subject. Other concerns are the high cost of flea market registrations, the lack of adequate indoor facilities at swap meets and the need to establish some consensus among the collector/restorer/dealer as to just what defines good to excellent condition ratings.

Next to collecting and restoring cars and buying parts, there is no aspect of the old car hobby that commands more attention than literature. Buyers, sellers and collectors themselves, the people who offer old car literature at automotive flea markets and by mail are a special breed. These people are proud of the service they provide to automotive collectors, restorers and historians.

Sooner or later, every old car enthusiast will look for literature relating to his car or area of interest. The literature vendor tries to satisfy that need. A few years ago, at Hershey, a middle-aged man wearing a Ford cap and carrying a shopping bag, approached Ford literature dealer Colonel Bill White about a 1931 issue and supplement of *Ford News*. "I have the issue, but not the supplement," the man explained. "Would you consider selling the supplement alone or trading it for some Model T literature? I really can't afford to put out the price for two items ($25 at the time), one of which I already have."

Bill looked over the Model T literature. "I'd like to trade with you, but Model T material is (selling) slow right now." White said. "However, since I really don't like to separate the two items, why don't you give me $20 for them? I'll break even and you'll have a good deal." The bargain was quickly sealed and, a pleased and satisfied customer left Bill's booth. Without a doubt, that man will buy from Bill White again. And that's what literature selling is all about.

Acknowledgements: The author thanks Shelby and Howard Applegate, William L. Bailey, Dick McKnight and Walter Miller for their invaluable assistance in preparing this article. Thanks, also, to the following literature dealers who so kindly provided information: the late Nat Adelstein (and his wife Betty), Del Bates, Grace Clark and George Ward (Clark, Ward & Company), John Conde, Phil Dumka, Mrs. Robert Eckel, Gus Garton, Tom Hilton, Howard and Gladys Hoelscher, J.B. Hoffert, Thomas R. Kerr, Jay Ketelle, Dan Kirchner, Joe and Shonda Lane (Sun State Auto literature), J. David Lee, Bill Lester, Jere Longrie, Bob Olds and Harry Paquin (Hash's Antique Auto Parts).

Photographic memories: old car photos

By Henry Austin Clark, Jr.

Automobile photographs can be grouped in three general categories. First we have old photos of old cars, such as you're likely to find in an antique shop. Second comes, current photographs of old cars, like the kind you try to take at a car show while some idiot walks in front of you. Third is current photographs of new cars, often taken shortly after the purchase of same and hopefully before the first accident. We would like to spend most of the time now talking about the first category, as it is in many ways the most interesting.

Old photos, of old cars, can be found in all sorts of places. We almost never visit a flea market, large or small, without finding and buying at least one interesting old photograph. This year at Hershey, we only found a few. However, they were good ones. Sometimes we have run onto entire albums or collections.

The purchase of a new car was an excellent excuse to gather the family around the vehicle for a photograph. This picture was taken in the teens or 1920s. Can you identify the make of the new car?

The art of photography has been pretty much perfected for a much longer time than most people think, especially as regards black & white pictures. We have all seen reproductions of the marvelous Civil War scenes shot by Matthew Brady. He used a wet plate camera.

Even those who do not worship steam cars are aware that the Stanley Brothers made their money perfecting the Stanley Dry Plate, which they sold to Eastman Kodak at some time or other. This left them free to turn their hobby into a business. In any case, almost since the dawn of the automotive age there has been the means to make good photographs of cars. Fortunately, this was often done, probably because the car was much more of a novelty than it is today.

The earliest photo of a self-propelled vehicle which I have found is of the Dudgeon steamer, taken when it was running around the New York area in about 1866. Car enthusiast Joe Tracy had this in his papers. He gave it to us some years ago.

Generally speaking, the new car in town was a newsworthy subject and it was standard procedure for the local professional photographer to make a picture of it. This was often run in the town newspaper. The picture was also printed-up, mounted on a fancy mat with a tan border (so that it could be framed as desired) and sold to the proud owner of the Winton or Maxwell. Usually, the owner was seated aboard with his mustache curled, hat at a jaunty angle and with the air of a man of the world enjoying his new plaything. This is the sort of a photo that has class. The car being new and shiny, looks well. So does the owner.

Whenever there was an organized event, be it the annual outing for the orphans or the Glidden Tour, there was a field day to be had by photographers, both professional and amateur. Our own favorite specialty, in event photographs, was the Vanderbilt Cup Races on Long Island. These were held in 1904, 1905, and 1906. There was no race in 1907, but they ran again in 1908, 1909 and 1910. Over the years, we have collected hundreds of shots of these races, sometimes a single photograph, but more often in lots.

One coup, of respectable proportions, was the result of a lead from a collector friend on Long Island. A fellow, who worked with this fellow, reported that a neighbor had found a bunch of glass plate negatives in the attic of an old house he had rented in Queens, New York.

Following up the lead, we arrived at the address and received no answer at the door, although curtains were seen to move. A car parked across the street drove away hurriedly. Finally, on about the second or third visit, we did get an answer to the back door and found out what all the mystery was about. We looked like a detective, to those in the house, and they were not about to let any detective in, as the family occupation was the "numbers" racket. On the last try, we were on the way back from one of our "junk hunts," as my wife calls them, and looked less suspicious. We were dressed in dungarees and riding in our dirty old, beat-up IHC stake truck loaded with old iron goodies like Firestone rims.

This fit into the decor of the neighborhood better. The house was on Ditmars Boulevard, a quarter-mile from Laguardia Airport. It was an area where, if you parked your car overnight and flew out of town, you would likely return to a bare frame and chassis. Once inside though, all was cordiality. While we could not buy the glass plate negatives, we were allowed to borrow them and have prints made ... one for us and one for the owner. This was done and we picked up a nice run of previously unpublished photographs of the last two Vanderbilt Cup Races. We have made copy negatives from our prints and can now reproduce them.

Of course, this was doing it the hard way. However, it was more exciting that just borrowing Willie K. Vanderbilt's personal album, full of fine Spooner & Wells prints, which was housed in a logical place ... the Vanderbilt Museum in Centerport, Long Island. We did that too, and got hundreds of photos from that source.

Our means of effecting a loan of photos, from either a museum or an individual, is to offer to make a copy negative of each picture for the lender. This we do in our own basement and the cost is not great. We used this same incentive to borrow the Byron photographs from the Museum of the City of New York and thereby added some very fine shots of the Mobile automobile factory in Tarrytown, New York. Later, the same factory made Maxwells. There were prints of them in the collection, too. We also got some great photographs taken at the Brewster Body Company plant in Brewster, New York. They were the importer of several fine European cars, as well as body builders.

Enough on where you find old photos. It is sufficient to say that you should touch all the bases. Ask elderly relatives, visit church rummage sales, antique shops, junk shops, flea markets (non-automotive as well) and, last but not least, check with other collectors who may care less about them than you do. Of course, here we have the advantage of being able to borrow a photo and return same intact with a copy

This photo should intrigue any car photo collector. The 1949 Kaiser hatchback is set up as a camera car, complete with a dark hood to keep light out and a large format bellows-type camera mounted on the passenger side.

negative. It is important not to waste time on modern photos of old cars or bad snapshots. They made lousy pictures in the old days too.

What do you do with them once you have found a few, you ask? Well, sometimes they are in handsome old-fashioned frames of the kind they don't make anymore. You can hang these in your den or garage, to lend atmosphere. If you find any really good ones, the national car club magazines are always looking for something, with a glow of nostalgia to it, to put on their inside covers. Even *Old Cars* might print some. Who knows? In any case they add to the sum total of collected material in our hands.

After getting a photo, it is fun to research it and try to find out what kind of a car it is and, if possible, what year it was made. In the case of event photos, it is very satisfying to determine, somehow, what event was taking place and then to look it up in *The Automobile* or *Horseless Age* (old automotive trade magazines) to read about what happened and how the car did. Car numbers in races or tours are a very helpful clue when visible and, in almost every case, you can actually zero in on the right event with a little luck.

Not too long ago, we purchased a framed 8 x 10-inch photo of a group of men surrounding what looked like an early Panhard bearing the number C2. It was parked by the curb with two white-capped officials holding stop watches and charts. The photographer was J. A. Seitz of Syracuse, New York. He was proud enough of his work to sign it. It was no trick at all to discover that this was the entry of Mr. Albert Shattuck in the 1901 New York to Buffalo Endurance Run. This run was canceled in midstream, after the assassination of President William McKinley. We enjoy the photo much more after learning all the details about it.

All sorts of tricks are helpful in identification. A jeweler's loop is a great help. Often, nameplates and the letters on hubcaps can be read with the help of one. Even license plates can be a clue; we have been able to look up the owner of a car and its make in one of the early registration lists that used to be published in little books. Never pass up one of these invaluable aids.

The largest collection of old photographs we ever encountered was the Mack Truck Collection. Years ago, John Montville spent a summer working at our Long Island Automotive Museum. A bit later he was employed in the advertising department of Mack in New York. He found that they were closing down the Long Island City branch. Stored there were 69 transfer cases of photographs of Mack and Saurer trucks. The word reached John that they were about to be thrown out. He went to his boss, advertising manager Leonard Matzner, and pleaded to be allowed to save them. The Long Island Automotive Museum, he explained would pick up the photos, all three tons of them, store them and make them available for any future company needs. Mr. Matzner agreed. The photos were given to the museum. They were trucked, in more than one load, to our Library.

This interesting photo shows a woman in a checked dress riding in the curb-side jump seat of an old runabout that wears 1915 New York license plates. Was it snapped as a car photo or a street scene? What kind of car is shown?

Old street scenes can tell us as much about life as they tell us about cars. This picture of an early limousine of an unknown manufacture illustrates life in the city. The year it was snapped is not recorded. (Al Maticic photo)

Photos of tours can often be related to news of events in old automobile trade journals. These cars of unknown make took part in the Automobile Club of America's "Sealed Bonnet Tour" in Detroit. Additional facts are lacking.

Photographer David B. Hillmer of Second Avenue in Detroit, Michigan took this photo of the NYATA event. A magnifying glass reveals a Maxwell-like radiator script on the lead car and 1909 New Jersey license plates on the second one.

Early racing photos are a treat. This one shows a Christie which was the first American car to compete in the French Grand Prix and which had the largest displacement engine ever used in any grand prix. (Al Maticic photo)

The late Henry Austin Clark, Jr., who authored this article, saved three tons of old Mack Truck photos with the help of John Montville. They were placed in his Long Island Automotive Museum for safe-keeping. (Mack Truck photo)

Quality artwork is a big plus for car catalog collectors

By Rolland Jerry

Why do collectors find some automotive sales catalogs more interesting and desirable than others, which are merely so-so ... some even a disappointment when we get them?

One reason is simply the standard of artwork which manufacturers used to illustrate their cars in sales literature. It takes a reasonable standard of artwork to make an interesting catalog. Some manufacturers were better at it than others.

By artwork I mean drawings, sketches and renderings; non-photographic illustration. At times, catalog artwork reminds me of the little girl who, when she was good, was very, very good. But, when she was bad ... oh boy! The swings and variations in catalog art are just as wide. That's why I usually prefer catalogs with photographs, given a choice.

Of course, the trouble from a collector's standpoint is that photographic-type catalogs were on the decline by 1924 or 1925 with the shift of many manufacturers to artwork for their sales literature. Artwork had become more fashionable than photography by then and color was the coming thing in commercial art, displacing the black and white realism of photography.

This is an example of car illustrations used in the 1920 Oldsmobile catalog. The artwork used in a companion catalog called *Oldsmobile Details of Construction* was larger and more interesting. (Henry Austin Clark, Jr.)

There were other reasons for the change, too. One was the emergence of the graphic arts, hand-in-hand with new advertising concepts; "sell the sizzle and not the steak" became a directive, which found expression in the artwork catalog. The results were often uneven, as collectors know.

Much of the period's glass plate photography, which characterized earlier catalogs, proved hard to beat for clarity and sharpness. Some of it never was. Chassis, engines and mechanical components always photographed well, but these features went out of fashion with the switch to artwork and a new emphasis on style and color. That's why pre-World War I catalogs, with their profusion of technical photographs, are so sought after now. And so expensive. Take Reo's catalog for 1909 covering the firm's one- and two-cylinder cars. These are described in a nice 24-page, 8 x 9-3/4-inch catalog which features page-sized photographs of the cars with only the merest suggestion of the retoucher's brush. The photography is excellent.

The Reo models ... touring, gentlemen's roadster and the runabout ... emerge from the pages just as they must have appeared in showrooms at the time. There are no "speed lines" or contrived distortions. No artistic license was taken to make them look larger than life. Every nut, bolt and grease fitting is clearly and unashamedly visible. Similarly, chassis and mechanical details are reproduced with the lavishness and clarity of a modern shop manual, which is the only place you'd find comparable illustrations today, what with the banishment of technical details from most catalogs.

Doubtless, dealers in sales literature would describe the Reo catalog as "real nice." This is exactly what it is, thanks to the outstanding photography. No wonder brass car restorers hunt high and low for original sales literature to guide them in their restorations. The same can't always be said of artwork catalogs, where drawings can be wrong or misleading.

Other early photographic style catalogs were even more pretentious than Reo's, which was a modest effort by standards of the day and in keeping with the car's price field. By contrast, Renault put out a whacking 54-page, 9-3/4 x 12-1/2-inch catalog to cover its many 1913 models. All types; from the tiny, single-cylinder, nine-horsepower model to the big-horsepower jobs, are shown in large photographs and as complete cars, as well as in chassis form. Nor did the company spare technical details. Renault's detachable wheels, the rear-mounted cowl radiator and the firm's back axles are depicted in excellent photographs of shop manual clarity.

Of course, there's no color in these early catalogs (although some manufacturers provided color borders and ornamentation for their catalogs and, occasionally, for the cars themselves). However, this scarcely detracts from their interest and the nature of the contents.

Most early catalogs were so complete and comprehensive in their coverage of the cars that it's difficult to think of a question which the customer could still ask. It's all in the catalog. If a manufacturer lacked dealers ... and many did ... then the catalog had to do a selling job, unaided by a salesman.

Some catalogs are a mixture of photographs and artwork. This was seen particularly during the early 1920s, when photography was on the wane. I have an undated 15-page, 8 x 10-inch Elcar catalog (I think it's 1925) covering the company's fours and sixes, but not the big eight. The difference between the same cars illustrated by photographs and artwork amounts to the difference between night and day.

The Elcars in the photographs are clearly recognizable, the cars depicted by drawings are not. The balloon tires shown in artwork cars are clearly out of proportion, while the artist has failed to capture the characteristics of the company's angular radiator and hood lines on the sixes. Similarly, the absence of even nominal clearance between the wheels and the fenders adds another jarring touch, which reaffirms my preference for photography.

Elcar's artwork reminds me of the catalogs issued by another Indiana manufacturer, Auburn. Some Auburn catalogs from the 1920s suffered the same defects; essentially, over-sized balloon tires and discrepancies in length, height and width relationships. Later Auburn catalogs were better, while Cord's ... most of which were photographic ... are hard to fault.

If I had to name some of the worst car art that I've seen, I suppose it would be the artwork used by Chrysler of Canada, in some of its catalogs for 1937 and 1938. Unless one knew what a Dodge or Plymouth looked like in those years, the catalogs wouldn't have been of much help.

Inaccurate and badly proportioned, the drawings simply fail to convey the lines of what was an attractive range of cars. If Chrysler wanted caricatures or even cartoons for their catalogs, they certainly got them. But, somehow, I don't think that was the idea.

On the other hand, Canadian Chrysler's catalog for the Custom Imperial and Imperial is a very desirable piece. In fact, this 22-page 8-1/2 x 11-inch catalog has good color artwork and comes complete with

Layout used in 1917 Oakland catalog used photograph of car and artwork in background. The illustration depicted the Model 34 roadster in a regal setting near the entrance court and garage of Shipton Court. (Henry Austin Clark, Jr.)

A sketchy depiction of trees, a house and the horizon appeared in the catalog artwork used in Elcar's 1923 sales literature to depict the Model 4-40H Speedway Sport Touring. (Henry Austin Clark, Jr.)

a plastic spiral binding. Even allowing for the fact that the Dodge and Plymouth artwork was prepared before the cars were available, I can't see how they were considered acceptable at the time.

At that, though, Dodge and Plymouth were topped in the art department by a few European manufacturers. I have some scarce prewar catalogs, on the Belgian Miesse truck and several French makes, where the artwork is so abstract that the vehicles defy identification.

I think a catalog with wild artwork is almost as bad as a piece of literature without an illustration of the make. There are a few of these, too, namely Rolls-Royce (1912), Willys-Knight (1930) and Cole (1920). Perhaps there are more that I am not aware of. The best that can be said for these and catalogs with stylized artwork is that they suffice as something on the particular make. We all have pieces like these in our collections.

Packard made excellent use of artwork. This rendering depicts the 1924 Packard Single Eight sedan. (Henry Austin Clark, Jr.)

There isn't much choice between Packard's artwork in later catalogs and the photography more typical of earlier literature. All of it was good. I have some early Twin Six material in which both are used with impressive results. Packard's original artwork for catalogs served a variety of purposes. It had to, since artwork was very expensive (and still is). The same illustrations crop up in such speciality pieces as the *Attributes of Packard*. That is the title of a 1926, eight-page, 8-1/2 x 10-inch catalog showing color choices that used the same art seen in Packard's magazines *The Packard* and *Passenger Transportation*. These were publications which featured catalog art from time to time. Cadillac did much the same with its artwork.

Dodge catalogs were excellent all through the 1920s, with much originality of artwork and in the choice of type faces for the copy. The illustrations appear to be pen and ink sketches. I don't have any myself, but those which I have seen are certainly specimens. I believe Norman Bel Geddes, the stage designer, had a hand in Dodge's artwork.

Oldsmobile used art color illustrations for the cars and photography for mechanical features in separate catalogs from 1928 until 1931 (perhaps earlier or later, but these are the years I have or have seen). The car catalogs are big at 7-3/4 x 11-1/2 inches, but the standard of artwork strikes me as uneven; proportions seem out here and there and the cars are populated by the "pinhead family."

More interesting, personally, are the companion catalogs titled *Oldsmobile Details of Construction*, which are larger than the vehicle sales catalogs at 24-odd pages on a 9-3/4 x 15-1/2-inch format. They explore the Oldsmobile F-29 and F-30 chassis, body work and engine features in great detail, plus illustrations of factory assembly and manufacturing techniques.

I've seen other technical catalogs which attempt the same thing, but not quite so effectively as the Oldsmobile pieces. Mine are for 1929 and 1930, but I believe they were also issued in 1928 and 1931. Publication numbers are Form 202 for 1929 and Form 0-2-30 for 1930. They're nice items for any collection.

Technical details were artistically highlighted in many sales catalogs, such as this 1928 Oakland piece. (Pontiac Historical Photo)

Cadillac's *Open Cars* for 1919 or 1920 (mine's undated) is a charming period piece. It is, in fact, a folio of inked and sepia wash drawings of the touring car, roadster and phaeton. The plates are 7 x 11 inches. Artist friends of mine can't decide whether the pieces are artwork or heavily retouched photography. It doesn't matter much, as the work is attractive, regardless of the source. All are suitable for framing if I wanted to break up the set, which I don't.

The Studebaker President catalog for 1935 was a signal effort. It was easily as grand as anything put out by Packard, Lincoln or Cadillac at the time. With 10 x 12-inch format and 16 pages, it's a quality effort on a heavily textured bond for the best display of the full-page-size charcoal sketches of the cars. At least, I think they're charcoal drawings with shading and contrast. Of course, they look like the President. This catalog reminds us of the better grade of European sales catalogs at the time. Delage, AC and MG did much the same in some of their material.

My comments as to preferences in catalog artwork are my own and I hardly expect universal agreement. I have little interest in them as art forms (although many certainly are), but rather their reference to the actual car. And, of course, none were ever intended to be assessed by collectors; the purpose was to sell the product. How they fared in this respect, we can only guess. I suppose that is part of the catalog collecting game.

Reproduction auto posters make beautiful art

By Rolland Jerry

They're great as mood and conversation pieces and have quite a different appeal than catalogs and sales literature. Classic car wall posters make nice additions to any collection. It's even better if you have a "rec" room or a restoration shop attached to the garage where they can be displayed to best advantage. Bright and colorful, they're part of automotive history. Original and authentic specimens are even more difficult to find than scarce and rare sales catalogs, but many good reproductions have been produced.

Frankly, I'm pleased with the very high standard of reproduction characteristic of most of the vintage car posters now available. More seem to be coming on the market every year as the interest in them widens. Autographics' showroom poster of the 1929 Model A and Banner King's wall display of the 1935 Ford V-8 engine illustrated, years ago, just how faithfully original posters could be reproduced in color. Since then, others have been issued.

Both Ford posters were duplicates of early sales promotional material made for dealer use. The originals were designed for showroom wall displays, rather than for the public. The originals were scarce because so few of the posters were released in the first place. Nearly all went to Ford dealers. The print runs were small compared to the thousands of sales catalogs released into general circulation. Few dealers bothered to save the posters, too. Thus, the survival rate of originals was vastly lower than for other types of sales literature, where print runs were much larger.

In addition to the posters mentioned above (and perhaps others that I'm not aware of) there are the posters which have been reissued and reproduced by car manufacturers as novelty items for dealer use. I don't know how freely available they are, but they are attractive specimens if you can get your hands on them. Presumably, the dealers concerned would be as good a place as any to make inquiries, since they were reissued for showroom display purposes.

As many literature collectors know, Fiat catalogs and sales literature set a very high standard of quality down through the years. From the lush pieces issued around World War I, to the latest items on the Dino, all of them are good; every piece is a nice addition to any collection. Fiat has also reissued vintage posters which maintained their standards admirably.

I don't know how many of these early posters Fiat reissued for new-car dealer use in the past 15 years. I have five or six. Presumably there were a few more, too. The originals were done by big name European poster artists back in the early 1900s to 1920s, with a few from the 1930s as well. A number have achieved fine-art status now, with originals hanging in art galleries. They combine a high degree of artistry with a soft sell approach.

Indeed, Fiat left the sales pitch up to the salesman and the catalog. The posters were meant to convey corporate prestige with a flair that couldn't be anything but Italian. Fiat issued them in English, Italian and Spanish and probably other languages as well.

The "Balilla" poster by M. Dudovich was issued in 1934 or 1935 with introduction of Fiat's new, small-car. The Vatican protested the length of the lady's skirt in version one. Fiat withdrew the original and reissued this one.

Artist C. Riccobaldi created the "Manifesto Fiat" poster for the Fiat 1500 in 1935. French automakers spent lots of money on posters in lieu of advertising in big-circulation magazines and newspapers like American companies.

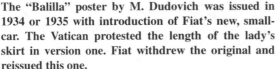

The Fiat "Balilla" poster is a celebrated piece issued in 1934 or 1935 with the introduction of Fiat's new, small-car. The Vatican took exception to the length of the lady's skirts in the first version of the poster. Fiat hastily withdrew the original and reissued one with a lower hemline. This kept the company well out of controversy. It's a good poster and, perhaps, one of Fiat's last purely artistic efforts. Later posters increasingly carried a selling message.

A Fiat 509 poster another famous one. The half horse, half man centaur depicted on it must be symbolic of something, but it's lost on me. The Fiat 509 is plain enough and so's the company's big Turin plant. This one's a great conservation piece and apparently full-sized at around 30 x 25 inches in full, livid color.

In another Fiat poster, a couple in a Victoria add up to a charming item. It is, apparently, Fiat's first car and makes this the firm's earliest poster. The artwork is dated 1899 and it's been used in a number of automotive histories. It measures out to 30 x 25 inches. The reproduction contains some of the creases and minor tears in the original. Fiat obviously had to hunt around to find a copy that could be reproduced.

Fiat's reproduction posters seem full-sized. The color reproduction is excellent (in fact by Fiat's own publications and printing facilities). If you can latch on to a set, they're well worth having. They will probably become quite rare in their own right as time goes on.

Renault also released a minor flood of what I call "near posters" some years back. They're poster format, but not copies of originals, although they seem to incorporate some original artwork. I have nine or 10 items covering all years from 1900 to the 1980s. These are somewhat smaller than Fiat's and stand, I think, as advertising and sales promotion novelties, rather than pure poster art. However, the cars come through nicely. Many, in fact, are models which are less familiar. All are photographic posters.

The significance of a "Renault 1930" reproduction poster escapes me, but the car seen in it is one of Renault's big and less familiar classics called the Reinastella. It's carrying a nice example of custom body work, too. If I didn't know better I'd say the little throng and the cop in the poster were looking at some-

European manufacturers were addicted to poster art promotional methods, particularly during the early years of automaking in France. They plastered posters, such as this 1925 Renault "Aviation/Automobile" design, on any available wall for outdoor display purposes.

Another famous poster was designed by M. Sironi and entitled, "Dipinto Fiat 500." It pictured the manufacturer's badge, the car and an example of ancient Roman art honoring the founding of Rome. The inference was that this popular 1936 Fiat model was comparable to great Italian art.

thing in the city dump, which is what the background seems to be. Whatever the background was, it appears to have been edited out in the re-issue, all of which makes for a rather strange setting without it.

American manufacturers were never much addicted to poster art promotional methods. European manufacturers were, though, particularly during the early years of automaking, when they plastered their posters up on any available wall for outdoor display purposes.

French manufacturers spent a lot of money on their posters, presumably in lieu of the big circulation magazines and newspapers, which is where American companies placed their advertising. Poster advertising was in the European tradition and car manufacturers were not about to change the habits and tastes of their customers.

Some of nicest (and scarcest) of all French art posters, however, are the Ford of France posters which promote, of all things, the Model T. They were beautifully done and project the Model T just the way Hispano-Suiza and Delage did with their costlier cars.

Cigarette cards depict brass to milestone models

By Walter E. Gosden

The collecting of automotive related paper material such as sales catalogs and folders, postcards and magazine ads has been written about a number of times. Another form of collectible paper that depicts cars, which little has been written about, is the cigarette card.

The cigarette card was first used for a purely practical purpose; to stiffen the paper wrapper the cigarettes came in to protect them from being crushed. Eventually, advertising found its way to the cards in the form of a simple line telling the brand name and maker of the cigarettes. The quality of the cards continued to improve. An improvement in printing processes was developed and color was introduced, as was the text on the back of the cards telling about the subject they featured. The first cards to show pictures came out in the late 1870s in the United States. They showed a picture of the Marquis of Lorne, the symbol of that brand of cigarettes.

The end of the 19th century and the beginning of the 20th century was a time when television, movies and radio didn't exist. For relaxation and entertainment, people turned to the collecting of postcards that they mounted in albums to show to friends. The introduction of the cigarette card, with its colorful appearance and informative text, gave the masses a whole new area to look to. The cigarette cards featured many different subjects, such as sports figures, birds, presidents, actresses, sea captains and their ships, etc. The list was endless.

The tobacco manufacturers were not interested in providing a hobby for the people, but saw that the cards they enclosed with their product could build up their business as interest in collecting the cards increased. In the early 1900s, there was very active competition between the tobacco tycoons on both sides of the Atlantic ocean. The tobacco or cigarette card had originated in the United States, but had

Lambert & Butler cards: British Crossley.

Lambert & Butler cards: An early Sunbeam.

Mobil Oil: A "Great Days of Motoring" Locomobile.

Mobil Oil: The Stearns touring was also depicted.

Mobil Oil: Oakland was the parent of Pontiac

Mobil Oil: A Chevrolet Royal Mail roadster.

spread to England and Europe. These countries would eventually be the leading producers of cigarette cards, while the cards issued in the United States would eventually lessen in popularity and, finally, be done away with.

The issuing of cigarette cards with illustrations or photographs of automobiles on them started when the automobile itself was only about five years old. Probably, the most colorful of the American issued cards that featured automobiles as their subject were the cards that came with Turkey Red Turkish cigarettes, circa 1907. The artwork on these cards is of the highest degree and in many instances is much better than the illustrations in the sales catalogs that the automobile manufacturers issued themselves to sell their cars!

The various cards were usually issued in sets of 50, with each showing a different make of automobile. However, many of the sets of cards issued with cigarettes in Europe numbered over 200 to each set. For a slight fee, many tobacco manufacturers offered albums to their customers to keep the cards in. Not all cards issued were strictly alike in size. Not all were made of cardboard. There were many cards that had a linen finish and some were not used as a cigarette package stiffener.

In 1957, a German firm issued an excellent set of cards that were printed on thin, glossy paper. They depicted both European and American automobiles. The two-seat Thunderbird, Cadillac Eldorado, Henry J, Packard Clipper, Lincoln Mark II and Edsel all found themselves featured on one set of German cigarette cards when they were new. In the early 1930s, the firm of Bilderdienst, in Berlin, issued a beautiful set of color cards that were gilt-edged. They showed automobiles of German manufacture, such as Horch, Hanomag, Mercedes Benz and many others.

Probably the best known series of cigarette cards came from England. In the mid-1930s, John Player & Son started to issue sets of cards with their cigarettes. They featured both British and American cars of that era. These cards illustrated mainly British cars, but also had a few V-8 Fords and Lincoln Zephyrs among the sets they offered. These cards from John Player & Sons had a complete description of the cars shown on the back of the card. The cards also had an adhesive on the back and could be mounted in an album especially prepared to hold the complete series. Such albums were available from local tobacconists for one penny.

Later sets of cigarette type cards were issued for other purposes. In 1966, Mobil Oil Company released its "Great Days of Motoring" collection, which is becoming very collectible now. Full Speed cigarettes of Holland offered a beautiful set of colored cards illustrated by Piet Olyslager. He went on to use many of these same illustrations in his book "Illustrated Motor Cars of the World," which was published in 1971.

Collecting factory photos

By Howard and Shelby Applegate

Photographs are one of the most popular versions of automotive literature and, next to sales catalogs and folders, have the highest collector demand.

Photography is a Greek word that means, literally, a printing process of diagrams made by light. A modern definition would be the process of reproducing actual life and scenery by images and sensitized surfaces by the action of light. Thus, the photograph itself is the effect or the resultant product of this process.

In 1902, the Studebaker Brothers Manufacturing Company, one of America's leading builders of carriages and other horse-drawn vehicles, decided to sell electric horseless carriages. When the electric models were introduced, Studebaker sent press kits to newspapers and magazines using techniques that had been practiced by the company since the 1870s, when the first carriage photos were sent to newspaper editors. The press kits included several articles describing the new models and seven photographs, two of which were re-touched scenes of electrics on the streets of South Bend, Indiana. The other five pictures were shot by company photographers inside one of the factories. These latter scenes were profiled in front of large white sheets or drapes. The photographs were printed on 9 x 12-inch paper for newspapers and 8 x 10-inch paper for magazines. The photo paper was dull, quite different from the glossy stock used today.

Also of interest to collectors are photos with maids, butlers and chauffeurs. This chauffeur driven 1929 Studebaker President Eight State Limousine shows a typical retainers uniform of this period. (Applegate & Applegate photo)

Other carriage companies who developed lines of gasoline-powered vehicles quickly followed suit. This indirect and usually unpaid form of advertising came to be called public relations, which still is an offshoot of corporate marketing or the paid form of advertising. These photographs, captions and public relations blurbs are now called press kits, because they are sent to media personnel at the time of new model introduction. Today, the photographs in press kits are either 4 x 5 inches or 8 x 10 inches in size. For years they were usually black and white, unless the photographic material was being supplied to a national magazine using a four-color printing process or to a television station. Today, however, most press kits are featuring more color transparencies than black and white prints.

In both the automotive trade and the old vehicle hobby, this type of photograph is still called factory-issued. Originally this phrase meant that the photograph was produced by and/or distributed by the auto-maker itself. In the intervening years since Studebaker's 1902 photos, the definition of factory-issued photograph has expanded to include other types of photos. Some photographs were authorized by or taken for vehicle manufacturers, but were not issued directly by them. Distribution of these items has been indirect through commercial photographers or advertising agencies. For example, Manning Brothers, a famous and venerable Detroit photographic studio, did considerable work for the independent auto-makers. Much of this work was incorporated into their literature and press kits. Wisely, the owners of Manning preserved all their negatives, not a common practice in that industry. When their automaking clients went defunct, Manning proved to be the only major source of original official photographs. Some of the best photographs for Ford, Lincoln and later Mercury for the years 1935 through 1941 came from the files of their advertising agency, N.W. Ayer, then of Philadelphia, Pennsylvania. Ayer, which supplied all the photography for press kits and literature, retained all of the work of the various photographers. It apparently sent to Detroit only what was approved for printing and distribution. The rest of the material remained unpublished for years, until it was given to a variety of automotive museums and libraries. Thus, these institutions and some collectors have photographs of Ford products that are not even preserved in the vast Ford Archives. Such custom body makers as Willoughby, Derham, Brunn, LeBaron, Judkins, Dietrich, Murphy, Rollston and Weyman, who built special bodies for America's luxury cars, kept extensive photographic records of their work to show dealers and prospective customers.

Dealer-created photographs are now also known by the generic term factory-issued, when in fact few dealership photographs had anything to do with the factory. Dealership material often lacked the professional quality of photos issued by the manufacturers. Dealership photos are collected primarily because they are unique and do not follow any set subject patterns. However, most of these shots are of showroom interiors, service areas, used car lots, dealer personnel and building exteriors.

Some companies, like Studebaker, used dealership photos in various corporate publications including house organs, annual reports, advertisements, literature and franchise marketing materials. In the late 1940s, Studebaker required each dealer to submit a minimum of one showroom photo showing display of new cars and one exterior photo with a new car or truck parked by the main showroom doors. In the 1950s, Diamond T required its branches and dealers to photograph each unit that they delivered to customers. This company demand for local material created an incredible number of unusual and interesting photos, but also an equal number of poor and useless items.

Also getting into the photographic picture were companies that manufactured aftermarket accessories. In the late 1940s and early 1950s, some firms produced continental kits for installation on many makes. As these accessory companies usually did not print literature, they sent press kit type photographs, often in color, to dealerships for use as marketing aids. Similar photos were issued by firms that made fender skirts, bumper guards, non-stock hoods and, in the 1970s, T-roof open-top conversions.

Restorers and collectors both agree that the best photographs are those commissioned and distributed by the automotive factories themselves. Some companies, like Studebaker and General Motors, had their own photographic departments with staff photographers, darkrooms and production laboratories. Others like Diamond T, Reo and Crosley had no photographic personnel or facilities, preferring to pay for outside professionals on a contract basis.

Why do collectors and restorers avidly search for factory-issued photographs? First, the price is most attractive; rarely does an original cost more than $25, while quality reproductions rarely exceed $5. Thus, a person can become a photograph collector without investing the vast sums of money required to purchase original printed literature. Or a restorer can acquire authentication material inexpensively to aid in the rebuilding phases of his vehicles. Second, most photographs are associated items that were issued in limited quantities by motor companies. Packard historians like collecting Packard factory photographs. So do historians of every other make of car and truck.

In 1902, Studebaker introduced horseless carriages and sent the first press kit to newspapers and magazines. It included articles and seven photographs of cars on the streets of South Bend, Indiana. (Henry Austin Clark, Jr. photo)

Auto photo collectors diligently search for materials relating to important historical personages of the industry. This photo shows actress Jean Harlow with her 1932 Packard dual cowl phaeton. (Applegate & Applegate photo)

Automotive factory photos are also collected as minor works of art that reflect on the social history of the period. Where else can one find so many quality shots of storefronts, residences, parks, national historic sites, fashions, architecture, labor, marine scenes and amusements?

Restorers also place a priority on detail photography such as specialized shots of parts of actual cars including engines, interiors and interconnecting parts. These are illustrations that simply are not available in sales or service literature. Detailed photography is least likely to have been changed by the airbrush in the art studio, as we shall note later.

What types of automotive photographs are collected? As with any other collectible, the hobbyist should acquire only what is of personal interest. Some collectors ... a knowledgeable minority ... are interested in quality photos regardless of make. They will buy a DeSoto photo as quickly as a Pierce-Arrow picture because of the composition or scenery in the photo. Others specialize in the companies or marques that interest them for a particular reason, while some seek period material and restrict themselves to chronological eras such as the 1930s or the 1960s.

Other than collecting by make or company, collecting by body style has the greatest number of followers, primarily because there are so many subjects from which to choose. Photographs of specific body styles are avidly collected, with emphasis on open cars, police cars, taxicabs, woodie wagons, sedan deliveries, professional vehicles, business coupes and fire apparatus. For example, station wagon collectors usually seek photos of all makes. Some specialists seek photographs of corporate experimental, dream or show cars. Most of these shots were taken in company styling studios or at major auto shows. The great historical value to photography of experimental cars is that, except for General Motors, most experimental cars are eventually destroyed and the photograph becomes the only permanent record of the vehicle.

Some hobbyists search for the unique historical photographs that depict important people, places and events in automotive history. They like commemorative photos of the first, last or millionth car of the same type; or the 1906 photo of John Mohler Studebaker seated in a car on the roof-top proving track at one of his South Bend, Indiana buildings; or pictures of Preston Tucker standing next to Tucker car number one; or shots of Raymond Loewy pictured with his great masterpiece, the 1963 Avanti.

Racing is a subject that intrigues many collectors. They seeks photos of track scenes, drivers, still shots of cars (whether winners or losers) and pace cars. The latter category has become the hottest photo collectible today. Photographs of Indy 500 Official Pace Cars appeal to almost every type of hobbyist.

Other collectors seek photographs of famous personalities. Many automakers paid entertainers or sport figures to endorse their products or exploited famous owners. Studebaker went so far as to encourage dealers to make cars available, on a complimentary basis, to dignitaries who visited their towns and cities, provided that the famous person would agree to be photographed in or next to the car. This photo negative would be rushed to South Bend, printed in the next issue of *Studebaker Wheel* and distributed to major newspapers and magazines throughout the country.

Corporate use of personalities reached its zenith in the 1920s and 1930s. John A. Conde in his *The Cars That Hudson Built* shows that Hudson distributed photographs of such famous car owners as actresses Constance Howard and Patricia Ellis, singer Morton Downey, cartoonist Rube Goldberg, auto test driver Cannonball Baker, aircraft inventor Orville Wright and adventurer Lowell Thomas. Hudson also featured aviatrix Amelia Earhart and racing driver Barney Oldfield several times, in 1930s photographs, based on paid endorsements. Not to be outdone, Hudson's competitor, Nash, featured Babe Ruth with his 1937 Ambassador Eight sedan and actress Constance Moore with her 1939 Ambassador Six sedan.

In 1932, Studebaker paid comedians Stan Laurel and Oliver Hardy to pose with a 1932 Commander Regal Sedan in front of the Hal Roach Studios. The resulting photo was extensively used in Studebaker publications, including special foreign language editions distributed in Europe and South America and widely circulated among American newspapers and magazines. Not to be outdone, Packard featured Jean Harlow with a 1932 phaeton and Marmon used the Latin actress Lupe Velez with her 1930 Model 78 sedan. Adventurer Lowell Thomas seems to have been the most fickle endorser. He worked originally for Hudson, then Nash and later for Mercury and Pontiac. Thomas, eventually, helped sell Kaisers in the early 1950s. Although personality endorsements have declined substantially over the last generation, Chrysler Corporation still employs two stars, Frank Sinatra and Ricardo Montalban, to plug their cars in advertisements and photographs.

Commercial vehicle pictures have become very popular with photograph collectors. Some hobbyists collect by make or vintage, others seek material related to certain types of vehicles, including beverage

Racing interests many collectors, especially Indy Pace Car shots. A 1949 Oldsmobile 88 is pictured by a General Motors office building. This is not an Indianapolis Motor Speedway official photo. (Applegate & Applegate photo)

trucks (especially those with the logo of famous beer and soda pop companies), military vehicles (any type and vintage), railroad trucks, inter-urban busses, ice cream trucks, and delivery trucks that supply goods and merchandise to retail stores. One of the commonest themes to be found in commercial vehicle photography ... and perhaps the ultimate to the collector ... is the photograph of the truck at work. In fact, this theme underlies Krause Publication's recent picture-book entitled *American Work Trucks*.

The farmer loading milk cans into the bed of his pickup truck or the bread truck driver unloading boxes of his fresh wares, in front of the A & P, typify the most exquisite form of commercial vehicle photography. Photos of oil tanker trucks delivering gasoline to service stations are highly collectible and appeal to the growing numbers of people who collect service station memorabilia. Unlike photos of most passenger cars, there is an important relationship between the commercial vehicle and the individual pictured with it.

Over the years, we have found that many automotive photograph collectors have organized their material around precise subjects, other than make, body style and time period. One woman was interested in any photos of vehicles which also included a thoroughbred dog. Several men collected photos that had both horses and cars. Uniformed chauffeurs appealed to a woman from Connecticut, while an author sought stereotypical photos that showed black Americans in servile situations to document his book on racial stereotypes. Another scholar studying American architecture was more interested in buildings than vehicles, while an art teacher bought photographs to use in classroom presentations on the history of industrial design.

There are also many types of photographs that are not collectible. Family photos of Uncle Frank and his 1932 Buick on the beach at Asbury Park, New Jersey are shunned by experienced photo collectors. They want official photos that have authenticity, company association and composition. Dozens of flea market vendors have hundreds of these family photos reasonably priced, but collectors consider them virtually worthless. Some veteran photo collectors, however, always look through piles of family Brownie camera photos in the hopes of finding that special gem ... like an amateur photo of President Eisenhower in his official Lincoln Limousine during the 1956 parade in Sarasota, Florida. Such gems will be rare, indeed.

Almost as worthless as family photos are photos taken at car shows, because there is rarely any opportunity for good photo composition. At a recent national one-marque club show, we observed dozens of members struggling to get poor shots of vehicles. The cars had average restorations and some had glaring errors in authenticity. This is not the way to go, when quality factory photos are readily available at reasonable prices. Dealers and distributorship photos should be looked at carefully before purchase. The item must either be unique or be a quality composition unmatched by the regular factory-issued photos.

Experienced automotive photo collectors even look at factory photos from a critical point of view. Most reject photos, of artwork or design studios, unless exceptionally unique. They also avoid photos that have been extensively doctored in the photo lab, especially when the background or the foreground have been white-inked out. Highly re-touched or airbrushed photos are similarly rejected, since they simply are not professional looking. Often, they are likely to be inaccurate. The studio tampering sometimes makes them different than actual production models, adding incorrect hubcaps, chrome, lights, windows or details.

Veteran collectors prefer exterior shots of vehicles where background and foreground add to the reality of the scene. People may be shown in the composition, provided that they add an important dimension to the shot and do not detract from the car by being too large and overwhelming or blocking part of the car or truck. After all it is the vehicle, not the person, that usually is important. The mature collector tends to avoid shots taken inside buildings, especially views of new car shows. In such cases, the results are usually similar to the odd shots produced at antique car shows and views taken in styling or photographic studios. There are exceptions to this rule, of course. Good views of manufacturing plant interiors, particularly assembly lines, are sought by some hobbyists.

Unless the vehicle illustrating the photo is rare, collectors also avoid shots which include only part of the car or truck. A photo showing the rear half of a 1960 Jeep pickup is not a collectible photo, while one depicting the front half of a Tucker outside the Chicago plant may be. Most collectors also tend to take a dim view of full side shots, preferring first the left front three-quarter view or, secondly, the right front three-quarter view.

Contrived photos are as easy to spot as the proverbial three dollar bill. In 1959, Studebaker issued a photograph of a convertible next to a Miami Beach hotel. The basic problem with the photo is that the hotel had been torn down two years before the picture was alleged to have been taken. It's easy to explain how this happened. The Studebaker photo department super-imposed a photographic cut out of the convertible onto an existing photo of the hotel, not realizing their chronological error. Plymouth, in the early 1940s, issued a photo of a station wagon parked in front of a small tropical railroad station. The Plymouth photo crew doctored the photo by whiting-out the name of the original town and having an artist paint in the name Miami. Not only was the scenery inconsistent with Miami, Florida, but the small station was not used by any of the three railroads serving Miami at the time.

Publicists for trucks long have realized that the most acceptable photos were of trucks at work. In the 1950s, when stylists began to promote annual model design changes like cars, marketing people had major problems getting good illustrations for press kits and printed literature. One genius at International Harvester Corporation solved this problem by using several handmade trucks as the basis for all photography. To give both authenticity and variety to a portfolio of trucks-at-work photos, he painted the name of a company or industry on the side of the vehicle in water color paint. One day, the bottler's truck would be designated Cardwell Brewing Company and shown next to a National Tea Company store. The next day, after washing and repainting the same truck, it would reappear as Booth's Bottling Company and be photographed unloading at a Jewel Tea outlet. These "dramatic" scenes set-up by corporate photographers usually looked exactly like what they were ... contrived and artificial street scenes.

Many photographs are of more interest to restorers and vehicle owners than to collectors. Those involved in the restoration process use photographs to authenticate their cars and trucks. Photographs often are more reliable than the art in sales catalogs and folders, some of which has usually been doctored. The best restorers, however, have learned to look at photographs with a questioning eye. Even though the process of photography is supposed to be a faithful reproduction of what the lens of the camera has seen, certain things take place in the photographic process about which the viewer may not be aware.

One immediate problem is to determine whether the photograph is of a pre-production mock-up, a handmade vehicle or a production vehicle. Photographs of the former may include accessories never used on production cars or have the wrong hubcaps and taillights or a number of exterior cosmetic changes. Even when you know that the photograph is of a production car, try to determine when during the model year the photograph was made. Sometimes, exterior changes are made in the styling of a car during the year and the restorer should determine when the photograph was taken. No doubt the restorer has already determined when his car was made by consulting one of the standard references on serial numbers, like Cars & Parts "American Car I.D. Numbers" books for the 1950s, 1960s and 1970s.

Detroit marketing people have proven to be compulsive photo doctors. If they like a certain composition with a Corvette next to a large tree, near a man and woman picnicking, they may be very unhappy

A 1902 Packard Model F Touring photo was sent out in press material issued to newspapers and magazines. It is not exceptional and possibly not shot by a professional. The driver is J.W. Packard. (Applegate & Applegate photo)

with the way the light changes the appearance of the car. They'll send the original negative to a photographic lab, which then airbrushes dull separator marks on the bright spots of the car. In doing so, they may have done nothing fundamental to change the appearance of the Corvette. On the other hand, they may have. Also, a wrong photo can be included in a press kit. The 1957 Chevrolet press packet included a photo labeled 1957 Corvette. In actuality, it was a 1956 Model with non-standard tires. This certainly has confused restorers for years.

In 1942, Studebaker's photo lab technicians used an original photo of a President Eight Deluxe Cruising Sedan and retouched it to make it look like a Commander Custom Cruising Sedan. However, they forgot to remove the large chrome strip under the three side windows. This incorrect photo was widely distributed to the media.

The introduction of the 1942 DeSoto, with its hidden headlights, led Studebaker management to request styling director Raymond Loewy to prepare some artwork using the hidden headlamp concept and wraparound skirts and trim. Loewy and his staff used the inaccurate Commander photo as the basis for their redesign work. This was all done with airbrushes and black and white artists' paint. Some copies of the Loewy print are being sold at swap meets as a typical 1942 Commander. In reality, it was a styling study for postwar models based on an incorrect original. Like anything else, factory issued photographs must be used with caution and knowledge about the marque.

There are two standard classifications of factory issued photographs: original and reproduction. Normally, original photos are defined as items authorized and distributed by and for companies. Yet, this definition is not very precise or accurate. Let's use the N.W. Ayer creation of photos for 1935 Lincolns as an example. Ayer had photographers shoot various models of Lincolns in many different backgrounds. Negatives were made in either 4 x 5-inch or 8 x 10-inch sizes. These are original photos. Ayer's staff then chose which prints to recommend to Lincoln and sent along sets of 8 x 10s for their review. The photos sent to Lincoln were made from original negatives. Lincoln marketing people selected the items for use in press kits and literature and had Ayer make 8 x 10-inch negatives from which to print the thousands of photos required for press kits. These 1935 press kit prints were second-generation originals.

When companies reprint photo papers in, say, a historical photo portfolio on Firebirds, new negatives are often made because the originals were lost or damaged. These Pontiac prints are factory-issued reproductions. Other makes known to have issued their own reproductions include Cadillac, Chevrolet, Plymouth, Chrysler, Dodge, Ford and Oldsmobile. The standard definition for reproductions are those prints made today by professional photo labs from first- or second-generation factory photos. That is, new 8 x 10 inch negatives are made from good clear original prints. The loss in clarity in such reproductions ranges from five to ten percent.

Amateur reproductions like the Auburn, Cord, Duesenberg and Lincoln-Zephyr prints that have been in the hobby marketplace for over 10 years are not even classified as reproduction, because their quality ranges from fair, at best, to poor. In addition, Manning Brothers sells prints made from their original negatives. Is an 8 x 10 Manning photo of a 1925 Wills Sainte Claire an original, because it was made from the original negative or a reproduction because it was made 50 years later for someone other than Wills? Most collectors would classify such photos as reproductions. How would you classify a photo of the 1949 Mercury coupe secretly taken by Kaiser-Frazer photographers prior to the public introduction of the new cars? It's an original all right, but not one issued by the right factory.

It is difficult for some hobbyists to distinguish between original and reproductions. Older photos are brittle and sometimes break and flake at the edges. Some show signs of "browning" or suffer advanced aging due to over-exposure to light and heat. Originals often had rubber stamp markings on the reverse indicating manufacturer and negative number. Many reproductions are now being made on resin backed photographic paper, which would not have been used until recently. The two leading producers of current reproduction automotive photographs advertise their material as reproductions, not originals, and all photos are stamped with their names on the reverse.

Some purist hobbyists seek only original material for their collections and refuse to accept reproductions. Other photo collectors acquire both originals and reproductions, depending on quality and availability. Availability of material varies. Quality reproductions exist for over 4,000 different factory photos. Late model originals for 1970 to 1981 may still be found at many swap meet literature stands. Earlier originals issued prior to 1969, especially truck and foreign cars, are much harder to find. This is because press kit material for commercial vehicles was distributed in limited quantities, while photos for foreign cars prior to 1965 were sent only to national magazines and the largest urban newspapers. Thus, only 100 photos of the 1948 Austin were originally made, compared with 10,000 for the 1980 Corvette.

Automotive photo prices depend on type and demand. Reproductions usually sell for no more than $7 each, with lower per unit charges for large-quantity purchases. Originals range in price from $5 to $150, depending on year, make, and rarity. One owner of an original 1955 Chevrolet Indy 500 Official Pace Car photo has refused an offer of $75, even though the photo is available in reproduction format. Fleetwood Body Company photos taken in the teens and 1920s range from $10 to $50 each, depending on marque and body style. Original complete Shelby Mustang press kits are often sold for $150 to $300 each.

If you don't already collect automobile photos and want to start, may we suggest that you use one cardinal rule ... buy only those items that you find visually appealing and attractive or that relate directly to your personal automotive interests. If you want to start with only reasonable investments of money, consider buying quality reproductions or acquire the newest material first. By attending major flea markets, one can still find most of the 1970s and 1980s press kits.

For example, American Motors issued two press kits a year, one each for passenger cars and Jeeps. You would need to acquire 24 different kits. Each of these probably has a minimum of five photos. These 120 or more photos should not cost more than $250 or about $2 each. We hope that you find the collecting of factory issued photos both informative and interesting.

Experimental and dream car photos are highly collectible. This one of Ford's experimental Mustang II, built in 1963, is more so because of the current popularity of the marque. (Applegate & Applegate photo)

A brief history of Chevrolet postcards

By Jay Ketelle

For about 100 years, postcards have been an inexpensive, yet highly visual way of communication in our country. And no collection of Chevrolet memorabilia would be complete without a representative selection of advertising and dealer postcards. Advertising postcards show the current model car or truck. Dealership salesmen would send these out to prospective buyers. Dealer postcards depict the outside of the dealership or the used car sales lot.

In this article, I will be talking about just some of these postcards (along with other variations) that have shown Chevrolet cars and trucks down through the years. I am certain there are many of you who could add further interesting comments to this article. Also, perhaps after reading this article, some of you will decide to begin collecting this type of postcard. Better yet, maybe you'll rummage around your grandparents' attic or in that old desk and dig up some of these postcards and give them to a friend who already collects them.

There are several types of postcards, besides those used by salespeople to help sell new cars and trucks. In the 1930s, black and white postcards showing actual photos of the different models were issued by a variety of companies. These postcards were sold to dealerships handling all makes of cars. They were designed for sending out to help sell used cars in a dealer's inventory. Also, some manufacturers

Speath Chevrolet was a neighborhood dealership that made good use of factory window displays. This post-card shows the dealership in 1956, judging by the appearance of a "Lucky Traveler" promotion piece in the window. (Jay Ketelle)

such as Buick, Cadillac, Dodge, Chevrolet and others issued these "used-car" postcards to their dealers, to help them sell their trade-in vehicles.

After the World War II, from 1946 through the early 1950s, Beurmann-Marshall Company issued a large number of black and white postcards. In addition, Dealer's Supply Company issued sepia or brown-toned postcards from 1946 through 1958. In later years, Chevrolet issued a large variety of postcards featuring its "OK" used cars, but most of these were of overall poor quality and did not show any cars in detail. Therefore, this type of card has less collector interest and value.

Museums, oil companies, other private businesses and individuals have issued postcards showing Chevrolets. Many of these postcards offer really nice photographic work, but they are less collectible, in almost all cases, because of their generally easier accessibility and because they just are not "the real thing" issued by Chevrolet.

Many Chevrolet dealerships have issued postcards showing pictures of their dealership, showroom, used car lot, service department or announcing a special sale. These, too, are quite collectible.

Probably the most sought after group of advertising postcards issued by any automobile company are the Corvette cards issued by Chevrolet. These postcards continue to be in increasing demand by collectors all over the world. Corvette postcards were first issued in 1954, when the same card was released with both red-tone and a green-tone tints. I've been told that these photos were taken with two different colored lenses.

No Corvette postcards were issued for the years 1955, 1956 and 1957. Beginning in 1958, postcards were issued for each year through 1984, with the exception of 1967 and 1983. Just one card was issued for both 1970 and 1971 model-years together, but in 1963 and 1964, two postcards were issued per year. One showed the coupe and the other depicted the convertible. In addition, a 1978 Indy 500 Pace Car postcard was privately issued, by a West Coast collector.

Chevrolet truck postcards from as early as 1923 have been found. However, only a very few of these postcards are known to exist from before 1954. They have been published yearly since then. They come both in standard size and (occasionally) larger size postcards. The latter were used to announce special midyear models, Bonanza packages or other special sales or models.

Postcards advertising Chevrolet cars can again be found from as far back as the early Teens. Coming up through the years, for 1927, 1928 and 1930, we find some nice postcards featuring various models, in

Postcards of the 1930s and 1940s made heavy use of "cameo" type insert photos. Pictured here are the owners of Land-Goddard Chevrolet in Kansas City, Missouri. (Jay Ketelle Collection).

Pictured on this postcard is Bob MacGillivray, a salesman for Roger Dean Chevrolet who sold the most Corvettes in the state of Florida for several consecutive years. (Jay Ketelle Collection)

a small circle or box, with Atlantic City, New Jersey in the background. There was probably a set of full-color postcards for the 1933 model year, although only one card has shown up so far. A nice set of 12 different color postcards was issued for 1937 (the same pictures were used on Chevrolet calendars that year). Additional nice color postcards were issued for 1940, 1941 and 1942. Postwar postcards, which are slightly taller in size, are known to exist for 1952. Since then, postcards have been published from 1954 until current times.

Chevrolet published large-size postcards for the 1967 and 1969 Camaro Indy 500 Pace Car, but did not issue cards for other Pace Cars. Other special varieties of postcards include those used to remind dealership customers of recommended maintenance on their vehicles, cards suggesting that you come in and order your new car, cards on the Soap Box Derby, cards inviting you to come to the showroom to see the new models and, in modern times, cards announcing low interest rates and estimated fuel economy. There are other types, too.

Postcards offer an easy way to display automotive history and, also, are an interesting way to keep up with the changes in clothing and hair styles. If automotive postcards are your thing, you'll want to think about attending the annual National Automobile Postcard Collectors' Meet. It is held every fall around the time of the Carlisle, Pennsylvania Flea Market and the Antique Automobile Club of America's Fall National Meet at Hershey, Pennsylvania.

This is a great event to attend if you would just like to look around and become more familiar with this area of collecting or if you have postcards you want to buy, sell or trade. For more information write to: Jay Ketelle, 3721 Farwell, Amarillo, TX 79109. You can also call (806) 355-3456 or fax (806) 355-5743.

Classic 1957 Bel Airs are showcased at Tom's Chevrolet in Wheaton, Maryland and depicted in this heavily re-touched color-tinted photo postcard. The "OK" Used Cars sales lot also features a 1956 Bel Air and a T-bird. (Jay Ketelle)

The low-priced 1954 Chevrolet 150 two-door sedan was promoted in this color postcard bearing the imprint of Park Circle Motor Company, a Chevrolet dealership in Baltimore, Maryland. (Jay Ketelle Collection)

Cars on Christmas cards

By Terry V. Boyce

Christmas. A grand time of year for families and for most retail businesses. It can be a slow time for car dealers, though. Manufacturers and dealers have long recognized the need to keep the product and the dealer before the customer's eyes during the holiday season. Christmas greeting cards are one method of reminding customers that they are appreciated. For a few pennies per customer the dealer can present his good tidings, while massaging the egos of potential buyers. Christmas greetings from a car dealer speak of one's importance and status in the community; cars are, after all, high-ticket items.

Like other cultural artifacts, old Christmas cards reflect the periods in which they were created. Pictured here are three automotive Christmas greeting cards, each a representative not only of the factory and dealer, but of their era.

December 2, 1927 was a historic day for the Ford Motor Company and the auto industry. Henry Ford unveiled his all-new Model A Ford on that day. Thousands of people crowded into Ford showrooms for a first look

Ford introduced the Model A just a few weeks before Christmas in 1927. Ford's Christmas card featured the new 1928 Fordor in an atmosphere of splendor. (Terry Boyce Collection)

The Model A was born into an era of Tudor homes, ornate design and cultured pretenses. Automobiles were evolving, changing from purely functional machines into four-wheeled works of art. The Model A was beautifully proportioned and exuded an elegance that belied its low price. Still, it maintained a virtuous simplicity that did not compromise the traditions of quality and service set by the plebeian Model T it succeeded.

It would be hard to imagine a Model T Ford in the gilded, tapestried scene used for Ford's 1927 Christmas card. Ford's 1928 Model A Fordor sedan, "the Baby Lincoln," looked quite comfortable in such surroundings, however.

The Ford card, with its embossed, heavy paper and gilded highlights bespoke quality. No message other than the traditional "Merry Christmas" was used. Even though the Model A was only days old, Ford felt no need to identify the car. The Ford logo said it all. Although cut to postcard size, the card was probably mailed in an envelope, since there is no printing on the reverse at all.

Twelve years later the Chevrolet Christmas card shown arrived at an Oklahoma family's mailbox. A terrible depression had wracked the nation during the years since the 1927 Ford card was sent. A reshaping, a streamlining of American culture and design had resulted. The new 1940 cars in the showrooms by Christmas, 1939, were clean and advanced in appearance. The design of Chevrolet's Christmas card was also clean and dynamic. Cropping in tightly on the illustration, which showed Santa at the wheel of a green 1940 Chevrolet Special Deluxe Sport Coupe, suggested action and speed. Things were moving again. The nation, all of it, was beginning to recover economically. Even a family in Norman, Oklahoma might dream of owning a new Chevrolet such as the one on the card. Only $750 would buy this six-cylinder car with its modern sealed beam headlights, column gearshift and "Royal Clipper" styling.

The 1939 Christmas card wished all a "Happy and Prosperous New Year" and for many it would be

Annual Christmas greetings continued into the exciting 1950s, with the cards continuing to reflect the changing tastes, customs and attitudes of Americans. The 1950s were years of great promise; television, jet aircraft, a polio vaccine. Everything was changing for the better. Automation promised a life of leisure for all. Mother enjoyed her Vegamatic, while father guided the family's new car with the aid of Rotomatic power steering.

Ford salesman Elmo Koger mailed this Auravision card to the Fred Coopples, of McPherson, Kansas, on November 5, 1965. A recording of Rosemary Clooney and Mitch Miller's Orchestra was bonded over the face of the card. (Terry Boyce Collection)

A cheery Santa at the wheel of a 1940 Chevrolet wished customers of the Hughes Motor Company in Norman, Oklahoma a Merry Christmas in 1939. (Terry Boyce Collection)

Technology even produced a new, improved Christmas card. Columbia Records developed the "Auravision" card by pressing a phonograph record into clear plastic, which was then bonded to the face of the card. Ford used an Auravision card for their 1955 Christmas mailing. Rosemary Clooney, in appropriate Christmas garb, was shown with a 1956 Ford Victoria in two-tone green. Rosemary and Mitch Miller's orchestra provided the music.

"Play it on any standard 78 RPM phonograph machine and take Rosemary's advice for Christmas enchantment and year around satisfaction," the card read on the reverse. The direct sales messages in print and in song remind us that the golden 1950s were also the years that our traditions were irrevocably commercialized. The little postcard-record does have great appeal, though. It begs to be heard. One can imagine how often it must have been played in the baby-boomed, energetic, optimistic suburbs of Christmas 1955.

Christmases past. On them we build the individual memories that make Christmas something personal for each of us. Memories of toylands, electric trains, snowy downtowns, paper sacks rustling in closets, tables laden with abundant foods, aunts, uncles, cousins and Christmas cards. Merry Christmas.

The Nash Ambassador Airflyte, styled in the continental manner by Pinin Farina. Hood ornament by Petty, white sidewall tires extra.

To the Boy who wanted
a Stutz Bearcat...

REMEMBER *how you hungered for it? Remember how your pulse raced to its engine throb? That was it . . . that old Stutz Bearcat, Heaven-on-wheels to that boy you used to be!*

Today we invite you to be young again—to thrill to the wonder and romance of travel again.

Come and take command of the proudest car ever styled by Pinin Farina of Europe—this new Nash Ambassador "Country Club"!

Come and wonder at *true* continental styling attuned to American standards of room and comfort . . . the luxury of custom interiors—with the widest seats, the greatest eye-level visibility ever built into an automobile. Relax in airliner reclining seats that ease dawn-to-sunset travel.

Then—feel the pounding of your pulse when the mighty "Le Mans" Dual-Jetfire engine lets loose. For this is the Nash custom power option that holds the top American record in the 24-hour road race at Le Mans, France!

Never have you known such performance . . . and never have you known such handling ease as you have with new Nash Power Steering.

And as the road unreels and new enchantments greet your eye you'll know why we even built sleeping beds in a Nash. For you're going to travel as you've never traveled before!

Let us put this great car in your hands. Discover why this brilliant Nash Ambassador is today's heaven-on-wheels for you!

Take the Key and See—
You'll Find None so New as **Nash** *Airflytes*

Nash Motors, Division Nash-Kelvinator Corporation, Detroit, Mich.

AMBASSADOR   STATESMAN   RAMBLER

1953 Nash: Packard boys still wanted Packards, but Stutz boys had to settle for a Nash Ambassador Airflyte Country Club. Oh, well. (*National Geographic*, 1953)

Comparison type auto advertisements were popular for 50 years

By Bill McBride

To a copywriter, nostalgia is a tempting, often irresistible hook on which to hang an advertising campaign, Yet this frequently goes against the idea most companies espouse: today's products are better than those we made way back when. So the battle is set; the copywriter says talking about the past successes can support the present hopes for success. While the advertising manager for the company says we want to talk about today and tomorrow, not yesterday

In automotive advertisements, the tradition of comparing yesterday with today is at least 50 years old. Manufacturers in the late 1920s were already conscious of how far the industry had progressed. And they were anxious to point this out to customers. In addition, they wanted to prove that even those early products were superior examples of the automaker's art when they were made.

Pierce-Arrow, in 1929, ran a series of advertisements introducing its new straight eight. A large painting of the new car was balanced by a smaller reproduction of a painting used in a Pierce advertisement of the 1900-1915 era.

Both paintings in each advertisement were by the same artist and the settings were duplicated as well. Two advertisements in particular use the artwork of Adolph Treidler. One is captioned, "Reproduced from a painting which has hung in the Pierce-Arrow Boardroom since 1912. A full decade earlier, Pierce-Arrow had established its fame as America's finest motor car."

The second caption says, "Twenty years ago, Adolph Treidler did the illustration alongside. It was conceived, not as a Pierce-Arrow advertisement, but as a portrayal of the distinguished figures of that day. And, save for changing fashions, the same subject serves equal purpose today ... with the aid of Pierce-Arrow and Mr. Treidler." The message is that the eminence of Pierce-Arrow in 1929 was undiminished since the Teens.

Thus, an ironic idea is established. On the one hand, the car makers wish owners to trade in their cars with regularity. On the other hand, they wish us to believe that the old cars were at least as good, in their time, as the new models. And, on a larger scale, the old car hobby reveres the old and disdains the new, until the new gets to be old.

The Brass Era car lover once had nightmares about, the car show with, line after line of perfectly restored Model As. Today's Model A lover dreams fearful of future car show with line after line of equally perfect Mustangs. And tomorrow's Mustang devotee will worry about acres of Fairmonts and Pintos. Yet, the advertising we will now examine shows us that the past means a lot to some car makers or at least to their copywriters and art directors. Pierce-Arrow must have found success with its 1929 series, because it continued through 1932. A 1930 advertisement is particularly powerful. It shows a 1919 Pierce-Arrow touring (small) and a 1930 Pierce-Arrow dual-cowl phaeton (large) with the headline: "The Tyranny of Tradition." The copy reads, "Only the stern mandate of very, great pride ... and no lesser legislation on earth ... may command always the finest a man or an organization has to give. Such is the tradition which governs the creation of America's finest motor car . . . It would be far easier to build Pierce-Arrows of average quality, and infinitely more profitable to produce them in greater numbers. But the tyranny of tradition forbids."

In 1931, Pierce went to even larger paintings of the new car with a black and white photograph of the older model. This time, a car still in service with its original owner is depicted. Famous people of wealth, like Adolphus Busch of St. Louis: New York banker Stephen Baker and Governor Horace White, of New York, are named. Their old Pierce-Arrows are shown. The copy states that each car is still used frequently. What isn't said is that these famous men now own a Pierce-Arrow. But such ambiguity is typical of advertising. One puts the pieces on the page and lets the reader assemble them.

A 1932 advertisement reveals how remarkably effective mass production had been in reducing fine car costs. A small 1908 advertisement is reproduced along with a 1932 Pierce-Arrow 12 Club Sedan. The 1908 car sold for $7,100. the 1932 model for a mere $3,650.

Packard begins a tradition of looking backward in its advertising. A black and white advertisement is headlined, "Buy your car in '33 the way they did in 1903." The illustration is an Albert Dorne drawing of a 1903 Packard showroom. The copy includes: "Perhaps you weren't old enough in 1903 to buy a car ... but you can imagine what a momentous event such a purchase was in those days. The buyer didn't act on preconceived opinions. He studied every car whose price was near the amount he intended to pay. He compared them in every way. Then, he did what too many people fail to do nowadays; he rode in each car and compared them all. Packard believes this year you should go back to the 1903 way of buying a car."

"In the fine car field, revolutionary changes have been taking place. Spurred on by the fierce competition of the depression years, fine car manufacturers have striven as never before to advance their cars mechanically. And Packard has made the greatest strides of all. Name any quality a fine car should have ... brilliant performance, long life, comfort, quiet ... Packard has combined all these qualities in its new 1933 models."

The tack is different than the Pierce-Arrow advertisements. Packard uses its 1903 model as a focus for the reasoning of the copy. Buy today as you bought then, carefully and thoroughly. In the depression, this was maybe too obvious to mention. But then, many people for whom the depression was a mere financial inconvenience probably bought by brand name, rather than by comparing. So for a struggling car maker, getting the potential customer to evaluate, before writing the check, would be a means to increased sales ... especially if his product was superior.

Packard did another advertisement of this sort in 1934. But this time, it does something unusual and suggests that the older car was less than perfect. The headline says, "Maybe You Were That Boy." The illustration shows a youngster on a bicycle watching a 1907 (or so) Packard touring car roar past. The copy: "Sometime 25, perhaps 30 years ago, you saw a Packard for the first time. Measured by the standards of today, it was a crude affair. But there was something about it that spoke the language of fine things. Something that brought a lift to your heart and a boyish resolution to your lips. 'When I get to be a man, I'm going to own a Packard.' Today, you are a man. Have you kept that youthful promise to yourself?"

Three years later, Packard does almost the same thing with a change of point of view. Instead of third person, the advertisement is written, in part, in the first person. The headline says, "I'm keeping a promise I made to this boy." The illustration shows a boy and his collie looking down the road at an unseen Packard. A Packard Six touring sedan is shown at lower left. The lead paragraphs tell the story: "Years ago, a little freckle-faced boy watched with envy as a magnificent new motor car went by. To that boy, it was more than a motor car. It was a symbol of a way of living that reached above the mere necessities of life. It was an emblem of success. And as his longing eyes followed the disappearing car, I promised him that some day, he, too, would own a Packard. Yes, I was that boy, and today, I'm keeping the promise I made to myself some 25 years ago. I'm going to get my Packard."

While these last two advertisements don't actually show earlier Packards in comparison with modern Packards, they do take note of, and pay homage to, the car's history and heritage. After the war, Packard, like most other manufacturers, was trying to get into production as quickly as possible to capture the willing postwar seller's market. Like the others, Packard offered a rehash of a prewar car called the Clipper. Their advertisements cranked away at the old Packard slogan: "Ask the Man Who Owns One."

One 1946 advertisement, however, uses the heritage approach. It shows three Packards: a 1902, a 1923 and a 1946. The oldest is "Old Pacific," the Packard that made a "trail-blazing coast-to-coast run." The 1923 car is "the first production car powered with a straight-eight engine." The 1946 is a Clipper Deluxe

Eleven years elapsed between the painting of the two Pierce-Arrow portraits on this page.. both by the same artist, both the same size, both portraying America's Finest Motor Car.

The Tyranny of Tradition

ONLY the stern mandate of very great pride ...and no lesser legislation on earth.. may command always the finest a man or an organization has to give. Such is the tradition which governs the creation of *America's finest motor car.*

No rules ever conceived could be more exacting than the set of ideals which freely operate in every phase of Pierce-Arrow manufacture.

There is in Pierce-Arrow precincts an always-burning fire of determination never to depart from a principle which puts *fineness eternally first.*

In every car of this patrician line is expressed a courage which scorns the accepted standards of excellence as commonplace, compared with Pierce-Arrow's own.

And there is ever present a pardonable disdain of any process less fine than the hand-crafts-manship which has always distinguished Pierce-Arrow motor cars.

It would be far easier to build Pierce-Arrows of average quality, and infinitely more profitable to produce them in greater numbers. But the tyranny of tradition forbids.

THE NEW PRICES
$2695 to $6250...at Buffalo
(Canadian Made up to $9,000)
In the purchase of a car from income, the average allowance on a good used car usually more than covers the initial Pierce-Arrow payment.

THE PIERCE-ARROW MOTOR CAR COMPANY · BUFFALO, N. Y.

PIERCE-ARROW

1930 Pierce-Arrow: an 11 year old Pierce in the inset photo, and the new dual cowl phaeton on a countryside excursion. (*Country Life*, April 1930)

four-door sedan. Here, the thread of logic is based entirely on the slogan and the fact that the Packard was always a leader in the industry.

In 1953, Nash ran an advertisement that seems stolen from the Packard advertisements of the 1930s. This time, the new Nash isn't compared with Nash cars from the past, but with the legendary Stutz Bearcat. This unlikely pairing seems silly given the subsequent history of Nash/AMC, but the advertisement is dead serious. The headline says, "To the Boy Who Wanted a Stutz Bearcat." The large illustration shows a Nash Ambassador Country Club hardtop. The small illustration is of a boy eying a passing Bearcat. The copy: "Remember how you hungered for it ... all saucy red and bright with brass? Remember how your pulse raced to its engine throb? That was it ... that old Stutz Bearcat, heaven-on-wheels to that boy you used to be!"

At first thought the comparison seems absurd, but remember that this was the era of the Nash-Healey sports car, which campaigned successfully at the 24-hours of LeMans and improved on the record of American engines held by Chrysler's hemi (which was used in Briggs Cunningham's sports cars). So there can be a small justification for the Stutz/Nash link.

By the 1970s, the era of nostalgia was upon us. There seemed to be little or no originality in so much we did and said. Popular music returned to the 1950s, dancing echoed the 1940s, movies revived the 1930s and politics went back to the 1920s. Auto advertisements looked back as well. Buick, Cadillac, Chevrolet, Chrysler, Ford and Lincoln all used older models in advertisements, usually to support the new ones with their fame and history.

This is a curious phenomenon to examine. For decades, it was always this year's car that was the best. "New! New! New!" was the trumpet call since the 1930s. But new had become an old word; we wanted a new word. And the word was "old."

As the 1970s opened, Ford introduced the Pinto. A teaser advertisement shows an array of desirable Ford cars of the past with a small, shrouded Pinto in the background. The headline says, "Ford's Pinto would be worth more in 20 years than you'll pay this September." A sub-head says, "It's happened before." And an over line says; "Put a Pinto in your portfolio."

The array of old Fords is impressive, as is the little price notes under each. Since then, of course, these prices have become outdated in the collector car market. For those with active tear ducts or weak stomachs, don't read the list:

Car	Original Price	Remarked value ($)
1903 Model A	$850	$12,000
1909 Model T Touring	850	8,000
1929 Model A Woodie	650	3,500
1932 Lincoln V-12	4300	12,000
1932 Model B Cabriolet	460	3,500
1955 Thunderbird	2,944	4,000

And what, may I ask, is an eight-year-old Pinto worth?

Ford continued to compare the Pinto with both the Model T and Model A through 1974. For the "fringe ad" collector, these advertisements make an interesting addition to your book. (Fringe ads are those advertisements not produced by the car maker at the time the car was new, but which do show the car in question. Examples are tire, battery, wax and accessory advertisements using cars as props. Also, advertisements of a later era which show the older car.)

Chrysler joins the craze in 1973 with an attractive series using a 1924 Chrysler sedan, a 1941 Town & Country and a 1946 Town & Country convertible. Headlines follow this thrust: "The 1973 Chrysler. The car changed. The idea didn't." Copy supports this with mention of Chrysler's long tradition of engineering firsts and leadership.

Corvette uses two older cars in one 1975 advertisement. A 1954 and a 1965 Corvette follow a 1975 along a test track. The headline: "Introducing a More Efficient Corvette." More efficient, maybe, but more desirable? Hardly.

Cadillac also features older models in its 1975 advertising campaign. Among the handsome Classics are a 1930 Series 452-A roadster, a 1933 convertible sedan, a 1931 phaeton, a 1933 Model 355 dual-cowl phaeton and a 1932 Model 355-B convertible coupe. Again, the thrust of the advertisements are to say that what we did well back then, we do even better today.

The fever was catching. Buick uses a 1953 Roadmaster in a 1976 advertisement for the Regal. And, in a 1977 Riviera advertisement, a 1963 Riviera hovers in the clouds as the headline proclaims, "Riviera

Will Foster painted the lower illustration for Pierce-Arrow in 1912. Eighteen years later, Mr. Foster pictures the same scene (alongside) with 1930 models of the same kind of girls, the same kind of car.

Three New Groups
of Straight Eights by
Pierce-Arrow

IN FOUR NEW WHEELBASES

In the purchase of a car from income, the average allowance on a good used car usually more than covers the initial Pierce-Arrow payment.

HAVING created a Straight Eight line of such rare symmetry as to utterly outmode its field, Pierce-Arrow has gone brilliantly farther in a new series of fine car developments.

The new models are in three groups and four new wheelbases, three of which are longer. All are of delightfully increased spaciousness within .. all are in the custom manner, with appointments of a beautiful and distinguished modernness .. all share the slender, low-swung, patrician grace so truly and exclusively *Pierce-Arrow*.

And these new and ultra-modern Pierce-Arrows are as richly endowed mechanically:

With gears which silently and easily shift *at any speed* .. with an "intermediate" that operates with the smoothness and swiftness of ordinary high .. with a wheel which handles with magical ease .. with super-safety brakes, non-shatterable glass, low gravity centers, hydraulic shock absorbers, etc. .. these latest models embrace every device known to the engineering of fine motor cars and *worthy of Pierce-Arrow adoption*.

NEW PIERCE-ARROW PRICES .. at Buffalo .. From $2695 to $6250

(Other Custom-built Models up to $10,000)

MAR 1930

PIERCE-ARROW

1930 Pierce-Arrow: Will Forster painting of 1912 Pierce-Arrow vestibuled limousine and new sedan. "Same kind of girls, same kind of car," reads copy. (*Country Life*, March 1930)

69

rides again." This advertisement is something of a record setter: for the first time we are asked to be nostalgic for a 1960s car.

In summing up, the battle between nostalgia and progress will always be with us. But in the car business, one wonders if promoting today's cars on the virtues of cars past isn't admitting that the idea bin is empty?

For the "Ad Collector," here's a representative list of advertisements which feature cars of two eras in the same advertisement.

Buick		**Packard**		**Date**	**Magazine**
Date	**Magazine**	**Date**	**Magazine**	6/8/29.......	*Literary Digest*
10/27/75...........	*Newsweek*	5/33.......................	*Fortune*	8/31/29.....	*Literary Digest*
11/75....	*Psychology Today*	5/34.......................	*Fortune*	9/14/29.....	*Literary Digest*
10/76....................	*Esquire*	3/37.......................	*Fortune*	10/19/29...	*Literary Digest*
10-11/76...............	*Classic*	2/13/37	*Post*	11/2/29.....	*Literary Digest*
		11/14/46....................	*Post*	11/29	*House Beautiful*
Cadillac				3/30......................	*Fortune*
12/74....................	*Fortune*	**Nash**		3/30..........	*House Beautiful*
1/20/75............	*Newsweek*	8/1/53	*Post*	4/30........	*House & Garden*
				5/3/30.......	*Literary Digest*
Chrysler		**Pierce-Arrow**		6/7/30.......	*Literary Digest*
10/72....................	*Fortune*	2/29..........	*House Beautiful*	9/30....................	*Sportsman*
2/73...............	*Smithsonian*	2/29..............	*Country Life*	9/30.........	*House Beautiful*
4/73.....................	*Fortune*	2/2/29	*Literary Digest*	9/6/30.......	*Literary Digest*
3/5/73....	*Sports Illustrated*	3/29..........	*House Beautiful*	10/30.......	*House Beautiful*
		3/16/29	*Literary Digest*	10/11/30...	*Literary Digest*
Corvette		4/13/29	*Literary Digest*	4/31....................	*Sportsman*
11/14/74	*Sports Illustrated*	5/11/29......	*Literary Digest*	4/31	*House Beautiful*

What we said 38 years ago still goes

The 1969 Lincoln Continental

1969 Lincoln Continental: Ad promoting Wisconsin Lincoln dealers uses 1931 *Saturday Evening Post* Lincoln advertisement to enforce a theme.

THE NEW
PIERCE-ARROW
TWELVES

Model 53 Club Sedan . . . $3690 at Buffalo (Special Equipment Extra)

Another Page in
Fine Car History

IN the first few moments of demonstration, any model of the New Twelve line registers as a brilliant example of engineering discovery and creation.

No other fine cars are like or even comparable . . . none has so completely harnessed and controlled the amazing power of twelve cylinders . . . or made this power so obedient to every wish and whim of silent, luxurious motoring.

The New Twelves are endowed, as well, with the enviable social preferment that is ever Pierce-Arrow's own.

In brief, Pierce-Arrow gives timely and characteristic expression to the twelve-cylinder type of fine car . . . offers economic warrant for its present purchase . . . and again supremely justifies the faith of two generations of well-bred Americans.

THE NEW TWELVES ARE IN TWO GROUPS: 142" to 147" wheelbase . . . 150 horsepower . . . $3995 to $4500 137" to 142" wheelbase . . . 140 horsepower . . . $3295 to $4050

THE NEW EIGHTS ARE PRICED FROM 137" to 142" wheelbase . . . 125 horsepower **$2495**

All prices f.o.b. Buffalo

THE lower picture, first published by Pierce-Arrow in 1908, portrays a car which sold for $7100 — the very finest automobile of that day . . . The illustration above shows one of today's new Pierce-Arrow Twelves — the greatest fine car value of the present searching and sophisticated hour.

THE NEW TWELVES are priced, at Buffalo, from

$3295

1932 Pierce-Arrow: Lower picture from 1908 portrays a $7,100 Pierce. The new Club Sedan pictured cost $3,650 at Buffalo. (*Country Life*, February 1932)

1946 Packard: A man has to be sentimental about his first Packard ... and his latest one. (Life, 1946)

Full-line advertisements stretch collectors' buying power

By Bill McBride

For the general collector, focusing an automotive advertisements collection is probably the hardest thing to do. You can't collect everything. You'll run out of storage space, if you don't run out of money first.

In the 80-odd years automobiles have been advertised in America, there have been probably 150,000 different advertisements placed in magazines. This, of course, covers everything from one-inch-long, black and white advertisements for Black Motor Buggies and Success Auto-Buggies on up to multi-page, full-color advertising inserts for the full Chrysler Corporation or General Motors lines. So the enormity of the collect-them-all Syndrome will usually overpower almost every collector.

Eventually, the collector has to place some limits on what to collect in earnest. A series of representative or exhaustive single-make collections is a possibility. A few favorite cars or trucks, done very thoroughly, is quite satisfying. Collecting for the quality of illustrations, typography, photography, or copy writing is also useful. It's simply a matter of drawing the line somewhere, until you decide to redraw it.

As a sidelight, let's define "exhaustive" and "representative" as they apply to collections. Exhaustive means *every* advertisement for a car or year of car ever published, including all variations in size, color, layout, typography, paper and magazines in which they were published. Representative means an advertisement or advertisements for every car/year/model included in the collection, but not every one. An exhaustive collection of Packard advertisements, for example, would fill volumes and take forever to compile. But, an exhaustive collection of Chrysler 300 letter car advertisements might not fill one album.

1955 Chevrolet: Part of a 1955 Chevrolet full-line ad. Olds' were Futuramics and Chevys were "motormatics." (*The Saturday Evening Post*, 3/5/1955)

73

NEW 290-HP TURNPIKE CRUISER—MERCURY'S NEW LUXURY SERIES—The most advanced car you can buy at any price, with features found in no other car. These innovations include Floating Ride with special Air-Cushion Suspension, a Skylight Dual-Curve Windshield that curves *up* as well as around each side, special superhighway instruments, Breezeway Ventilation with roof-level air intakes and power-operated back window, distinctive styling shared by no other car.

NEW MONTCLAIR PHAETON COUPE—ONE OF 4 NEW MONTCLAIR MODELS—This sleek new hardtop is a brilliant example of Mercury's new Dream-Car Design. Gone is the plump look of most other cars. Bulging curves have given way to bold, clean-cut lines. Other Montclairs include a new convertible, a 4-door sedan, and a 4-door hardtop. A new 255-horsepower Safety-Surge V-8 engine with Power-Booster Fan is standard. A 290-hp Turnpike Cruiser V-8 engine is optional.

NEW MONTCLAIR CONVERTIBLE—FIRST CONVERTIBLE WITH SEDAN ROOM—There's room for six adults—new leg room, knee room, shoulder room, and headroom—in both front *and* rear seats. And you'll find this new "sedan room" in both the Montclair illustrated, and in the Monterey convertible. New features include a two-tone top and the biggest back window you have ever seen in a convertible—almost 6½ feet wide for "hardtop" visibility when the top is up.

1957 Mercury: Many full-line ads took two-page spreads to illustrate models from each series. The first page of this ad shows the Turnpike Cruiser on top, the Montclair Phaeton Coupe in center and the Montclair convertible on bottom. (*The Saturday Evening Post*, 1957)

and price for everyone in the Big M fleet!

COLONY PARK, ONE OF 6 BIG M STATION WAGONS—ALL TRUE HARDTOPS—
The most advanced station wagons you can buy. First with a true passenger car ride. First with true hardtop design. A power-operated back window eliminates the lift gate, provides a unique all-clear loading platform. There's a giant 87.4 cubic feet of cargo space. In addition to the Colony Park shown, there are 2 Voyager models and 3 budget-priced Commuters—the biggest choice in the field.

NEW MONTEREY 4-DOOR SEDAN...PRICED JUST ABOVE LOWEST PRICE CARS—
Mercury's lowest price series includes the concealed-pillar sedan shown, and a 2-door sedan, 2-door hardtop, 4-door hardtop, and a convertible. All new Mercurys are more than 17½ feet long, over 6½ feet wide, with new oversized interiors, and exclusive Floating Ride. In this series, 255 hp is standard. 290 and 335 hp is optional. Never before has so much bigness and luxury cost so little.

NEW MONTEREY PHAETON SEDAN, NEW HIGH IN "SEE-ABILITY"—You're surrounded with 28 square feet of glass for excellent all-around vision. And, as in all Mercurys, you can get dream-car features such as Merc-O-Matic Keyboard Control and a power seat that "remembers." And air conditioning is no longer a luxury. Mercury's unique new system combines air conditioning and heating in one low-cost unit. Get the full story today at your Mercury dealer's showroom.

THE BIG MERCURY for '57 with DREAM-CAR DESIGN

MERCURY DIVISION • FORD MOTOR COMPANY

1957 Mercury: The second page of this full-line advertisement starts off with the Colony Park station wagon. The Monterey four-door sedan is in the middle and the new Monterey Phaeton Sedan, or four-door hardtop, is at the bottom. (*The Saturday Evening Post*, 1957)

1955 Chevrolet: A way to expand your full-line ads is an all-wagon ad. First ad showing the midyear Nomad, too. (*The Saturday Evening Post*, 4/30/55)

On the other hand, a representative collection of anything could be as large or small as you wish.

For the collector looking for a way to stretch his ad-buying dollar, a collection of "full-line" advertisements may just do the trick. Full-line advertisements are one-make advertisements. They show all or nearly all of the models of a particular make of car for a single model-year.

Not all manufacturers ran this type of advertisement. Our files show ones for Chevrolet, Buick, Edsel, Ford, Mercury, Pontiac and Buick. Ford Motor Company, ran advertisements in 1957 and 1958 which showed every model made by every division, but these aren't true full-line advertisements. They are not limited to one make.

One of the benefits of full-line advertisements is a chance to see many of the obscure or rare models of a given year, many of which appear nowhere else in that year's advertising.

By far, Chevrolet ran the most full-line advertisements, starting as early as 1928. Other advertisements of this type appeared during model years 1931, 1932, 1934, 1935, 1936, 1939, 1940, 1949, 1952, 1954, 1955, 1956, 1957 and 1958. During 1955-1957, special all-station wagon advertisements also ran in several magazines. It is also possible that they ran a full-line advertisement every year from 1928 through 1941, but our files do not show them. Still, that's what collecting can compel you to do: find out if those advertisements did appear and where. Then you can go after them.

In the late 1920s, the cheaper cars were usually limited to a few models, usually a coupe, a sedan (two- or four-door), a roadster and a touring car. At the other end of the price spectrum, the luxury cars offered dozens of models, some custom-built and specially-equipped. A curious turn of history has reversed this practice.

Today, Chevrolet will sell you any number of body styles of Cavalier, Beretta, Corsica, Camaro and Caprice Classic, as well as one or two Corvettes. In the recent past, there were other models, such as the Chevette, Citation, Impala, Monza, Monte Carlo, Chevelle/Malibu, Corvair and Chevy II/Nova. On the other hand, Cadillac, which offered 50 body styles and types in 1927, now offers only the deVille, Seville and Eldorado in a very few variations.

Of course, one must remember that the high profits on those inexpensive Chevrolets allowed General Motors (GM) to keep the Cadillac name alive right through the Great Depression, even though the profit on those Cadillacs was small or nil. Today, the profit on the Chevrolets still pays most of the GM bills, since there are more people in the market for the Chevrolet name than for the Cadillac name. When gasoline costs so dearly, luxury can come from other sources; such as wines like Chateau Briand or Grand Marnier.

Continuing with full-line Chevrolet advertisements, the 1928 advertisement shows seven models, including the "ritzy" Imperial Landau sedan priced at $715. The 1931 advertisement appeared very late in the year ... in September ... and includes an astonishing 20 models. The copy reinforces the trend to wider choice for the low-priced car buyer: "Chevrolet now offers buyers in the low-price field the same advantage that custom-car buyers have long been enjoying: the privilege of choosing from an exceptionally wide range of cars, with a variety of color schemes." A closer look reveals that the 20 models weren't quite so varied.

There are no dual-cowl phaetons, town cars, depot hacks or limousines in the advertisement. However, the variety still is impressive when you realize the country was three years into the depression. Like many of the full-line advertisements, the 1932 version was published in the late spring. That's when dealers, as today, were clearing out the current models and getting ready for the next year's cars. However, the 1932 Chevrolet was introduced late in the year and it seems odd to be shoving the "new" model aside so soon.

1949 Oldsmobile: "Here they come, (all of) the new Futuramics" from Oldsmobile. (*The Saturday Evening Post*, 1949)

Prices were the focus: "New reduced prices make America's most popular car a greater value than ever!" The bottom of the line standard models appear in an April advertisement. Selection is enhanced by the "26 brilliant new colors," new two-tone color combinations and the roadster at a paltry $445.

The 1934 Chevrolet full-line advertisement ran in February and shows 14 models. The phaeton disappeared, but four open cars were offered: two cabriolets and two roadsters. The phaeton returns in the handsome 1935 full-line advertisement, which is done in black and gold with the 11 different models in red. An interesting fine-print paragraph states that "with bumpers, spare tire and tire lock, the list price is $20 additional."

For 1936, Chevrolet offered 12 body styles. Again, there was no phaeton. This time, apparently, it was gone for good. Also gone is the true roadster. The only open car is a cabriolet. A Chevrolet station wagon makes its advertising debut in the 1939 advertisement. Seven models are shown and "reduced prices" is the hook for the advertisement. A 1940 advertisement qualifies for full-line status, but only barely. Five models are shown, but Chevrolet made a station wagon that year. It doesn't appear.

The full-line Chevrolet advertisement disappears until 1949, when it is reborn under the headline "All Star Revue." Seven models are shown, including the convertible and station wagon. Three years later, in 1952, there are 10 models with new color-matched interiors in all Deluxe sedans and coupes."

"Fourteen wonderful ways to see the USA," proclaims the headline of the 1955 Chevrolet full-line advertisement. This is an advertisement which clearly demonstrates the utility of the full-line idea. Several models which never appear in any other Chevrolet advertisements are illustrated in the advertisement: the One-Fifty Utility sedan and One-Fifty Handyman wagon are examples.

As we've seen, the number of models offered changes each year. For 1956, it's 19. For 1957, it's 20 including the Corvette, which is not in the 1956 count. For 1958, it's "Sweet Seventeen." By putting together a collection of these advertisements, you can get a clearer idea of what a make was selling year by year and what models were dropped, renamed or replaced. Useful color scheme information is presented as well.

Chevrolet was beginning to incorporate model names into its selling plan in the mid-1950s. The One-Fifty and Two-Ten designations were replaced with monickers like Yeoman, Del Ray, Biscayne and Brookwood by 1958.

Over at Pontiac, the full-line idea ran all through the period 1938-1942. It then picks up again in 1948. For 1941, two full-line advertisements appear, one as an introductory advertisement in October 1940 and one as a "get a car for spring" advertisement. The first shows 10 models, the second shows 11. The extra model is the Torpedo Six Business Coupe.

The portent of war shows in the 1942 Pontiac fun-line advertisement. A sub-head intones "Pontiac for 1942 is even better built to serve you extra long and extra well." The copy lead says, "This year your choice of a new car is going to depend ... more than ever before ... on how many years it will last." And, indeed, such were the worries and fears people had about the dreadful war America seemed inevitably to join.

In the spring of 1948, Pontiac proclaimed itself "An automobile show all by itself." 'Nine models crowd a highway and the copy repeats a familiar theme: "You will find a car precisely suited to your requirements." This was a common theme running through many of the full-line advertisements and a fair justification for them. The more possibilities a potential customer sees in your product, the more likely he is to buy it. In 1949, Pontiac used the same "Auto Show In Itself" idea. Eight models including the convertible and station wagon were illustrated.

Plymouth turned out two full-line advertisements that we know of, in 1942 and 1953. The 1942 advertisement is particularly handsome in full color. Seven cars are pictured, including what must be the rarest of 1942 Plymouths, the woodie. In 1953, the idea is "A New Plymouth for every taste, every need, every pocketbook." Chrysler Corporation was in its pudgy period of design and these Plymouths are particularly pudgy. Even the convertible is rendered mundane by the lines, grille and proportions.

Style and fashion were Buick inclinations in the late 1940s. Three full-line advertisements, all in color, were produced by Buick. One of each appeared in 1946, 1947 and 1948. Again, they were published in the spring. All three are as close to true full-line advertisements as Buick gets. They show the basic models, but not all variations. Each advertisement has a convertible, sedan wagon and sedanet.

Ford used the show-'em-all idea in 1955. In 1956, it produced an all-wagon advertisement similar to the Chevrolet advertisement of the same period. Again, we get to see the cheaper models in the 1955 advertisement. The Mainline Business Sedan, Customline Tudor Sedan and Ranch Wagon are good examples. Of special interest here is the Thunderbird and Fairlane Crown Victoria.

Mercury's full-line advertisements appear in 1955 and 1957. Eleven models are illustrated in the 1955 advertisement, including the valuable and scarce Montclair Sun Valley with its clear green sun roof treatment. Likewise, the 1957 advertisement shows a desirable collector car, the Turnpike Cruiser with its power-operated rear window, air suspension and "space patrol" radio antenna sticking out of the roof line over the windshield.

In summing up, the full-line ad collection allows you to get a lot of models covered quite thoroughly in just a few advertisements.

For The Ad Collector

As usual, our ad list is representative. There are likely many more. Supplementary lists are invited.

Date	Magazine
Buick	
6/22/46	*The Saturday Evening Post*
1/31/48	*The Saturday Evening Post*
Chevrolet	
2/11/28	*The Saturday Evening Post*
9/12/31	*The Saturday Evening Post*
1/9/32	*The Saturday Evening Post*
6/11/32	*The Saturday Evening Post*
2/17/34	*Literary Digest*
2/24/34	*The Saturday Evening Post*
3/30/35	*The Saturday Evening Post*
4/4/36	*The Saturday Evening Post*
3/25/39	*The Saturday Evening Post*
4/6/40	*Collier's*
7/9/49	*The Saturday Evening Post*
4/19/52	*The Saturday Evening Post*
3/29/54	*Life*
4/3/54	*The Saturday Evening Post*

Date	Magazine
3/5/55	*The Saturday Evening Post*
4/30/55	*The Saturday Evening Post* (all wagons)
5/56	*Holiday* (all wagons)
3/30/57	*The Saturday Evening Post*
4/13/57	*The Saturday Evening Post* (all wagons)
Pontiac	
10/26/40	*The Saturday Evening Post*
4/19/41	*The Saturday Evening Post*
10/25/41	*The Saturday Evening Post*
4/19/48	*Life*
3/16/49	*The Saturday Evening Post*
Plymouth	
11/17/41	*Life*
Mercury	
3/12/55	*The Saturday Evening Post*

The Auto Ad Collector

By Bill McBride

Automotive advertisements provide an interesting look at the rich tapestry of motor car history. This brief article looks at four different categories of automotive ads and provides a longer listing of representative specimens, including the name of the magazine, the issue and the date(s) they appeared.

Lincoln-Zephyr advertisements

The streamlined automobile was a creature of the 1930s. Flying, like automobiling, had passed from novelty to reality. America's auto designers looked to the airplane as their inspiration for style and technology. The Franklin Airman, the Pierce Silver Arrow and Buckminster Fuller's Dymaxion were early streamlined cars. Chrysler's attempt to mass-market the streamlined Airflow is the best-known example of aircraft design translated into automotive terms. However, the first *successful* streamlined automobile was the Lincoln-Zephyr. This Edsel Ford designed vehicle inspired some beautiful advertisements.

Edsel advertisements

A less successful (but no less interesting) Ford product, from a later era, was the Edsel. It was launched in 1957 and lasted just three model years. As a totally new product, designed for a distinctive market niche, the Edsel received heavy advertising support. In addition to its appearance in 1957, 1958 and 1959 Ford advertisements, it also showed up in advertisements placed by spark plug, automotive wax and gasoline companies.

The Edsel was known as the "Big E," but an "E" car that proved to be bigger in terms of popularity was the Cadillac Eldorado. "El Dorado" was the name of a mythical land of great wealth, sought by early explorers of Central America and South America. Literally translated, El Dorado means "The Gilded Man." It is probably derived from the custom of the Chibcha Indians of Colombia, who anointed their chief, rolled him in gold and washed him in a lake, into which gold and jewels were thrown.

Eldorado advertisements

The Cadillac Eldorado, introduced in 1953, was made for such a man who was "rolling in wealth." Through the years, the prestige automaker retained this name for its top-of-the-line automobiles. It

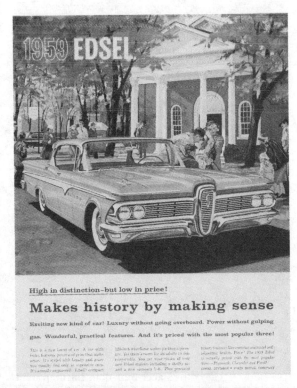

1959 Edsel: Do you think they were attending church to pray for the marque's survival? (*Life*, 1959)

1957 Edsel: Champion welcomed Edsel to a roster of 36 automotive makes using its spark plugs as factory equipment. (*The Saturday Evening Post*, 10/12/57)

1957 Edsel: Even Ford advertised the new car! However, "The Edsel Look is here to stay" proved an inaccurate prediction. (*Life*, 1957)

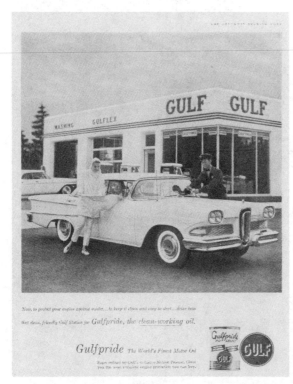

1957 Edsel: The white Pacer four-door hardtop went with the Gulf filling station's sanitary white appearance. (*The Saturday Evening Post*, 12/7/57)

was originally seen on a line of luxury sedans and convertibles and, later, wound up (from 1967 on) as the name of a separate model in the personal luxury car field. As a rich, upscale model in both of its guises, the Eldorado generated many handsome and fancy advertisements, which are all very collectible now.

Color car advertisements

For the automotive advertising collector who cherishes the small, but elegant things in life, there is a type of advertisement that is equivalent to the gorgeous "illuminated" manuscripts (with miniature paintings) that friars and monks produced in the 17th and 18th centuries.

In the teens and the 1920s, American "literary" magazines proliferated. These were generally about 7 x 10-inches in size and were loaded with articles and book reviews. The list of well-known titles includes, *Harper's, The Century, Review of Reviews, The Outlook, The World's Work* and *Atlantic*.

Typically, these magazines contained some automotive advertisements. These were produced in both black and white and color. The small color advertisements are especially collectible. Some are simply reduced-size copies of advertisements that ran in larger-format magazines. Some, however, were created especially for the smaller-size publications. Collectors appreciate both kinds. The small versions of big advertisements always seem to have greater richness of color than their larger counterparts, while advertisements produced exclusively in the smaller formats are precious and rare to find.

The following columns contain representative lists of Lincoln-Zephyr, Edsel and Eldorado advertisements, plus a list of color advertisements that appeared in the small format periodicals.

Lincoln-Zephyr advertisements 1936-1942

Date	Magazine
1936 — Model Year	
2/36	*Fortune*
3/21/36	*The Saturday Evening Post*
4/36	*Fortune*
7/36	*Fortune*
1937 — Model Year	
10/12/36	*Time*
11/36	*Fortune*
12/36	*National Geographic*
12/36	*Fortune*
2/37	*National Geographic*
3/37	*National Geographic*
4/37	*Esquire*
7/3/37	*The Saturday Evening Post*
8/37	*National Geographic*
1938 — Model Year	
11/20/37	*The Saturday Evening Post*
12/18/37	*Collier's*
1/38	*National Geographic*
3/38	*National Geographic*
3/38	*Esquire*
3/4/38	*The Saturday Evening Post*
5/38	*National Geographic*
1939 — Model Year	
12/10/38	*The Saturday Evening Post*
2/39	*National Geographic*
2/18/39	*The Saturday Evening Post*
3/39	*Fortune*
3/4/39	*The Saturday Evening Post*
4/1/39	*The Saturday Evening Post*
5/39	*Fortune*
6/12/39	*Time*
7/15/39	*The Saturday Evening Post*
7/15/39	*Time*
8/12/39	*The Saturday Evening Post*
1940 — Model Year	
10/14/39	*The Saturday Evening Post*
11/27/39	*Time*

Date	Magazine
3/4/40	*Time*
3130/40	*The Saturday Evening Post*
4/27/40	*The Saturday Evening Post*
6/10/40	*Time*
1941 — Model Year	
9/28/40	*The Saturday Evening Post*
10/12/40	*New Yorker*
10/12/40	*The Saturday Evening Post*
11/40	*National Geographic*
11/11/40	*Life*
12/2/40	*Life*
12/2/40	*Time*
12/40	*Fortune*
12/14/40	*The Saturday Evening Post*
12/16/40	*Life*
1/41	*National Geographic*
1/13/41	*Life*
2/3/41	*Life*
2/22/41	*The Saturday Evening Post*
2/24/41	*Life*
3/41	*National Geographic*
3/8/41	*The Saturday Evening Post*
3/17/41	*Life*
3/22/41	*The Saturday Evening Post*
4/7/41	*Life*
4/28/41	*Life*
5/41	*National Geographic*
5/5/41	*Life*
5/17/41	*The Saturday Evening Post*
5/19/41	*Life*
6/16/41	*Life*
1942 — Model Year	
9/29/41	*Life*
10/20/41	*Life*
10/25/41	*The Saturday Evening Post*
11/10/41	*Life*
11/15/41	*The Saturday Evening Post*
1/42	*National Geographic*

BUT WHAT LIES BENEATH THE STYLE?

Many people speak of the 1939 Lincoln-Zephyr as the most beautiful yet built. That is true. This car has never been handsomer. It is the style leader of today!

But style alone does not set a car apart as this car is set apart. What lies beneath outward beauty? Why is the 1939 Lincoln-Zephyr still unique?

It is because the distinctive combination of features in the Lincoln-Zephyr is not to be matched in any car, at any price!

Beneath the graceful streamlines, in all closed types, is a bridge-type framework of steel trusses —to which panels of steel are welded on the top, the sides and the bottom. Body and frame are unified in a single structure—rigid and safe. The Lincoln-Zephyr is the only car of its kind.

The Lincoln-Zephyr V-type 12-cylinder engine has a brilliant record of performance on roads good and bad. And it gives 14 to 18 miles to the gallon of gasoline! This is the only "twelve" in the medium-price field!

Yours to enjoy, also, is the flowing ride of the Lincoln-Zephyr. Passengers sit "amidships." Hydraulic brakes, new this year, offer gentle, even stops under all conditions. Springs, axle assemblies and engine are completely rubber-insulated from the body-frame unit. The result is greater quiet in a car already quiet.

As you consider any new car this year, look deeper than style! Judge every feature, seen and hidden. 60,000 Lincoln-Zephyr owners admire a car as modern in every way as in appearance!

BENEATH ITS OUTWARD BEAUTY

A combination of features that makes it the only car of its kind. 1—Unit-body-and-frame—steel panels welded to steel trusses. 2—V-type 12-cylinder engine—smooth, quiet power. 3—14 to 18 miles to the gallon 4—High power-to-weight ratio —low center of gravity. 5—Passengers "amidships"—modern comfort for six in chair-height seats—the gliding ride—direct entrance onto the floor of car—high visibility. 6—Hydraulic brakes.

LINCOLN MOTOR COMPANY—DIVISION OF FORD MOTOR COMPANY, BUILDERS OF FORD, MERCURY, LINCOLN-ZEPHYR AND LINCOLN MOTOR CARS

STYLE LEADER FOR 1939 *Lincoln-Zephyr V12*

1939: Aircraft styling and technology. This 1939 Lincoln-Zephyr advertisement highlights the technical. (*The Saturday Evening Post***, 12/10/38)**

1970 Eldorado, Cadillac Motor Car Division

Eldorado. What better credentials could a car have? The exclusive and brilliantly responsive new 8.2 litre V-8 engine (500 cubic inches) in the 1970 Fleetwood Eldorado, performing in concert with front-wheel drive, will captivate you with driving pleasure unmatched anywhere in the world. And Eldorado's boldly individual styling and elegantly appointed interior tell you that it is unmistakably Cadillac in every detail. Your authorized Cadillac dealer invites you to experience the vitality, luxury and distinction of this, the world's finest personal car.

1970 Eldorado: What better credentials could a luxury car have than the Eldorado name? (*National Geographic*, 1970)

Edsel advertisements 1958-1959

(Dates for 1960 advertisements unavailable).

Date	Magazine	Date	Magazine
7/22/57	Life	11/2/57	The Saturday Evening Post
8/5/57	Life	11/11/57	Life
8/19/57	Life	11/16/57	The Saturday Evening Post
9/2/57	Life	11/25/57	Life
9/9/57	Life	11/30/57	The Saturday Evening Post
9/14/57	The Saturday Evening Post	4/14/58	Life
9/30/57	Life	6/16/58	Life
10/5/57	The Saturday Evening Post	11/29/58	The Saturday Evening Post
10/14/57	Life	12/22/58	Life
10/19/57	The Saturday Evening Post	1/19/59	Life
10/28/57	Life	4/1/59	Holiday

Edsels in other companies' advertisements

Date	Magazine
10/12/57	The Saturday Evening Post (Champion Spark Plugs)
12/7/57	The Saturday Evening Post (Gulf Oil)
2/10/58	Life (Simonize)

Edsel Articles

Date	Magazine	Date	Magazine
8/31/57	The Saturday Evening Post	9/57	Harper's Magazine
9/2/57	Life	12/7/57	Business Week
10/57	Hot Rod	4/58	Consumer Reports
11/24/56	Business Week	11/30/59	Time
11/26/56	Newsweek	11/28/59	Business Week
6/8/57	Business Week	11/26/60	New Yorker

Edsels in Ford Corporate advertisements

Date	Magazine	Date	Magazine
11/16/57	The Saturday Evening Post	3/24/58	Life
11/25/57	Life	3/29/58	The Saturday Evening Post
12/21/57	The Saturday Evening Post	4/28/58	Life
1/25/58	The Saturday Evening Post	5/58	Holiday
3/58	Holiday	6/16/58	Life

Eldorado advertisements 1953-1966

Date	Magazine	Date	Magazine
2/24/53	Look (AC spark plugs)	3/56	Fortune
8/29/53	The Saturday Evening Post (AC spark plugs)	3/56	Holiday
9/7/53	Life (AC spark plugs)	11/12/56	Life
8/23/54	Life	12/16/57	Life
3/55	Holiday	3/58	Fortune
4/55	Fortune	10/11/58	The Saturday Evening Post
5/55	Holiday	2/60	Holiday
6/55	Fortune	3/22/63	Life
7/55	Holiday	4/63	Holiday
8/55	Fortune	11/66	Holiday

1920 Standard Eight: What a powerful car the automotive department of Pittsburgh's Standard Steel Company built. (Color, *Century*, February 1920)

Leadership rests on Achievement

.. AND LEADERS ARE *MADE BY DEEDS*

When the writer of history dips his pen and starts his record of life, he looks about him for accomplishments and deeds. The hopes and aims and aspirations of those who walk across his pages are interesting, of course, but only in *things done* does he find the substance of which his record must be made. . . . And as in the history of human affairs, so is it in the chronicle of business. When the buyer of anything that's built looks into the record of him who built it, he goes beyond the claims and creeds, and hopes for fame and wealth. And this is the reason why Cadillac has won first place in the fine-car field. Out of the welter of claims and hopes, the record of Cadillac stands clear. For, true to the spirit of Cadillac himself, intrepid discoverer and leader of men, the motor car company that bears his name has constantly been a pioneer. The electric self-starter, the 90-degree V-8 engine, the 16-cylinder engine, the Syncro-Mesh transmission, interchangeable parts, the thermostatic carburetor, enclosed bodies—these are but a few of the Cadillac "firsts" which have contributed so much to the development of the automobile. . . . It is out of this long record of achievement that the new Cadillacs and La Salles of today have had their being—the finest cars, in every way, that Cadillac has ever built.

CADILLAC MOTOR CAR COMPANY · · · Division of General Motors

Cadillac

CADILLAC V-12 5-PASSENGER SEDAN

1933 Cadillac: Leadership rests on achievement and Antoine de la Mothe Cadillac was a leader, like his name-sake. (Color, *National Geographic***, 1933)**

A beginner's list of color advertisements

Cadillac

Date	Magazine	Date	Magazine
3/25	*Harper's, Review of Reviews, Century*	2/33	*National Geographic*
4/25	*Harper's, Review of Reviews, Atlantic*	3/33	*National Geographic*
5/25	*Harper's, Review of Reviews*	4/33	*National Geographic*
11/25	*Harper's*	5/33	*National Geographic*

NOTE: These are the first color car advertisements to appear in *National Geographic*. Buick followed shortly thereafter, as did Dodge.

Chalmers

6/20 .... *Century*

Diana

9/25 .... *Harper's*
10/25 .... *Century*
11/25 .... *Harper's*

Franklin

Many magazines 1918-1920

Haynes

12/22 .... *Schribners*
3/23 .... *Century*
3/24 .... *Harper's*
4/24 .... *Harper's*

Jordan

2/18 .... *The World's Work*
4/20 .... *Century*
6/20 .... *Century*

Lincoln

1/24 .... *Harper's*
3/24 .... *Harper's*
5/24 .... *Harper's*
7/24 .... *Harper's*
9/24 .... *Harper's*
10/24 .... *Harper's*
11/24 .... *Harper's*
12/24 .... *Harper's*
1 through 8 and 12/26 *Harper's*

Marmon

In several magazines 1917-21 including *Atlantic, Century*, etc.

Maxwell

11/22 .... *Review of Reviews*
12/22 .... *Review of Reviews*

Moon

6/ .... *Review of Reviews*
4/25 .... *Harper's*
5/25 .... *Review of Reviews, Atlantic*
7/25 .... *Review of Reviews*
8/1/25 .... *Harper's*

Oldsmobile

6/17/11 .... *The Outlook*

Pierce-Arrow

9/11 .... *Everybody's Magazine*
10/13 .... *Century*
1/14 .... *Century*
7/14/15 .... *The Outlook*
10/20/15 .... *The Outlook*
1/15 .... *Century*
11/21 .... *Century*
10/27 .... *Atlantic*

Rauch & Lang Electric

3/19 .... *Review of Reviews*

Standard

2/20 .... *Century*
2/21 .... *Harper's*
11/21 .... *Century*

Studebaker

6/19 .... *Review of Reviews*

Stevens-Duryea

11/13 .... *Harper's*

Woods Electric

6/18/10 .... *The Outlook*

These additional makes advertised during the year(s) indicated. The publication and date are unknown. (All advertisements in color.)

Make	Year	Make	Year
Cole	1919	PanAmerican	1917
Hal Twelve	1917	Peerless	1912
Mercer	1920	Templar	1920
National	1919		

All advertisements are not different, that is, the same advertisement may have appeared in different magazines in different issues.

1933 Cadillac: The leader in this ad is LaSalle, explorer of the Mississippi, but the car is a Cadillac V-8 Town Sedan. (Color, *National Geographic*, 1933)

The car magazine collecting bug

By J. Neal East

I have suspected, for some time, that human beings who avidly collect things have a screw loose somewhere in their psyches. In my own case, my wife is absolutely convinced of it. It would probably make a fairly interesting psychological study to investigate just what it is that makes certain, otherwise fairly normal, people collect all kinds of things. I find it hard to believe, but I have actually heard of people who have no interest in collecting anything. Bless their souls, they don't know how fortunate they really are not to have that strange, irrepressible drive to have one of every last something-or-other known to man.

At one time, I was bitten by the car magazine collecting bug. It was many years ago, when I was working for the old *Rod & Custom* magazine. *Old Cars's* former publisher LeRoi "Tex" Smith was working for the companion publication, *Hot Rod Magazine*. He is one of those lucky people who doesn't have to collect things. He still can't understand why I decided I had to have a copy of every issue of *Rod & Custom* that had ever been printed. When Tex and others at the publishing house, who were unafflicted with the collecting disease were enjoying their lunches, I was digging through some musty Hollywood bookstore, searching for those missing back issues.

As with all who have a screw loose on some subject, I can give some pretty rational reasons for collecting magazines. As a budding young automotive journalist, I felt it could be instructive to see what had been done in earlier issues. I also knew that there could be considerable reference value in the back issues, for times in the future that I might be working on articles on related subjects. In addition, not only was it my job to work for a magazine, but I was also a car hobbyist. Thus, the back issues could probably help me work on my cars. All of these reasons proved to be valid in actual practice.

The author recommends using the classified advertising section of *Old Cars* to find magazines to add to a collection or as a good way to reach other magazine collectors who may want to exchange periodicals.

Scientists and engineers who belong to the Aerospace Corporation's Old Car Club look over some vintage car publications from the collection of author J. Neal East.

However, Tex still wondered about the day I came in from my "lunch hour" of grubbing in some bookstore all glassy-eyed and dusty, but with a weird smile on my face. Clutched in my sweaty hand was a May, 1953 issue of *Rod & Custom*. This was the first issue, the vaunted Volume 1, Number 1. Poor Tex, that was just another day for him, but for me it was a great day, a memorable day and a very satisfying day.

Something must be said, at this time, about one of the major hazards of collecting magazines. It is not the black widow spiders one meets or the time and money spent. It is that, someday, the collection is actually completed. You look proudly at these stacks of magazines ... all in proper order, of course ... and you know that you actually have one of every issue. There is a little sadness that creeps in at the same time. The search is over. The possibility of an adrenalin-releasing "find" is no longer there. Even that is not the hazard. The real hazard is the next thought: "Well, now that *Rod & Custom* is complete, what shall I do? I know! I'll collect *Hot Rod Magazine*!"

If you don't think that is a real hazard, consider that at one time or another, I have had complete collections of *Rod & Custom, Hot Rod, Car Craft, Road & Track, Rod Action, Old Car Illustrated, Sports Car Graphic, Car Classics, Special Interest Autos* and a number of other automotive titles you might not even recognize. Honest Doctor, I'm not sick, my wife just sent me here to talk to you.

Since this section of *Automobilia* has an emphasis on automotive literature collecting and I have warned you of the hazards of magazine collecting, let's get on with some of the details. In all seriousness, the collecting of magazines which deal with subjects that apply to your interests can be extremely helpful. The initial cost is really quite reasonable. Obviously, the current and future copies cost you whatever the subscription or face value is. A good percentage of the back issues of recent dates can often be bought for face value or less. Older back issues become more costly, often depending on the age and the title of the magazine, regardless of the contents. The first issue of *Road & Track* can't compare editorially to later issues, yet its scarcity is such that it commands a very high price. By the same token, if you decide to collect every issue of a publication and are able to do so, the value of the collection is enhanced.

Perhaps the first thing to decide is what your purpose in collecting magazines is. If you really want only the information contained in the magazine, then each issue will have to be considered on its own merits. You should plan to take the time to look through each magazine to determine if it has material which applies to your interest. The title and publisher are of no importance, because you will want to get the information on your subject from any source. The age of the magazine is of little importance, too, if the material is not of the kind that gets out of date.

After years of collecting old car books and magazines, author J. Neal East managed two automotive book shops in the Los Angeles, California area before opening another one in Denver, Colorado.

If you decide to collect all the issues of a magazine which you find interesting, you should fully admit it to yourself and go ahead full steam and do it. By full-steam, I mean within the limits of the budget and time which you can afford, which brings us to another decision. You do need to give some thought to the money and time you think you can reasonably spend at it. This is a personal kind of thinking and you may find that your time/money budget for collecting will change, in relation to changes in your personal life, as you go along.

Whether you decide to collect for content only or for a complete collection, the next step is very important. You must begin some sort of record keeping. You will find somewhere, fairly soon, that you just can't remember if you have a certain article or issue. I found that 3 x 5-inch index cards could hold plenty of information and could be carried with me when attending swap meets and book stores. Not only should you have a record of what you already have, but you should also have a list of what you want. You will discover that you will learn what you want faster than you will find it, so the want-list will become very important.

One last consideration, before actually going out to collect, is to figure out someplace where you have space to store magazines. You may think that you are only going to collect a few items, but I can almost guarantee that you will soon find that you have far more than you expected. More on this later, just take the advice and figure on some storage space, making sure it is in a dry area.

One more little item which may help you: if the publishing company is still in business or the magazine is presently being published, contact them and request information on publication dates and whether or not they have back issues. Sometimes the publishing house can't take the time to answer, but if they do, you may learn some important information. For instance, many magazines have gaps in their publishing. Maybe they were only published quarterly or bi-monthly in the early years or had a title change somewhere along the line. Sometimes, the volume and issue numbers do not correspond with the cover dates, which can be confusing. If you can get this information from the publisher, you are ahead of the game.

Okay, it is finally time to get out there and scrounge! Swap meets, both the automotive kind and the general kind, are excellent sources of car magazines. Prices are usually reasonable and, if you buy in quantity, you can usually work a better price for the lot. Used book and magazine stores are also good places to check, although prices may be a bit higher because of overhead and their increased awareness of the value of back issues. You may also find that the people working in the used book stores will know quite a bit about the history of the publication.

Advertising your needs in hobby publications is an important and necessary aspect of collecting. You will find issues you need and make connections with other collectors. You should make up copies of your want list to send out by mail. You will find other advertisements from people like you (who have a similar screw loose). You can correspond with them directly. Don't ignore this part of the game, because it is a prime source of information. Even if the other fellow doesn't collect the same titles as you do, he may have information about the titles and also know where some stock is.

Another aspect of advertising, that is a must, is to use non-hobby publications. Examples are the local newspaper and throw-away "advertiser" or "trader" type tabloids. There are lots and lots of people who think that the only thing to do with last month's magazines is to throw them out, so the prospect of some-one paying for them is real news.

Well, so much for some basic advice on collecting magazines. You will find things that work for you which are not mentioned here. Maybe you are already doing all of these things. At any rate, let me give you a few examples of my experiences to back up my advice.

Earlier in this article, I mentioned needing space to store extra magazines. I discovered that I had peo-ple contacting me who didn't want me picking out certain magazines and leaving the rest. The lady whose son has married and moved away, leaving stacks and stacks of car magazines, simply wants them out of the closet. If you get them at all, you have to take the whole works. I literally bought so many col-lections of this kind that I began a mail-order business of selling the extras. I ended up getting the ones I needed. I also could upgrade the condition of the ones I kept as I got replacements that were in better con-dition. Having so many to sell, the collection soon began to pay for itself. I eventually had some of my collections hardbound for my library. This was all paid for by selling extra issues.

Like any other kind of literature collecting, magazine collecting offers the excitement of making the "big find." This is really enjoyable. I remember buying a box of miscellaneous car magazines from a lady who could hardly believe somebody would actually give her money for them. The price was so cheap, I figured they were worth it, without looking through them. Then I later discovered that the box contained

Ray Calloway (left) and Dave Pierson (right) belonged to the Aerospace Employees Car Club when the author (center) talked to the group about car magazine collecting. He holds a copy of the defunct CAR EXCHANGE magazine.

one mint-condition copy each of *Road & Track* number 1 and number 2, among other magazines. Since I had neither at the time, I was really excited by my good fortune.

I found part of the fun of collecting magazines was in solving the little mysteries I kept running across. Once you get used to comparing cover dates with volume and issue numbers, you discover they often don't add up right. My index cards had all kinds of notes with question marks next to them.

Collectors eventually figure most of the mysteries, but there is fun to be found in the process of doing so. Some magazines, such as *Car Classics*, have gone through numerous owners. Even Krause Publications, the world's largest hobby publisher, owned it for a time. Tracing the history of magazines can be fascinating.

Other magazines have had title changes, such as *Honk!* becoming *Car Craft*. Some change size, as did *Hop Up, Car Craft* and *Rod & Custom*. Others are sporadic in publishing dates, stopping altogether, then being revived and so on.

All-in-all, magazine collecting can be fun from the standpoint of the exciting finds, the people you meet, the things you learn and the unusual places "treasure hunting" takes you. Besides, when somebody gives you a hard time about collecting, you can give them your "straight" lecture about how important the contents are to you, how they have actually saved you money in fixing your car, how you are able to write them off your taxes, etc. I assure you, it is easier for a car buff to explain collecting automobile magazines than it is for a non-smoker to explain why he collects old-time ashtrays. But, then, that is a loose screw of a different thread anyway.

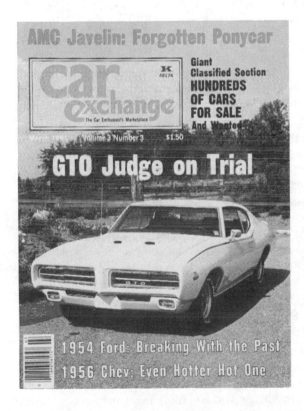

Car Exchnge magazine was published in the early 1980s. This is the March 1981 issue with GTO on the cover.

Muscle Car & Truck Buyer's Guide is another discontinued old car magazine with a special focus. It's now a book.

Stamps trace man's evolution from pedal to petrol and piston

By Diane Thomas

Collecting old cars can be fun, but also budget-busting. Another way is to collect them on stamps of the world. By careful selection of stamp issues, the history of the development of the automobile can be traced and a fine collection assembled, either for entering philatelic competition events or simply as a personal display in the home.

The invention of the present day motorcar depended on two earlier inventions the bicycle and the internal combustion engine. Why the bicycle? Because it was the first device on which man propelled himself on wheels. Before that he used a wagon, and the propelling (or pulling) was done by a horse, mule, oxen or other animal. The bicycle made man independent of animals for locomotion.

The first bicycle invented was the pedestrian hobby horse, on which it was necessary for the rider to use his feet, in a scooting motion, to get around. It had a seat, but no pedals. Still, it gave the local gentry a real feeling of freedom in the early 1800s. A two-franc stamp issued by the Republic of Mali showed an 1809 version of this type of vehicle. Depicted on a 10-franc stamp in the same set was a French bicycle of 1861. By then, the rider used pedals connected directly to the front wheel. Even ladies had their own version in a three wheeler. It looked very much like the senior citizen bikes of today.

A ladies bike of 1861 influenced the design of the first motor car built by Karl Benz in 1886. Tricycle cars were built until well into the 20th century. Benz's tricycle was pictured on one of a pair of stamps issued by Germany in 1961, to celebrate 75 years of automotive history.

The ingredient needed for a successful evolution of car from bicycle was the internal combustion engine. Two men are responsible for this and both have had stamps issued in their honor. One was Le Bon, who in the late 1700s discovered illuminating gas. The other was Lenoir, who patented a petroleum vapor engine in 1860. Lenoir used illuminating gas with a Ruhmkorf coil for ignition and the same jump spark coil issued on later cars. His milestone was commemorated on a Belgian stamp.

From this two-cycle engine of Lenoir, Siegfried Marcus developed a simple car in Vienna in 1864. It was powered by a four-cycle engine. Unfortunately, he was a Sunday dabbler and never seriously introduced the car to the public. An Austrian stamp of 1971 showed his early motor car.

Marcus did inspire Karl Benz and Gottlieb Daimler to perfect his humble invention and stamps from several countries have honored the early cars of these two pioneer German automakers. Daimler-made cars were shown on stamps issued by the republics of Niger and the Congo. A German stamp, of 1961, commemorated the 75th year since Karl Benz introduced his gas-engined tricycle.

In the United States in 1893, two Illinois farm boys, Charles and Frank Duryea, built what is rightly called the first American automobile. It looked very much like the Daimler. They spent a year making the first model and another year perfecting it. Finally, in 1896, they had a car running that was exhibited in the Barnum and Bailey Circus. San Marino issued a series of car stamps in 1962. The early Duryea was shown on the one-liter value.

The oldest name still surviving on an American automobile was that of Ransom E. Olds, who first built the Oldsmobile and later gave his initials to the Reo. Experimenting with steam, Olds decided very quickly it was not the power source for cars of the future and turned to gasoline-powered cars. The Curved Dash Olds of 1904 was seen on the 50-liter stamp that San Marino issued.

The first United States car manufacturer to make precision parts was Henry M. Leland, who entered the car business by the back door. He had been producing engines for Olds, but made them too powerful. Leland was unable to convince Olds that extra horsepower was a good thing. Left with engines on his hands, Leland designed the first Cadillac. He was part showman and shipped three cars to England. There, they were disassembled. The parts were mixed in a heap. Mechanics from the Royal Automobile Club put the cars back together from the random pile of parts. All three cars ran perfectly for a 500-mile test run. On a stamp of their 1961 series, Monaco used the 1906 Cadillac.

The Dudgeon steam carriage of 1866 was depicted on a four-cent United States stamp.

The car that did the most to change the American way of life was the Model T Ford. Henry Ford's first Model A, built in 1903, was used on a United States first-day cover cachet in 1963, when the United States Post Office issued a Henry Ford commemorative stamp. Monaco chose the 1908 Model T as one American car in their 1961 series. Even Hungary paid homage to the indestructible Model T on one 1968 issue. Its imaginative design showed a cowboy driving a Ford with two other cowpokes, one mounted on horseback, looking on. Qiwain and the Congo also honored Henry Ford on postage stamps.

Various sheikdoms and African nations who have recently become autonomous have issued stamps picturing the cars of the past, despite the fact very few cars were ever a part of their history. While their philatelic value is questionable, they do complete a collection telling the story of the horseless carriage. From such countries as Umm Al Qiwain, Republic of Niger and Republic of Congo have come attractive stamps showing antique autos.

Steam cars and electrics have also been used on stamps. The Dudgeon steam carriage of 1866 was depicted on a four-cent United States stamp from not too long ago. For collections extended to include racing cars, there are two series from Monaco and one from Berlin. The latter, a 1971 issue, included four stamps commemorating a 1921 race between two German cities, Berlin and Pottsdam. Pictured on these stamps were the Opel

The United States issued a three-cent stamp of 1952 recognizing the 50th anniversary of the American Automobile Association.

rocket car, an Auto Union, a Mercedes-Benz SSK and both of the latter two rounding a curve.

There are many other facets of the motor car that can be used to expand collections. The United States issued a three-cent stamp of 1952 recognizing the 50th anniversary of the American Automobile Association. It depicted an early pioneer car and a generic postwar streamliner.

One modern United States issue honored the tow truck industry with an 8.5-cent stamp depicting a Ford-like 1920s tow vehicle.

Many countries have issued traffic safety stamps. Issues showing such related items as military vehicles, postal busses, ambulances, fire trucks and delivery vans are easily available. Several countries have issued stamps on traffic signals, highway markers and road building. Another motor car theme found on European issues was designed to combat drunk driving.

A collector can go as far as he wants to with this illustrated history of the motor car stamps of the world or can also start with very recent stamps. One modern United States issue honored the tow truck industry with an 8.5-cent stamp depicting a Ford-like 1920s tow vehicle.

In 1988, the United States Postal Service decided to bring automotive art to the American people by issuing a commemorative stamp collection featuring five classic-era automobiles. The art featured on this set was done by Ken Dallison, a member of the Automotive Fine Arts Society who lives in Indian River, Ontario, Canada. These stamps were dedicated, by postmaster general Anthony M. Frank, during the 102nd annual convention of the American Philatelic Society, where the original Ken Dallison art works were also displayed.

The cars depicted on the set were a 1928 Locomobile Cabriolet, a 1929 Pierce-Arrow Sport Phaeton, a 1931 Cord L-29 Coupe, a 1932 Packard Phaeton and the rare 1935 Duesenberg short wheelbase SJ roadster built for actor Clark Gable and owned today by Alfred Ferrara. Each of the five stamps had a value of 25-cents, which was enough to mail a first-class letter when they were issued.

Artist Ken Dallison designed this 1928 Locomobile stamp on the 60th birthday of the car depicted.

All of Dallison's stamps, including the 1929 Pierce-Arrow stamp, were valued at 25-cents.

Packard contributed an extraordinary number of innovations to the motor car industry and the inspiration for this stamp.

The thrill of owning and driving a Duesenberg was reserved for the rich and famous, but anyone could afford to buy this stamp.

Pumps / Plates / Parts

Visible gas pumps are hot collectibles

By Paul Hatmon

The visible gas pump stands in rusted disarray amid the debris of the abandoned farmyard. Its glass cylinder is pockmarked by BB shot or maybe cracked beyond repair. In a lot of instances, the glass is missing entirely. Shreds of bird nests drip from the open top, where once a glass globe gleamed. The hose and nozzle were pirated for use on a modern, overhead gravity-feed fuel tank. The hand lever was long since removed for use as a prop for the barn door.

At least that is the way it was during the 1940s, 1950s, 1960s and into the 1970s. The fickle taste of the American public then caused a radical change. In order to keep up with the Jones family, the car collector *must* have a renovated visible pump in his yard. Possibly, it is utilized as a yard light. If he has a high-beamed ceiling in his den, the old pump sits prominently there. It is displayed in all its glory, 10 feet high from the top of the globe to the floor. Maybe the pump is in the living room with some three feet cut out of the middle, the innards removed and guppies swimming to and fro in the glass cylinder. The brass nozzle and hose connections gleam and are still functional to remove the water from the fish tank. Some very high-class furniture dealers carry this item.

An electric pump with what was left of a flimsy plastic globe. This "late model" showed its age by advertising premium gasoline. (Paul Hatmon photo)

The country is being scoured for derelict gas pumps. There are commercial firms building the aquariums from them. A local car dealer has one man restoring pumps on a full-time basis. That piece of equipment (once scorned by the junk dealers because of having too much glass) is almost as sought after as Uncle Ben's gold elk tooth.

Early visible pumps varied in shape and size. The first pumps were extremely heavy, with an abundance of cast iron. Just prior to the debut of the electric pump, the heavy cast iron bases, intricate cast doors and debonair overhead canopies had degenerated into tinny metal cover skins, angle iron bases and pressed tin tops. Gas pump manufacturers no longer bothered to tint the cylinder glass or etch the gallon levels into the glass.

Once upon a time, those manufacturers were as numerous as tree leaves. Hays Equipment, Ameri-

98

This Gilbert-Barker lighthouse-type gasoline pump awaited some collector. Its beautiful blue-tinted glass was unsullied by holes or cracks. (Paul Hatmon photo)

A restored "Mae West"-type Fry cast iron pump stood in an exclusive Kansas City suburb. It boasted of once-costly 13.9-cents a gallon gasoline. (Paul Hatmon photo)

can Pump, Bowser, Gilbert-Barker, Clear Vision Pump, Wayne, Butler, Bennett, Rush and Fry were just a few companies. An old-time DX distributor said that, during the depression years, you could get a 500-gallon gasoline tank buried and a pump mounted on a concrete base, all hooked-up, for $50. Now it takes over $50 to fill up some of the gas tanks on some recreational vehicles.

The smallest general store had at least one pump when the price of a gallon of gas was in the teens. The squeaking of the hand pump could be heard for blocks when the stuffing boxes or oil can were neglected. One resident, who lived next to an old-time station for many years, was awakened each day, at six a.m., by the screech of a pump next to his bedroom window.

The outside covers of the pumps are known as "skins" to the collector. The early Fry had a cast iron skin. It was familiarly known as the "Mae West," due to its resemblance in shape to the famous buxom lady. Two hands could easily span the pump, just below the cylinder. The Fry was a bit off the beaten track with its 10-inch diameter cylinder, when most pumps used a 12- or 12-1/2-inch glass. This caused the glass of the Pennsylvania-manufactured pump to be some 36 inches long. The Fry generally had two arms extending out to the side, each fitted with a light bulb and reflector. A light socket in the center lit up the glass globe. The pump handle was also a bit odd, differing from others because it had a crescent shaped hole. There was no commercial interchange here. These long-necked, slender-throat pumps are the aristocrats of the visible pumps. They were built with care and attention to detail.

The American Pump, manufactured in Wichita, Kansas, is an eight-sided pump with an ornate cast iron base. It featured the near-standard 12-1/2-inch diameter cylinder, which was some 26 inches in length. Of near standard dimensions were the height of some eight-feet-six-inches from floor to top. By adding the glass globe, it rounded out to nearly 10-feet high.

Since most early gas stations had a canopy or roof that would accommodate the trucks of the day, the pumps were somewhat protected. The pumps out on the big ranches and farms were mostly in the open. When found, these pumps are much more difficult to restore than the service station units, because of rust problems.

An American slab-side pump that was still in use in the 1980s. It would take lots of work and be a real headache to restore this one. (Paul Hatmon photo)

A Missouri farm employed this early Hays pump for daily use. This design has short iron rods around the cylinder and sports a rare all-glass small-grilled top. (Paul Hatmon photo)

The Hays Equipment Company, also of Wichita, Kansas, manufactured a square pump whose skin also came off in two pieces. The first pumps were square and of neat appearance with a simple design. Most Hays handles were made of pipe over the base of which slipped very a long shaft, sometimes held by a drift pin. These handles are almost impossible to remove without damaging them, due to rust. Since the handle must be removed before that piece of "skin" can be removed, they are a real pain to work on.

Another model Hays pump was also square, but with a tapering shape. It illustrated heavy use of cast iron for the base, center, top and doors. This made for a very attractive pump. This early Hays had a huge cast iron bonnet. It resembled an old-time nun's headdress and had covers for two outrigger lights. This top unit probably weighed 30 pounds. Most all models of the Hays pump had a hole in the cast iron door for storage and locking of the pump when it was not in use. The nozzle was placed inside, with just the hose sticking out.

The Butler pump was built in Kansas City and Indianapolis. This pump resembled the Hays in style. It also had square sides. Some early Butlers had fancy canopies on top, making them look extremely top heavy. A few deluxe models sported brass decorative strips around the base. They had blue glass with acid-etched numerals to mark the gallon levels. The Butlers used a unique type of brass nozzle that differed from that of peer brands. It weighed a bunch and had a large, heavy tube on the nozzle. Complicated locking mechanisms made of brass helped the looks of these pumps.

The Wayne Pump was manufactured in Indiana. It seemed to be one of the most popular latter-day visible pumps. These "lighthouse" types were clean of line, with a minimum of gingerbread. They had simple glass cylinders that were unmarked. There were internal tin numbers, mounted on a shaft, to reveal the gallons of gasoline pumped. The latter-day Waynes weighed half as much as the early ones. The skins were made of lightweight metal and the bases were stamped from thin metal. These pumps also had tops made of tin. The handles were stamped with a nice palm-fitting grip on the lever and a square-shaped hole and fitting on a short shaft. Most of these handles had a small set-screw, in the base, to keep them from coming off.

Some pumps, like the Fry, used a rotary-type pump, while others used one- and two-cylinder pumps in the fashion of an old steam engine. A few pumped only on one stroke, but some pumped when the lever was moved both ways. The advent of the electric pump spelled finis for the hand-operated jobs.

Whatever brand of pump you come up with, each has its own unique features that may appeal to you.

Gas globes glimmer with the glow of faded glory

By Paul Hatmon

The gasoline globe collector has been with us ever since there were hundreds of varieties of gasoline and gasoline pumps. The current rage for antique pumps has set the globe market on fire. "Old line" globe collectors are sometimes difficult men to deal with. The prices are high and superior knowledge of globes is on their side. The neophyte collector can probably amass a collection of maybe 50 different globes, of the later variety, without digging too deep in his jeans. Any efforts over that or attempts to get some of the older globes are difficult.

This original Royal Crown Ethyl globe was once used as a yard light on a small Missouri farm. It may still be there. (Paul Hatmon photo)

Sinclair's dinosaur is on this mixed plastic/glass globe. (Paul Hatmon photo)

The different kinds of gasoline globes snows Heinz 57 varieties completely under by both type and amount. From glass, metal and plastic to the swan song of flimsy all-plastic globes that fall apart at the first wind storm, the gasoline globe has run the gauntlet.

Globes came in one-piece glass with molded logos. They came with one-piece glass with attached logs. There were metal centers with glass units. There were glass centers with glass inserts. There were round globes, shield shaped tops and oval football shapes. One collector I know has some 600-plus different globes.

The manner of placing the units in a three-piece globe or four-piece globe also vary. The older 15-inch and 16-1/4-inch unit inserts could be placed in a metal- or glass-bodied center with snap rings on the outside. Some of the glass-bodied centers had inserts with two small holes to accommodate bolted-on inserts. Very little pressure on these bolts cracked the glass insert.

The beginning of the end was the standardization of the plastic center number 216 with glass inserts. Almost all companies used this center with their own custom-painted glass logos.

This beautiful, old glass-centered Texaco globe served as a door light at a rural mechanic's home. Perhaps he uses it today. (Paul Hatmon photo)

This is a one-piece etched Red Crown gasoline globe used by Standard Oil Company of Indiana. The red paint is faded. (Paul Hatmon photo)

A good example of a mixed plastic/glass oval globe is this one advertising Site brand gasoline. (Paul Hatmon photo)

The number 218 oval center, shaped like a football, was used by Shamrock, Zephyr, Site and others. These inserts fit into slots.

Collecting the earlier gasoline pump globes is really difficult. Most are already in the hands of the long time collector. There were many styles of bodies. There were glass, large Gill, small Gill metal, round plastic and oval plastic globes and many sizes of each. The standardization of the number 216 and number 218 plastic center for the 13-1/2-inch inserts and oval inserts lowered the prices.

Probably the most sought-after one-piece glass globes are the Royal Crowns used by Standard Oil Company years ago. They were very large and heavy globes made of a type of so-called milk glass. These came in several varieties. The rarest of the bunch was the Crown Ethyl Red Crown. These letters were molded into the rim of the globe. The globes were white with red trim for Red Crown and gold for Gold Crown. The white was unsullied with paint. A series of marble-sized bumps were molded around the rim. These globes command a top price from antique shops and collectors. They are still around.

This globe advertises Milton Oil Company's Dixcel gas. (Paul Hatmon photo)

A couple of brand new, never-mounted Gold Crowns and Red Crowns sit in a glass show case in a long-time Standard Oil dealer's office in a small, backward Missouri town. Two more Royal Crowns serve as yard lights on the obscure country farm of a local Standard Oil dealer. A White Crown globe sits forlornly in a flea market showcase with a $900 price tag.

Both the Crown and Shell one-piece globes are now being reproduced. The reproduction Royal Crown has a small hole in the top (just in case someone tries to sell you a replica for an original.)

People who want gas globes seem to prefer the "super-duper" grades of gas. The Boron, Dino Supreme, 100 Octane, Ethyl and Sinclair HCs are all wanted types. A local man advertised a couple of globes of the more common variety and received many calls wanting White Rose, White Eagle, Mustang and other varieties hard to come by. The glass or metal centered 16-1/4-inch insert globes seem to carry the highest prices. The 15-inch insert globes run a close second. A lot of old-time collectors sneer at the 13-1/2-inch glass insert globes with a plastic center, but there are more of them available now, due to standardization.

A defunct Ohio firm named Cincinnati Advertising Products Company made a great many of these latter day globes. By the 1980s, only three small oil companies were still using globes on their pumps and one of the three was planning to drop their use.

Since the gasoline market was a captive market, there was not much percentage in flaunting your logo when you could sell all the gas you have without expending the effort. Globes also grew quite expensive to keep on the gasoline pumps. Wind storms, snipers and accidents made replenishment an expensive affair.

If you want a couple of globes for your mantel or, maybe, one for your yard light, there are a limited number of globes available. If you are a gas pump fan it may take a bit of scrambling to secure an original globe. The following sources might be of help: Time Passages Ltd., PO Box 65596, West Des Moines, IA 50265 (phone 515-279-0194) or Weber's Nostalgic Supermarket, 6611 Anglin Drive, Fort Worth, TX 76119 (phone 817-534-6611).

Red Crown valve caps: an American tradition

By Cliff Reeves

Blue Dot taillights, Fulton sun shields, exotic radiator mascots and Red Crown valve caps are items of automobilia from another time. They are accessories that have spurred many tall tales about their role in, and contributions to, the automotive industry.

Many misconceptions were caused by their scarcity in certain parts of the country or the shortness of the time periods in which they were available to the automotive trade. Whether the tales surrounding such items were fabricated to meet certain situations or whether they were documented and proven facts is an interesting facet of history.

Nearly every old car buff has been intrigued by yarns of days gone by. Such a yarn was the reason behind my personal research into the history of an old automotive accessory. The Red Crown valve cap is the item that I studied in depth.

After restoring several 1940s and 1950s cars, I was continually involved with the old car hobby for several years. I picked up many noteworthy tips about factory and aftermarket accessories for early automobiles. At a gathering of old car buffs, the topic of oil company-related accessories for automobiles was being discussed. One recalled a rather unique tire valve stem cap molded in the shape of a crown. He remarked that he had obtained several of the caps, some years ago, from his neighborhood Shell Station.

I had discovered facts about such caps and advised him that the item he recalled was actually offered by Standard Oil Company and that the cap was formed of red plastic. My friend responded that there were also gold air caps. He also insisted that both color caps were offered through Shell dealers.

To get the facts, I started researching the Red Crown question. I remembered that my first encounter with Red Crown valve caps was in 1955, at age 14, but I suspected that the trademark was probably used many years prior to that time.

As my study progressed, it became clear that the research would have to be documented by personal observations and comments from those involved in various ways with the caps. With only faint memories of the caps from my youth, I felt it was important to obtain an example of an original. This was a decision that led to a five-month search through salvage yards, old service station store-

An example of Red Crown valve caps.

105

Gold Crown valve caps were available, too.

Standard Oil Company dealers got caps in boxes of 1000 to give away.

rooms and long-established tire shops. Finally, after several dead ends and wild goose chases, an aged and tiring gas station at the north end of Topeka, Kansas gave up a treasure. The owner was the type of fellow who never seemed to throw anything away.

A long wooden shelf at the back of the shop was lined with countless old and rusting coffee cans filled with lug nuts, Monkey Grip patches and cracked and deteriorated valve stems. It seemed the likely place to find a prize. In questioning the station owner, he recalled the caps, remarking that he used to remove them and put the regular style caps back on. He did not remember saving any of them, but ... with a little coaxing ... he consented to my rummaging through the old cans in hopes that some of the caps had found their way there.

From the mid-1940s to about 1957, Standard Oil Company products became simply Red Crown or White Crown gasoline. The glass globes used during this period did not display any names on the bottom band, only the raised jewels.

My search through each can yielded the usual amount of rust, cobwebs and odd nuts and bolts. Occasionally a corroded and badly worn brass air cap from the 1940s turned up. However, as I continued through the collection of cans I met with success. One rather strange appearing blue shape came rolling out of one of the cans. It turned out to be an original Red Crown valve cap. It had been painted, severl times, perhaps to match a vehicle's color. Upon showing my find to the shop owner, he recalled seeing the caps in various colors other than blue.

This recollection, and others regarding the colors of the caps, have proven to be a most aspect of my research. A month-long series of phone conversations with previous Standard Oil dealers located all over the country resulted in varying recollections of the caps, the dates they were offered and the colors they came in. One of the retired dealers recalled an article he had read in a company publication about the current historian for the company. This person was a great help in obtaining facts on the name Red Crown and its use by Standard Oil Company.

Back in 1937, this Studebaker tank truck and Standard Oil Company filling station created a scene familiar throughout the Midwest. The gasoline pump to the left of the truck displays a glass crown globe with Solite markings. (Applegate & Applegate photo)

The Red Crown symbol first appeared on visible gas pumps in the late 1920s. By the early 1930s, it spread throughout 15 Midwestern states. More than one type of glass globe was molded in the shape of a crown. These were produced from white glass. The one-piece etched Gasoline Crown globes of the early 1920s were red with white accents and said Gasoline around the bottom. Late 1920s models used on pumps dispensing regular gas were accented with red paint and had the words Red Crown embossed at the bottom of the globe. A circa-1928 design for ethyl gas pumps was completely white and had the words Red Crown Ethyl embossed around the bottom of the globe. In the mid-1930s, the words around the bottom were discontinued. The white globe was redesigned to display the words White Crown.

This theme of Red Crown and White Crown globes was used from the mid-1930s to the late-1940s. Early in this period, a blue globe that carried the word Solite appeared. This was a trade-name for Standard Oil Company's low-octane white gasoline. A fourth color also appeared during this period. Green was used for kerosene or diesel-type fuels. The green globe carried small raised areas around the bottom resembling jewels.

From the mid-1940s to about 1957, the products became simply Red Crown or White Crown gasoline. The glass globes used during this period did not display any names at the bottom, only the raised jewels.

In 1957, Standard Oil introduced premium gasoline and used a gold-colored crown to mark the premium pumps. The use of the crown globe, continued for only three more years and disappeared with the introduction of newer, low-profile pumps in the 1960s.

During this nearly 40-year span, Standard Oil Company promoted various changes and additions to its product lines. One popular method of promotion was the Red Crown valve cap. Although these caps were offered to patrons for many years, they have become a rare and hard to find item today.

The valve caps were formed from red plastic in the shape of a crown, like the gas globes. They were threaded to fit a tire valve stem to replace the regular air caps. The offering of many different colored air caps throughout the years seemed to be a likely possibility, considering all the different colored globes. However, upon further checking, I was advised that the caps were offered in only two colors. The most widely seen was the Red Crown valve cap, which was offered until the globes were removed in the early 1960s. The Gold Crown valve cap was used to introduce and promote the premium Gold Crown gasoline for just three years, from 1957 to 1960. They were formed from dark brown plastic and were vacuum-plated to a shiny gold appearance.

Through the years, the Red Crown and Gold Crown air caps were very Popular with the public and were seen on many vehicles. With the passing of the Red Crown trademark in the early sixties the glass globe, and air caps quickly became rare and nearly nonexistent items. Authentic reproductions of both the red and the gold air caps are now available.

On collecting license plates

By Tim Howley

A California license plate! The very name conjures up visions of sun and bronze-bodied surfers, giant redwood trees, little cable cars climbing topsy turvy hills, the timeless splendor of the High Sierra and Lake Tahoe, the glamour of Hollywood and the stars, and strains of Al Jolson pouring out those lyrics that still give California tourists goose bumps, "California here I come, right back where I started from. On an old car or new, a California license plate is the most colorful and romantic of all. It symbolizes the state that Michigan built, the place where the cars are fast cars, far out cars, old cars and new cars. Truly, California is the automobile lover's paradise.

California license plates have always aroused curiosity and interest anywhere "East of Laramie." Just think what a set of California plates will do on your car at a concours. "Hey, is that a California car? Wow!"

Vintage California plates are the most desirable of all, but they're not rare. California plates from most years (especially 1920 and later) are quite common at swap meets in the West. Plates from most any year can be purchased at the Hot August Nights Swap Meet in Reno, Nevada, and usually at quite reasonable prices. By the same token, caution should be exercised against purchasing California plates at "inflated" Eastern prices. As a general rule, no California plate is worth more than its counterpart from the other 49 states, provided the plates are in equal condition.

To many, the most desirable California plates are the earliest made in 1906 through 1913. Plates from these early years are highly collectible, but not particularly rare. These plates are quite elaborate. Some are all-leather with tin numerals. Some are leather over wood, with tin numerals. These are probably the earliest types. Later plates in this period are all-copper and all-aluminum, with embossed numerals. Some are metal, with the numerals affixed. A few are perforated metal to allow the air to slip through them when they are placed in front of the radiator.

During this period, it was even possible to make your own plates, as long as you registered your number with the state and paid your fee. Very little is generally known about California plates in these earliest years, but it would be difficult to say that any plate from this period is right or wrong, authentic or unauthentic.

Around 1908, the Automobile Club of Southern California began issuing porcelain license plates to its members. These carried the club's identity, as well as a blue on white (rather than the officially prescribed black on white) color combination. Also at about this same time, municipalities began issuing aluminum or brass badges which were placed on dash panels.

While California plates were made at Folsom Prison, in the early teens the state decided that these elaborate plate-making processes were simply too expensive. In 1914, California plates were finally standardized as all-porcelain. They had white numerals on a red/orange field. These plates are very desirable, but not terribly rare. 1915 was the first year that California plates were offered in the now familiar yellow and black colors. 1915 plates were black number on a yellow field. According to some collectors, 1915 and 1927 California plates are some of the most difficult to find, although no explanation has ever been offered as to why this is so.

In 1916, the state offered plates with blue numerals on a white field. These colors were continued through 1919, the last year of porcelain plates in California. The only differences in years were the small metal figures affixed to the plates. The 1916 plates had the California "Golden Bear." On the plates, the bear insignia was a dull silver, possibly because the bear was made of lead. 1917 plates had the California State Poppy. The poppy tab was yellow. 1918 and 1919 plates had a green mission bell and a red star, respectively.

Again, the state decided that its plates were too expensive to make. So, in 1920, tin plates were offered for the first time. 1920 plates are black with white numerals. 1921 plates are yellow with black numerals. 1922 plates, white with blue numerals. 1923, black with white numerals.

The 1924 plates are interesting in several respects. The white numerals on a bright green field provide a highly attractive color scheme. This was the only year that California plates had both six and seven digits. Earlier and later, California plates had no more than six digits. It's also a little difficult to come across 1924 California plates in good condition, again for no explainable reason.

California's 1927 plates are rather desirable. Some collectors say they duplicated the original 1914 colors with white digits on a red/orange field, but this is not so. The 1914 porcelains were white on a brilliant red. The plates for 1927 were white on dark red ... a big difference. Still, they are very popular with collectors. Some say 1927 plates are hard to come by, others say no. 1928 plates have yellow digits on a blue field.

In 1929, California established a color scheme and pattern that was continued through 1937. 1929 plates had "Halloween orange" digits on a black field. In 1930, this scheme was reversed to black digits on a Halloween orange field. The reversal of these two colors was continued every other year through 1937, which used orange digits on a black field. In 1938, the plates featured black symbols on a lemon yellow background.

The 1939 California plates are among the most colorful of all. The colors (orange digits on a blue field) resembled the still seen yellow on blue series that first came out in 1969 and is still valid today. The 1939 plates also read "California World's Fair '39." For extra cost, the motorist could have special decorative World's Fair plates. They showed the Golden Gate Bridge and a composite of the San Francisco and Oakland skylines. The 1939 World's Fair was held on Treasure Island, in San Francisco Bay, midway between the two cities.

There were actually two different plates depicting the bridge and the skyline. However, the rarest and most valuable 1939 California license plate doesn't show the bridge or the skyline, nor does it say "California World's Fair." The rarest 1939 California license plate (and perhaps the rarest California license plate of all) doesn't say anything but "Cal '39." Maybe it was sold only to embittered Southern Californians who chose not to acknowledge a World's Fair in the northern part of the state.

Who knows?

Beginning in 1940, California began issuing plates with rounded corners. These were continued until 1956. Granted, these plates were not as attractive as the earlier designs with the squared corners, but collectors say the state saved untold amounts money on the tin. In 1940, the plates had black digits on a yellow field. For 1941, they had yellow digits on a black field. A few 1942 plates were made, but they are quite rare. No plates were offered at all in 1943. Californians simply saved their 1941 plates and affixed small aluminum tabs for the year change. Small tabs with a red "V" for "Victory" were also given to plate holders.

In 1944, Californians were required to display a windshield sticker. Since most of these stickers were permanently affixed to windshields, they are almost impossible to find today without a car attached. For this reason, 1944 California stickers are worth considerably more than the plates of any year. It is not uncommon to pay relatively steep prices for a mint 1944 sticker.

In 1945, the state began offering plates again. The 1945 plates had white digits on a black background. These same plates were retained, in 1946, with a black-on-yellow metal tab. In 1947, new plates were offered again. They had black digits on a yellow field. These plates were retained in 1948 with a red-on-aluminum tab, in 1949 with a black-on-aluminum tab and in 1950 with a red-on-aluminum tab. New plates were offered in 1951 and continued through 1955. These were yellow digits on a black field.

The 1956 plates were quite a bit different. These are known as the "black on yellow multi-year series" plates. Even the bracket holes were repositioned, as the plates were somewhat smaller than in previous years. In 1957, California began offering reflective tabs to update the license plates. These tabs are worth as much as the plates, perhaps even more. The reason is simple. All of the older tabs are stuck to old license plates, usually under other old tabs

The new design of 1951 was also used in 1953. It was yellow on black.

The final appearance of the design introduced in 1951 came in 1955.

New 1956 plates were smaller than before. The bracket holes were moved.

The 1956 black on yellow multi-year series plates were replaced by a yellow on black series, which was introduced in 1963 and still valid today. However, for the last several years, California's plates have had blue symbols on a white background with the word California in red.

California motorcycle plates have followed the automobile plate colors. Motorcycle plates from 1914 through 1919 are porcelain and are contoured to fit the fenders.

Naturally, in buying California plates (like those from any other state) a pair is worth more than two singles. A pair of plates which was never used or is in mint condition is worth a premium. However, rusty original plates are always worth more than plates which have been repainted by some well-intentioned collector.

In collecting license plates, originality is the name of the game. You may get credit in a car show for a restored set of plates as part of the car, but in plate collector circles, restoration is akin to defacing the plate entirely.

Yellow on black was back again for 1963.

Most cars in "factory photos" have Michigan manufacturer tags, but this 1934 Ford publicity photo shows a Touring Car with California license plate.

Today's ancient license plates were usually homemade

By Keith Marvin

Probably no adjunct to the interest in automobiles and related subject has become more popular in the last decade than the collecting, studying and spotting of automobile license plates. A generation ago, the subject was prosaic indeed, with a handful of collectors keeping a weather eye out for rare and esoteric items. Complete runs of plates from the first to last issues decorated the interior of countless garages, barns and carriage houses across the land. Otherwise, when a set of plates expired, owners generally threw them away.

In Canada, the province of Ontario began automobile registrations as early as 1903. Those first Canadian plates consisted of black leather pads carrying silver metal numbers and the provincial coat of arms. Shown here are 1913 and 1914 license plates from Manitoba, Canada. (G. Chartrand photo)

Like postage stamps, license plates are collected for rarity, appearance, color, variety, specialties and, in rare cases, errors. More common is the collector interested only in the license plates issued by a single state, usually where he or she resides. A good example is this complete run of 1909 to 1928 Virginia license plates. (Virginia Division of Motor Vehicles)

Today, there has been a complete reversal in pattern. Thousands upon thousands of plate collectors dot the country. There is a successful auto-license plate society. Increased interest in the field is apparent. No where to be found are the runs of old plates which once dotted garage walls. They are now in license plate collector's hands in most cases, that's where. Now, it costs collectors plenty of the folding green to get the owner to pry them free.

Like postage stamps, license plates are collected not only for the sake of collecting alone, but for rarity, appearance, special colors, varieties, specialty varieties and, in rare cases, errors.

No one knows where or when the first registration numbers were assigned to vehicles, although it is known that chariots were registered in the Rome of the Caesars. We also know that there was a contest at times to try for low numbers, even as we see today. Hansom cabs were carrying number plates in Victorian London and we have but to look into the late Sir A. Conan Doyle's *The Hound of the Baskervilles* to get a classic example involving the talents of no less a personage than Sherlock Holmes!

Regular automobile registrations appear to have begun in Europe, where one historian places the first in Munich, in 1899, followed by Kristiania (now Oslo) later the same year and Belgium and Spain a year later. Another study lists Austria-Hungary in 1900, with Ardmore, Pennsylvania coming on-stream about the same time (the latter for steam cars only).

Whatever the answer, the credit for being first in automobile registration must go to Europe which, as well as most of the world excepting the Western Hemisphere, subsequently opted for permanent registrations. As we are concentrating on North America, we bid our European forebears a fond adieu and thank them for blazing a path in the field.

Before formal registrations went into effect, certain commuters were given license to operate cars in various communities through letters written by officials in authority. These were carried by the motorist. For example, on September 6, 1899, such a letter was written, at the request of Myron D. Adams of Lansingburgh, New York. It allowed him to operate his vehicle on the streets of Troy, a city that adjoined his community. This is the earliest record of such a registration in my files.

During the 1950s, Atlas Supply Company of Newark, New Jersey annually published attractive, four-color, full-page magazine advertisements showing the design of the license plates for all 48 states, the District of Columbia and 12 Canadian provinces or territories. This one shows 1954 issues.

Thousands upon thousands of plate collectors cover the country, today. No where to be found are the derelict old plates once nailed haphazardly to garage walls. They are now in license plate vendors' or collectors' hands. Prices are still affordable, but rising year-by-year. This was one vending booth at the 1984 Hershey, Pennsylvania swap meet. (Dennis Schrimpf photo)

The first state in the United States formally passing legislation for motor vehicle registration was New York. It happened in 1901. All automobile owners were obliged to submit to the Secretary of State their name, address and the make and horsepower of their car. They also had to enclose one dollar.

Up in Albany, the Secretary of State filled in the data (probably in a ledger in a fine Spencerian hand) and put the buck in a cash box. He then sent a postcard to the registrant advising him to get a leather pad and attach his initials thereon, hanging the same from the rear of his vehicle. There weren't all that many car owners then, but certainly there must have been some duplication.

This apparently didn't bother Albany. Back then, the chance of any two similar sets of initials on the license pads, as they were called, becoming involved in accidents or other confusion, was a remote one. In almost every case, three initials were employed on the pad, although at least one four-letter combination is known to have existed.

Two years later, in 1903, New York State looked over its past two years of registrations. Some 954 vehicles were registered and running before the end of 1901. This meant that, in its initial year, the state had gleaned $954 from the motoring public. That isn't much from today's standards, but the Secretary of State was doubtless sharp enough to see, philosophically, that this represented $954 that the state hadn't gotten in 1900! And registrations boomed far above 954 in 1902 and early 1903.

On May 15, 1903, New York State, becoming cognizant that sets of initials had long since run out, formed a new code of registrations. It announced that, as of that date, all motorists would be obliged to re-register and a numeric series was commenced. The numbers would be assigned by a small metal seal about the size of a half dollar. Upon receipt, the owner would be required to have this number attached to the rear of his car. The specified colors were black on a white background. The plate material was optional. This meant, in most cases, that metal or painted numbers would be attached to a stitched leather pad or tin or composition background. No further state identification was required and Number 1 was assigned to G.P. Chamberlain of Harrison. By May 3, 1904, the inclusion of the abbreviation letters, "N.Y." were also made mandatory in the display of one's number.

It should be pointed out here that more than half the states and most of the Canadian provinces began their registration systems in this primitive way and the do-it-yourself type of registration pad or plate was in favor in many parts of the country. Elsewhere, however, a more carefully thought out type of registration would gain rapid favor.

On September 1, 1903, the Commonwealth of Massachusetts began issuing license plates that were heavy steel affairs coated with dark-blue porcelain enamel. They carried a number and the legend "*Mass. Automobile Register.*" These porcelain plates were made with high-gloss finish and were highly legible.

They also had a tendency to chip, if struck by a stray rock or pebble. They were expensive, but they would come to dominate the field for more than a decade.

In 1903, other places had other ideas. Although Pennsylvania adopted registrations that year, generally do-it-yourself pads with metal numbers on a black leather pad (with a "P" prefix or suffix) were used. Then, the cities of Philadelphia brought out dated porcelain enamel plates. Having such local options was fine, provided the vehicle so registered didn't move from that community. Otherwise, another state pad would be required. Many motor vehicles, consequently, carried both local plates and state pads.

Ontario, Canada also began automobile registrations in 1903. Its plates consisted of black leather pads carrying silver metal numbers and the provincial coat-of-arms.

In 1904, the first plates appeared in St. Louis, Missouri, Rhode Island, Chicago, Illinois and Montreal, Quebec, Canada. 1905 saw the advent of the first official issues of Connecticut (which had used the do-it-yourself system until then), as well as Maine, New Hampshire, Vermont and Wisconsin. Ontario put its leather pads into obsolescence and issued a new series, made of rubber, which carried neither identification of origin or date, except in their latter years of use. Then, a small, aluminum plate containing the embossed letters "Ontario" was fastened in the top center, above the numbers. These would remain in use until January 1, 1911.

A year later, plate debuts were noted in Pennsylvania, Virginia and West Virginia, as well as Cincinnati, Columbus and a few other Ohio cities. With the advent of the Pennsylvania porcelain enamel plates, the hand-made leather jobs went into discard. In Philadelphia, the municipal authorities, perhaps unaware of the new state series, issued a new series of Philadelphia locals. Then, the state maintained that the motor vehicle law was all encompassing and automobilists in the City of Brotherly Love were obliged to carry both state and local markers on their automobiles.

Only one new license plate issue appeared in 1907. That was in the District of Columbia. Plate number 4515 was assigned to the United States President's car.

This was the threshold of the movement of the states and provinces to jump on the bandwagon in the matter of registrations. What had started as a practical and necessary thing, became a fanciful thing as well. Designs of license plates would begin to show imagination. Elaborate color schemes would be tried ... some to rather poor advantage. Increased inter-city and interstate travel would prevail.

In Europe, where plates had no identifying marks as to the country of origin, one was obliged to include an oval on his or her car when crossing frontiers. The letter or letters on that oval identified the country of registration. In America, plates explained themselves, more or less. However, it was about as simple to motor out of state with one's own set of plates, as it was to cross a frontier in Europe without the needed oval.

Not only license plate collectors look for old license plates. The owners of antique and classic cars collect them for various reasons, which range from decorating their garage to displaying them on their old cars. In some states, such as Wisconsin, "year of manufacture" (YOM) license plates are legal to use on properly registered collector cars. (Old Cars photo)

Here is a close-up of "The 50th American Presidential Inaugural" license plate. Note that the date 1985 does not correspond to the date of the election year, but to the actual year of the inauguration. This design also carries the date of 1789, when the George Washington was inaugurated.

In 1907, the District of Columbia released its first license plates. Plate number 4515 was assigned to the United States President. A specialized area for license plate buffs is United States Presidential Inaugural plates. This collector displays some of these unique issues from the District of Columbia.

The international oval explained and cataloged

By Keith Marvin

Of the many aspects surrounding international motor travel, perhaps the most interesting and least understood is the use of the international oval or traveling plaque. The international oval carries a combination of one to three letters. It is attached to the rear of a vehicle to identify the country or home base of the car in question.

Now, it may seem odd, to the casual observer, that such a symbol is carried on a motor vehicle, when it travels outside its own land. This is especially true, if the license plate clearly identifies the country of origin. However, this is not always the case. Most countries are not clearly identified on their number plates and, in the earlier days of international motor travel (primarily in Europe), none did.

Except for short, over-the-border jaunts, traveling from one country to another, 70 years ago, was a complicated and interesting experience. Only the affluent could own the new toy ... the automobile. It was flimsy at best and impossible at the worst. Roads outside metropolitan centers were, for the most part, barely adequate or nearly nonexistent. The international traveler was obliged either to bluff his way about on his own number plates or to go through the rigors of obtaining temporary, visitor registrations. The more adventurous automobilists had their problems intensified each time they crossed another frontier.

Since no license plates gave a hint of their origin, only a few seasoned travelers even attempted to guess where this or that car came from. In nearly every case, except in the United States, the markers were white and black. The only possible way one could spot a "foreign" plate was to note an unorthodox numbering system.

As concern into clarifying the mystery of where an automobile was registered intensified, a number of countries, represented by their various touring clubs, set up an agreement accepting the "International Travelling Pass." This allowed cars to travel in and out of those countries, provided they had, in addition to their regulation number plates, the international sign.

"The plate must be oval, 30 centimeters wide, 18 centimeters high and must carry one or two black letters on a white ground," read a stipulation to the agreement. "The letters must consist of Roman capitals and have a minimum height of 10 centimeters; their outline must be 15 millimeters thick."

These stipulations were laid down at the outset of the new system, on October 11, 1909 and the regulation was strictly adhered to for many years. The rule is not as rigidly kept today. Now, it is not unusual to see ovals in black with silver letters or simply with the letters themselves attached directly to the body of the car, sans the oval-shaped plaque.

In the first four years of oval display, motoring, on an international basis, increased by leaps and bounds. Automobile production also increased, while average prices on cars decreased. This made them more readily accessible to a larger number of buyers. At the same time, roads were vastly improved and more new roads were being constructed nearly everywhere.

By the end of 1913, the following letter combinations were registered by subscribing nations:

A=Austria, B=Belgium, BG=Bulgaria, CH=Switzlerland, D=Germany, E=Spain, F=France, Algeria and Tunis; GB=Great Britain, H=Hungary, I=Italy; MC=Monaco, MN=Montenegro, NL=Netherlands, P=Portugal, R=Russia and S=Sweden. Egypt was also a subscriber to the agreement by this time, but for some reason, unknown to me, was not assigned a letter combination. Oddly, motorists from both Algeria and Tunisia (two nations under French control) were required to display the French oval when crossing frontiers. However, the case of tiny Monaco having its own oval, in the early days, seems extraordinary. Although it was an independent principality, as it remains today, its cars were registered with French number plates from the Marseilles District. Not until 1928, did Monaco issue its own license plates.

There were some notable countries that were not in on the ground floor of international participation, including Denmark, Norway, Greece and Turkey. Another peculiarity affected motorists from Luxembourg, who used the D oval on their cars. This nation was not a subscriber to the original 1909 agreement. Therefore, despite its independent Grand Ducal status, it was treated as a part of Germany under the agreement. Another surprising omission was Romania. Serbia was not included, too.

On June 28, 1914, Archduke Francis Ferdinand (heir to the Austro-Hungarian throne) and his wife were assassinated. This occurred in the Bosnian town of Sarajevo and the world plunged into four years of warfare. Four years later, Serbia and Montenegro were combined into a new nation called Yugoslavia. With this change, the MN oval became obsolete. Other emerging nations included Finland, Poland, Czechoslovakia and the Baltic States. The Russian Empire also disappeared and with it its R oval letter. This letter was transferred to Rumania, a new subscriber to the agreement.

As the patchwork quilt of new nations appeared, so did a preponderance of new letter combinations adopted by succeeding International Congresses on Motoring. As we all know, the changes continue to occur, with some regularity, into modern times. For the latest information, see the chart of ovals, both active and inactive, listed at the end of this history.

I'm not entirely certain what the mystique is surrounding the display and use of the oval, but it is there. Several attempts to properly identify number plates and others to eliminate international letter combinations have come to nothing.

In Europe, for example, it would be a relatively simple matter for each country to list its name on the plate, which would be similar to the practice employed by the United States and Canada. Belgium, for example, might solve its problem by imprinting "BEL-GIE-BELGIQUE" on its tags, thus eliminating the necessity of carrying the B marker. Somehow, though, the international letter idea has taken hold in such a way, that it is more than likely to be with us forever.

Prior to its subjugation by the Soviet Union, in 1940, the license plates of Latvia did carry proper identification. It made no difference. When a Lett elected to cross his own frontier for another country, he carried his LR oval. These days, license plates of both Andorra and Monaco carry the country names on them. However, when motorists living there travel outside their own domains (and they all do, as there is precious little area within their own borders) they carry their AND and MC letters, too.

Over the past 15 years, there have been additions affecting motorists in other countries in which undated series of license plates give a clearer idea of a car's home "turf." For example, Austrian license plates now include the provincial coat-of-arms in their design. Hungary and Rumania carry their flags, in full color, under which H and RD, respectively, appear. Russia is planning to follow suit. Its 1994 series will carry the nation's flag over the letters RUS.

The Aland Islands, a dependency of Finland, now use plates with the name Aland, the island's coat-of-arms and its flag, all presented in full color. Current Irish plates are now adopting the city or county name to appear, in Gaelic, above the numeric/letter combination. Thus, a car registered in Dublin could be readily identified by "Baile Atha Cliath," the city's Gaelic name, on its tags. San Marino (the country, not the California town), shows both its coat-of-arms and the country name on its license plates. Malta is readily identified by the Maltese cross on its license plates. Nevertheless, when motorists living there travel, they must have the international oval on their car.

The variations of letter combinations, over the seven decades since the inception of the international oval, have been interesting, even if a bit confusing. Some of the original codes assigned have never changed to this day. Others have been augmented, such as the GB. It originally applied to cars in England, Scotland, Ireland, Wales, the Isle of Man and the Channel Islands. Later, an alphabetical suffix was added, here and there, to differentiate these places. GBA, GBG and GBJ, respectively, were adopted for the Channel Islands of Alderney, Guernsey and Jersey; GBM was used for the Isle of Man; and GBY and GBZ identify Malta and Gibraltar. All of these, except the Maltese designation, remain in effect to this day. Upon achieving independence, in 1974, Malta adopted the letter M, which had formerly been assigned to the defunct state of Palestine. The GBY combination then passed into limbo.

By the same token, following the formation of the Irish Free State, in 1922, the GB combination was withdrawn there. However, it has been maintained, to this day, in Northern Ireland. The Irish Free State first adopted the letter combination SE, which stood for the Gaelic term "Saorstat Eireann." By World War II, the Irish Free State had proclaimed its independence as a republic. Then, the SE combination was scrapped in favor of EIR, which stands for the Republic of Ireland or Eire. This, in its turn, was phased out in favor of an IRL designation.

For many years, the F (France) was used in all French possessions. The same pattern was followed by both Spain and Portugal. In the latter case, the P (Portugal) applied, for years, not only to the homeland, but also to its possessions of Angola, the Cape Verde Islands, Mozambique, Guinea (now Guinea-Bissau), Timor Sao Tome and Principe, as well as Macao. In less than four years, this changed. All former Portuguese possessions, with the sole exception of Macao (which still swears allegiance to the motherland and, presumably, still requires the P oval on any motor vehicle leaving the island) declared independence. Angola and Mozambique did use PAN and MOC letter combinations for a time. They reverted back to the P, for awhile, preceding their independence. Timor was absorbed into Indonesia. I have no current information on the current letter combinations in use for any of these former Portuguese colonies.

Another change, in recent years, concerns use of the D insignia. Included in the original 1909 combinations, the D has applied to Germany ever since then. After the proclamation of East Germany (German Democratic Republic) following World War II, the D oval continued in official use, both in that country and West Germany. Later, Communist East Germany opted for the letters DDR on its oval. This indicated "Deutsche Demokratische Republik." It was used until the two Germanies were reunited in 1990. Following that momentous event, the D became the official insignia of unified Germany again.

One of the odder things about this international oval game is that, these days, certain combinations are not entirely official, although they are generally accepted as proper identification. Some combinations are registered with the Geneva Road Traffic Board and are filed with the United Nations. Some are registered and not filed with the United Nations. Others aren't officially noted, but are generally accepted wherever they are seen. Compounding the confusion is the fact that some countries have never gotten around to adopting a combination of letters at all.

Bermuda is a good example of a country without an oval. There has never been a letter combination assigned there, yet a good many cars leave the islands for travel in the United States and elsewhere. The reason for the lack of a combination can probably be traced to the fact that, until World War II, motor vehicles were prohibited by law in the colony. The five former British West Indian colonies, which are now independent (Bahamas, Barbados, Jamaica, Trinidad and Tobago), were assigned official combinations. They have all retained them. The Windward Islands of Dominica, Grenada, St. Lucia and St. Vincent long ago adopted WD, WG, WL and WV respectively. The Leeward Island chain, which includes Antigua, Montserrat, St. Kitts-Nevis-Anguilla and the British Virgin Islands, were never assigned combinations. However, the British Virgin Islanders do use the unofficial combination BVI, when traveling abroad.

No combinations have been assigned to the Cayman islands or the Turks and Caicos Islands either, but there will be official combinations, at least for the Cayman Islands. They have become a noted tourist attraction and automobiles have become abundant. These vehicles do travel off the Cayman Islands, especially to Florida and the southeastern United States.

One might well ask how a car, from Bermuda, can be identified as such, when the number plate carries no legend of origin. I can cite one incident, isolated to be sure, of an acquaintance of mine from Hamilton. He painted "Bermuda," in block letters, on his license plates, directly above the numbers. "The plates were otherwise unidentifiable," he explained. "I got sick and tired answering questions about where the car was from. Everyone asked: the police, kids and almost everyone else. After I painted the word Bermuda on those plates, the questions stopped.

There was another more serious consideration which went through my mind," he added. "What would ever happen if I happened to forgot to carry my personal papers and got into a serious accident? There would be absolutely no way that those (regular Bermuda) plates could be identified." Certainly, this danger would arise in any other cases where letters are not, or never have been, assigned to a locality's license plates.

Now and then, one may encounter a car carrying an obsolete combination of letters on its international oval. Symbols such as the KT and KWT used in Kuwait are examples. These might still be in limited use.

119

Others, which also have never been approved or officially accepted, crop up from time to time. Examples include US instead of USA and, previously, Y in place of the approved Yugoslavian YU.

The latter brings up a most significant point; there is constant change going on. For instance, since the break up of Yugoslavia (which is still going on) began, the parts of the old republic continuing to use the YU oval are Montenegro and Serbia. At this writing, Montenegro is getting "shaky" and will possibly leave Serbia to fend for itself. However, Montenegro's motorists continue to use the YU international oval, at least for the time being.

The other parts of what had been Yugoslavia have declared there independence. Accordingly, they have issued both new number plates and international ovals. The symbols used include BiH for Bosnia and Herzogovina; CRO and HR for Croatia (CRO is now being phased out, though); PM, standing for The Republic of Macedonia in the Cyrillic alphabet, for Macedonia; and SLO for Slovenia.

As to how the break up of the Soviet Union affects international ovals used there, uncertainty reigns. Those symbols that I know have been adopted, so far, are as follows: BEL=Belarus; EST=Esthonia; LV=Latvia; LT=Lithuania; MLD=Moldova; RUS=Russia; and UA=the Ukraine. As for other so-called Soviet "republics" that remain, including Armenia; Azerbaijam; Kazakhstan; Kyrgyzstan; Tajikstan; Turkmenistan; and Uzbekistan, the final decisions about international oval designs remain to be determined.

Another recent break up occurred in the former Republic of Czechoslovakia, which heretofore used the CS oval. Now, two different states exist. The Czech Republic has chosen CZ and Slovakia is using SK.

The only other state, in Europe, which comes to mind for consideration is the Turkish Republic of Cyprus, which has existed since 1983. That's when the Turkish populace on the northern part of the island (numbering about 175,000 people) declared its independence. It now shares mainly one thing only, the capital city of Nicosia, with the Republic of Cyprus. Otherwise, the two have little else in common. Turkish Cyprus flies its own flag, even though it is not internationally recognized. If an international oval is used, on those rare occasions when a motor vehicle crosses the border to the south, it would, undoubtedly, be the TR of Turkey.

Other countries have experienced a sort of metamorphosis, much like the variations used in Ireland. One of these involves the progression of combinations used in Lebanon and Syria. For a time, one set of letters applied to both countries. This took two forms, SL and LSA. Then, Lebanon adopted LIB and Syria took SYR, which it has kept. Lebanon, however, made another change to its present RL.

Another place which changed, twice, after its initial set of letters, is Sarawak. This is the exotic land, on the northern part of Borneo, ruled for three generations by a dynasty of white rajahs. Sarawak shared its first combination of SNB with neighboring North Borneo. Then, it adopted SK. Ultimately, Sarawak was absorbed into Malasia. It uses the letters MAL today.

In at least one instance, a letter combination was changed, due to the official name change of a country. This occurred when Siam became Thailand and the SM combination was scrapped in favor of the then-vacant T.

After India became a republic in 1950, the former British Indian BI insignia was replaced with,the current IND letters. In the early 1950s, France gave up its claim to Pondicherry and other communities comprising the 196 square miles of French India. Then, the letters IND replaced the French Indian IF sign. Ten years later, Portugal ceded Goa and the 1,426 square miles of enclaves making up Portuguese India. Thereafter, India's IND sign was substituted for Portugal's P.

In Malaya, the story was more complex, but nonetheless fascinating. For one thing, Malaya was divided into two political subdivisions, the Federated and non-Federated Malay States. The primary difference was supposed to be that the native sultans in the non-Federated group enjoyed a good deal more independence and less British interference. Be that as it may, two ovals were used by residents of Negri Sembilan, Pahang, Perak and Selangor, which comprised the federated group. The automobile owner, when traveling abroad, had his choice of FM (Federation Malaya) or PTM. This stands for "Parsekutuan Tanas Melayu," which means exactly the same thing as Federation Malaya in Malay. The non-Federated States of Johore, Kedah, Kelantan, Perlis and Trenggan were assigned their own combinations. Then, all five were phased-out, in 1948, when all of Malaya adopted the FM designation. Malaya is now Malaysia and the MAL oval is in current use.

For general oval confusion, British East Africa probably takes first place. In the beginning, there were only two: EA included Kenya, Uganda, Nyassaland, Tanganyika, Zanzibar and Northern Rhodesia; SR was assigned to Southern Rhodesia. Then, these were changed. Kenya was assigned EAK; Tanganyika took EAT; Uganda got EAU; Zanzibar adopted EAZ; Nyassaland used NP and Northern Rhodesia grabbed NR. Next, came a second change for Nyassaland. It substituted RNY for the earlier NP and RNR and RSR for Northern and Southern Rhodesia, respectively.

The final changes, currently in use, are the letters MW for Malawi (formerly Nyassaland) and the Z favored by Zambia (formerly Northern Rhodesia). The former Southern Rhodesia became Rhodesia. It has retained the RSR combination. Kenya and Uganda which, oddly enough, have remained Kenya and Uganda, have kept their EAK and EAU letters. Tanganyika and Zanzibar became the Republic of Tanzania, but have retained their former EAT and EAZ symbols.

Another obsolete combination is NF, which was used by Newfoundland. This was prior to its entry into Canada, on April 1, 1949, as that country's 10th province. Theoretically, any Newfoundlander who travels outside Canada these days would use the proper CDN letters. However, the Newfoundlanders are a proud and independent people. Many of them resent Newfoundland's absorption into Canada. They still think of themselves as Newfoundlanders, rather than Canadians. So, even today, one may encounter cars still carrying around 45-year-old, obsolete, NF international ovals. The good old folk of Newfoundland (pronounced with the emphasis on the last syllable) have always been proud that their island was the older of the two former dominions. Its incorporation into the British Empire dated to 1498, versus 1534 for Canada's.

Actually, international oval letters are seldom used by anyone from the United States, Canada, Mexico or Central America, when travelling in Central and North America. One can see that it really isn't a necessity, as it is in other parts of the world. Over here, all license plates proclaim their country, state or province of origin.

The use of the obsolete NF oval brings me to the concluding subject in this study; those ovals carrying letter combinations which are neither officially recognized or accepted by road traffic boards and enforcement agencies. These badges generally reflect the political thoughts of the car owner. They project a sense of peculiar pride and a desire to be associated with what the ovals imply. These badges, though not official, are commonly seen today and no one seems to care very much.

Unofficial symbols on international ovals should not be confused with combinations reflecting the affectation of a driver's homemade oval, such as the GBW seen by my late friend and colleague, automotive historian Michael Sedgwick. He spotted this on a car registered on the Isle of Wight. Also, while vacationing on Prince Edward Island, Canada, in the early 1970s, I saw an oval with PEI on it.

Some international ovals, seen rarely today, have no official status, but are generally recognized for what they represent. These include BzH, C, CYM, ECOSSE, FRL, Q and VL. Explanations of their "meanings" are presented in the chart below.

The changes in these international letter symbols, as can be seen, are as rapid as the political changes throughout the world. They have to be watched closely, if one is to understand them at all.

Provided below is a listing of all international letter combinations known to me, past and present, official and non-official, but accepted. The writer would be grateful for any omissions or addenda on the part of the readers.

INTERNATIONAL MOTORING LETTERS PAST AND PRESENT

(Country codes in capital letters denote combination is currently in use)
* Not in official use (i.e. United Nations not notified)
** No official recognition of name change in country previously using another name
*** Unofficial status, but seen and/or frequently "recognized."

Code	Country	Code	Country
A	Austria	AZ	Azerbaijan
(and, until 1918, used by the Austro-Hungarian monarchy)		B	Belgium
		BA	Burma **
ADN	The Peoples Democratic Republic of Yemen	(See Myanmar)	
		BDS	Barbados
(Formerly in the Crown Colony of Aden)		BEL	Belarus *
AFG	Afghanistan	BG	Bulgaria
AL	Albania	BH	Belize
AND	Andorra	(Formerly British Honduras)	
AOE	Spanish Sahara	DI	British India
AUS	Australia & Territories	BiH	Bosnia & Herzegovina *

121

Code	Country
BL	Lesotho
(Formerly Basutoland)	
BOL	Bolivia
BP	Botswana
(Formerly the Bechuanaland Protectorate)	
BR	Brazil
BRG	Guyana
(Formerly British Guiana)	
BRN	Bahrain
BRU	Sultanate of Brunel
BS	Bahamas
(Formerly British Somaliland)	
BUR	Burma **
(See Myanmar)	
BVI	British Virgin Islands **
C	Cuba
CA	Canada
CAM	Cameroons (early)
CB	Belgian Congo and Ruanda-Urundi
CC	Consular Corps
(Not considered a letter combination)	
CD	Corps Diplomatique (See CC)
CDN	Canada
CFS	French Somaliland
CGO	Congo Kinasha
(now Zaire)	
CH	Switzerland
CI	Ivory Coast
CL	Sri Lanka **
(Formerly Ceylon)	
CNB	Colony of North Boreo and Labuan
CO	Colombia
CR	Costa Rica
CRO	Croatia * (Also HR *)
CS	Czechoslovakia
CU	Curacao and Surimane
CY	Cyprus
(Formerly Palestine)	
CZ	Czech Republic
D	Germany 1910-1949; Federal Republic of Germany 1949-1990
	Unified Germany since 1990
DA	Danzig
DDR	German Democratic Republic 1974-1990
DK	Denmark and Greenland
DOM	Dominican Republic
DY	Benin
(Formerly Dahomey)	
DZ	Algeria (El Djezair)
E	Spain and Possessions
EA	British East Africa, including Kenya, Northern Rhodesia, Nyassaland, Tanganyika, Uganda and Zanzibar (1932-1938)
EAK	Kenya
EAT	Tanganyika
EAU	Uganda

Code	Country
EAZ	Zanzibar
EC	Ecuador
EIR	Ireland (Erie)
EQ	Ecuador
EST	Esthonia
ET	Egypt
ETH	Ethiopia (Abyssinia)
EW	Esthonia
F	France and currently used for French Depencies. (Also formerly used for Algeria and Tunis)
FI	Finland and Aaland Islands (SRF is still in use, but being phased-out)
FJI	Fiji
FL	Liechtenstein
FM	Federated Malay States including the Sultanates of Negri Sembilian, Pahang, Perak and Selangor
G	Gabon
(Formerly Guatemala)	
GB	Great Britain including England, Northern Ireland, Scotland and Wales
GBA	Alderny (Channel Islands)
GBG	Guernsey (Channel Islands)
GBJ	Jersey (Channel Islands)
GBM	Isle of Man *
GBY	Malta
GRZ	Gibraltar
GEO	Georgia
H	Hungary
HK	Hong Kong
HKJ	Jordan
HR	Croatia (Also CRO)
HV	Upper Volta
(See Burkina Faso)	
I	Italy And The Sovereign Military Order of Malta Recognized by many nations as the smallest independent country in the world, but surrounded by the City of Rome
IF	French India
(Pondicherry and surrounding land)	
IL	Israel
IN	Dutch East Indies
(now Indonesia)	
IND	India
IR	Iran
IRL	Ireland (Erie)
IRQ	Iraq
IS	Iceland
J	Japan
JA	Jamaica
JO	Johore, Malaya

Code	Country
K	Kampuchea or the Khmer Republic (Formerly Cambodia)
KAT	Katanga * (A province of Zaire which attempted secession. Distinct oval license plates were used in 1960-1963.)
KD	Kedah, Malaya
KL	Kelantan, Malaya
KT	Kuwait
KWT	Kuwait
L	Luxembourg
LAO	Laos
LAR	Libya
LB	Liberia
LIB	Lebanon
LR	Latvia
M	Malta
MA	Morocco
MAL	Malaysia
MC	Monaco
MD	Moldova (1991-1993)
ME	Spanish Sahara
MEX	Mexico
MLD	Moldova
MN	Montenegro
MOC	Mozambique (Previously used 1932-1956 also) *
MS	Mauritius
MT	Tangier
MW	Malawi
N	Norway
NA	Netherlands Antilles
NAU	Nauru *
NEP	Nepal
NF	Newfoundland
NGN	Netherlands New Guinea
NIC	Nicaragua
NIG	Niger
NL	Netherlands
NP	Nyassaland Protectorate
NR	Northern Rhodesia
NZ	New Zealand and Territories
P	Portugal and Possessions
PA	Panama
PAK	Pakistan
PE	Peru
PI	Philippine Islands
PL	Poland
PM	Macedonia
PNG	Papua New Guinea
PR	Perlis, Malaya
PS	Persia (now Iran)
PTM	Malaysia
PY	Paraguay
Q	Qatar
R	Russia 1910-1926, Rumania 1930-1931

Code	Country
RA	Argentina
RB	Botswana
RC	China (Taiwan)
RCA	Central African Republic (Central African Empire 1976-1979)
RCB	Congo (Formerly French Congo)
RCH	Chile
RF	Russia 1991-1993 (Previously used by Ruanda-Urundi)
RG	Guinea
RH	Haiti
RHV	Burkina Faso (Formerly Upper Volta)
RIM	Islamic Republic of Mauritania
RL	Lebanon
RM	Madagascar
RMM	Mali
RN	Niger
RNR	Northern Rhodesia
RO	Rumania
ROK	South Korea *
ROU	Uruguay
RP	Philippines
RPB	Benin (Previously Dahomey)
RSM	San Marino
RSR	Southern Rhodesia
RU	Burundi (Formerly Russia)
RUC	Cameroons
RW	Rwanda
S	Sweden
SA	Saudi Arabia (Formerly used by The Saar)
SAU	Union of South Africa
SB	Serbia
SD	Swaziland
SE	Irish Free State (Saorstat Eireann)
SF	Finland and the Aaland Islands (In use, but being phased-out; see FI)
SGP	Singapore
SHS	Kingdom of Serbs, Croats and Slovenes
SK	Slovakia (Previously assigned to Sarawak)
SL	Syria and Lebanon
SLO	Slovenia
SM	Siam (See Thailand)
SME	Suriname
SN	Senegal
SNB	Sarawak and North Borneo
SO	Somalia * (Also assigned to Slovakia 1939-1945 * and 1992 *)
SP	Somaliland Protectorate
SQ	Slovakia *

Code	Country	Code	Country
SR	Southern Rhodesia	VN	Vietnam
SS	Straits Settlements	WAC	Gold Coast
SU	Soviet Union	(See Ghana)	
SWA	Nabibia	WAG	The Gambia
(Formerly Southwest Africa)		WAL	Sierra Leone
SY	Seychelles	WAN	Nigeria
SYR	Syria	WD	Dominica
T	Thailand	WG	Grenada
(Formerly Siam)		WL	St. Lucia
TC	French Cameroons	WS	Western Samoa
TCH	Chad *	WV	St. Vincent
TD	Trinidad and Tobago	Y	Yugoslavia
TEG	Spanish Guinea	YAR	Yemen
TG	Togo	(Formerly Yemen Arab Republic *)	
TN	Tunisia	YMN	North Yemen
TR	Turkey	YU	Yugoslavia
TS	Trieste	(Currently used by Montenego and Serbia)	
TT	Trinidad and Tobago	YV	Venezuela
(Formerly assigned to French Togoland)		Z	Zambia
TU	Trengganu, Malaya	ZA	Republic of South Africa
U	Uruguay	ZM	Zimbabwe *
UA	Ukraine	ZR	Zaire
USA	United States of America	ZRE	Zaire
V	Vatican City State	ZW	Zimbabwe

THE NON-OFFICIAL OVAL

Although numerous ovals, not officially recognized, are used profusely throughout the world, there also exist downright fakes. These are frequently seen in areas and "accepted," by those residing in those areas, for what they are meant to represent. Because of this curious custom, I am listing those most frequently seen today, with a brief explanation of each.

BzH   Once very commonly seen on British cars returning from holidays in France. The combination, in translation from the Breton language, stands for Bretagne or Brittany and, though not as commonly encountered these days, they are not infrequently seen.

C   Although this oval is universally recognized and has been assigned to Cuba for decades, this crops up regularly, throughout Western Europe, and stands for Catalan. Few Cuban cars are seen in Europe, aside from those assigned to Cuban Embassies.

CYM   This stands for Cymru. This means Wales, in Welch, which is a difficult language (at best). CYM ovals are commonly encountered throughout Great Britain. The combination GB, of course, would be mandatory for any Welch car leaving Great Britain. However, within the nation, the CYM combination is properly used, generally by Welch Nationalists who would like to see Wales independent.

ECOSSE   This combination is not commonly seen. It is the French word for Scotland. The ECOSSE oval is popular with Scots who would like to see the restoration of the Scottish Kingdom. It is the only known oval carrying this many letters. Why the French terminology is used remains a mystery.

FRL   Frysland is a province in the Netherlands and this oval combination is frequently seen. It is used only within the Netherlands. When I spent a week in Amsterdam, in 1976, I must have seen at least 50 of these. Cars leaving the country, of course, carry the official Dutch oval NL.

Q   Although Q is the officially recognized oval symbol for the Persian Gulf state of Qatar, it is also commonly seen in the Province of Quebec, in Canada. It is favored by Quebec separatists, who would like to see the province secede from Canada.It is not as commonly seen as it was in the days of Rene Levesque, Quebec's ex-Premier and head of Le Parti Quebecois. The Q symbol, pretty well, identifies the owner of a vehicle as a separatist.

VL   A Belgian counterpart to the Fryslanders of Holland, the VL sign indicates the political thought of the user in regard to Flanders (Vlanders). It is used only within Belgium. The regular B oval is required for travelers driving outside the kingdom.

British license plates

Edited by Keith Marvin

Most of us see English films in theaters or on television. Very often, these films are replete with English street scenes. These scenes often illustrate very well, many types of British and other European cars. For me, this was the case for many years and, try as I might during all this time, I could not make sense out of the license plate patterns for British cars. Yet, I knew that some licensing systems do have plans and patterns which discriminate locales, types of vehicles and so forth.

Sometimes, the number patterns used for English license plates are not easily discernible on the surface of things. If this thought has struck you or you are planning a trip to Great Britain, then this little piece may be of some use to you.

While living in Nottingham, England last year, I took the opportunity to study English vehicle licensing patterns a bit. By doing so, I resolved the confusion for myself, at least somewhat. I also noted that there were numerous aspects of the British structure of licensing that quite possibly might have some direct application to our diverse and often confusing series numbering systems used in the United States.

A three-wheel 1933 Morgan Super Sports wears a number that pre-dates the more modern British registration systems. This one has two letters, a space and four numbers. Numbers stay with a car for life.

Here, there are over 50 different jurisdictions. Each one has its own license plate issuing system complete with its own rules and laws covering a wide variety of special types of plates. These include passenger cars; trucks; recreational vehicles; buses; motorcycles; government vehicles; handicapped drivers; taxicabs; farm vehicles; classic cars; collector cars; antique cars; special interest cars and so forth.

Dates, fees, length of plate use, plate design, number of plates, position on vehicle, transference of plates and many other aspects all may vary from state to state. In some cases, the plates may vary within a single state, such as with the special ones issued by the Minnesota Red Lake Reservation Council.

All of this variety, as delightful as it may be to the license plate collector, creates a great deal of confusion among motorists. On the other hand, Great Britain (which includes England, Scotland, Wales and Northern Ireland) has a combined population about one-fourth as large as that of the entire United States. It also has one basic license plate system. For the most part, it is a unified system for the entire area.

The system used in Great Britain, with few variations which I'll discuss later, encompasses nearly all vehicles, whether they are cars, trucks, trailers, buses, motorcycles, mopeds, tractors, farm vehicles, construction equipment or forklift trucks, as well as some other vehicles.

Under the British scheme, any observer with a small amount of knowledge can identify almost any vehicle as to the year and location of its first registration in England. License numbers are assigned to a vehicle when it is first registered. However, the purchase of the specific number plate to mount on the vehicle is the responsibility of the owner.

If a certain vehicle remains legally registered in Great Britain, the number remains assigned to that vehicle. It is used for its entire existence, until the vehicle is "actively altered" by disposal, sale overseas or designated transference at the time of the vehicle being junked.

The current design of licensing in Great Britain began in 1963. Some license numbers from that date on are based on a pattern which includes 3 letters, one to three numbers and one letter at the end. An example would be the designation ABC 123 A. Others have the pattern reversed, with one letter, one to three numbers and three letters. For example, the designation A 123 ABC.

The basic premise of both systems is the same. A portion of the three letter grouping is a key to where the vehicle was first registered in Great Britain. Within that three letter combination, the last two letters are indicators of a specific licensing authority. For instance, the last two letters OL are among those used to designate a vehicle registered in Birmingham, while WB is one code used to denote a vehicle registered first in Sheffield). A list of what combinations designate different communities is readily available in a wide variety of books and brochures that are very easy for a motorist to obtain. Although cars and other vehicles are moved and traded over various parts of the nations, some continuity does remain. Many times, one will see cars that have remained in one general area for their entire lifespan.

The single letter at the end or beginning of most number plates is the indicator of the year of first registration. The system began in 1963 with an A at the end. It proceeded, more or less through the alphabet and years, dating cars and other vehicles a this scheme. The table for this is: [suffixes] A=1963, B=1964, C=1965, D=1966, E=1967, F=1968, G=1969, H=1970, J=1971, K=1972, L=1973, M=1974, N=1975, P=1976, R=1977, S=1978, T=1979, V=1980, W=1981, X=82, Y=1983, then [prefixes] A=1984; B=1985; C=1986; D=1987; E=1988; F=1989; G=1990; H=1991; J=1992; K=1993; L=1994.

From 1967 on, the year letter changed on August 1 to, more or less, coincide with the start of a new model-year in the car industry. This was a change very much encouraged by that industry and the automobile dealers. Due to this change, the letter E was used only from January 1 to July 31, 1967. Prior to 1967, letters were changed at the end of the calendar-year.

The symbols 1, 0, Q, U, and Z have not been used. The reasoning given has to do with the potential confusion between numbers and letters or letters and other letters in terms of clear recognition.

Thus, with the knowledge of the first or last letter for vehicles registered after August 1, 1983, the approximate age of most vehicles can easily be determined. It is helpful to note that, in British society, conversations and discussions about cars go according to the letter of registration. The enthusiasts may not mention a model-year at all. Used car advertisements, police reports and so on, refer to most cars by that last letter of registration.

There is a big "to do" every summer, around the first of August, when the new registration letter begins. Quite a few buyers will hold off purchasing vehicles, until after that date, in order to ensure getting the new registration plate. This is due to the perceived higher re-sale value for a car with the more recent model letter on its number plate.

This is the most exciting English transportation since Lady Godiva's horse. And that was only a one passenger model.

A few hundred years ago all eyes were turned on English transportation. A young lady went riding with her top down and got 2 or 3 miles to a stallion. It was quite an event.

Now Ford's Model C Cortina has everyone watching again. And they're not just watching, they're buying. And no wonder.

This car gets up to 30 miles to a gallon of gas. The 2-door deluxe model (above) costs only $1873* or $40.95* a month. It's built with the tradition of Ford's Model A firmly in mind.

The engine is larger than that found in many imports. And the seating room is larger, too. Automatic transmission and GT styling are available. Front disc brakes are standard.

Those are the features that help make Ford's Model C Cortina the largest selling car in England. And these features make it so right for America. (Sales more than doubled in the U.S. last year.) One other thing helps in this country. Parts and servicing are available at hundreds of Ford dealers across the nation. They never horse around.

Ford's Model C

CORTINA

An E-suffix registration plate seems properly British for this 1967 Ford Cortina Model C. This advertisement described this $1,873 car as "the most exciting thing in English transportation, since Lady Godiva's horse."

Once aware of this concise system, it is quite easy to identify most British vehicles. In fact, it is much easier to understand this system than that used in most places in the United States. Here, the number patterns are often hard to understand. This is true even in small states with only three to four million people.

There are a lot of exceptions in the British system. These can cause confusion and misunderstanding. Even that withstanding, using their scheme, one can probably categorize over 90 percent of the vehicles one encounters. This is not bad, to be sure.

Below, is a brief description of some of the more common exceptions found in Great Britain:

1. Vanity plates: Personalized number plates and letter combinations may be purchased, if the registrant wishes to pay the added fee to do so.

2. Old registration numbers, usually white or silver characters on black plates: these can be distinguished from more recent plates by color. The newer plates are black on yellow for the back plate and black on white for the front plate. Old patterns usually indicate cars or other vehicles which were registered prior to 1963, which are still valid.

3. Old registration numbers that have been transferred to newer cars: some car buffs and others are willing to pay a high price to purchase the rights to a number plate from its owner. Costs for this range up into the hundreds of pounds (one British Pound is worth about $1.50). A brisk business flourishes in this area, as seen by advertisements in Sunday papers and car magazines placed by people having certain numbers for sale.

4. Cars coming into England, from outside of the country, as used cars: many American and Canadian cars arrive in Britain this way. They are given the letters for the year they arrived in Great Britain. For example, a 1976 Chevrolet Camaro Sporting a Y-registration would indicate that it came into Great Britain in 1983.

5. British military and government vehicles have special plates assigned while in service. When they are sold off as surplus equipment, they are given the registration letter for the year in which they were released to be sold off to the public. There was a large disposal of such cars and trucks in the Nottingham area in the spring of 1983 and several hundred vehicles from 1977 and earlier subsequently started appearing on the streets with Y-registration plates.

6. British military and other government personnel, assigned to overseas posts (usually on the European continent) are allowed to purchase vehicles for their private use. These may or may not be new British cars. While on assignment, the vehicle is assigned a special number plate with a letter B in between two number sequences. When returning to Britain, the vehicles are given standard registration numbers. The number plate assigned reflects the year the car entered Great Britain, which may be one or more years after it was originally purchased. I noted a 1981 British Vauxhall Cavalier bearing a Y-registration for 1983. Model changes for many cars are not drastic, and this subtle situation can also cause confusion for some.

7. Northern Ireland, the Isle of Man, the Channel Islands and some other localities have their own plates. Their number patterns are different.

8. British registered cars sold or transferred overseas and subsequently returned bear a number plate for the year they are re-registered in Britain. We observed a beautiful 1957 Bentley that had once been purchased by a United States service person who shipped it home. When the owner was re-assigned to England, the car was brought back in. It was then assigned a Y-registration plate.

9. Private cars belonging to United States military personnel and families that are shipped in from abroad, as used vehicles, are expected to obtain British plates with the registration letter of the year registered in Great Britain. If the vehicle is new and not of American or British manufacture, and the intention of the owner is to ship it out of Great Britain within a specified time, an alternative type plate is assigned. It has a different number pattern from that normally used. Volvo is one manufacturer that sells many cars to United States service personnel this way, as some taxes can be avoided.

10. United States military vehicles are issued special British license plates.

11. Diplomatic vehicles, in general, and cars belonging to diplomatic personnel, have special British plates.

Even with all these exceptions (and perhaps others I've missed), if one is in Britain's proper, the vast majority of vehicles observed will easily fit into the boundaries of the regular registration system. When model styles do not change very much for many years, the British system makes for an easy identification of vehicles. The caution raised by the exceptions makes understanding the system it even simpler. It categorizes the majority of non-regular plates one sees into specific groups. These can be helpful in identifying cars and trucks that one encounters when visiting Great Britain or when looking at photographs and motion pictures of that interesting, automotive playground.

Cuter'n a bug's rear

Before you take off in the Queen Mary of small cars
check for stowaways. Cortina's "boot" (trunk to you) takes
21 cubic feet of gear (about 5 normal suitcases), even
golf bags. There's room for a crew of 4 big sailors
and a lot of booty, too! Even with a load like that, Cortina's 67
well-engineered horses accelerate fast past the petrol
pumps. As for service, it's everywhere—strictly
American—with domestic type nuts and
bolts. Now that Cortina's hit the U. S., there'll
really be some sourkrauts around!

FORD'S CORTINA

This 1967 Ford Cortina advertisement showed a "British license plate" with no letters or numbers on it. Most of the regular plates issued to motorists in Great Britain carry alpha-numerical designations that tell you several things about the vehicle and owner.

A 1962 Austin-Healey roadster with registration number LKE326. This license plate was issued one year before the numbering system that's most commonly encountered today went into effect.

Under the system, an N-suffix registration number would suggest a 1975 automobile, but this photo is labeled "1978 Jaguar XJ12." Our guess is the photo is mislabeled, but the owner might have a number that breaks the rule.

Tag toppers as collectibles

By Randy Rundle

Sooner or later, along with owning and driving a collector car, the desire comes along to gather memorabilia associated with the era of your car. One of the more popular accessories to collect is the "tag topper," so-called because it mounts on top of your license plate (or vehicle tag) and advertises a local business.

Quite often, such toppers were installed when you purchased a car from the local auto dealership. This helped the car dealer advertise his brand of automobiles and the services he provided.

Auto-related businesses also took advantage of the toppers' constantly displayed promotional messages. Local body shops, auto supply stores and hardware stores soon began to utilize this inexpensive form of advertising.

Also popular were topper from various insurance companies, as well as some designs offered as novelties by auto accessory companies. For example, a cat with a wiggly mouth and eyes appeared around 1948. It was sold by Western Auto parts stores, as well as other automotive component suppliers.

Toppers first appeared around the early 1920s, with many of the first examples being made of cast aluminum. Good examples include specimens produced for Brewer Motor Company, Livingood Lincoln-Chrysler-Plymouth and the Griffith Motor Company of Carthage, Missouri.

In the mid- to late-1930s, toppers made of flat aluminum and sheet metal began. The printing of advertising messages on flat metal was much faster and cheaper. It speeded the production of tag toppers and made them less expensive to produce.

Using a silk screen process, the toppers could be lettered quickly. They were then baked in an oven to "heat set" the ink. Additional advantages of the new production process were the ability to offer multiple colors and much greater design detail.

The 1940s were the "good years" for tag toppers. Many elaborate designs were turned out during the decade. A good specimen is the Ed Rudolph Chevrolet topper, produced for a Chevrolet dealer from Phoenix, Arizona. This "Super Service Garage" offered "all night service for all cars." An actual picture of the dealership, which was located at 316-400 East Adams Street, appears on the topper. This was truly a deluxe tag topper.

Through the mid-1950s, tag toppers were in high demand and readily available. Then, as cars changed, it became more difficult to display a tag topper on license plates that were set into specific size recesses in the body. The demand for tag toppers slowly began to fade away.

Bicycle tag toppers also became popular. Children could display a tag topper on their "wheels," just like dad did. The Goodrich Silvertown Safety

Chevrolet dealership appears on this specimen.

Livingood dealership sold Lincolns, Chryslers and Plymouths.

Car dealers used toppers to promote brands they sold.

State Farm Insurance and American Automobile Association toppers.

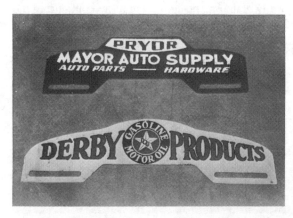

Auto parts and product suppliers used tag toppers to promote their lines.

League was a club for young bicycle riders. It promoted bicycle safety. When dad went in to buy new Goodrich tires for the family car, the children could join the safety league and get a little tag topper of their own to fit bicycles. They featured a red reflector marble and were quite a prize for kids. These bicycle tires were made for Goodrich by the Matthews Company of Pittsburgh, Pennsylvania during the 1940s and 1950s.

Some of the other companies that manufactured tag toppers included The Douglas Company of Minneapolis, Minnesota and the Dura Products Manufacturing Company of Canton, Ohio. Dura Products produced the Ed Rudolph Chevrolet topper. Most of these tag topper makers have now gone out of business. Some have merged with other companies and survive, but they no longer manufacture tag toppers.

One old car hobby company has begun manufacturing tag toppers on a limited basis. It offers reproductions of an authentic 1940s style design. Information about these tag toppers can be obtained from Fifth Avenue Antique Auto Parts, 415 Court Street, Clay, KS 67432.

The tag toppers that were once a popular an inexpensive form of advertising are now being saved and treasured. What was once given away for free can now have substantial value to collectors. The lowest prices are paid for single color tag toppers. Fancy designs, like the Ed Rudolph Chevrolet topper, can cost two to three times as much as the single color type. Falling between both on the value scale, depending on rarity and condition, are the cast aluminum toppers.

Most local tag toppers from your area are probably inexpensive to buy and fun to collect. They can be dated by checking advertisements in old telephone books, school yearbooks or newspapers. The toppers look great on your old car or the wall of the garage it's stored in. They are a great addition to any automobile advertising collection.

Carthage, Missouri car dealer gave this topper away.

Primitive signals gave drivers "a sense of direction"

By Diane Thomas

It would be nice to know the name of the first man who installed a turn signal to notify the car following him of his intentions, but there is no historical record of this.

Undoubtedly, the earliest signaling device was the rope-controlled hand. Surely, it was used first on a bus or truck. Trucks had been in use at least since Winton made its first commercial delivery wagon in 1898. With small motor cars, it was possible to extend an arm and have motorists see it. After all, they were driving either tiller steered or right-hand drive cars. However, when the closed-in and overhanging wagon body came along for trucks, an extended signal was a necessity. Also, when some cars changed to left-hand drive, the driver's signal wasn't as consistently visible. Therefore, the installation of manually-controlled turn indicators evolved.

The easiest signal to rig was the lightweight wood arm. These were often painted to resemble a hand and coated arm. They were controlled by a rope and pulley. One was used on each side of the vehicle. It was hoisted halfway to signify a stop, part way to show a left turn and up to the 10 o'clock position for a right turn. The same hand signals are taught today, though rarely put into use. Some of the vintage signal arms can be found today in antique shops or even on some old commercial vehicles.

By the time that cars were electrified (1913 for most models) night driving made it necessary to have lighted signals for indicating turning and stopping. Many manufacturers designed signals to fit on whatever type car the public might buy, whether they had tops and with or without rear seats. The signals were optional equipment. The price was nominal and, in most cases, the car owner had to attach the accessory himself. The automakers figured they were purely an extra-cost option, not a proven necessity.

Three years later, in 1916, several cars incorporated three safety accessories as standard equipment: hand-operated windshield wipers, rearview mirrors and electric stop lights. These stop lights usually included turn signals in their design.

When the 1917 cars came out, many were closed models with heaters. Both were real firsts in the popularly-priced auto market. This meant that the windows were rolled up for cold weather driving. It became accepted that electric signals on a car were here to stay, as witnessed by the increasing number of cars using them as standard accessories. Those people driving around in last year's models could buy add-on signals at their favorite auto parts store. They installed easily. Soon everyone was blinking and winking at corners.

One would guess that standardization would quickly be adopted in the design of signal lamps. After all, they had a definite purpose, fitted a specific vehicle and signaled in a certain way. However, standardization wasn't the case. There were as many designs as there were accessory companies making them. Some used arrows, some employed hands and others had alphabetical letters. Many worked by a toggle switch, but others were operated by buttons. There were ones that swung like railroad semaphores to attract the attention of indifferent motorists. Some were made with letters so small they surely could not

v in
a il-
sig-
olar
hich
uni-
ent

The Outlook combination stop and tail light of the 1920s had a beehive-shaped dome of prismatic glass that directed light on the license plate.

A popular 1920s combination taillamp/stop lamp was the Solar Stop Signal. It came with a universal attachment.

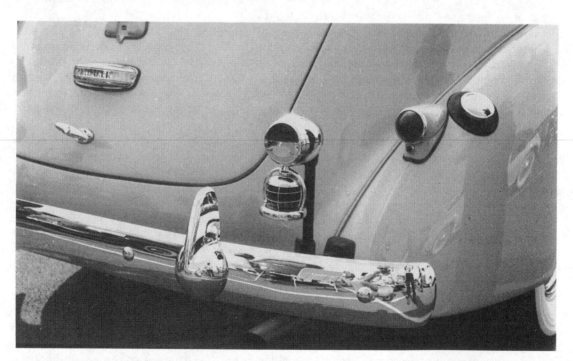

A rare "wig-wag" taillamp was a nice touch on Larry Warner's right-hand drive 1938 Studebaker export model, when it was exhibited at Hershey 1993. This signal lamp swings like a railroad semaphore to attract the attention of indifferent motorists following behind the car.

be read by middle-aged drivers as little as five feet away, let alone 15 feet. Some models worked by lever-and-cable (for those whose cars were not electrified). Some signals worked by vacuum. One intriguing design rolled the signal back and forth on a revolving drum.

Like so many small auto accessories, most of the bolt-on signals have disappeared. Occasionally, they turn up at swap meets. When regulations were passed in some states that all right-hand drive antique cars had to have stop and turn signals, it became harder than ever to locate them.

Those regal hood ornaments were victims of government

By Tim Howley

The hood ornament is dead. The little zinc gods in the United States Department of Transportation have decreed that any permanently affixed hood ornament ... yes, even the proud United States Eagle ... is unsafe, unlawful and illegal. In the case of naked flying ladies, perhaps they are also illicit. The last once-noble ornament to fall was the Lincoln Continental's "square star," which adorned the 1967 model, but fell in 1968

Manufacturers can only use them by attaching a spring device underneath, so that they will give under impact. This has relegated the hood ornament to the area of an expensive, accessory shelf item and makes it easier prey for thieves. In these days of safe, homogeneous pieces of transportation, there is hardly room for a knight or ... worse yet ... an archer. In a reckless moment, he might aim his arrow directly at the seat of Ralph Nader's pants.

True, the hood ornament all but vanished in the 1950s, after being reduced to but a "blob" atop the whale it rode on. But, in the 1970s, spurred by a new nostalgia, hood ornaments were poised to make at least a small comeback. Now, the good ship Mayflower shall never return to sail on the prow of the Plymouth. Nor shall we ever again see the brave chief guide the Pontiac along the highways and byways of America. And never again will be allowed to feast our eyes on the lovely and naked Cadillac goddess.

But, once upon a time, when there were no freeways or super-highways, when life moved no faster than the 40 miles per hour rural speed limits, automobiles wore a different air. They were guided along their way by graceful birds and fair ladies. Some had as their mascots Greek or Roman gods or knights of old. Perhaps, like old-time cars, the mascots, too, were only playthings. But, like running boards and sidemounted tires, the automobile was so much more of an automobile when each make had its own distinctive radiator ornament.

The idea of using deities for mascots on vehicles apparently goes all the way back to the Romans. Considerable evidence exists that little images of the Roman gods were commonly used for "good luck" on chariots. In 1896, Lord Montagu revived the custom by having an image of St. Christopher made for his early motor cars. The Italians made the former saint their official mascot in 1907, attaching his image to the radiator cap.

The practice caught on and was especially popular with the French, who called their little radiator idols "mascottes," but hardly took them seriously. The irreverent French enjoyed such delights as cupids that urinated when the water in the radiator boiled, Kewpie Dolls and even little devils who thumbed their noses at pedestrians. This flippant approach to mascots was picked up by the American accessory manufacturers and their wares became very popular in the 1920s and 1930s. But, such nonsense was not to be tolerated on the radiator caps of staid manufacturers on both sides of the Atlantic. There, pomposity ruled.

One-inch wing spacing identifies 1938-1940 Packard pelican.

One of the most officious of all was the Rolls-Royce "Spirit of Ecstasy," created in reaction to French vulgarity. More commonly called " The Flying Lady," this most traditional of all hood ornaments has graced the Rolls-Royce since 1911. It was commissioned to the famous sculptor Charles Sykes and his signature still shows on the base of many of the first Rolls-Royce mascots. The early ones are hand-finished silver. Later, they were bronze with nickel plate and, still later, chrome plate. Finally, Rolls-Royce took over manufacture of the "lady," making her of stainless steel.

The Mercedes three-pointed star goes back to the marque's earliest years. It has always been one of the most delicate and restrained of all the automotive mascots. Conversely, the mascots of the Nazi high command staff cars, showing the German eagle and swastika, were the boldest of any.

In Belgium, Athena (the Roman goddess of War) defended the Minerva driver's battle through traffic. Isotta-Fraschini is associated with a winged figure of a man known as "Triomphe" or more colloquially, "the doughnut slinger." The factory turned thumbs down on this figure designed by the French sculptor Bazin. So, Triomphe was mounted only on cars sold by the New York Agency. He was so popular that the American Public came to regard him as authentic.

Hispano-Suiza's stork was also designed by Bazin. It appeared shortly after World War I, being taken from the squadron insignia of Captain Charles Guyne mere, the French ace of aces. The stork embodied the gracefulness of a bird in flight, indicative of Hispano-Suiza's power and ease of ride.

No other radiator ornament was quite as bizarre as the white elephant on the Bugatti Royale. Undoubtedly, the eccentric Ettore Bugatti was so turned off by the pretentious ornaments mounted on what he considered to be lesser marques, that he decided to mount his ornament in mock seriousness. Le Patron's elephant stands on his hind legs, with his trunk raised high in the air. The solid sterling silver elephant was a gift from the builder. Indeed, Ettore Bugatti didn't have to prove anything to anybody.

The 1928-1929 Pierce Arrow archer with foot down.

Animals ... especially birds ... have always been favorites as mascots. The Peerless eagle was one of the first. There was also the Wills St. Claire flying goose, the Ford quail, the Chevrolet eagle and the Studebaker duck (or was it a goose?). Eventually, almost every bird known to man was used.

Some automakers preferred the hard sell, using the first letter of the car's name: the Austin A, the Bentley B, the Rockne R, the Jewett's flying J and the Hupmobile's encircled H.

One of the first mascots in this country was the brass globe and the route of the Peking-to-Paris "Great Race." This was proudly displayed on the Thomas-Flyer radiator cap in commemoration of the event won by Thomas In 1908.

Before mascots, cars made lavish use of brass-scripted nameplates attached to the radiator core. Then, along about 1912, the Boyce Company came out with their famous MotoMeter. Immediately, every manufacturer sold a Boyce MotoMeter with

Even with damaged (bent) neck a 1930-1932 Cadillac/LaSalle heron looks great.

The aero engine style mascot (shown on Model A) appeared as early as 1910.

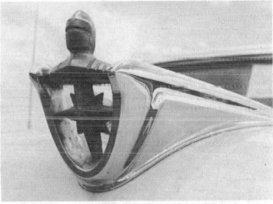

This "Lalique" type glass ornament is probably by Corning Glass.

Among postwar automobile mascots is the 1956 Lincoln knight.

Wings flank the MotoMeter that is used on early Oldsmobile.

The goddess on 1933-1936 Cadillac V-12s and -16s was special-ordered on V-8s.

the name of his car inscribed under the glass. Soon, MotoMeters were sprouting wings and all sorts of decorations. The "t-bone" type cap was, however, not decorative. It served the very practical function of unscrewing the hot radiator cap.

World War I, with its surge of patriotism, brought forth a profusion of eagles, waving flags and even figures of Uncle Sam and the Statue of Liberty. But, it was not until about 1928, when the temperature gauge was moved to the dash, that the radiator ornament reached its zenith. Some of the finest jewelers of the classic era were commissioned by classic car builders and many of their creations were cast in silver and gold-plated. Even mass-produced cars offered exotic radiator ornaments. Usually, these were made of pot metal or low grade zinc.

The most coveted of all the ornaments were (and still are) the works of the French crystal-glass artisan Rene Lalique. His crystalline creations were the sensation of Paris early in the century. He was the master of the technical process of "vitrification." That is the transforming other materials into glass through heat and fusion. His keenest interest was the luminescence of crystal.

Lalique produced lamps and vases and his crystal flasks revolutionized perfume packaging. During the Classic era, Lalique crystal became the international symbol of elegance. It was only natural that custom Lalique creations would appear as hood mascots on the world's finest automobiles. Duesenberg owners were likely prospects for Lalique ornaments and they can be seen on Duesenbergs occasionally. The most beautiful ones are lighted from beneath.

Beautiful hood mascots were not exclusive to the most expensive automobiles. One of the most striking ornaments of the 1930s was an eagle that was optional on the petite 1932 Chevrolet. Throughout the decade, Chevrolet continued to offer distinctive winged-type mascots.

Pontiac's "Chief of the Sixes" was a beautifully detailed, copper-faced, nickel-plated ornament depicting a Native American visage. The best ones appeared on 1928 to 1932 Pontiacs. Later, the poor chief became more stylized and less ornate, but he was always striking. In some years, a brave or an Indian maiden appeared instead of a chief.

By the mid-1930s, six-cylinder cars had one ornament and eight-cylinder cars had another. There were two versions after the war, too, but they were available with either engine. The deluxe type had an illuminated plastic Indian head insert. These later ones are reasonably good imitations of Rene Lalique's style. Pontiac's parent marque, the Oakland automobile, used a Golden Eagle hood mascot from 1928 to 1931.

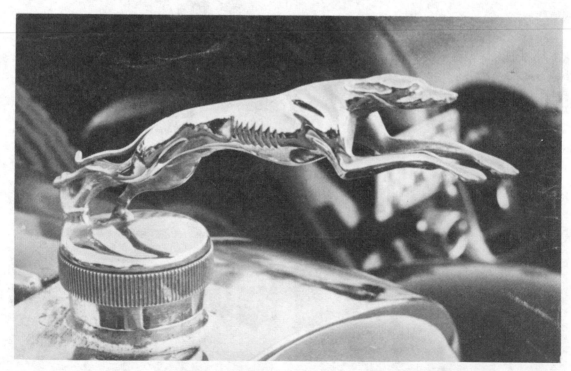

This style of Lincoln greyhound mascot was used on 1934-1937 models. According to Bill Williams, the author of a book that gives complete details on many collectible mascots, this one was zinc die-cast with chrome plating.

In the late 1920s, Buick had a succession of female mascots in semi-Indian headdress. These mascots are pretty, but have no particular significance. Later, Buick ornaments copied the Cadillac goddess. A 1938 Buick "dream car" carried the first cigar-piercing-donut bombsight hood ornament. It was quickly adopted as a symbol. By the 1950s, it was as much a Buick trademark as the hood-side "port holes." Experts at the Museum of Modern Art concluded it was the ideal symbolism of the relationship between Detroit and the American public.

The sensuous Cadillac goddess and the graceful Cadillac heron were used from about 1929 on, although later they became nothing more than devices for opening the hood. It's surprising that Cadillac never saw fit to use an image of Antoine de la Mothe Cadillac. The Cadillac family coat of arms remains the official emblem for the marque to this day.

A pirate or "Minute Man" on an aftermarket design.

It's even more surprising that Lincoln never capitalized on the majestic image of old "Honest Abe." Perhaps this was because the "Great Emancipator" was Henry Leland's hero. He was not held in quite as high esteem by Henry and Edsel Ford.

The Lincoln mascot was always the famous Greyhound or "dog" (as buffs now call it). Commissioned by Edsel Ford to Gorham, the nickel-plated dog became standard and was announced in the Lincoln service bulletin dated September, 1926. Most Lincoln owners presume it is incorrect on pre-1926 models. Not so. A Lincoln sporting the dog on its radiator cap appears in a 1923 issue of the Ford Motor Company magazine *The Lincoln*.

The dog was continued as an accessory throughout the production of the Lincoln models L, KA, KB and K, but was never used on the Lincoln-Zephyr or Continental. In the late 1940s, the Lincoln mascot became a knight. He appears on all the "Mexican Road Race" Lincoln Capris and on later Premieres. The Continental Mark I used a simple ball-and-sphere, but since the Continental Mark II of 1956, the Lincoln Continental symbol has always been the four-pointed star.

While Lincoln mascots have always been inspiring, Ford ornaments were as basic as the car itself. The Model A quail was old Henry Ford's idea. Edsel didn't like it any better than Henry liked the dog. A clay for the quail was made by an artist in Ford's employ, but the final modeling and actual accessory were designed and produced by a small machine shop in Connersville, Indiana. An original quail is not especially rare now, but is highly-prized. The only other truly collectible Ford ornaments are the 1936 "lazy 8" and the 1934-1936 greyhound, which was sired by the Lincoln mascot.

Mercury ornaments, on the other hand, are truly distinctive. This is especially true in the 1950s, when designers decided to make the most out of "The Messenger of the Gods."

Chrysler Corporation has had a number of attractive ornaments over the years, perhaps the most notable being the classic Imperial's felled bird. The Chrysler Gazelle was first used on 1932 models to symbolize grace and speed. DeSoto and

Crescent moon appeared on 1912-1928 Moons

Many different styles of accessory, commercial, organizational and personality hood ornaments were available in the automotive aftermarket from the early days. This one is marked "Nation" on its base.

Plymouth, in 1931 and 1932, had quite similar winged women ornaments. The mundane DeSoto had a long list of interesting ornaments, ending up in the 1940s with some fairly good Lalique imitations lighted from beneath. Even an old Hernando DeSoto head from the late 1940s and early 1950s is worth collecting. The Dodge ram is another collectible mascot. It appears on some fairly late-model cars and trucks and frequently in advertising. Plymouth's Mayflower first set sail in 1933 and was continued into the late 1940s. It is the earlier versions, of the ship mascot, which are beautifully faithful in detail. The later galleons are little more than stylized blobs.

Not all of the classics have classic hood ornaments. Auburn's winged man and winged woman are good, but not nearly as exciting as the cars. The fantastic Cord had no hood ornament at all. Apparently, Marmon never went in for exotic ornaments, but McFarlan had Atlas holding up the world.

Pierce-Arrow, still one of the less sought-after classics, has one of the most sought-after ornaments of all. In fact, the distinctive and delicate Pierce-Arrow archer is far more prized than any of the 10 different Packard ornaments. He evolved from the wheel-and-arrow symbol used between 1922 and 1927. He first appeared in 1928, helmeted and partly clad. In 1929, he decided to appear bare headed. By the early 1930s, he was statuesque, unhelmeted and totally unclad. Instead of leaning forward, he held his head in an aiming position. In later years, he tired of this position and decided to kneel on a grassy mound. The archer's bow was either bronze, copper or brass. While some of the Pierce-Arrow archers are cast in bronze, others are made of pot metal.

Packard's cormorant (sometimes called pelican) probably evolved from the graceful bird with its head humbly bowed. It is one of the most understated and beautiful of all mascots, seen during the Classic Car Era. From 1928 to 1932, Packard offered a mascot featuring Daphne (a young nymph from Greek mythology) at the well. Packard's advertising agency, Young & Rubicam, renamed the statue Adonis, but collectors seem to prefer calling him the "sliding boy" or the "boy at the well."

Another one of the famous Packard ornaments is the flat-chested "Goddess of Speed." This scantily-clad, winged woman is actually holding a wire wheel, but most of us call her "the Lady with the dough-nut." The last Packards continued to carry the cormorant, but by the end, he must have been hanging his

Packard's 1929 "Goddess of Speed" ornament. According to mascot expert Bill Williams, this wreath cap had two diameters, 2-3/4-inches for Standard Eights and 3-1/4-inches for Super Eights. Design patent 73026 was issued on it.

Egyptian sun-god Ra by Renzetti and Brown was on 1926-1935 Stutz.

Rembrandt Bugatti designed the elephant mascot for the Type 41 Royale.

head in shame rather than humility. The cormorant, by the way, was part of the Packard family coat of arms.

This was also true of Franklin's lion rampant. He first took his kingly position on the Franklin hood in 1924. That was shortly after old John Wilkinson, Franklin's chief engineer, left the firm. (Old John never would have permitted a radiator ornament on a car that didn't need a radiator cap.) From 1925 to 1927, the lion became lazy and sat on his rear quarters. Some say he was "swatting insects." This joke is the perpetual bane of Franklin owners. Insects were perpetually clogging up the radiator.

The next time you see the Franklin lion, note the inscription below him. "Aura Vincit" means air conquers. In 1928, Franklin used a small replica of the Spirit of St. Louis on their Airman series. This was to commemorate Charles Lindbergh's historic trans-Atlantic flight of 1927. At the time, Franklin had built a whole advertising campaign around aviation. Towards the end, Franklin resorted to a bird. Gone with the wind was imagination. Gone soon, too, was the Franklin.

Stutz is remembered for a mascot sculpted after the Egyptian Sun-God Ra, symbolizing supremacy in all things. The Rollin automobile had a Griffin type ornament with the head of a Sphinx and the body of a winged lion. This was symbolic of silent speed. Gardner, a St. Louis assembled car, had a fantastic Griffin. In fact, the Gardner Griffin is one of the rarest and best of any mascot. It was alleged to scare off evil spirits on the road. Who knows? It may still scare off evil judges in a antique car show.

All cars built under Knight sleeve-valve engine patents were entitled to carry a knight on their radiator cap. The Willys-Knight is one of the handsomest. In 1930-1931, its knight was even mounted on a steed. Kissel had an eagle, but only on the 1928 "White Eagle" speedster. In 1929, Kissel's white eagle was embossed on the front of the radiator shell.

Of course, Wills St. Claire had a grey goose for its emblem and hood ornament. A really rare mascot was the distinctive quarter-moon design of the Moon automobile. The Moon-built Diana had the finest radiator ornament of all. It depicted Diana, the huntress and Goddess of the Chase. She stands tall and bare breasted (though modest enough to wear a gossamer shirt), with her bow pointed toward the stars. The detail is flawless. Diana would be fit for a Duesenberg. Yet she is sentenced to ride forever atop one of America's most obscure motor cars.

The collecting of hood ornaments can be an enormously satisfying pursuit. For one thing, the ornaments take up considerably less space than a car. How many people could hope to have a car collection the size of the one William F. Harrah amassed? Yet, anyone could probably collect that many mascots in a few years of serious pursuit.

Mascots are not hard to find. Many rare ones are still going at bargain prices. It's one aspect of the hobby that really hasn't caught on. Sure, we all have a Boyce Motor-Meter and a few other trinkets on our shelves, but how many collectors do you know who can simply overwhelm you with their hood ornament collection?

Hood ornaments show up in all sorts of places: at swap meets, non-automotive flea markets, pawn shops and your neighbor's attic or garage. Just about everybody in the world has an old hood ornament or two tucked away somewhere. In the old days, when people hauled their cars off to the World War II wreckers, they often kept the ornament as a souvenir. This was especially true if it was an unusual one. Junk dealers often kept them when they wrecked the car. Sure, a lot of them were stolen. However, even the stolen ones are still likely to be around somewhere. Surely, the survival rate of mascots has to be hundreds of times greater than that of the old cars.

Most of the European mascots are brass, aluminum, copper or bronze. So are many from the American Classic era. However, during the 1920s, pot metal and cheap zinc started coming into play. Almost all of the low-priced cars used pot metal or zinc mascots. So did some of the classics.

A problem is that such materials deteriorate with age. Ornaments made of them are also difficult to replate and braze. Many restorers have gone to the trouble of making new castings. So, while brass replicas are not the real thing, they are certainly faithful to the original and are a lot more durable.

One important thing to remember in collecting hood ornaments is don't shy away from the more recent ones. Many cars of the 1940s and 1950s had really nifty ornaments and they're now going at give-away prices. Don't discount ornaments from low-priced cars, either. Some of the best ornaments appeared on the dumbest cars. DeSoto is a perfect example. It had a "family car" market niche, but there was often a beautiful bust of the Spanish explorer on top of the hood.

We have not attempted to cover all the ornaments. Hood ornament knowledge in the hobby today is mainly word of mouth. We all seem to be somewhat expert on the mascot or mascots for our own favorite make, but how many of us have a fair knowledge of hood ornament lore on a wide range of cars?

A number of books have been written about mascots and collecting them. Two out-of print titles are *Car Mascots Enthusiasts Guide* ($80) by G. Di Sirignano, which was published by Crescent in 1977, and *Motor Badges & Figureheads* ($50) by B. Jewell, which was printed in 1978 by Midas. Both of these books are heavily focused on European mascots. (The prices given in parenthesis are 1993 value estimates provided in *The Car Book Value Guide and Bibliography* by Thomas E. Warth).

Motoring Mascots of the World: First Edition, by William C. Williams, is another book that was first published in 1977 by Motorbooks International. It covers both European and American mascots and factory designs as well aftermarket types (including Lalique). This book was unavailable for a time. However, according to Motorbooks International, *Motoring Mascots of the World* is not out-of-print and will be re-issued again in 1994 at a price of $60.

F.F. Burr designed "Sieur de LaSalle" used in 1927-1930.

Mercury runs on this American-made aftermarket cap. It's not from a Kissel!

This is likely from a Pan automobile of the 1920s.

Large-size "wall plaque" replica of circa-1949 DeSoto hood ornament art.

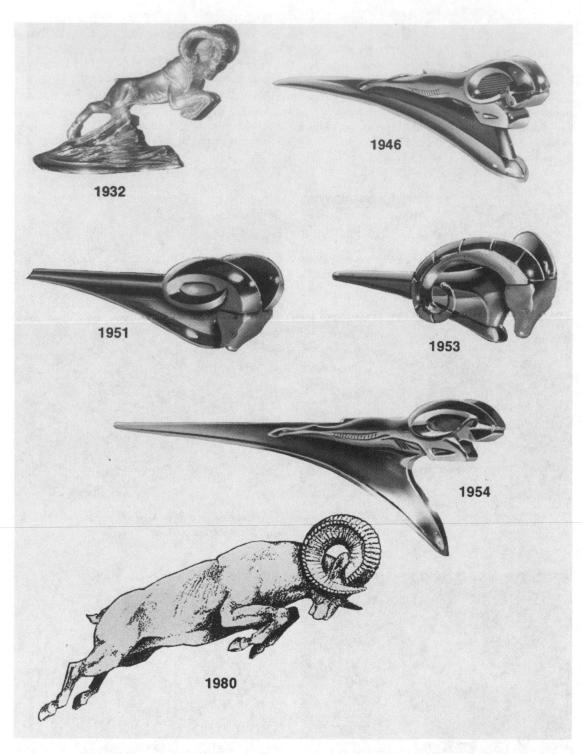

Six hood ornaments trace the evolution of the Dodge ram mascot from 1932 to 1980. Bill William's research shows that the earliest design was created by Herbert V. Henderson and had design patent 86370 dated March 1, 1932.

Hood ornaments reveal history of price and individuality

Edited by John A. Gunnell

Man's inherent need to be different from his fellow man planted the seed of an art form that has only recently been recognized ... the hood ornament.

Known to collectors as mascots, automobile hood ornaments originally functioned as radiator caps. When modern radiator caps moved under the hood, some innovative automotive designers wanted to keep them on top for decorative and identifying purposes. Today, many hood ornaments are works of art that could proudly stand among the world's finest sculpture and glass collections.

There are major collections of ornaments and mascots throughout America and the world. More than 1,100 mascots are featured, alone, in one of the largest at the Merle Norman Classic Beauty Collection at San Sylmar, in Sylmar, California. The experts there wrote this brief history of mascots.

The factory mascot, supplied by the manufacturer as either standard equipment, a deluxe accessory or a company identification feature (as with the Mercedes-Benz and Cadillac) originated with the Vulcan in 1902.

Not every factory mascot was as constant as the Flying Lady.

Companies rarely felt obligated to retain their original design. Pierce-Arrow's original arrow-inside-a-wheel evolved into an archer. The bow man then gained weight, lost his clothes and got himself into more comfortable shooting positions.

Fraternal organizations got into the act, often with quite elaborate ornaments. The "Liberty Bell" design for the Odd Fellows, created in 1926, had an insignia that lit up with red and blue jewels. Its bell also had a clapper that could be operated and rung from a button on the instrument panel.

Personalized mascots were often one-of-a-kind items. They varied from elegant and intricate sculptures to outrageous and gauche designs. One of the most famous mascots, picturing a lifelike coiled cobra, was given to Rudolph Valentino by Mary Pickford and Douglas Fairbanks upon completion of Valentine's film "The Cobra."

Eventually, mass-production, streamlining and cost-cutting led to the general demise of the hood ornament and mascot. By the mid-1930s, most were reduced to ordinary knick-knacks. By 1942, they had all but disappeared.

The first mascot, as we know it today, was merely an artist's conception. It was never made. It dated from 1827, when an Englishman sketched a design for a three-wheeled steam carriage that he called the Docudep. Perched upon its tiller bar pivot sat a regal bird with outstretched wings. Though never brought to life, it was the first recorded use of a mascot for a motorized vehicle. An actual mascot didn't appear until almost 70 years later, when Lord Montagu of Beaulieu placed a St. Christopher (patron saint of travelers) image on his dash.

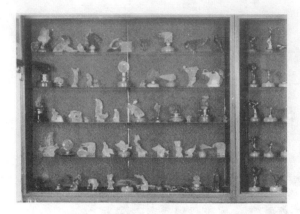

One of the display cases which houses the hood mascot collection.

The "foot-down" version of the Pierce-Arrow archer in metal.

The earliest documented American mascot was a gnome-like creature created for the hood of the car by L.V. Aronson in 1909. This "Gobbo, God of Good Luck" was the predecessor of many Aronson designs, including the much-copied "Speed Nymph" of the Packard. As mascots became increasingly popular, many flagpoles were stripped of their ever-present eagles. However, most "after-market" hood ornaments of the day were found in jewelry stores and accessory shops.

In 1915, a master craftsman of jewelry and crystal named Rene Lalique created the first of 27 designs that are considered the most exquisite of all mascots. His crystal-glass sculptures were mounted on either a short metal base with a stout stud for mounting or a tall, fitted base with a light that connected to the car's electrical system. Color discs were sometimes added, creating a colorful, rainbow-like effect.

Times are changing again and the mascot has been making a cautious comeback. In addition to Rolls-Royce, Mercedes-Benz, Cadillac and a few other enduring automobiles, other manufacturers and enthusiast car builders are now attaching mascots to their hoods. One 1980s Chrysler luxury car, for example, was adorned with a Cartier cut-crystal mascot. And, not too long ago, England's Prince Charles commissioned a silver frog mascot to squat on the hood of Princess Diana's Ford Escort. It may have been predictive of his feelings about the princess in more recent years.

In the 100-year-plus history of the automobile, over 5,000 mascots have been created. Many are locked away in small, private collections and hidden from public view. However, the hood ornaments at the Merle Norman Classic Beauty Collection can be seen during pre-arranged tours that allow the public to view them. Write: San Sylmar, 15180 Bledsoe Street, Sylmar, California 91342 or call (818) 367-1085 to get visitor information.

One unique version of the Pierce-Arrow archer mascot in glass.

A rooster in Lalique crystal-glass.

Race driver Phil Hill and representatives of the Merle Norman Classic Beauty Collection at San Sylmar, in Sylmar, California, view the hood ornament gracing a 1934 Duesenberg Model J in the collection.

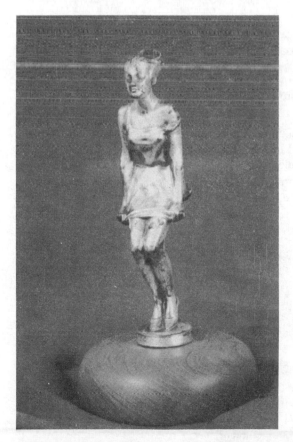

This lady seems to be fighting a headwind.

In 1911, Rolls-Royce commissioned English sculpture Charles Sykes to create a unique mascot for their very special car. This resulted in the now famous "Spirit of Ecstasy." Popularly known as the "Flying Lady," this mascot is still available for those discriminating Rolls-Royce owners who want that extra touch of class.

Collecting is a "disease" that changes course of life

By Paul Hatmon

Collecting, contrary to popular belief, is not a hobby. It is a disease; a crawling, insidious thing that burrows deep down to the very fiber of your being. It's with you night and day. A serious, dyed-in-the-wool collector never lets up. It's an eat and sleep thing, continuing around the clock. Of course, it's occasionally interrupted by some minor detail, like your job or maybe your daughter's wedding. But, such trifles pass and it's back to the search and restoration.

There are people who collect buttons; lamps; coins; dishes; stamps; locks of hair; used bagels; campaign buttons; cigar bands; and wooden Indians ... even shrunken heads. However, the one that gets the brass ring is the antique car collector. He'll tell you 950 reasons why he goes rooting in long abandoned estates where "keep out" signs abound. He'll explain why he spends all of his vacation time (and even some of his boss's) running down phony leads. But rarely, will you get a logical explanation.

Car collecting has grown from a handful of old car worshipers, to thousands of happy bolt-twisters from coast-to-coast. This hobby, in turn, has attracted more sideline wrinkles than a pudgy matron, who has forgotten her two-way. Many moons ago, before I felt the pangs of car collecting fever, I was assisting a contractor friend in clearing ground, in the middle of an inner-city district, to make room for a new freeway. One of the older wrecking yards in the city had been on the same spot as long as I could remember.

A large, early IHC radiator emblem is the centerpiece of this assortment.

The wrecking yard operator received such a handsome sum for his land he left about a third of the oldest stock, cars dating back to the 1920s, up for grabs. This forced the contractor to move them. The bright bits of baked glass and chrome on the radiator shells of those cars from the 1920s, 1930s and 1940s interested me. So I stripped the cars before they went to that big wrecking yard in the sky.

That was the beginning of my first automobile nameplate and emblem collection. This is a hobby I continue to work on to this day. Each nameplate and emblem has a unique story all its own. It involves not only how it was made, but its basis for

148

naming, its design and the circumstances of its pro-curement. This is lecture material in its own right.

Those first 35 or 40 nameplates and emblems gave me a start to collecting thousands of insignias in later years. That first batch included such rarities as Jones Six, Cole 8, Peerless, Erskine, Empire and Locomobile insignias. For some time, I merely threw the plates and emblems into a small box. I took them out, from time to time, to show someone or to just admire them like a miser admires his money.

It became apparent this was not a good method of displaying nameplates and emblems. So, I began mounting them under glass on black panel board (the type used in truck interiors in the old days). Soldering small bolts on the back of those examples that did not have attachments, I mounted all of them firmly to the board. This was then placed into the framed glass.

The Olds script, Chevy bow tie and Mack bulldog are some logos seen here.

Being of rather a parsimonious (which is egghead talk for tight) nature, I raided used furniture stores for picture frames with good glass. In those days, the rate was from 25-cents to 50-cents for a picture of a cross-eyed deer or the diploma of some long-departed herb doctor. From then on, whenever I amassed 25 nameplates or emblems, I'd mount them on the walls of my garage. I tried to mix them up, using maybe one insurance badge, one or two brass scripts, a body plate and maybe a small city license.

One of the most unusual items I ever found was a plate that looked just like a car badge, although it bore the emblem of the Anti Horse Thief Association. People placed these on their barn doors to tell crooks to beware. Being a natural-born wag, I also placed, in almost every frame, one logo that resembled a car emblem, but was actually from a sewing machine, water heater, or air conditioner. I don't know how many times some wide-eyed character looking at my collection told me, "Why my grandpa had a car with that name and I remember it well." Of course, the nameplate plate or emblem he was proudly showing to his wife or buddy was from an old toaster we threw away the previous fall.

One hot August day, while fishing for bass in an abandoned strip pit, I was dragging a discouraged worm slowly across the bottom. While seeking to attract a "lunker," my hook snagged into something that seemed to weigh about 12 pounds, but didn't fight back. Reeling it in, it turned out to be a badly rusted radiator shell from an early model Willys-Knight. It had a perfect enamel and brass "WK" emblem on it.

One company that changed their radiator emblems with the tide was the Hupmobile. Almost every year, they used several different Hs in their logos. There were even one or two emblems that spelled out Hupmobile.

In my early days of collecting, I would infrequently find original brass scripts that were on early 1900 to 1912 cars hanging on garage walls, along with the expired license plates.

I recall one antelope-hunting trip in the wilds of Wyoming miles when we ducked into a ram-shackle building, in a ghost town, to get out of a blizzard. After building a fire, I noticed a reflection off one wall. Hanging there was a perfect nickled namescript from an Interstate automobile, as well as a Non Pareil brass bulb horn. On that same trip we came across an ancient mine that was still in operation. Its hoisting power was a gargantuan Cunningham V-8. The nameplate from it cost me three bottles of beer for the grizzled old miner.

Another discovery came on a car-hauling trip in southwestern Oklahoma. I stopped on an asphalt secondary road, miles from the nearest town, to check a worked-out wrecking yard. It had been converted into a 40-acre hog lot. Evidently, when they salvaged the brass from old car radiators, they

A Cadillac script sets off this grouping of club badges and one nameplate.

Here's a grouping of mostly obsolete logos from Auburn to Terraplane.

just tossed the radiator shells helter skelter. They all landed on one side as they fell. Those acres resulted in almost 100 nameplates, among them rare examples for a Texan, an Empire, a Duesenberg and a Wolverine (with a red inset). I was later to find a Wolverine emblem that was exactly the same, except it had a blue inset.

After several hours of searching and probing in the ground, what I also came up with was a liberal amount of hog manure on my clothes and body. I also detected a royal offense to the olfactory senses and equipment. The motel clerk stayed on the leeward side of me, at some distance, and, instead of showing me to the room, simply pointed the way.

I also began to pick up motor club badges. They were originally made of brass. A few years later, they began to make some like car insignias, with ceramic-type glass colors poured into a pre-molded brass background. The finish was then baked on. These used to be readily available in wrecking yards. Usually, you unscrewed one end of the license plate, where they were ordinarily attached, to remove them. On some older models, they were attached directly to the radiator, with long bolts going clear through the core.

At the time I was a traveling trucker, most of the older wrecking yards would allow you to help yourself to motor club badges, so long as you damaged nothing and took your insignia from portions of the

Eight nameplates and badges set off this grouping of vintage car parts very attractively. Many collectors of such items prefer to mount them in frames so that they can be hung on a wall and displayed for the pleasure of others.

car that were no longer resalable. Try that in one of these ultra-modern yards where they keep Dobermans or German Shepherds. To get past the gate, you need clearance from the Pentagon.

Many automotive nameplates have quite a story behind them. The Beggs Six was an assembled car put together in Kansas City. For many years, the huge Beggs sign was still visible, painted on the side of a brick building on the banks of the Missouri River in the downtown market area. That's where the cars were built.

The nameplate had a red glass background with the word Beggs on it. It was reputed to have $25 worth of gold dust mixed in with the red porcelain. I had one Beggs nameplate and there is definitely a glittering substance in with the red. Maybe it was gold.

The Diana automobile had an oval black background about the same size as a Packard hexagon. It showed the head of the huntress Diana, which was reported to be from cast silver. I never tested one, but I would guess that German silver or white brass was used. That's probably closer to the truth.

The postwar Kaiser featured a chrome buffalo on its large nameplate. The significance of depicting a bison is unknown to this writer. The Frazer, its stablemate, used a flamboyant coat-of-arms measuring almost six inches by four inches. It had many beautiful colors, but was extremely fragile. Out of about 20 examples, I found only a couple without chips or cracks.

Bentley put out unique sets of wings in the 1920s and 1930s. They all featured a "B" with a different color inset (black, green, red or blue). This was supposed to denote a certain model and year, but all bets were off if the wealthy buyer wanted a color to match his paint job. Bentley emblems were very scarce on the older cars. It was many years before I managed to acquire a red-label Bentley nameplate and then, only because it was loose and coming off the gas tank of my Bentley Super Sports.

Bugatti nameplates are also as valuable as gold. I secured one new Bugatti nameplate from a dealer in France, during a period of lassitude on his part. Dealers can be a good source of some nameplates. Another source is the car collector who picked up one or two nameplates or a brass script because they were handy, even though he had little interest in collecting the plates themselves. These fellows will usually sell or trade the nameplate for another old car part.

By 1955, I had accumulated some 50 frames of different nameplates and badges. Harrah's Automobile Collection (The National Automobile Museum now) made me an offer I couldn't refuse. I sold the complete collection, but kept all my duplicates. Of course, I immediately started another collection with the duplicates. This time I standardized the frame size at 16 x 20 inches, sawing my own frames. This resulted in a collection with much more eye appeal when displayed on the wall.

Older nameplates and car emblems are very hard to come by now. They are still around, though. Once I was just rummaging in the back room of a wrecking yard shed and came upon a half-gallon syrup bucket full of some rare porcelain plates of the 1920s. Some old-time "junkie" with an eye for beauty had evidently saved them, because he thought they were attractive. Ten dollars bought the bucketful. Such discoveries are often a once in a lifetime event.

This sideline hobby has furnished me with some of the most entertaining and relaxing moments of my collecting life. When I think of the hundreds of people who have viewed my collections, it pleases me. I realize that I have shown several different generations things they might never have seen if it had not been for my pack-rat tendencies.

Of course, the collecting of emblems will continue. Even some modern emblems are very attractive. There are enough different sporty car emblems to fill a couple of frames. If the whole car is too expensive for you or takes too much room, maybe emblem collecting could be your thing.

It was easier to find nameplates for pioneer automobiles years ago.

A cast iron 1928 Model A Ford Tudor Sedan manufactured by Arcade Toy Company is dwarfed by CorCor's version of the 1932 Graham Blue Streak four-door sedan in this Mark Thiessen photograph, distributed by the National Geographic Society for its recent automobilia exhibit in Washington, D.C.

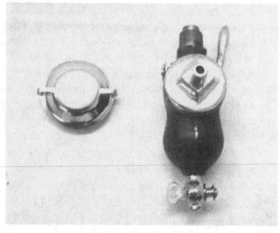

Spark plug fans also collect priming cups like this one.

Magazine ads for vintage tires, as well as old cars, are sought after.

Stoplamps and lenses make interesting collectibles, especially when lit up.

152

The collection

By Jack Martell

Only a devoted collector would drive 700 miles in 14 hours, spend $80 on fuel and live in a gypsy camp to go treasure hunting. Only a true enthusiast would endure heat, cold, rain, mud and junk food and, then, confront sanitary facilities beyond description to find an obsolete antique item.

In case you have not guessed what kind of collector I am describing, it is the old car parts swap meet addict. This describes a real "rust junkie" who will put up with all sorts of adversity to acquire a rusty, license plate or a greasy hubcap.

However, after two or three days of this kind of activity, a true old car buff is usually on such a "high" that he or she won't mind a 700-mile trip back home.

Upon arriving home, they are still so elated about their newly acquired booty, they just have to tell someone. While unloading the car they spot a neighbor across the fence (a neighbor who just spent the entire weekend manicuring the lawn with a surgical scissors). "Boy, I have been looking for this one for some time!" screams the collector. The neighbor, with a sort of half smile, notices the $7 price tag still attached, says "nice", and walks away mumbling something like, "and I thought I was nuts for chasing a little white ball around the golf course."

Oddly enough, neither of these people are likely to give up their favorite habits. Collecting old cars and their related automobilia has to be in your blood. It is not an acquired habit.

As antique car prices escalate, it becomes increasingly difficult for most Americans to own one. However, many people are resorting to collecting bits and pieces of cars and auto trivia.

The collecting possibilities are endless. They include common car parts like, hubcaps, nameplates and headlights, as well as unusual items such as vases and automatic headlight dimmers. All of these and more are sought after specimens.

On top of this, there are paper collectibles, such as old magazine advertisements, owners manuals, sales literature and factory photographs. Then there are the auto-related items, including tools, signs, oil company paraphernalia, tire company promotional items and more. The levying of user fees and road taxes has also generated many collectibles in the form of license plates and chauffeur badges.

When you were 10 years of age, a large assortment of new toy cars and trucks would gain the envy of your peers. At 15 years of age, toy cars would draw laughter from your peers. But, at 35-years-old, a collection of antique toy cars would bring you much praise.

Many toy cars were styled after production models of the same time. This often proves helpful in dating a toy like a cast iron Model T Ford, a hard rubber 1935 Auburn or a plastic postwar Ford.

Some people are fond of only one make of car. They collect everything related to that particular marque. Others advocate variety. They go after virtually anything tied-in to cars.

Hubcap collecting suggests a mental image of large silver saucers laying alongside the interstate. Reality can be quite the contrary, as a true antique automobile hubcap collector would not give those stainless steel monsters a second glance. Collectible hubcaps are of the screw-on variety, manufactured before 1930.

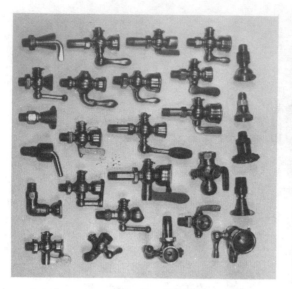

A variety of brass priming cups for antique automobiles.

Screw-on hubcaps, seen here on a sedan with disc wheels, are popular.

Screw-on hubcaps were predominantly made of brass or aluminum and measure from two- to seven-inches in diameter. Some bear names that most people have never heard of like Pope-Hartford, Minerva, Dort, Krit and Velie. Others advertise marques that are no longer produced, but are nostalgically remembered, such as Pierce-Arrow, Packard, Stutz, Maxwell, Studebaker and so on.

Collectors usually like to start with an accumulation of about a half-dozen hubcaps for popular cars that are (or once were) quite common to see, such as Ford, Essex, Dodge, Oakland, Nash and Cadillac. Then the bug bites, and soon they feel the desire to have one of every kind. This is a goal that serious collectors of anything will tell you is impossible to achieve. But, it is fun to try.

Collecting screw-on hubcaps can be interesting, but finding original matching wrenches can be even more challenging. Very few of these tools had car names on them. Those that do are very desirable.

Spark plug collecting is now sweeping the nation like beer can collecting once did. Serious interest is on the rise. Anyone interested in mechanical gadgetry would be fascinated by early spark plugs. To combat the problem of poor quality gasoline in the early 1900s, many innovative devices were incorporated into spark plug designs. What has evolved into a simple product today, was once a highly competitive market.

With the exception of flat tires and boiling radiators, spark plugs were probably the greatest source of problems on early cars. Manufacturers knew this and tried dozens of things to overcome the problem. Each company's attempt is reflected in early advertising claims directed at the end user. Spark plugs were affixed with air breathing devices, priming cups, spark intensifiers, self-cleaning devices, multiple-point electrodes, viewing windows and many varieties of electrode design. Amazingly, more than 2,000 corporate names have adorned spark plugs over the years.

License plate collecting can be an interesting and colorful hobby. However, it is space-consuming. With 50 states issuing plates for almost 80 years, that amounts to over 4,000 possible specimens. Plate collectors usually try to collect just their own state, or their birth year, or perhaps just interesting plates. In addition, there are hundreds of license plate add-ons that bolted to the tags in "piggyback" fashion. Most were advertisements, club badges or political endorsements.

License plate collecting is somewhat easier to get involved in than most other automotive-related hobbies, as there is an abundance of old plates to be found. Although some are quite rare, many are common to find. Newly-issued designs can also be interesting. For instance, pictorial plates and sample plates seem like good additions to a collection.

Stoplight lenses make an interesting collectible, too, especially when mounted and lighted from behind. Equally as interesting, but more scarce, are lenses with car names on them.

The Hard Stuff

Collecting old car shaving mugs

Edited By John Gunnell

Collectors of vintage automobiles are not uncommon around the country. Neither are antique shaving mug collectors. If you added both of these interests together, you might wind up with a collection like that assembled by William Pollock, of Pottstown, Pennsylvania, years ago.

At the time, Pollock owned and operated the "Pollock Auto Showcase" museum in Pottstown. It housed a collection of some 65 automobiles including a 1903 Cadillac, 1903 Ford, 1900 Oldsmobile and the oldest running car in America, a 1891 Peugeot. The museum also contained 60 very early bicycles and motorcycles, automotive toys, antique radios and telephones, vintage typewriters and, of course, shaving mugs.

In 1985, due to medical problems, parts of the collection were liquidated. Today, only 10 of the cars remain in William Pollock's possession and he is running a complete antique car restoration shop, where his 40 years of producing prize-winning work continue. The rest of the museum cars and his collections of bicycles, typewriters and shaving mugs were sold.

Before the mugs were liquidated, Pollock was the only known person to seriously combine the hobbies of collecting cars and shaving mugs. He pursued both hobbies with the interest and enthusiasm of a born collector. His research indicated that early autos and shaving mugs had at least one thing in common in common. To a degree, they both reflected technological changes that took place through the demise of the barber shop shave and shaving mugs, back in the mid-1920s.

Perhaps the commonality evolved from centuries ago, when primal man invented the wheel and made the first wagon. About the same time that this forerunner to the automobile appeared, man also began to trim his hair and beard with crude stone axes or knives. Thereafter, the ingenuity of man refined the technology of both wheeled vehicles and shaving methods and tools.

We can also go back 100 years, to a point in time when the barber shop shave and the shaving mug held a place of high esteem and distinction in society. They were regarded almost as highly as the automobile was a few decades later. At the time, a barber used the same mug, brush and soap for lathering all of his customers prior to shaving.

This technique was changed when new public health laws were enacted to prevent the spread of so-called "barber's itch." That was the slang name for a skin irritation or disease caused by unsanitary practices. This, of course, paved the way for individually-owned shaving mugs. When this change occurred, it became necessary for shaving mugs to bear distinguishing marks for quick identification.

First, the owner's name was added. At this point, American ingenuity took over. Soon, the manufacturers of barbering supplies started decorating mugs in a host of designs. They were sold at prices ranging from 10-cents to 25-cents. Near the end of the 19th century, countless varieties were available. By then, prices rose to the range of 25-cents to $3.

The creative talents of the early china painters (mug decorators) promoted the sale of shaving mugs in both a practical and artful way. Each came with its own particular type of American heraldry, as ordered by the owner. Creating miniature paintings on shaving mugs became an American folk art. It became a

DeRosa mug (left) shows body being painted. Mug on right shows mechanic.

Two types of trucks are seen here; van on left, canopied express on right.

The old car pictures were hand-painted on the china mugs.

Mr. Mitterich (left) started driving before Mr. Quigley (on right).

Truck is seen on left mug and the other shows an auto engine.

These mugs depict non-automotive transportation scenes

very unique form of the decorative arts, but one often unrecognized by passing generations. Perhaps the most interesting aspect of the decorated mugs was that they depicted Americans of all classes, in all walks of life, whether professional, merchant, tradesman or farmer.

Every conceivable type of decorative motif or design could be found on these relics. Transportation was a very popular subject. In fact, if all mugs bearing transportation scenes and emblems were collected together, one could probably trace the complete history of transportation in the United States, pictorially, from its beginning.

Railroad design mugs were in high demand. Other forms of transportation, such as horses, wagons and carriages, also inspired many mug painters. It was natural for automobiles and aircraft to appeal to mug artists. Airplanes, however, did not come into general use until shaving mugs began to disappear from barber shops. Therefore, aircraft designs are not seen.

Most mug collectors like to concentrate their efforts in a particular category. William Pollock was such a collector. His specialty mug collection grew closely related to his interest in early automobiles.

Pollock's was the largest known collection of auto-related shaving mugs in the country. Though all the vehicles pictured on his mugs were not considered classics by car enthusiasts, the mugs with their hand-painted autos were, indeed, classics to shaving mug aficionados.

Auto-related mugs are much sought after by all mug collectors. One reason is that they were made until only the mid-1920s. In fact, any automobile made after 1924 would not have been featured on an antique shaving mug, because the last firm to decorate mugs in the United States was the Koken Barber Supply Company of St. Louis, Missouri. Its mug-decorating department was closed in 1924.

The mug collection that Pollock assembled included designs depicting both American-made and foreign-made vehicles. Shown on his mugs were original paintings of a 1902 Oldsmobile, 1902 Crestmobile, 1904 Winton, 1904 Peerless, 1906 Royal Tourist and 1909 Winton truck. Other vehicles seen included a 1910 Peerless six-cylinder, 1911 Locomobile six-cylinder, 1913 Haynes, 1914 Hupmobile, 1915 Star, 1915 Chevrolet Bakery Truck, 1916 Cadillac and 1917 Chevrolet Touring.

The auto-decorated mugs each bore the name of the original mug owner. In many cases, the particular car shown denoted, with great pride, the make and model of automobile that the mug owner drove. However, there were some instances where the picture on the mug depicted the mug owner's profession. For example, one mug depicted an automobile mechanic working on a car.

Another variation was reflected in the Pollock collection by his "J. Field" mug. This name appeared in old English lettering, in gold, above the steering wheel of a car. Mr. Field was employed, for many years, as a chauffeur for the Luden Cough Drop Company. His shaving much commemorated this fact.

Another example of a design depicting a trade or occupation was Pollock's "Frank De Rosa" mug. It featured an auto body painter coating the body of a car with new finish. Mr. DeRosa was obviously involved in this field. The year 1916 appeared under his name on the mug, so he did not work with quick-drying nitro-cellulose lacquer, which wasn't in use at that time.

A more personalized version of the shaving is the photographic mug. According to advertisements in early barber equipment supply catalogs, it had an actual photograph burned into its surface. A mug bearing an actual photograph of its owner was considered very desirable. It cost the barber who ordered it $3. Generally, the hair-cutter then added a small fee to the retail price for his trouble. Back then, this kind of shaving mug was the most expensive of all types.

The Pollock collection also contained the "H. Erickson" mug. It was a rare photographic type showing two men standing beside a 1909 Winton truck. One of the two men in the photograph was obviously H. Erickson, the owner or driver of the commercial vehicle.

As the tempo of life in the United States began to change to a faster pace, the once-popular barber shop shave finally faded into obscurity. It disappeared by the mid-1920s. No longer did the average American male take time for his frequent regular trip to the barber shop for a shave. The safety razor had made great inroads into the barbers' business, so they began placing more importance on haircuts.

For its part, the automobile played a dominant part in shaping America's future, even though it hurried the passing of the shaving mug. However, for collectors of nostalgic Americana, shaving mugs of all types (including those with automotive designs) have only lost their lather ... not their luster!

Exonumia is side effect of incurable "automania"

By Bob Lemke

"Exonumia? Wasn't that a Frazer model made in 1951?" the average old car enthusiast might ask.

No, exonumia is a generic term used by numismatists or coin collectors. It describes that branch of their hobby that has to do with tokens, medals and other items that were issued as commemoratives, coin substitutes, etc., but that had no legal tender status.

Many exonumists (collectors of tokens and medals) collect by topic. In recent years, with interest in old cars booming, the number of collectors of automotive-related exonumia has been increasing at a rapid rate. Most of the items discussed herein represent automotive-related promotional pieces of the 1930-1960 period. Not considering minor varieties, there probably are only some 25-40 different types of automotive tokens and medals known to be available.

Nearly all exonumia items have considerable collector appeal (hence, value) today. However, at the time they were issued, most examples were giveaway items offered as enticements to draw prospective customers to the showrooms. Although some tokens and medals were issued before the turn of the-century, many seem to date from the 1930s. This is logical. That was the depression era and few new cars were being purchased. The auto industry tried every avenue it could think of to increase motor vehicle sales.

It is hard to say whether the promotional tokens handed out at new-car shows, special events and car dealer showrooms had any appreciable effect on sales before, during or after the depression. However, these items certainly are gaining appreciation today as interesting collectibles. They are part of an ancillary field for old car hobbyists.

Older and rarer than most automotive promotional tokens are their forerunners issued by buggy companies. Many buggy tokens are of interest to old car enthusiasts because the same firms went into making automobiles. An example of this is Parry Manufacturing Company of Indianapolis, Indiana. One token identified it as a manufacturer of "high grade" buggies and surries. In 1910, the firm turned out a car with a four-cylinder overhead valve engine. It failed, however, and Parry disappeared by 1912.

Probably the earliest automotive token was a pot metal souvenir of the Columbus Buggy Company of Columbus, Ohio. It was issued in 1892, during the Columbian Exposition in Chicago, Illinois. That event was the first World's Fair. The piece illustrates a rather unconventional portrait of the explorer Columbus on obverse (front) side. A Columbus motor-buggy is represented on the reverse side. Like many buggy manufacturers, in 1903, Columbus went into horse-less carriages production. It offered both gas and electric models for a decade. In 1913, the firm produced a large six-cylinder car. It proved to be its last contribution to the transportation scene.

Tokens and medals issued by the major automakers appear to be the most popular type. Many people collect "Big Three" cars, so there is a lot of competition for medallions related to Ford Motor Company, General Motors and Chrysler Corporation models.

The majority of Ford exonumia dates from the pre-World War II years. Ford's exhibition at the 1933-1934 "Century of Progress Exposition" in Chicago, Illinois was one of the most popular on the site of that World's Fair.

For the first year of the expo, Ford issued a souvenir medal marking its own progress. Thirty years had passed from the company's start in 1903. A 1933 Ford radiator grille on the front and a stylish V-8 emblem encircled by a laurel wreath on the back combined to give the medal a classic look. Today, this piece is popular with collectors. Apparently, it was re-struck in 1975. The re-strike specimen differs from the original by the addition of a 1975 date after "Thiry Years of Progress" stamped around the circumference on the reverse side.

The term V-8 still was the watchword again, in 1934, when the second Ford expo medal was released. This symbol appeared on both sides of the souvenir. The dynamic V-8 symbol on the obverse side of the medal was a near preview of the logo used later on 1936-1938 Ford hubcaps and badges. The emblem featuring a rotund 8 and intersecting V on the reverse side of the token was similar to the Ford car emblems of 1932-1933.

There are some postwar Ford medallions, including some relatively modern issues. In fact, as recently as 1978, a medal was struck to honor the 50th anniversary of the Model A Ford. It shows the grille, head lamps, headlamp tie-bar and ahoo-ga horn of a Model A Ford. Is it a factory item or an aftermarket commemorative? Probably the latter.

By the 1950s, General Motors was pretty much alone as a major issuer of promotional medals. Many of those struck by General Motors in the early postwar period were true commemoratives. They often recognized milestones in General Motors' corporate history.

This seems to be a recent four token issue honoring Auburn (right), Cord (left) and Duesenberg (top center) automobiles. The reverse side of the Duesenberg medal, on bottom, denotes the Classic Model J of 1930.

As the 50 millionth General Motors automobile rolled off the assembly line on November 23, 1954 a commemorative medal went into production. A milestone automobile, the 1955 Chevrolet Bel Air two-door hardtop, was pictured on the medal. Another automotive commemorative that marked the same occasion was a special production run of Bel Airs with custom gold paint and matching gold and white interiors.

An enigmatic Chevrolet token from late in the decade celebrated the "Best of Best '59 Jubilee." Just what this event was is unclear. The back was stamped "Chevy Showboat, Greenbrier, White Sulphur Springs, West Virginia." The new-in-fall 1959 Corvair (a 1960 model) did not yet offer the Greenbrier Sports Wagon model. Thus, the inscription probably refers to a Chevrolet sales promotion, a press gathering or a dealer outlet. It's possible the piece marks some sort of anniversary for a dealership.

A popular General Motors token that is much in demand and scarce is a piece issued to spur sales of 1940 Oldsmobiles. The obverse of the attractive nickel-silver medal shows a roadside rat's-eye-view of an oncoming Oldsmobile and the slogan "America's biggest money's worth: 1940 Olds." A prolific advertising message is packed into the reverse face of the medal.

Among many early Pontiac tokens was one issued during the period when the company's product was known as the "Chief of the Sixes." On this

Rocketships appear on both sides of the 1956 Motorama medal

token, the front has an Indian brave's profile. The reverse side is given over to the slogan "Product of General Motors" that establishes the car as a GM product. Pontiacs of the time were a "companion car" to the larger and more expensive Oakland. Introduced in 1926, the Pontiac became so popular that, by 1931, it had completely eclipsed Oakland and the parent marque was discontinued.

One of the great automotive styling identification symbols of all time was the Pontiac Silver Streak. It was introduced on 1935 models and capped with another famous symbol, the head of Chief Pontiac. Both are shown on a Pontiac commemorative token of the same vintage. A frequent issuer of tokens in the 1930s, Pontiac pieces are quite common today. They exist in many varieties.

Many collectors specialize in "encased" coins. Encased silver dollars of any kind are extremely rare. This makes the encased dollars that Buick Motor Division issued in 1940 and 1941 very rare and expensive. Their values are enhanced by the fact that 1940-1941 Buicks are among the most popular collector cars of the immediate prewar period. These pieces usually sell at high prices, when available.

The General Motors "Motorama" events were a popular showcase for new cars and dream cars in the early postwar years. Cars of the future, models of the present, pretty girls, electronic gadgets, stage shows and giveaways combined in a seductive sales pitch for General Motors products of the 1950s. The touring extravaganza brought forth a trio of "spinner" tokens between 1954 and 1956. A raised dot in the center of each token allowed it to be spun on a hard surface ... say a bar ... while an arrow on the other side indicated who paid for the round of drinks. Beginning with the round issue of 1954, each year's souvenir went a little farther in styling. The futuristic dream cars are depicted on those pieces of 1954 and 1955.

Ford and General Motors weren't the only automakers to commemorate significant dates in corporate history with tokens and medallions. The silver anniversary of Ford's Mercury division, celebrated in 1963, was marked with the issue of a heavily chromed commemorative medal. The 1939 car, introduced in November 1938 to fill the price gap between the Ford Deluxe and the Lincoln-Zephyr, was rather

The back of the 1954 Motorama medal shows a dream car.

In 1978, a medal was struck to honor 50th anniversary of the Model A Ford.

crudely represented on the medal above the latest Mercury with its reverse-slanting "Breezeway" rear window.

Chrysler seemed to prefer issuing medals to celebrate important transitions in styling. A bold, but infamous styling move made by the firm was the 1934 introduction of the Chrysler and DeSoto Airflow models. Public reception of this kind of design was only luke-warm. However, a medal showing a 1934 Chrysler Airflow and the slogan "A century of progress in a decade" on one side was struck for the Chicago Worlds Fair. It also marked the 10th anniversary of Chrysler and depicted a 1924 touring car on its reverse side.

Another Chrysler Corporation medal, from 1956, denoted the company's bold new "Forward Look" styling. It showed a double "arrowhead" logo on one side and the names Plymouth, Dodge, DeSoto, Chrysler and Imperial on the other. Today, this design concept of stylist Virgil Exner is best remembered as the "tailfin look." It seems distinctive, but certainly dated.

Scarce in the automotive token series are truck promotional items. However, Dodge Truck Division did strike at least one token. It probably dates from the mid-1930s. The sales pitch on the piece contrasted Dodge's advanced features over those of its competitors, which still used cable brakes, splash lubrication, etc.

One of the most recent automotive medals is an aluminum "Sensible Spectaculars" giveaway made for an AMC/Rambler sales promotion. Each of the 1966 American Motors lines (American, Classic, Ambassador and Marlin) is named on the piece. The opposite side says, "Rambler extra value features make your Rambler dollar a bigger dollar." This is the only known AMC promotion medal.

During the 1960s, television was found to be a very effective means of giving the buyer a preview of each year's new cars and of luring them to the showroom. As television's promotional value was more fully explored, the use of medals as a sales motivation tool was impacted.

Today, automotive-related exonumia is still seen from time to time. Most of it is in the form of special collections or precious metal commemorative issues. These are certainly not giveaway items. Still, while no tokens and medals are being issued as factory sales promotion items, the automobile continues to be the theme of various commemorative medals and silver ingots.

Several private mints have devoted single items and whole series to old cars. Several examples are noteworthy. The Madison Mint issued a one-ounce .999 fine silver ingot illustrating a Stanley Roadster. In Hershey, Pennsylvania (home of the world's largest old car show) a coin club medal honoring the 1903 Cadillac was created. Three hundred of these medals were struck.

Old car decanters are a growing collectible field

By Diane Thomas

Who says alcohol and cars are incompatible? With the energy shortage, alcohol and gas are being mixed in tanks, just like in the good old days. In the tanks of antique car decanters, the gas is often replaced with "high-octane" liquid fuel.

Fancy-shaped containers for food and drink are no recent trend. Log Cabin Syrup cans once dominated the Sunday breakfast table, little brown jugs held cider and ceramic cows gave milk for cereal. However, containers in the shape of old cars were not as popular.

Once in a while, a small glass car surfaces in a collection. These were filled with tiny sugar candies. After the contents were eaten, the car became a child's toy that got pushed along a carpeted roadway. Today they are kept in glass cabinets and their "empty" price is many times the original candy-filled price.

It's been said the difference between a man's toys and his son's toys is simply the cost. In the case of old car decanters, this is certainly true.

The earliest old car liquor bottles were quite crude. An example of this is the Garnier bottle. It represented an open car of undetermined make, presumably of pre-1912 vintage, with no front doors. It also lacked a steering wheel and the tires were non-rolling ceramic.

Even a 1912 Rolls-Royce Silver Ghost Town decanter car was poorly copied. It had what car restorers would call a home paint job. The windows were pasted-on bits of printed paper and the non-rolling wheels had plastic tires.

A Jewel Tea delivery wagon was a better copy of the real thing. It it would never have earned 100 points at an old car show, although it did have metal fenders and running boards, large rolling wheels and rubber tires. It was a passable representation of a mid-teens model. Car memorabilia collectors were quick to buy it in 1974.

This item started a veritable rush of old car decanters and the larger distilleries made it a point to duplicate real cars as closely as possible. However, federal regulations regarding the closure of liquor bottles have made some minor authenticity compromises necessary.

Racing models attracted collectors who found a copy of the 1906 Renault that raced to victory in the Grand Prix at LeMans. It looked super elegant on a shelf, due to its long length. The three spare tires in the rear concealed the cork and the long length was necessary to provide content capacity. Although the white rubber tires were ceramic, the car's detailing was excellent.

Another early race car decanter is a replica of the 1911 Marmon Wasp that won the first Indianapolis 500-mile race. This chrome yellow racer has respectable detailing, but a sloppy paint job.

Many police officers purchased the Model A squad car decanter.

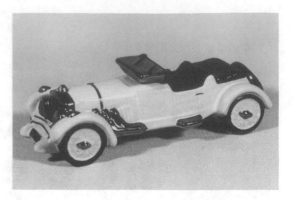

This early roadster decanter has a fold-down windshield.

One Embossograph's Jim Beam Duesenbergs set against a Gatsby style backdrop.

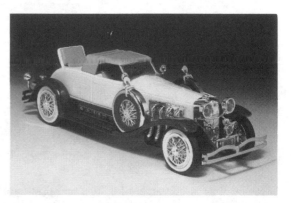

Beam's sporty 1935 Duesenberg roadster, also made by Emossograph Corporation.

The earliest old car liquor bottles were quite crude. Windows were pasted-on bits of printed paper and the non-rolling wheels were molded to the body, though some had plastic tires.

164

The bottles came out with budget-busting regularity. As the quality of reproduction went up, so did the price. When the decanters were introduced in the late 1950, holding approximately $5 worth of spirits (usually whiskey), original pricing was under $20. Each time a new design appeared, the price rose at least $5.

Buyers grumbled as they paid, not because of the price, but because so many of the decanters had mistakes obvious to collectors of old cars. When the rumbles grew loud enough to reach the distillers' ears, one company approached one of the old car clubs and made a deal. For a pre-production evaluation of design authenticity, the club would receive a royalty on each decanter sold.

The initial result of this arrangement was a 1909 Thomas-Flyer Flyabout. It came complete with an "owner's manual" giving the historical background of the car and testifying to its authenticity. The detailing included a brass crank and steering column, brass head, tail and side lights and dog-leg windshield. Owners could return a card that "licensed" the car in their name.

The success of the first such authenticated decanter brought more "pedigreed" bottles for collectors. And for those whose transportation tastes deviate, fire engines, ambulances and trucks have appeared over the years.

In fact, if you're a serious collector of old car decanters, you'd better build a 20-car garage-shelf. The decanters keep coming. At any price, they are always cheaper than the real cars.

Collectors often compare decanter's features to real car.

A veritable rush of early old car decanters included this 1919 Stutz.

Postwar car decanters were a natural evolution following collector trends.

The 1934 Duesenberg Collapsible-Front Town Car in a different color scheme.

Distilleries tried harder to duplicate real cars like the 1913 Cadillac.

Embossograph's Jim Beam Model A Ford has appeared as a fire truck.

After success of the police car, a paddy wagon was issued by Jim Beam.

The 1931 Model A Ford ambulance is a highly detailed decanter.

The 1917 Mack firetruck is a detailed decanter.

Automotive history reflected in Jim Beam bottles

By Bill Siuru

The James B. Beam Distilling Company is probably best known for its Jim Beam brand of whiskey. The company has been around since George Washington served his second term as president.

However, for many people, the distinctive decanters that the company often packages its product in are what's important. The collecting of Jim Beam bottles has become a big hobby, with annual conventions drawing thousands from all parts of the United States and foreign countries. The hobby has even spread to such far away places as Australia and New Zealand.

The first distinctive decanters appeared in 1941, with bottles shaped like bowling pins. Incidentally, this design was continued right into modern times, with annual updates. The first decanter issued to commemorate an event appeared in 1955. Appropriately, it honored the 160th anniversary of the company. This was followed by dozens of other special bottles commemorating everything from statehood birthdays to sporting events and political conventions. Special bottles are even issued for the annual convention of Jim Beam bottle collectors clubs.

While just about every subject, from the 101st Airborne Division to Zimmerman's "world's largest liquor store" in Chicago, Illinois have been depicted on bottles, one of the most popular topics through the years has been automobiles.

Naturally, motor sports has been a popular subject. The first automotive bottle appeared in 1970 and, appropriately, honored the Indianapolis 500 Memorial Day classic. Also in 1970, the first in a series of bottles to commemorate the Mint 400, the "World's Greatest Off-Road Race" sponsored by the Del Webb Hotel and Casino in Las Vegas, Nevada was issued. One of several sports heroes honored on Jim Beam bottles was Bobby Unser, whose Olsonite Eagle was modeled in very fine detail on a 1975 decanter. Like many Other organizations and associations, the Sports Car Club of America got its bottle in 1976.

Of particular interest to collectors of automobilia is the "Beam on Wheels" series of bottles. The first in the series was a beautiful replica of a 1904 curved dash Oldsmobile. It came out in 1972, on the 75th anniversary of the original Olds Motor Vehicle Company. Typical of the Jim Beam automobile replica bottles, this one is detailed right down to its red spoke wheels and brass lights. This was followed, in 1973, with decanters that were scaled-down models of the Volkswagen Beetle. They came in either red or blue.

Fords have been seen on many decanters. The first one, a 1913 Model T runabout replica, came out in 1974. However, unlike Henry's cars, which came in any color as long as it was black, the Jim Beam cars also came in green. In 1978, the company brought out its version of the 1903 Ford Model A on the 75th anniversary of Ford's first mass-produced car. This decanter was stunning in either black with red trim or red with black trim. Both had an abundance of simulated brass.

Various versions of Ford's second Model A have also been depicted on Jim Beam decanters. In 1980, there was the 1928 Model A roadster, complete with rumble seat. In 1981, this car was painted fire engine red and became a fire chief's car that looked like the real ones used by many fire departments of the era. In 1981, there were also two rare versions of this Model A roadster replica produced. One hundred yellow ones were given to Jim Beam salesmen attending a sales meeting and 25 black ones were presented to salespeople who made their quotas in Jim Beam products.

Also in 1981, two decanters modeled after the 1929 Model A four-door phaeton were offered. One was light blue. The other was dark blue and detailed like the police cars used in the 1920s and early 1930s. Two more decanters depicted a 1928-1929 Ford Model A pickup truck and a 1930 Model AA police paddy wagon.

Fire apparatus has been an important part of the Beam on Wheels series. As far as motorized vehicles go, the first one modeled as a decanter was a detailed copy of a 1917 Mack pumper. This AC "Bulldog" Mack was copied from the original housed in the Mack Museum in Allentown, Pennsylvania. It is one of the largest Jim Beam speciality containers. Another fire engine, patterned after a 1930 Model A Ford truck, was added to the series later.

In 1976, Jim Beam replicated the 1907 Thomas Flyer 6-70 Model K "Flyabout." This was the car that won the 1908 New York-to-Paris race. The decanter came in either white or blue.

The 1914 Stutz Bearcat was the subject of a 1977 edition decanter. The models, which came in either yellow and black or gray and black, were detailed right downtown the monocle windshield mounted on the steering column.

Like the original, Jim Beam's 1981 version of the 1934 Duesenberg Model J town car was impressive with it blue body, white top and chrome trim. The decanter is authentic right down to the sidemounts and external exhaust system for a supercharged engine. It is over 18 inches long. In 1982, a special midnight blue edition of the Duesenberg decanter was brought out as the official commemorative issue for "Auburn '82," the 27th Auburn-Cord-Duesenberg Club convention.

Another addition to the stable of Jim Beam cars was the 1978 Corvette decanter.

The first Beam fire engine was this 1917 Mack, which also one of the largest bottles the Jim Beam Company has issued.

One of the fanciest "Beam bottles," as they are often called, is this elegant 1934 Duesenberg Model SJ town car. Two different color versions of it exist.

All decanters in the Beam on Wheels series are noted for their authenticity and excellent detail. In several cases, the replicas have been authenticated by marque experts or old car clubs, before they go into production. While the bottles themselves are crafted from Regal China porcelain, the wheels, interior and exterior trim, and other detail parts are made of plastic (or metal in the case of some early editions.)

Since the decanters are functional, in that they carry Jim Beam's liquid refreshments, they must incorporate a stopper. The decanter designers have usually cleverly hidden the stopper from view. For example, on many of the antique and classic car decanters, the stopper is found under the removable trunk.

The bottles were designed by Embossograph Corporation of Lake Bluff, Illinois and produced by the Regal China Corporation, a subsidiary of the Beam Distilling Company. Ideas for the bottles come from many sources, but many come from artists at Regal China and from Beam executives.

Because of the craftsmanship that went into the decanters, the bottles in the Beam on Wheels series were relatively costly when new. They are now among the most valuable items sought by both Beam bottle collectors and collectors of automobilia in general. While only the automotive bottles have been mentioned here, the series also includes equally attractive decanters ranging from circus wagons to locomotives.

Fords are predominant in the Beam on Wheels series, but General Motors has not been forgotten. Three decanters that appeared in 1977 and 1978 depicted familiar General Motors products. First there was the bottle shaped and painted like an AC spark plug. This was followed by a bottle dedicated to "Mr. Goodwrench," GM's personification of its parts division. Finally, the Delco Freedom battery became the model for another decanter. The 1957 Chevrolet Bel Air and aforementioned 1978 Corvette are part of this group, too.

For enthusiasts interested in further information on Jim Beam decanters, an excellent book with color pictures and current values was published. It is titled *A Guide to Jim Beam Bottles*. Al Cembuza and Constance Avery were the authors. To learn about the multitude of Jim Beam bottle collectors clubs, hobbyists can also write: International Association of Jim Beam Bottle & Specialties Clubs, 2015 Burlington Avenue, Kewanee, IL 61443.

Ford's Model A has come in many decanters. Here we see the Model A Phaeton police car, regular phaeton and cabriolet behind a Duesenberg roadster.

The Jim Beam 1934 Duesenberg J decanter also came in a roadster version.

Collecting automotive porcelain ad signs

By Paul Hatmon

At certain phases of the moon, the old car collector goes off on a tangent. It is not enough to hoard license plates, radiator ornaments, car posters, literature or old automotive magazines. Remember, several years ago, when you could see small porcelain oil company signs at the edge of some farmer's field? These small signs withstood the weather, impervious to rust, risking only the hazard of an odd rifle shot from some disgruntled hunter. You don't see them there any more.

A battered Phillips gasoline sign in my collection survived 30 years on the outskirts of a small Oklahoma town, way back on a secondary road. The weatherbeaten old rancher stated the oil company paid

Donald Duck slugged a snowman to drive home Standard Oil Company's "A knockout for winter" promotion. This rare set of round signs advertising Standard gasoline, RPM motor oil and extra service features Disney characters.

him $1 a year for over 25 years just to leave it on an iron post, at the front edge of the ranch, near the highway. He said, "They quit paying me, so I took it down."

For the next five years, the sign covered a hole in the bed of his pickup truck. He remarked to me, as he handed me the bullet riddled sign, "I reckon I'm through with it."

Oil companies were one of the biggest users of ornate porcelain signs. A sign would last until a change in design was needed. Each company did its best to make its own sign unique and colorful. A company sign can be identified by the pattern and colors without being able to read the slogans.

One of the most sought after oil company porcelains is the Mobil red horse that pranced across stations, signboards and gas pumps for many years. A 30 x 45-inch example from the late 1930s is very expensive. The company made some very colorful small logos for the gas pumps. One old-time gasoline station operator, whose building dated back prior to World War II said he sold a sign off the end of his 40-year old station for 10 times what the horse cost him new. When he told me of the sale he remarked with a wry grin, "I had to sell that one, they stole the other one off the opposite end of the building when I was in the hospital."

Other goodies hotly pursued are the white glass eagles from the White Eagle Oil Company. These grand old birds have peered down at many an antique car, when they were new. How many of those glass eagles survived the wanton vandalism of a couple of generations of target shooters?

There has always been a great interest in glass gas globes. The most desired are the one-piece globes from the manually-operated pumps. These fragile works of art have always brought high prices. Now, they have now boomed clear out of the stratosphere.

Also hotly sought after are the three-piece globes. These featured a center of metal. Later the center was plastic, with glass inserts used on the newer manual pumps and still, later, on the electric pumps that went up to 49-cents a gallon. I can barely remember those.

Filling station owners could buy the center and order the proper glass inserts from their oil company. These inserts later also became plastic. They were all meant to be lighted from within. These were the grand daddy of the modern plastic lighted sign.

You are going to need a lot of loot if collecting these globes is your thing. And, as in anything from the past that becomes valuable, the duplicators jump in for a ride on the band wagon. So if you lay out a bundle of green, at least be sure you are buying what you are paying for and not some quick-buck artist's reproduction.

The small pump signs used on the older type machines are very desirable and getting very hard to find. The fire helmet used on Texaco's Pumps of the 1930s-1950s was one of the more attractive porcelains. These can still be seen once in a while in some out of the way two-pump station. The small gas pump signs can be obtained for a semi-reasonable sum they make an attractive addition to a den or finished garage.

For many years, the familiar double-faced porcelain sign of the AAA emergency service hung in front of service stations and garages, that furnished aid for this national motoring club. In more recent years, the club switched to lightweight aluminum signs. The same type older sign was used for motels and hotels. These have converted to the interior-lighted plastic signboards.

There are still a few metal AAA signs in remote areas but they are coming down rapidly. In the small town of Van Buren, Missouri, immediately underneath the huge modern plastic lighted AAA sign, hangs the small AAA porcelain sign of 30 years ago. It is streaked with rust from the iron hanger and bolts.

The standard sign of the nationwide AAA said "Emergency Service" around the AAA logo in the center. It is difficult to find one without some bullet chips. They are most common. The AAA signs with the name of the state are the rarest, because you only have one-fiftieth of the market. Any collector who is lucky enough to have a duplicate is busy hunting for the fellow, in another state, who is in the same boat. These signs will hang for 20 years and, if they escape the bullets, will shine-up like new.

The AAA badges, that were originally made of brass and mounted on radiators in the teens, turned into poured glass or a type of porcelain in the 1920s. Next, they changed to the stamped or die cast type that bolted on the license plate bracket. That was when the artistic appeal went out of the AAA badge. In the 1950s came the plastic stick-on version, which gave way to the decals of today.

Signs can still be found in the least expected places. We stopped at a small general store deep in the Ozarks. It had once been a service station, as evidenced by the obsolete, half-junked pumps still standing in front. A weathered Mobil porcelain sign, with small red horse and all, still creaked from an overhead hanger at the side of the store. After a bit of dickering with the crotchety old store keeper, the sign was mine.

Another type of red Socony flying horse sign showed only the horse.

If you need a reason to collect, consider the decorative aspect.

Oakland dealer sign was seen at Fall Carlisle '90 swap meet.

A red, white and blue Havoline Motor Oil sign has a very attractive design.

This Pontiac logo was well known for many years; last seen in 1970s.

Chrysler and Plymouth dealers used this sign in the 1930s.

The oil companies put out a steady flow of porcelain, tin and glass items that are now collector's items. Examples range from large signs, to one-gallon containers to quart-size motor oil cans.

When I asked if he had any more or knew of any other porcelain signs he began to ask me a flock of questions. Where I was born, how old I was, did I have any relatives in the area? Evidently, my answers suited him. He locked the front door and beckoned me to follow him to the rear of the store. We went through a store room, down some stairs and through a heavy oak door, into what seemed to be a storage area carved out of solid rock.

Showing me a cloth-covered disc on the rock wall, he removed the cloth to reveal what appeared to be a glass or porcelain sign about two-feet in diameter. In the 1920s, he had been chief dragon of the local Ku Klux Klan. This had been the meeting place. The insignia had been made for them by one of the same companies who made the porcelain gas signs. He had kept it all these years and left instructions in his will to destroy the emblem and the cavern after his death.

He let me take a couple of photos, with the promise I'd never reveal my source. Said he had given up that foolishness 30 years ago. The other members of the Klavern had long since shuffled off this mortal soil. If I didn't have the photo in hand, I would not believe it myself.

On the same trip, I spotted an old porcelain sign at the side of a deserted- looking, old-time service station. Knocking at the house next door, I talked with the wife of the former owner. I asked about buying the sign. She invited me into a living room that had not changed in 30 years. After agreeing on a price for the sign, she mentioned there was a Prince Albert porcelain sign on the back of the old station door. Taking me over to the old station, we found the sign as described. While I was taking it down, the lady pulled down two big boxes covered with the dust of years. The boxes contained the two glass globes from the last two gasoline pumps. They had been removed some 25 years ago. The nice lady received a goodly sum and I picked up some rare items.

The oil companies put out a steady flow of porcelain and glass items that are now collectors items. A rare White Eagle sign was found nailed to a machine shop wall with two glass, two-foot high eagles peering down from a shelf above. The defunct India Oil company put out some of the most colorful pump signs. A Norse Oil sign is hot property. That oil company covered the country with the big Viking, underlined by "Business is Good," mostly in black and white. Another Oil company that used black and white, for a time, on its porcelain gas signs was the Cities Service Company. It utilized a black triangle on a white background. The slogan was "Once-Always."

Tire and battery companies are a good source of colorful signs. One Montgomery Ward tire sign dates from the 1930s, as do many Willard Battery signs. Almost every collection I have seen includes a Willard sign. The company put out a lot of them and they lasted well. The prices range from reasonable to asinine.

A decent gas pump sign, not too rare, should be affordable for anyone. On the other end, a big automobile dealer's sign of extreme rarity, such as the 1931 Nash porcelain, is worth up to 40 times as much. A good Packard dealer sign is expensive, too, if it is in good shape. The rare India or Humble gas pump signs are climbing in value, as well. Of course, the antique dealers smell a new fad miles away, months early. Their prices don't always make sense.

The pleasure in porcelain signs is not only in the hunting or finding. They are beautiful works of art that were carefully designed. If arranged with consideration given to color and shape, they make a beautiful display on the wall. The smaller gas pump signs, such as a Standard Red Crown design, are suitable for den or game room. The larger signs are fine for garage or hobby room.

One local custom shop has a wall some 20 x 60-feet in size, which is covered with porcelain signs, mostly from oil companies. There are several huge five-foot signs from the 1930s. They are arranged with taste. This results in an eye-appealing display that puts some modern art murals to shame.

Some time ago, I stopped collecting automobile nameplates, because I ran out of room. They covered some 120-feet of wall space on, at least, the top three feet. This left the same length strip underneath the nameplates. It about four and one-half feet high. Porcelain signs filled up the gap between the nameplates and the floor quite nicely. There is always a "good reason" to find something new to collect!

You are going to need a lot of loot if collecting porcelain signs is your hobby. If you plan to lay out a bundle of green at the next swap meet, at least be sure you are buying what you are paying for and not a reproduction.

Handsome logo identified Mobil Oil Company's Gargoyle brand lubricant.

A Packard dealer's porcelain sign.

Scarce and popular are the Mobil flying red horse signs. Unfortunately, like most other porcelain signs that hung in rural environments, they are often found riddled with bullets and buckshot.

The "snitching post" started in Oklahoma City

By Kristie Lynn

The "snitching post" was the timely name given to the first parking meters, when they replaced the old Western hitching posts on Oklahoma City streets, in 1935. The nation's first parking meters ... 150 of them ... were the brainchild of the late Carl Magee, an attorney and newspaper editor. He dreamed up the idea as a device to increase the turnover in parking space on busy streets. Then, a mechanical engineer from Ohio, named Gerald H. Hale, developed the clock-operated meter. He joined with Magee, as a partner.

From this rather modest 150 meter installation, in Oklahoma City, has sprung a controversial business; one which has been fought in the courts since the very beginning. There are over 1,650,000 on-street metered parking spaces; they earned millions last year.

Meter foes fought back from the beginning. They usually charged that parking meters violated an individual's basic constitutional rights. Lawsuits by the hundreds hit courts all over the nation, but judges continually ruled in favor of the mechanical monster.

One case of particular interest was that of attorney Rice Line, in San Angelo, Texas. He contested the city's legal right to own and operate parking meters on one certain street. The deed to that street property dated all the way back to horse-and-buggy days. It specifically guaranteed the citizens free use of the thoroughfare. He lost the case in the courts.

Speaking of horse-and-buggy users, parking meters have even brought the Amish to heel, in Millersburg, Ohio. These people scorn modern transportation and still drive only horse-drawn vehicles. Still, one finds parking meters around Millersburg's courthouse square. They are restricted to daytime use only, by horse-drawn wagons.

Howard Henry, a wealthy wheat farmer in Minot, North Dakota, took city officials to court over an overtime parking ticket. "I had just come out to put in another nickel," he protested. He then went on to express his view that North Dakota, of all places in the country, had more than ample room for free parking. The case went against Mr. Henry and he was fined $1. He was fighting mad and refused to pay the fine. This man then initiated a campaign against parking meters. In 1948, there was a voter's referendum and parking meters were outlawed throughout the State.

This certainly wasn't the end of the matter. Battle lines were drawn and great political pressure was brought upon the state legislature, in an effort to legalize meters. Why the pressure? Because eight cities in North Dakota had parking meter investments of over $300,000. Minot, alone, had $43,000 tied up in parking meters. The legislature did legalize parking meters, in 1951, but another state-wide referendum, again led by Henry, later outlawed all parking meters in the state of North Dakota.

Cities defend parking meters, and rightfully so, with the argument that they keep parking spaces "rotating," for the fuller use of all citizens. In addition, such meters prevent bad traffic jams. However,

177

Trying to get time on the meter with a Bank Americard may be difficult. This meter was used in San Francisco. The photo dates from 1965.

the revenue collected is really the major concern today, not the convenience it might afford the average shopper. Small coins dropped into such meters add up to a small fortune annually and fines for overtime parking total over $45,000,000 each year. The general upkeep and operating expenses take less than 30 percent of the gross, which of course comes to a very fat net profit.

In the early days of parking meters, the profit argument was not of any importance, because the cash flow was earmarked for the improvement of traffic control and street repair. All of this changed over the lapse of a few short years. Now, most towns and cities use meter money for everything under the sun, even things unrelated to traffic control. San Antonio, Texas, for example, doubled its parking meter fees and put the revenue into its police department and fire department retirement funds.

One of the biggest moneymaking parking meters ever recorded was located in Toledo, Ohio. It was placed near the collections office of a public utility and set at five-cents for a mere 15 minutes of parking. This strategic meter made $256.65 in one year of operation. Parking meters seem to do rather well, wherever they might be installed. For example, even those on the Arctic fringes make decent profits. The initial 35 meters put on the streets of Kodiak, Alaska, averaged $69.59 the first year they were in service. Parking meters usually pay for themselves within the initial year. They require little, if any, maintenance and often last for as long as 20 years. So the profit margin is obvious and huge.

Citizens have hilarious ways of sending in their parking fines, after they find their vehicle ticketed for overtime parking. One irate driver, in Seattle, Washington, paid $1.50 just to mail in a chunk of welded steel with the words, "check enclosed,"

Double parking meter for municipal parking lots was good for up to 12 hours.

painted in bright red on the outside. A college student in Pueblo, Colorado, spent 72-cents on postage, simply to mail in 100 pennies as full payment of her fine. A judge in Billings, Montana, was sent a large squash, made out as a check. This unique "check" was accepted and cashed by a local bank. And a businessman in Carson City, Nevada, explained to the judge that the meter he had parked by was frozen and didn't work. The judge didn't believe the violator and fined him $1. Soon after, the court received its payment. It came in the form of a new silver dollar, which was frozen in a block of ice.

Millions of people, throughout the world, have now become accustomed to doing business with parking meters, on the mechanical monster's terms. The ugly little metal box stands solemnly by the curb, like a robot policeman. It has become accepted as a normal part of everyday life. Although most people lose their court battles with the meter, others have been known to take more direct physical action. One angry woman in Detroit, Michigan, kicked a parking meter and broke her big toe. While she was at the doctor having it set, she received an overtime ticket for parking in front of the clinic!

Opposition to parking meters has died down, for the most part, and many communities have tried to glamorize the business with attractive "Meter Maids." In some cities, such as Waco, Texas, these policewomen also act as smiling goodwill ambassadors. They assist travelers in finding their way, while handing them pamphlets extolling local tourist attractions. No doubt, the parking meter is with us to stay. Perhaps the initial 46 years were the most difficult.

(Editor's note: The parking meter statistics in this entry date from 1981, when it was first published as an article in *Old Cars*. Today, the parking meter industry is a $17.9 million business, but revisions of the specific statistics mentioned in the text are not available.)

Seen here is a Duncan-Miller parking meter with a two-hour time limit.

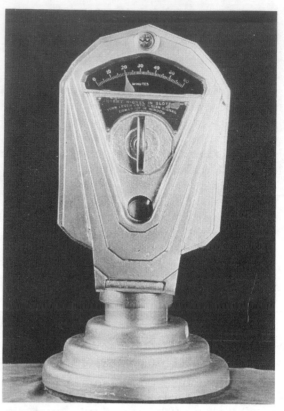

It took a nickel to purchase 20 minutes on this art deco styled meter.

A Duncan Model D-2 parking meter converted into a table lamp.

Early photo taken in the pre-meter maid days.

Guide to motoring garb of yesteryear

By Keith Marvin

Back in what is regarded as "the good old days," nearly every aspect of living presented some problem. Eighty years ago, life in general was more formal and rigid. Nearly every action, from table manners to proper attire, was governed by the book.

There were right and wrong ways of doing things then. By the book referred to the principle of acceptability in general terms. But, when it came to determining what was acceptable in the area of clothing, there was a book which was much more explicit. This was *Burberry's Proof Kit Number XVI*, which was published in London in 1904. It is one of the most revealing ... if not THE most revealing ... catalog of its time on clothing for fin de siecle ladies and gentlemen.

The hardbound, 324-page volume, replete with pen-and-ink drawings reminiscent of Charles Dana Gibson, is very rare. It is considered a collector's item today. But, 80 years ago it was considered de rigeur in the households of anyone who cared about the style and quality of their wardrobe. A great many did.

Burberry's Proof Kit Number XVI was published by Burberry's, of 30-32 Haymarket Street in London. They also maintained branches in Basingbroke, Paris, Berlin and New York.

Included in the book's pages was the absolute word on the proper attire for sport and play, formal occasions or a leopard-hunting expedition. It was a sort of English counterpart to the *Abercrombie & Fitch* catalog. And, it is still going strong.

Today, a gentleman's trench coat may be had in gabardine for as little as $675. Milady's similar garment is available for $515 or, if she opts for a ranch mink lining with detachable collar, it will cost $2,990. Not bad.

One of Burberry's specialty lines back then was focused on the motorist. By 1904, automobiles had really taken hold throughout the United Kingdom.

It's true that the cars of that day left a good deal to be desired in safety, dependability and aesthetics. However, dating back to 1898 or 1899, when Lord Montagu took the Prince of Wales (later King Edward VII) for a spin in his Daimler, an increasing number of Dukes, Marquis, Earls, Viscounts, country squires and sachems of the business world were availing themselves of the new toy. A large number of manufacturers were working around the clock to supply the demand.

The English motor car of 1904 looked very much like its counterpart in other lands. They may be seen in the Burberry sketches, which provide apt backgrounds for the modeled items of motoring garb.

Most are chain-driven, rear entrance tonneau touring cars. Occasionally, they were depicted with a windshield and a roof as special, extra-cost equipment.

In *Burberry's Proof Kit* coverage of available motoring attire was not restricted to the owner and sometimes driver, but to chauffeur uniforms as well.

The clothing was designed with infinite care. It had to be. As an example, one of the most notable safety precautions in motoring garb could be seen in the gauntlet gloves. These mitts helped motorists avoid getting entangled with the spark and other levers which many automobiles carried on the top of the steering-wheel column.

Because of a lack of a top, in many cases, water-repellency was considered a must wherever possible. A large array of coats was always in stock, ranging from the greatcoat with Inverness cape (the style so loved by Sherlock Holmes) to the "slip on" (which resembled a tent more than a coat).

There were lighter outfits, too, such as tight-fitting uniforms complete with high-button collars and puttees. One style of gauntlet mitts was even favored and supplied to His Royal Highness the Prince of Wales.

The "Burberry fifteen guinea fur coat" appears to have been one of the more popular offerings and, although it wasn't specified which animals had given up their own coats to produce it, 15 guineas represented a great deal of money in that halcyon era.

In other drawings, the aviator and the Paletot coats were show. What were they? I don't know. I don't think many knew back then because, under the names, they were respectively described as being a "traveler or wayfarer" type and "a type of loose overcoat."

One of the more interesting materials used in motoring wear was gabardine. The book included a quote from *The Country Gentleman* which stated "rain-resisting Gabardine is equal to oilskin, but without its drawbacks," whatever that meant. In the opening pages of *Burberry's Proof Kit*, readers were reminded that "The words gabardine, slimber, urber, urbitor and the letters B.Y.P. (Burberry-Yarn-Proof) are registered." It is interesting to note that garbadine may now be found in any dictionary.

The section on motoring styles is of some importance, because it is history. In a sense, it reminds us that there was a time when one thought twice about going for a drive and had to plan accordingly and dress both sensibly and properly.

Burberry suit worn by operator of a 1904 motor tricycle.

Burberry's dust wrapper.

Car watchers' guide to music videos

By Charles Webb

Michael Jackson's "Thriller" is the most elaborate and expensive music video ever made. But old car fans may consider the best thing about it the 1957 Bel Air ragtop Jackson drives at the beginning.

Although they've been around for more than 20 years, music videos with old cars have suddenly become hot "automotive" collectibles. There is an entire network ... MTV ... devoted almost exclusively to showing videos and car collectors love to tune it in.

Many of these films feature special-interest automobiles. They are a natural for new 1950s-style "rockabilly" groups such as The Stray Cats and The Fabulous Thunderbirds. But, it also seems like almost every other group uses old cars in their videos. This is great for car watchers.

However, you don't have to sit through Billy Idol singing "Dancing With Myself" to the undead, to get a peek at your favorite car. The following is a partial list of music videos with cars in them, so you can be more selective about those you watch. There are lots more.

In a few cases, I saw the video or part of it only once. So, I was not able to precisely identify the vehicle featured. Some videos, such as Jackson Browne's "Tender is the Night," have a lot of nice cars in them. In such cases, I generally mention just the most prominent one.

You may want to cut this list out and place it next to your television. That way, if you find out a particular video is going to be shown, you'll be prepared to record it on tape.

Cars have long been associated with musical recording artists. This late-1950s customized "dream car" was connected to singer James Darrin and survives in a St. Louis, Missouri museum today.

Car watchers' guide to music videos

SONG	ARTIST	CAR
"Bad Girls"	Don Felder	Mercedes convertible
"Big Log"	Robert Plant	1955 Bel Air convertible
"Brass in the Pocket"	The Pretenders	1959 Cadillac four-door hardtop
"Church of the Poison Mind"	Culture Club	1959 Cadillac convertible
"Cry, Cry, Cry"	Neil Young	1957 Eldorado convertible
"Cut Loose"	Paul Rodgers	1952 Cadillac four-door sedan
"Gimme All Your Lovin'"	ZZ Top	1932 Ford "Deuce" coupe
"Hot Girls in Love"	Loverboy	1940 Ford coupe
"How Do You Spell Love"	The Fabulous Thunderbirds	1956 Thunderbird
"I'm Still Standing"	Elton John	Rolls-Royce convertible
"I Want a New Drug"	Huey Lewis & The News	Porsche
"I Won't Stand in Your Way"	The Stray Cats	1951 (?) Mercury coupe
"My Town"	Michael Stanley Band	1955 Ford convertible
"New Frontier"	Donald Fagen	1956 (?) Buick
"New Song"	Howard Jones	Rolls-Royce
"Our Lips Are Sealed"	The Go Gos	1960 Buick convertible
"Sexy & 17"	The Stray Cats	Various street rods
"Sharp Dressed Man"	ZZ Top	1932 Ford "Deuce" coupe
"Should I Stay or Should I Go"	Clash	1959 Cadillac convertible
"Street of Dreams"	Rainbow	Jaguar XJ sedan
"Tender is the Night"	Jackson Browne	1956 Chevrolet convertible
"Thriller"	Michael Jackson	1957 Chevrolet convertible
"Why Me?"	Planet P	1958 (?) Cadillac two-door hardtop
"Wonderin'"	Neil Young	1957 Eldorado convertible
"Uptown Girl"	Billy Joel	Rolls-Royce
"You Make My Heart Beat Faster"	Kim Carnes	1966 (?) Mustang convertible

The Ever Popular RICK NORCROSS and his Wonder Guitar

Some entertainers use old cars on albumn covers, as well as in music videos. This is the cover of the "Nash-Full" album featuring the "ever-popular Rick Norcross and his Wonder Guitar."

The "NashFull" album features several songs with "automotively" inspired titles, such as "Sleeping with My Lady" (remember the Nash Travel Bed?); "Plain Jane" (slang for base model), and "NashFull Rag."

Auto art in bronze

By Dennis Schrimpf

Artists are special people. We don't all agree on what makes an artist special, but we can all agree that some artists are special. Stanley Wanlass is one of those special artists.

I talked with Stanley Wanlass at Hershey several years ago. He was there for the unveiling of his newest sculpture, "The Passing of the Horse." This three- foot high masterpiece depicted the epic confrontation of the horse and the automobile.

Minute detailing was seen everywhere in the sculpture. The more you looked at the piece, the more little nuances you noticed, including a dog running alongside the car; a little girl in the back seat clutching her teddy bear; a picnic lunch, complete with bronze watermelon, strapped on behind; a worried expression on the face of a woman beside the driver; an old cowboy (who was fighting to keep a way of life from changing) with a weathered face; and a look of determination etched into the driver's countenance. All this and more is captured in this magnificent artwork.

Stanley Wanlass readily admitted that Peter Helck, America's premier auto artist, is an inspiration to him. It shows! The same fantastic flair for motion, that Helck is so famous for, is also accurately captured in bronze by Wanlass. The subject matter is similar, too. His focus is on the early era of automotive history.

Other well-known Wanlass sculptures include a depiction of the famous New York-to-Paris race of 1908. The car seen in this work is, of course, the famous Thomas-Flyer.

Wanlass doesn't confine his talent to just automotive subjects. A 32-ton sculpture commissioned for the city of Everett, Washington and a prize-winning bicentennial medal, designed for the state of Oregon, are other good examples of the Wanlass touch.

Being a history buff, Stanley Wanlass is used to extensive researching of his subjects. The sculpture commissioned by the Fort Clatsop National Memorial depicts the famous Lewis and Clark expedition's arrival at the Pacific Ocean. Although Lewis and Clark were never on the beach together at the same time, Wanlass felt comfortable taking artistic license to "stretch the truth" and bring them together in a dramatic recreation.

Stanley Wanlass with his sculpture "The Passing of the Horse."

The Wanlass sculptures are limited editions. Most are issued in editions of 30 numbered copies. They are usually sold out within a matter of weeks.

The sculpture pictured here originally sold for $27,000. It is probably worth a great deal more than that today.

It takes almost 1,000 man-hours to complete each bronze sculpture. Casting is a most intricate and delicate procedure and the amount of finishing time is enormous. The field of automotive art is expanding rapidly. This field is fortunate to have Stanley Wanlass as an active contributor.

Intricate detailing was an important element of the $27,000 bronze sculpture by Stanley Wanlass. The artist feels that his works depicting early motoring scenes were inspired by his appreciation for the art of Peter Helck.

"Two Thoroughbreds" is another Stanley Wanlass piece showing Phil Hill in a Ferrari race car.

Toy Autos

The pedal car: every boy's dream

By Al Marwick

A line drawing of a pedal car was the choice, when we established a logo for the business card announcing our antiques store.

We never owned a pedal car in our childhood. A tricycle, a coaster wagon and a two-wheel scooter we had. Being addicted to automobile mania upon graduation from cradle to playpen, any toy with wheels was imagined by us an automobile. For the collector headed in any hobby direction, the psychologists say it begins very early and continues both in or out of our subconscious.

The "Duesenberg" of the sidewalks, the pedal car, was the ultimate luxury of a youngster's imagination. As a wheeled toy, they were more plentiful than believed, but rest assured you, they never appeared in our neighborhood in the rollicking, golden 1920s.

You could make believe a tricycle was an automobile, but a pedal car really looked like one. In acceleration and handling, we could run rings around any pedal car with a three-wheeler, but it never really did resemble a runabout or roadster.

The decades rolled on. The adolescent years, the college years, the war years, the make-a-living years came and went. Then, the frivolous years arrived. Those grandiose, frivolous years brought our first pedal car.

The first person (they, we, us and our when applicable) includes my young partner, my son, who was even younger then. He didn't at all mind basking in the old man's frivolity.

If our first pedal car was a Cadillac, (that name was painted on its radiator) it didn't, otherwise, live up to Cadillac's image as a luxury marque. The Gendron Wheel Company of Toledo, Ohio obviously marketed it as a price-leader. When we purchased it, the pedal car still had $9.95 written in crayon, below the Cadillac script.

We had better make some differentiation here between the line drawing on our business card and our first pedal car. They both have Cadillac emblazoned across their radiators. However, the business card shows a more deluxe model with bicycle wheels instead of wagon wheels. It also shows fenders, stop lights and a hood ornament. I don't know who made the business card Cadillac. It could also be a Gendron.

When I brought the plainer (Gendron) Cadillac from Rock Island, Illinois to Monterey, California, I immediately put it in our antiques store window. However, the first customer interested in it pounded on the door the next morning. He hoped to hold us to our $9.95 crayon price or report us to the Better Business Bureau.

The toy came out of the window. We hung it from the ceiling and put aside immediate and massive inflationary ideas. Then, we erased the crayon price and placed a "not for sale sign" on it. Even with the regrettable erasure, the faint outline of the original price can still be seen.

With simulated headlights of wood (instead of metal) and no fenders, running boards, windshield, pneumatic balloon tires or fanciful accessories, our Cadillac-in-name-only qualified, not only as a price leader, but also as the most authentic stripped-down "cheapie."

Cars like this "Packard of the sidewalk" were the ultimate luxuries of a youngster's imagination. It has many accessories, an opening door, a folding top and functional rumbleseat. Such wheeled toys, now rare, were plentiful.

Pedal car expert Tom Crotty unearthed this example of the Model 153 Gendron Packard roadster in rough, but restorable condition. Crotty uses a drawing of this luxury pedal car on his business card. (Tom Crotty photo)

This pedal car bore an original license plate with the number 4-406. What it lacked in luxury options, was made up for with a rich personal history. Its condition was also mint and original.

The story related to us by the seller, another antique dealer, gave virtual pictorial title in the form of a round, framed photograph. It accompanied the purchase and showed a boy (maybe six-years-old) seated behind the wheel with his dog. An American flag was planted behind him, indicating that the picture might have been taken in celebration of a holiday.

The seller informed me the little boy died shortly afterward and the grieving parents kept the toy in the attic of their Davenport, Iowa residence for Over 50 Years. The treasured pedal car was a commemoration of remembrance. Upon liquidation of the estate, it came out of the attic. The antique dealer obtained it and sold it to us. We became the second registered owners, so to speak.

This ends the personal history of our Gendron juvenile auto, but to give expanse to the subject, we found a Gendron advertisement from the April 1930 issue of *Toy World*, a playthings marketing magazine. This pedal vehicle advertisement covered the entire market from the cheapie Cadillac to more sophisticated classic roadsters, supercharged racers and Tri-motor airplanes. The miniature rumbleseat roadster, with its bulb horn, vertically-standing spotlight, windshield wings and convenience step for the rumbleseat, was a Packard. Its marque is not named in advertising layout, but I've seen a specimen with a Packard nameplate affixed to the radiator. The Packard model for the advertisement carried the exact same style license plate as the cheapie Cadillac, but had license number 6-634.

It has always been (and perhaps always will be) in the very young child's imagination to want to get behind the wheel of something his or her size. Today, they may prefer a space ship or an airplane. Still, they want to steer something that's moving ... preferably moving fast. As space cadets, junior size, return to earth eventually, they also dream about learning to drive on earth. The pedal car is just the thing for this.

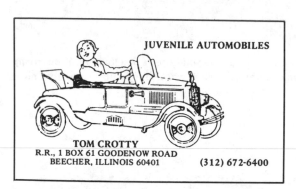

JUVENILE AUTOMOBILES

TOM CROTTY
R.R., 1 BOX 61 GOODENOW ROAD
BEECHER, ILLINOIS 60401   (312) 672-6400

Author isn't the only one that uses fancy Packard pedal car on calling card.

Most pedal cars found at swap meets need some restoration.

The juvenile motor car wasn't limited to the pedal style in the early days of the automobile, For the discriminating buyer there were gas, steam and electric miniature, too.

Some manufacturers of full-sized cars produced limited editions of electric and gasoline juvenile models. In France, Andre Citroen made one, along with a complete line of children's cars in various sizes. Citroen felt that, if a child grew up playing with a Citroen toy, he or she would be most prone to buy the real thing upon reaching adulthood. Bugatti also produced a line of electric-powered children's vehicles.

At East Moline, Illinois, in the mid-1920s, a man named Fred Lundahl advanced one of his pressed steel toy trucks into the first prototype of a Buddy L pedal truck. He never risked putting it on the market, since he had his hands full with manufacturing smaller push-and-pull toys. However, numerous other firms explored the pedal car market.

Besides the trade name Gendron, pedal car names also included Steelcraft (produced by Murray Ohio of Cleveland, Ohio) Garton, of Sheboygan, Wisconsin and American National. Certainly, there were others.

To help children associate their juvenile cars with dad's car, the makers gave them names of the real ones. The popular marques of the day included Essex, Nash, Oldsmobile, Buick, Packard, Cadillac, Dodge, Lincoln and Hudson.

This miniature rumbleseat roadster, with its double-bar bumper, headlights, windshield, screw-on hubcaps, door handles, upholstery and top was a replica of the 1925 Packard. Robert Schultz of Oakland Pedal Cars owns this one.

Profile view of Tom Crotty's unrestored Gendron Packard with the "passenger" door open and the rumbleseat in raised position. The runningboards are missing, but the fancy step plates are still attached. (Tom Crotty photo)

What's being done in pedal car collecting today? In contrast to hand-toys, they pose a slight storage problem, but they are being gathered just as avidly as any other automotive artifact. Advanced collectors are, of necessity, getting more and more into restoration. To find a pedal car of any vintage in good to excellent condition is much harder than finding a representative hand toy.

The antique pedal car has modern counterparts, with a limited selection still being produced, but production today is nothing compared to the past. Also missing, in most cases, is the quality and detail of the past.

We have come full-circle with the pedal car. It was one of the most affluent of toys for its era. It was found in the villas of Beverly Hills and Hollywood, the Gold Coast of Chicago's north shore and on the estates of Long Island in New York. But, it was also seen everywhere else, although often in stripped-down form. The *Sears* catalogs and *Montgomery-ward* catalog had plenty of pedal cars to be admired and desired by every red-blooded American child; particularly those smitten forever with the incurable disease called automobile mania.

To help children associate their juvenile cars with dad's car, the makers gave them names of the real ones. The popular marques of the day included Essex, Nash, Oldsmobile, Buick, Packard, Cadillac, Dodge, Lincoln and Hudson.

Kid cars

By Gordon Schindler

A typical "kid car" of the early 1920s heads this entry, merely because it is the most appealing illustration available. In all probability, it was a cyclecar, not strictly a kid car at all. It was part of some long-forgotten promotion contest, a slogan or subscription contest. "Hey Fred! I won this auto; it's a dandy," the young driver calls out.

Another popular magazine of 1910 ran a drawing of an interesting and obviously practical design created by Ralph W. Dunkle, a boy with a mechanical bent living in Greenville, Ohio. The article revealed, "The body of this homemade car consists of a light wooden frame and floor, from the center of which rises a galvanized shield."

Features of similar, contemporary kid cars with no springs, a plain wooden seat and a slipping rope clutch were "standard" features. The spare tire also served as the back of the seat. "The engine is rated at two horsepower and gets up a speed of 15 miles an hour" the article stated.

In 1918, under the heading "A Boys' Motor Car," a *Popular Mechanics* how-to article began "Even though the home-built bearcat roadster does not compare in every detail with the luxurious manufactured cars, it has an individuality that puts it in a class by itself.

"The amateur mechanic, or the ambitious boy, who is fairly skilled with tools, can build at least the main parts of his own small car. A motorcycle engine or other small gasoline motor is used for the power plant." A drawing detailing construction of this kiddy-type version of the then-very-popular Stutz Bearcat was offered.

Not to be out-done, *Popular Science*, also in a 1918 issue, presented somewhat simplified plans for a "Small Car Made of Bicycle Parts and a Motorcycle Engine." The wheels, sprockets, chains, etc., which were used in making this car, were taken from an old discarded bicycle, according to the article. The engine was rated at four horsepower. Like the *Popular Mechanics'* design, this one also used a slipping belt as a clutch. As power was only applied to one wheel, "it is not necessary to have a differential" the article added.

No springs were deemed necessary, as "The frame of the car is made of one-inch oak which gives a spring when the wheels pass over a bump," added the magazine. The steering gear, as well as the seat cushion and other small attachments were purchased from a second-hand automobile dealer. "An isinglass windshield protects the driver's face and permits a clear view ahead" the article concluded. (Remember isinglass?)

The Niagara Motor Bob appeared in a 1913 advertisement. Kid customers were given their choice of either an American-type hood or the French-type hood. The latter was patterned after the Renault's hood. For pure ugliness, it couldn't be surpassed. Plans for either model were available for only 20-cents. Parts were also available for these early kit cars.

A 1920 English car with compressed air motor. The kid-driver had a foot pump.

They also came with a direct-to-consumer arrangement. In the early days of the auto industry, many real cars were sold that way. In more recent years, Avanti II tried this form of merchandising.

An English kid car of 1920 was operated by a power plant that didn't use liquid fuel. It had a compressed air motor. As the magazine copy with the picture said "When his car is out of 'fuel,' this young driver charges the compressed air tank with a foot pump and drives on."

Disc wheels, full-length fenders and a windshield (pardon me, a windscreen), all added up to a very realistic little buggy. Unfortunately, no figures are available on the number of cylinders, displacement or air-power output of the engine. It was, however, apparently sufficient for the driver to roam around the backyard or to "hot rod" down the sidewalk to the accompaniment of its hissing exhaust. No muffler was necessary, or even desirable, to silence the hiss. The young driver could imagine he was at the throttle of a giant steam locomotive. No pollutants in the air exhaust either!

A really practical kid car was the buckboard powered by a "motor wheel." Buckboards were also powered by on-board gas engines and electric motors. They rode the crest of their popularity roughly from 1915 to 1925.

The motorized power wheels were made by several firms, including A.O. Smith and Briggs & Stratton. The buckboard, however, wasn't made primarily for kids. It could be street-driven with comparative safety, considering the traffic of the period, at speeds up to 25 miles per hour.

No clutch was used on such vehicles. Idling during standstill periods was accomplished by pressing on a clutch pedal, bringing up the motor wheel and breaking contact with the road. Letting out the clutch gently moved the buckboard forward. There was no reverse and only one forward speed.

Copy from a Briggs & Stratton advertisement of 1919 read in part: "This sporty little Briggs & Stratton Flyer is one of the most popular motor conveyances ever brought out for young America ... equipped with pneumatic tires steered by means of a wheel just like an automobile ... a foot-brake is provided in order to facilitate stopping the car.

" . . . Power is derived from a Type D Briggs & Stratton Motor Wheel ... Simple to operate and safe in the hands of any boy or girl . . . an ideal vehicle of transportation for young folks, although hundreds of grown-ups have taken enthusiastically to the use of the Flyer as a convenient and enjoyable method of transportation for both business and pleasure.

"... The upkeep is almost negligible ... Just imagine riding over 80 miles on one gallon of gasoline, at the rate of between 4 and 25 miles an hour, along some delightful boulevard or over the picturesque coun-

A typical "kid car" of the early 1920s. It was the prize in some long-forgotten sales promotion or contest. "Hey Fred! I won this auto; it's a dandy," the youthful driver calls out.

try road with a charming young lady for a companion ..." Even then, in advertisements catering to young Americans, they injected a little sex. Earlier, the makers of buggies had done the same thing.

The "easy-to-build" Shaw Cycle Car was not a real cyclecar, but another buckboard with an engine compartment. Plans to build it were available from Shaw Manufacturing Company of Galesburg, Kansas. No motorcycle parts appear to have been used in its construction. It was not powered by a motorcycle engine. The engine was listed as a 2-1/2-horsepower Shaw motor.

Advertising copy stated that the Shaw Speedster could carry two passengers, but a drawing showed only one seat for passengers. "A real automobile" the ad boasted. Hardly, but it must have looked very appealing to kids of the time.

An even more attractive kid car, circa 1932, was available from Syco Sales Company of Toledo, Ohio. This was neither a kit car nor a complete car offering. The copy merely suggested that interested boys "Send 50-cents today for detailed building plans, simplified so you can easily build this car." It does appear to have been a street-worthy little vehicle and was obviously patterned after contemporary dirt-track racers. Equally obvious was the fact that it was not a car that "any boy of 12" could build, as other advertisements proclaimed.

The end of the 1930s did not bring the demise of kid cars. A 1947 advertisement for a "Motor Car" powered by an automobile starter was placed by Constructive Enterprises of Dayton, Ohio. Such motive power was obviously incompatible with the claim in the copy that it was "a swell deluxe model that travels over the highways just like big car."

The safety factor was conspicuous by its complete absence. Operating such a motor car on the street would have been very dangerous, indeed, not to mention illegal in most areas.

None of these vehicles seem to have been very commercially successful and few, if any, later examples of the genre can be found. Mopeds and bicycles seem to have emerged triumphantly as contemporary transportation for the younger generation.

The home-built bearcat isn't luxurious, but had a classy individuality.

A really practical kid car was the buckboard powered by a "motor wheel."

An attractive 1932 car was available from Syco Sales Company of Toledo, Ohio.

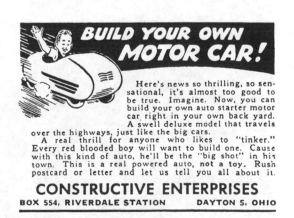

A 1947 ad for a kid car, powered by a starter, was run by a Dayton, Ohio firm.

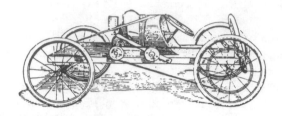

This kid car has a light wood frame and floor and galvanized center shield.

The easy-to-build Shaw Cycle Car was a buckboard with an engine compartment.

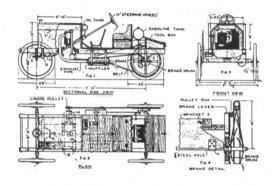

A 1910 kid car with no springs, a plain wood seat and a slipping rope clutch.

This very professionally constructed homemade kids' car came to an auction.

Historical survey of pedal cars 1900-1983

By John A. Gunnell

Pedal cars seem to be capturing the interest of more collectors than ever before. Older versions of these toys have been collected for many years, but now even the newer models of the 1950s and 1960s are rising in popularity and value.

This article is intended as a brief survey of pedal car history and recent collector trends. The information presented is based on a combination of personal research combined with facts extracted from a number of sources. Published references are listed at the end. The current prices given are from flea market vendors and dealer-asked prices. The article does not cover childrens' cars powered by electric, steam, gas, air or spring-wound motors, all of which usually sell at higher prices. It concentrates on metal-bodied pedal cars.

The Primitives: 1900-1908

The first pedal cars appeared during this period. They were basic in design and construction, being built on a simple frame of wood rails. Spoked bicycle wheels with thin, hard-rubber tires mounted on straight metal axles were attached via metal springs at the front and by metal brackets at the rear. Sheet Metal and wood parts were used to fashion a radiator, hood, cowl and bucket type seat. A direct-drive, pedal-type linkage system was most common, but some chain-drive versions may have been sold.

These cars were originally priced $4 to $10 dollars. Names of real cars such as Ford, Locomobile and Reliance, were sometimes painted across the radiator. Other models such as the Kirk Letty Flyer were "generic" types. Popular manufacturers included Gendron, Swan and Fenton.

Today, these cars are thought of primarily as "museum pieces." They look fragile and seem somewhat less durable than later types. Many owners use them for decorative purposes, as conversation items or as furniture (i.e. as a planter or liquor cabinet).

(Note: Toy collectors disdain restoration. They prefer replacing worn parts only. They feel that refinishing a toy will destroy original markings and decals, thus reducing its value. A nice original is generally most valuable).

The Racers: 1909-1919

These pedal cars were essentially larger, fancier versions of the more primitive types. They were often patterned after speedsters or raceabouts of the day. They measured about 12 to 14 inches wide and three- to four-feet long. Original prices remained in the $4 to $10 range, with the most expensive editions having dummy gas tanks and windshields.

Some popular models were the Star, Dodge, Green Auto Racer, "Speed King" auto racer, Dan Patch "Big Racer" and the American Auto Racer. The latter was one of the fanciest. It included a hood mascot, front and rear fenders, license plate, headlights, cowl lamps, bumpers and horn or siren. It was built by American National, of Toledo, Ohio. Other popular pedal cars of the day were made by Gendron, Garton, Murray-Ohio, Steelcraft and Wescott.

The first pedal cars were basic in design and construction, being built on a simple frame of wood rails. Spoked bicycle wheels with thin, hard-rubber tires were mounted on straight metal axles. This one is a racing car.

This looks like an antique toy collector's vision of heaven with toys from coaster wagons to bicycles. Note the classic pedal cars along the back wall and the pedal cars and airplanes along the wall to the right of the photo.

These "racers" bring moderately high prices. Some are much more valuable, though. They are actually sturdy enough for children to use, although such use is getting rare. Lucky kids who have an opportunity to "drive" one are supervised carefully by value-conscious adult collectors.

The Classics: 1920-1934

It would seen likely that the lightweight racers continued into the 1920s, but, by the early years of that decade, a new type of pedal car was also evolving. Sturdier and much more elaborate than earlier types, these classic- looking models marked a zenith of prewar pedal car development.

The more expensive models, selling for $25 to $40, looked like scaled-down copies of the Buicks, Packards, Cadillacs, Peerless limousines, Stutz raceabouts and Pierce-Arrow touring cars owned by the lucky childrens' parents. Full miniature coach work was fitted (sometimes with opening doors) and they were heavily accessorized with lamps, windshields, dummy folding tops, runningboards, step plates, sidemounted spare tires, upholstery and mini-sized touring trunks.

Pedal cars of this era ... at least the expensive ones ... had many realistic "technical" features such as electric lighting, functional gearshift mechanisms, Alemite lubrication, balloon tires mounted on roller bearing disc wheels, brakes, shock absorbers, functional springs, plated double-bar bumpers, nickle-plated trimmings and genuine Duco finish.

American National Toy Company cataloged over 30 models for 1923, including two which are considered ultra-valuable today. They are the Packard coupe and the tandem-drive Packard dual-cowl phaeton.

At Hershey 10 years ago, we once saw a banged-up Packard roadster for sale. The asking price, then, started at $200. Restored, it was worth about 10 times as much. It sold for $190. Today, it would be next to impossible to touch one at that level. Mint originals could go extremely high. Even more desirable, according to experts, were the Packard coupe and phaeton. The coupe was worth $8,000 a decade ago!

The Streamliners: 1935-1944

Although some of the very elaborate pedal car offerings might have lasted into the depression era, the late 1930s are generally characterized by stylish, but simpler models. The majority sported a highly streamlined appearance related to the look of real automobiles in this era.

These cars were still constructed of heavy gauge metal weighing 45- to 65-pounds. They sold for $11 to $25. They had eight-, nine- or 10-inch diameter artillery spoke wheels and measured 14- to 18-inches wide and 36- to 55-inches long.

Most of these cars featured elaborate grilles, hood ornaments, windshields, headlights, hubcaps and squeeze-horns. The majority had separate pontoon-type fenders and some even had fender skirts. External exhausts, two-tone paint treatments, electric lights and functional windshield wipers were common on deluxe types. Identifiable favorites included the Ford, Lincoln-Zephyr and Chrysler (Airflow). Others were generically named Streamliner, SuperCharger, Fire Truck and Dump Truck.

The leading makers of this period seem to be Garton Toy Company, the Toledo Toy Company, the Murray-Ohio Company, Steelcraft and Skippy. In 1937, Garton produced at least 200 streamlined "Silver Streak" roadsters which Pontiac Motor Division distributed at a factory worker's Christmas party. These are exceptionally rare.

Early Postwar: 1945-1954

Pedal cars of the early postwar years are basically similar to the Streamliner type, but usually slightly plainer. Separate pontoon fenders and bumpers were replaced by more integrated stampings, using one-piece bumper/grilles and faired-in fender lines.

The asking prices on these models seem to be $250 to $1,000 and they are popular. But, this period also brought in new types of pedal cars which command somewhat steeper values. One of these is a Murray-Ohio built replica of James Dean's customized 1949 Mercury. F.A.O. Schwarz, the famous New York City millionaire's toy store, also imported a limited number of Ferrari racing cars built by Giordani in Italy. Patterned after Juan Fangio's Grand Prix winner, this car sold for $395 new. It is valued $1,500 to $2,000 today.

Another desirable pedal car from the early 1950s is the Kidillac. This replica of a 1953 Eldorado convertible came in different trims and originally sold from $30 up.

The "Flat Hoods": 1955-1970s

Following the design trends of full-sized cars, pedal car makers modernized their creations in this period. Flat hoods, quad headlights and fin-shaped rear fenders appeared on both real cars and toys of this era.

Two of the most popular models of this period were the traditional Fire Chief car and its companion the Dump Truck. There is also an Indianapolis Pace Car version of one design. Murray-Ohio and AMF

Although some of the very elaborate offerings may have lasted into the depression era, the late 1930s are generally characterized by stylish, but simpler pedal cars. This is the popular Garton racer.

One of the earliest pedal cars was this 1912 Dan Patch roadster that Mark Thiessen photographed for the National Geographic Society during its 1990 exhibit entitled "Automobilia: Fact, Fun & Fantasy."

appear as the predominant manufacturers. Slowly, but surely, other firms were dropping out of the business or switching to molded Plastic, push-type miniatures. The author purchased a pedal car for one of his sons, in the early 1970s, and feels it must have been one of the last metal-bodied versions. Soon thereafter, the plastic "Big Wheel" trike appeared and the metal pedal cars gradually vanished.

The pedal cars of the "flat hood" era were characteristically longer, lower and wider than their predecessors. Materials and construction didn't change drastically until the end, although the sheet metal seemed to be of lighter gauge. It was, however, more corrosion-resistant than that used on older models. The use of plated metal ornamentation disappeared and plastic hubcaps and accessories came into use.

As with real postwar cars, asking prices on these toys go all over the board, although they are always increasing. A very nice Indy Pace Car version, displayed at Hershey '93, had a firm $700 asking price.

Even more valuable are low-production types which represent replicas of real automobiles such as mid-1950s Pontiacs, late-1950s Mercurys, Corvettes, Thunderbirds, Mustangs and GTOs. One candy apple red Mustang convertible, that was originally sold as a Ford dealer promotional item, will bring $250 in poor condition and an easy $500 in top shape with all of the hubcaps intact. There are replicas of the Mustang with prices starting around $250, which keeps the prices paid for originals from going too much higher.

At the Carlisle and Hershey swap meets a number of years ago, well-known automobilia dealer Charles Schalebaum, of Ridgewood, New Jersey, displayed a new-old-stock (NOS) 1957 Corvette pedal car. It featured a functional three-speed transmission and white fiberglass body.

Today, plastic-bodied pedal cars are the norm. Modern toy catalogs list dozens of different styles. These toys are both functional and durable, but they lack the nostalgic feeling evoked in car collectors by older pedal cars. At least one company, Hagstrom's Sales Limited of Atlanta, Georgia, re-entered the medal pedal car manufacturing business in the 1980s. It offered Fire Chief and U.S. Army cars. The owner of the firm, who collected vintage bicycles and Mustang pedal cars, saw a market for his new models among the children of adult collectors.

And why not? While dad restores his Gendron Packard roadster or Kidillac, junior can cruise the backyard without fear of scraping an irreplaceable fender or scratching original decals.

References: 1) *Automobile Quarterly*, Volume 12 Number 1, 1974 (three articles); 2) Beverly Hills Pedal Car Company, press release (Joe Molino Public Relations), September 1983; 3) *Best of Old Cars*, Volumes II and III ("Toy Symbols of Old Cars" by Al Marwick); 4) *Car Collector* and *Car Classics*, Volume 6, Number 12, December 1983; 5) *Antique Toy World*, Volume 13, Number 7, July 1983; 6) *Cars for Kids*, Edoardo Massucci, 1983 (available from used book dealers); 7) *Automobilia of Europe: Reference and Price Guide*, Gordon Gardiner and Alistair Morris, Antique Collectors' Club Limited (available from Motorbooks International, Osceola, WI 54020.

Most of the late 1930s pedal cars featured elaborate grilles, hood ornaments, windshields, headlights, hubcaps and squeeze-horns. The majority had separate pontoon-type fenders and some even had fender skirts.

One candy apple red Mustang convertible was originally sold as a Ford dealer promotional item. It's hard to find with all of the hubcaps intact.

Popular pedal cars of the 1920s came from Gendron, Garton, Murray-Ohio, Steelcraft and Wescott. Many had names of big cars on the radiator to help the kids identify with dad. This little clown's car seems to have a Chevy badge.

Battery powered Kingsbury

By Al Marwick

A trip found us in New England for the turning of foliage from summer to autumn. No one should be deprived of the beauty of this scene. While there, I made it a point to rendezvous, for a few days, at the base of the White Mountains in Keene, New Hampshire. The history of a toy's origin is part of the romance of the hobby, just as it is for the background of every big car. Keene is the home of the Kingsbury Machine Tool Manufacturing Company, once the maker of Kingsbury Toys.

The toy maker Arcade worked with cast iron. Kingsbury worked with pressed steel. The first firm went out of business at the start of World War II, some 52 years ago. Unlike Arcade, Kingsbury continued in business into modern times. It did this by producing custom-made parts processing systems, rather than toys.

If Kingsbury wasn't always toys, it wasn't always Kingsbury either. It started out as Wilkins Toy Company, another famous name. Harry T. Kingsbury, the young owner of a bicycle shop in Keene, bought out Wilkins in 1894. Then, in 1918, he renamed the company.

A third link in the Kingsbury chain was the, Keystone Toy Company of Boston. In 1942, they bought the manufacturing equipment for making the toys from Kingsbury. Keystone produced a few models for a short time following World War II.

David A. Piper, a company officer involved in development engineering, was our first contact at Kingsbury. He was a descendent of Dennis Piper, who started the firm before Wilkins and Kingsbury. It began, in 1875, with the manufacture of sewing machines, clothes wringers and the like.

To interject still another name, Piper later joined with members of the Colony family. They included a Colony son-in-law, named James Wilkins, Jr. In 1890, the Colonys and Mr. Wilkins founded the Wilkins Toy Company. Twenty-eight years passed before it became Kingsbury Machine Tool.

Kingsbury has never relinquished a feeling for the nostalgic toy business. At their Keene plant, they reserve an area called the Architectural Room for display of their toy products. These range from a horse-drawn carriage made of cast iron dating from the Wilkins days, through products of the transition period, to automotive and pressed steel types from the Kingsbury era.

Besides their own informal display, Kingsbury has loaned the best of the specimens to the Colony House Museum in Keene. The Colony family is a part of Kingsbury history and Horatio Colony, Keene's first mayor, made his home in the present museum.

The modern company frequently used pictures and text, in advertising and public relation materials, that referred to its participation in toy manufacture. It was quick to tie its heritage to what was termed the "last stronghold of Yankee craftsmanship."

From our contact with David Piper at the Kingsbury plant, we were led to the Colony House Museum on West Street in Keene. The imposing 160-year-old, brick, residence houses collections of the Historical Society of Cheshire County. Naturally, they include Wilkins and Kingsbury toys.

Kingsbury Toys are famous for their faithful replication of the automobile styles of the eras in which they were produced. It should be remembered that designing a toy automobile is not merely an effort in

A Kingsbury copy of the famous Greyhound "Silver Sides" bus.

minutely following the details of the original. The cost of producing an exact miniature would put the price of the toy far out of the mass market. The task is to blend details so that the car will have the appearance of reality with the smallest number of parts.

It was important, even years ago, that the toy be free of sharp edges. Hopefully, it could be designed with safety in mind and in a manner that would not damage mama's grand piano when the child was acting out a head-on crash with an immovable object. Kingsbury primarily made toys of a light sheet steel, while its predecessor, Wilkins, dealt mostly with cast iron.

Kids of the 1920s and 1930s (I was one of them) could usually pick a Hudson Terraplane from a Lincoln-Zephyr before they could read. Good replication was important then, just as it seems paramount now to serious collectors. As we grow up to be adult Collector's of the very toys we played with years ago, we tend to want the same things from them.

When Chrysler introduced its DeSoto and Chrysler Airflows in 1934, Kingsbury got into production with the miniature variety. The toy was 13 inches long overall, about an inch longer than models in the 1928-1932 "Classic" toy series that preceded it.

As Chrysler made running changes in designing the Airflow trunks and grilles from 1934 to 1937, Kingsbury followed suit with its toy versions.

A Kingsbury advertising layout, which did the Chrysler Airflow no harm, read "Son and Father Agree." It pictured Dad's real Airflow and Johnny's little one. Both father and son were smiling into the camera with their prized possessions. Had Chrysler's advertising agency been sharper, maybe it would have picked up the cue and used the father and son theme in national advertising. However, those were the depression years and most advertising space was devoted to "hard selling" of the car's features.

Kingsbury Toys had appeal to other advertising agencies, though. Many old-timers will remember the slogan, "Motorist's Wise, Simonize." Do they recall how Simonize portrayed an attractive young, lady sitting with legs crossed, with a Kingsbury Airflow in her lap. Of course, the toy's steel was polished to a maximum Simonize gloss.

Although the Kingsbury Airflow series was significant and pertinent to a car ahead of its time, the Classic Series far outshines it as a source of collectibles today. They were popularized as motor-driven units, made of first-quality, light-to-medium gauge steel. They were finished in baked enamel or automobile lacquer. The motor-drive springs were quite durable.

The Classic toys and Airflows differed in tire equipment, too. In the earlier series, made from 1928 to 1932, the rubber tires were vulcanized onto the steel wheels. Deeper into the depression, the Airflows used solid rubber tires on wood wheels. Some rubber tires on steel wheels appeared, but the rubber was not vulcanized.

The Classic Series models represented composite designs. They were styled like cars of the era with characteristic landau irons, rumbleseats and exposed trunks. By 1931, electric headlights and taillights were introduced. These were soon followed by Kingsbury music box radios. Still another option on Kingsbury toys, although it only applied to Airflows, was an electric horn. The accessories were operated by one standard flashlight battery mounted under the chassis. Toward the end of the Classic Series, some of the toys were given a touch of greater realism when a "Body By Fisher" decal was placed low on the front, cowl and right side.

Besides a Cabriolet Coupe and top-down roadster in the Classic Series, there were three closed cars: a two-window Brougham; a three-window seven-passenger sedan; and an open chauffeured Town Car. All were spun off the Brougham body shell. There was also a truck series and a Station Wagon.

A pair of British race cars and their respective drivers were renowned at the time. Kingsbury produced toy versions of the famed "Bluebird" driven by Sir Malcolm Campbell and the almost equally famous Sunbeam made famous by Major Seagrave.

The toy cars covered for this Kingsbury story had retail prices of $1 to $3.50. Foremost in every reader's mind at this point, I should imagine, is "What are they worth today?" This is a matter of condition, rarity, emotional identification, a willing buyer and a good, negotiable cheek.

For inspiration while writing about Kingsbury Toys, I placed my most recent Classic Series acquisition before me as I type. It's a two-window Brougham with landau irons embossed on the sail panel and an exposed box trunk towards center. The body is a deep forest green with lighter green fenders. A light tan fabric roof is simulated. Orange wheels and striping are set off with white rubber tires that mimic wide whitewalls. To replace the battery, one slides the metal cover back and inserts a 10-cent cell with its bottom towards the front of the toy. The light bulbs are 2.2-volt units. If necessary to replace, one unscrews the reflectors on the front lights or taillight and pulls out a brass clip.

This is my Kingsbury Brougham. A Classic that doesn't burn gas or use lots of oil. When I put it on parade, I don't worry about vapor lock. Will the lights work? If not, simply find me another battery.

When Chrysler introduced its DeSoto and Chrysler Airflows in 1934, Kingsbury got into production with the miniature variety. The toy was 13 inches long overall, about an inch longer than models in the 1928-1932 "Classic" series.

Early cast iron toy cars symbolize horseless carriages

By Al Marwick

I personally consider the description antique toy far too broad. Beyond the question of how old something must be to qualify as an antique, people ask things such as, "Antique what?" or "Are we talking about Greek, Roman, European, Oriental or American?"

The misuse of the word antique will never be eradicated. Nevertheless, I like to brush past it and get into specifics. Let's focus on some really old cast iron automotive toys, the kind patterned after turn-of-the-century, tiller-steered horseless carriages. We'll discuss three specimens that characterize very early cast iron toy cars. While, they may not necessarily be the oldest, they represent this category nicely.

Always remember, that toy cars are nothing more than symbols of big ones. At car shows, we can still see a few horseless buggies with engines under the front seat and a tiller for the driver's hands. Personally, I'd much rather view the esthetics of a classic era Pierce-Arrow Touring Car. It does more for me than a horseless carriage.

Taken a step further, into the realm of toy cars, I prefer the long hood of a Hubley cast iron Packard, the top-heavy contours of a pressed steel Buddy L Model T, the image of a stately Carette tin limousine or the bright colors of a milestone era Japanese tin Thunderbird.

This is all personal opinion. To many hobbyists, the true old-time cars still have their charm. I pay homage to them. However, they are being passed by, in volume of interest, as models from later eras gain favor among collectors.

Each of us, with our own era or decade of identification, puts primary focus on our favorite time and its memories of good-looking automobiles. I don't mean to intimate that we can't enjoy all periods of automotive history, but we each have our time periods of primary interest. The new automotive age and its toy vehicles have made collectors forget toy horse-drawn vehicles and tiller-steered toy buggy-type cars.

Let's carry on, then, with historical emphasis on very early cast iron toy cars. One of my favorites in this area is an early tiller-steered toy. I think (but can't prove) that it was made by Kenton of Kenton, Ohio. This belief is based on the nature of the casting, the type of wheels used (like those seen on other Kentons) and the popular Kenton color combination of red car with yellow wheels. In any person's toy collection, it would represent the beginning of the automotive age with the horseless buggy.

Kenton later made a cast iron toy limousine. It carried the usual red with yellow wheels and gold trim paint scheme associated with early Kentons. As to what kind of early automobile it represented, the answer is even more vague than its date of manufacture. I've gone through a lot of books on real cars covering the first decade of this century and didn't come close to finding one that matches the toy. The nearest thing I came across was a huge, French-built Hotchkiss limousine that was shown at the Importer's Salon, on the top floor of the R.H. Macy Building in New York City, way back in 1905

A third known specimen of the early cast iron toy auto is a Touring Car with post-type pillars supporting a canopy roof. With some variation, toys of this body style were made by both Dent and Kenton. The one I'm thinking of was manufactured both with and without the roof. We owned a tiller version of the toy. This example has been referred to as both a Franklin and a Renault. The research may go on for years. Who knows what will crop up? I claim no expertise as to authentic "blood lines."

Many early cast iron toy cars had figurines that "rode" inside them. Our touring car came with non-original driver and passenger figurines. They had obviously been switched over from a horse-drawn cast iron toy.

There have been at least a dozen more tiller-steered buggy-style toy made by different manufacturers. Probably the most sophisticated is a Harris model with a clockwork undercarriage. It is the only mechanical cast iron toy car I have ever heard of. It was offered with and without self-propulsion. It's very rare.

Still looming in my mind is the vision of one such mechanical Harris Tiller-Buggy perched on a shelf in the living room of Murrell Johnson, of Lincoln, Nebraska, 27 years ago. I had the opportunity to buy it. Murrell pitched me a proposition and I didn't bite. Like the baseball player who just tossed a home run hurl, it is one pitch I would like to get back again.

Nationwide, the leading collector of toy cars in this category is probably Lillian Gottschalk of Parkton, Maryland. Not surprisingly, she became the eventual owner of the Harris Tiller Buggy with the fancy clockwork mechanism.

Horse-drawn toys were also made of cast iron. (*Sears* **photo**)

209

This display at Henry Ford Museum held early cast iron toys styled after tiller-steer horseless carriages. At upper and lower center are front and rear views of a circa 1900 spring-wind toy made by Ives & Hubley. On right is an example of the first toy discussed in story, probably a Kenton, with correct driver. The car on upper left is not identified. The cast iron three-wheeler at lower left is German from about 1920. The late Dick Teague owned these.

Sears ahead of its time

By Al Marwick

In case you have never noticed, the toy collecting revolution in America was launched some years ago with the advent of the toy show. From coast to coast, counting toy auctions, there will be hundreds of all-toy events this year.

With the coming of the so-called "general" show, wheeled toys have taken a lead in popularity. It hasn't always been this way. The new interest in toy cars has ridden piggy-back on the mania for full-size old cars.

One catalyst that sparked it all came in 1970, when Sears, Roebuck and Company bought a huge collection of toys from a former Chicago automobile dealer named Ken Idle. Amiable and colorful, Idle was best described as a collector of collections involving many artifacts.

Sears made a gift of this mammoth collection to the Smithsonian Institution. It was subsequently assigned for stewardship to the National Museum of History and Technology, also in Washington, D.C. The museum divided some 2,800 units into 12 segments and displayed a representative portion of each segment in a large exhibition area in 1972. In addition, they formed four traveling toy displays and trucked them to museums all over the country through at least 1977.

Ahead of its time and out in front of the antique toy revolution, Sears made a most remarkable social contribution regarding the playthings of American culture. It didn't do as well in another facet of the antique toy hobby, namely reproductions. Let me tell you the story.

Upon acquiring the Idle collection and making the charitable donation, Sears decided to reproduce eight items which the Smithsonian held. Ironically, these toys were merchandised not through the retailer's toy department, but through its housewares department.

It seems that Sears was originally approached about handling the fancy brass castings of a Grand Rapids, Michigan foundry as an item of room decor. Sears became enthralled with the foundry's authentic old-time method of hand-molding. The plan was switched to molding copies of toys from the donated collection. Sears commissioned the job to be done at the same foundry.

Five cast iron horse-drawn vehicles and three automotive toys were offered in the 1971 *Sears Christmas Catalog*. Each toy had to be taken apart, the molds made and casting done in the same cast iron as the original. Then, they had to be assembled and painted in the original colors. As reproductions, each toy was bench-marked and sold with a certificate attesting to its authentic nature.

The toys were offered in a limited and numbered edition of 250 each, with a price range from $100 to $300. Sears agreed to break the molds following the production run, which they did. Any remaining and unsold toys were to go to the Smithsonian for national distribution to other museums.

The price range for the reproduction toys was a factor in the dreadful sales results that followed, though advanced collectors of today wouldn't bat an eye at such numbers. Each of the cast iron cars was priced at $150. I must confess I did bat an eye at the time, but I was motivated by the credit card system's main benefit, forestalling the agony of immediate payment. So, in November 1971, I lined up at the Sears mail-order counter to order, as a mature businessman, my very own Christmas presents from me to me. They were two of the three cast iron cars, which I still have in my possession.

The group of all eight toys was presented on pages 313 through 316 in the 1971 *Sears Catalog*. When the sales figures leaked out of Sears, the results were unbelievable. Something like less than 100 total

In addition to cars, Sears reproduced this cast iron hook and ladder wagon. It sold for $300 in 1971 *Sears Catalog*. **(Sears)**

copies of the toys were sold. Sales of the horse-drawns outsold the automobiles by a wide margin. Remember, it was 1971, not toy-collecting-crazy 1994.

The first of Sears, Roebuck's limited-edition collector's items was a Touring Car. Like the original manufactured by Kenton of Kenton, Ohio, the reproduction was 10 inches long. Although this toy was generic, its realistic folding top and people figurines inspired a certain lifelike naturalism. (Kenton also made originals with the touring roof raised, using the same interior figurines). The color is bright red with gold striping. It has silver-painted, simulated tires and black-painted fenders, top and tonneau.

According to a confidential source, only two of the top-down Touring Car reproductions were sold. I have never learned how many were produced, unsold and returned to the Smithsonian for museum placement.

The second reproduction I purchased was a big, 13 inch long reproduction, in cast iron, of the Kenton Sedan. The original toy also came from the Kenton factory, like most of the Ken Idle collection. This entry is more in the theme of replica design and reminds one of a Nash, Studebaker or Willys-Knight. It is painted in the same color and striping arrangement as the Touring Car.

The vintage of the original Kenton Sedan was 1926, and that date is neatly inscribed in the casting of the rear spare tire. This toy was produced originally in three scale sizes of nine inches, 11 inches and 13 inches overall. It was also offered with both spoke and disc wheel options (as were most of the full-size cars of that era).

More popular than the Touring, the reproduction Kenton Sedan checked in with a mail-order sales total of eight. If the company could resurrect the original mold and re-advertise the toy at the same price in a current catalog, they could sell 1,000 of the 13 inch sedans. Of course, this won't happen. The integrity of Sears, Roebuck and Company is without question. This is simply a commentary on timing and hindsight.

Controversy surrounds the third 1971 Sears reproduction. It was a Model T coupe of the teens. My personal claim is that it was never a genuine toy, but that it was adapted by the foundry from a contemporary plastic kit by Revell and made into an iron casting.

My sources say that Sears sold two of the Model Ts via mail-order, but not to me. Right from the start, I did not like the looks of this toy. Compared to an Arcade Model T, it's ugly. This doesn't mean that I am not looking for one right now. Ugly can sometimes be beautiful in an old car, big or small, just for the fact that it's so ugly.

My views of reproductions, in general, vary with the particular item. If done well, I believe in them. In fact, I believe in and promote every toy collecting category: repainted, restored, mint original, new-in-the-box, representative original, scratch-built, cracked and broken, rusted and busted and well-done reproduction. From my own collection, I can proudly show you splendid specimens depicting each of the above conditions of the toy artifact.

The future of the vehicular toy, as it relates to the hobby field of automotive nostalgia, is in reproduction and scratch-built. I respect the stance of the purist, but progress will not favor his determination.

Desire, ornamentation and possession will win out. On a reproduction drawing board right now, is the most revered of classic cast iron toy sedans.

My view is this. If someone can restore or virtually reproduce big cars, then why not little ones. The key to credibility is do it right, whatever the size of the car.

Spearheaded by the popular shows, toy collecting has taken on a soaring spirit and vehemence. But, as I glance back over my shoulder seeking reasons why, the Idle-Sears-Smithsonian triangle grows bigger and more romantic with each passing year.

Kenton sedan reproduction, over a foot long, represents composite styling of the 1926 era Nash/Studebaker/Willys-Knight. It's a cast iron replica, even to the tread on the running boards. (Sears)

The reproduction of the 1921 Kenton Touring was 10 inches long. The 1971 *Sears Catalog* showed all three toy cars offered. A Certificate of Authentication was received with each toy. (Sears)

The original Buddy Ls

By Al Marwick

Just the other day, someone stated, "Nostalgia is nice, but I wouldn't want to live there." It was a cute bit of abstraction. I really like the line, but nostalgia is my game. In my business ... I sell antiques ... it's there everyday. I guess I live there.

In 1925, Santa Claus left me a Buddy L hydraulic dump truck. It seems like it was only yesterday. I still can see it under the tree. But, my Buddy L hydraulic dump was stolen off the back porch not too long after the holidays of 1925 vanished. Then, the years went by.

The sports-crazed adolescent years came and went. Then, I found out about girls. Next, came my college, war and automobile dealer years. These were followed by marriage, children and wanderlust for travel.

I didn't get back together with a Buddy L hydraulic dump for 34 years. Then, around Christmas in 1959, I was driving down a commercial thoroughfare in Kansas City, not too far from the famous Country Club Plaza. Rarely failing to glance at automobile showrooms, I repeated this lifelong habit as I drove

This is Buddy L's number 206A closed cab 1924 tanker. It's another model with the look of the famous IHC "Red Baby" truck.

by one dealership. However, this time I stopped. Taking the place of a shiny new automobile was a table of old toys. You guessed it ... one was a truck, the likes of which I had not seen since 1925!

Nostalgia set in. The return to childhood was instantaneous when I spotted the Buddy L dump. It worked manually, not hydraulically, but that was close enough. There was also a Model T roadster pickup next to the Buddy L. It was also just like another toy I once owned. Instantly, I became a toy collector. Now I write about it, some 3,000 toys later.

The history of Buddy L of East Moline, Illinois is fascinating. The Moline Pressed Steel Company began making fenders for Model T Fords and other cars along about 1916. One day, early in the 1920s, owner and founder Fred Lundahl turned out a toy truck of pressed steel to take home to his only son, Arthur Lundahl. Arthur went by the nickname "Buddy." Since there was already a couple of boys called "Buddy" on the block, Arthur Lundahl became Buddy L. There you have the origin of a great trade name in the toy industry.

Fred Lundahl lost his company during the depression and subsequently, in 1931, died. The people in Moline felt he would be forgotten. He certainly hasn't been, though. The Buddy L trademark is still in existence and being used on products today. Of course, no one since has built a Buddy L the way Fred Lundahl built them.

The 1924 model 205 fire truck.

Swap meets and toy shows reflect growth of toy truck (and bus) hobby.

As for Arthur "Buddy L" Lundahl, he grew up, received a good education and joined John Deere and Company in Moline. You've heard the phrase, "The mill is the town." Well, Deere is Moline and Arthur became an executive vice-president.

Yes, the real life Buddy L did collect his own toys. Mother Lundahl put a few specimens up in the attic and Bud Lundahl has joined us in the toy collecting revolution.

The history of Buddy L encompasses three eras: the 1920s, the 1930s and postwar, plus numerous types of toys. We are covering the 1920s (the Fred Lundahl era) and restricting the topic to toy trucks.

In that era, toy truck makers preferred making toys that looked like real trucks. Sturditoy of Providence, Rhode Island configured the hoods of its pressed steel toy trucks in the likeness of real White trucks and stamped the running boards with the White script. Keystone Toy Company, of Boston, Massachusetts, copied the shape of Packard trucks and, through some sort of agreement with Packard, used the Packard script on the toy's radiator.

Buddy L was thinking of copying the International truck in shaping its toys, but didn't go quite as far in detail. They did a "Red Baby" version of International with IH decals affixed. This was made in the style of a closed cab express and sold by International truck and tractor dealers.

Most large-size Buddy Ls of the 1920s are essentially pressed steel toy trucks that measure about two-feet long and resemble International trucks. Two exceptions are the aerial ladder and the coach bus, which are both longer. In addition, the coach bus had no relationship to the International hood style. It was more of a composite Fageol-GMC model in design.

The second Buddy L truck series of the 1920s was termed the Model Ts or "flivvers" by Buddy L. They were roughly one-foot long overall, with one exception. The "one-ton express" truck was two inches longer. Also, since two of the flivvers were made up as a coupe and roadster, the Model T truck series covered has to be amended to include, technically, two passenger cars

In all, I can list 17 body styles of the large Buddy L trucks of the 1920s. Then, with extra versions of the express and two dump trucks having been offered, the grand total comes to 20. There could be even more variations. The list looks like this:

200	Open Express Truck
200A	Closed Express Truck
201	Dump Truck (manual)
201A	Dump Truck (hydraulic)
201B	Dump Truck (manual with A-frame hoist)
202A	Sand and Gravel Truck
203A	Lumber Truck
206	Street Sprinkler
202	Coal Truck
206A	Oil Truck
207	Ice Truck
203B	Baggage Truck
204	Moving Van
205	Fire truck (chemical)
205A	Fire truck (pumper)
205B	Fire truck (aerial Ladder)
205C	Fire truck (insurance patrol)
204A	Railway Express
208	Coach Bus
209	Auto Wrecker

All the above carried solid disc, one-piece cast aluminum wheels, with the exception of 200 and 200A, which had spoked aluminum wheels. The Closed Express, model 200A, represents the International Harvester "Red Baby."

What is there about the large, pressed steel toy truck that collectors love? I can tell you. It's huge, rugged, colorful and profound. Sitting on a shelf in den or office, it turns into an esthetic conversation piece that says something about the room it decorates. It becomes another symbol of our mutual battle cry, "I love old vehicles!"

To prove how merchandising, even in the world of toys, eventually catches on to what's going on, since 1976 the packaging for modern Buddy Ls (even those made in Japan) has carried the likeness of Fred Lundahl's toy flivver on every box. For us in the collecting and nostalgia game, it's a kind of tribute to a man who went broke producing a quality product.

Technicalities about the engineering of old Buddy Ls could go on and on. Personally, I'm more interested in the color and atmosphere that the image of the toy inspires. In this connection, during the spring of 1963, a certain Moline girl (my wife) and myself, drove one morning from Moline to the East Moline plant of Buddy L. After the usual routine tour of the assembly line the assistant superintendent took us to a room he referred to as "the morgue."

The 1924 model 204 moving van.

This was a storage facility. Covering from floor to ceiling were of all the Buddy L toys herein described and many more. The Fred Lundahl Buddy Ls, those of the golden 1920s, were all wrapped in blue and white striped paper and packed in their original, individual cartons. I opened the flaps from a couple of boxes and there were the thin pull-ropes that attached to the front axle so the child could pull his Buddy L truck along behind him. They came this way originally.

What happened to the East Moline morgue, I do not know. I didn't have the time then to pursue a search. Buddy L manufacturing went from East Moline to Japan, with a couple of years stopover in Missouri. The thought of what happened to the

The 1926 model 207 ice truck.

City baggage dray dating from 1934.

The aerial ladder and silver-blue 1927 coach bus are longer and more distinctive than other early Buddy Ls. This bus did not have the IHC look. It is more of a Fageol-GMC composite design.

This is the number 201B Buddy L Dump Truck with A frame hoist of 1921. The original pull cord is attached to the front.

morgue is something for the curious collector to ponder as he sips a drink, stares into the mystery of a roaring fireplace and muses.

There will be a Buddy L truck under the tree this Christmas, just as new and shiny as that first one in 1925. And alongside it will be one that is rusted and busted and tired of all the miles. Relativity has a charm. I like living in nostalgia.

Buddy L made cars, trains, boats and Ts

Besides toy trucks, Buddy L made a tug boat; a small monocoupe airplane with one- and two-door hangers; an industrial train with round house; and a famous backyard train, along with many other types of toys stamped from heavy-gauge steel.

Buddy L also produced seven separate styles of Henry Ford's Model T. These are described, below, with their model numbers:

210	Roadster Pickup
210A	Roadster Passenger Car
210B	Coupe Passenger Car
211	Dump Scoop Bed
211A	Dump Rectangular Sided
212	One-Ton Express
212A	One-Ton Express Huckster

Open cab version of 1929 Street Sprinkler truck bears a BL-12 decal on seat and says Buddy L Tank Line on side. It is about two feet long overall, with green tank, black cab and red cast aluminum disc wheels.

218

The Smith-Miller Company

By Al Marwick

In the initial years of my interest in collecting cast iron wheeled toys, I paid little attention to the cast aluminum Smith-Miller trucks. Time changed all this in a slow metamorphosis of recognition. In short, I came around. But I wonder why it took me all those years to figure out that cast aluminum toys were destined to join lithographed tin, cast iron and pressed steel toys as desirable collectibles?

It was 1971 and I was already into old toys for over a decade when I purchased my first Smith-Miller, in a second-hand store, on Franklin Boulevard in Sacramento, California. A $5 bill bought me a Mack "Blue Diamond" truck in presentable condition. It was all there: air horns, headlights and the Mack bulldog radiator emblem. The hydraulic lift action of the dump body was still working, too.

I palmed the configuration, took it home and placed it on a shelf. Then, I stepped back to gain perspective. I remember saying to myself, "Man, that looks real."

A couple of years went by and I found myself exposed to the possible purchase of a dozen Smith-Millers stacked, here and there, in a residential garage in San Diego. I passed them up. Today, I can only say to collectors everywhere, "When in doubt, never, never pass." See your banker, break the kid's piggy bank, mortgage the house, take your favorite sport coat to one of those recycled clothing stores called "Nice Twice, Act II" or "Encor Boutique." Just never pass. Induce your wife to do the same. (Won't that be fun?)

Just so you don't take me too seriously, let me also state that some of the best deals I ever made were those I never made. Think about that statement!

The most desirable of collectible toy trucks coming out of the post World War II era have been Smith-Millers. Like the original Buddy L Company, Smith-Miller originally turned out to be a financial disappointment for its investors. Related nameplates preceded and followed the Smith-Miller marque. Even more important, in recent years, the name has been revived by a collector who now produces original-quality Smith-Miller toy trucks of past and new designs.

When the product was first introduced, towards the end of 1944, it was called "Smitty Toy." Then Smitty was dropped from the decal appearing on the left and right door panels. In some sort of company reorganization by Ironson and Smith-Miller, the name became Miller-Ironson. All of this occurred over a manufacturing span of 14 years encompassing the early history of the company, before its current revival.

If I sound like an authority on Smith-Miller my plea is "nay." I criss-cross the country, sometimes in person and often on the telephone, and pick up enough information to make a story out of something. Bits and pieces are added to bits and pieces. I have confidence enough in my sources to believe that I am mostly accurate on Smith-Miller, but please don't "pop your eyeballs" if you encounter an inaccuracy.

As you may already know, these toys with the slogan "Famous Trucks In Miniature" were manufactured in Southern California. Smith-Miller began in Santa Monica, moved next to Glendale and ended up in Los Angeles (with Miller-Ironson added). A Culver City warehouse on Jefferson Boulevard was also involved. This address identified Miller-Ironson Corporation on the product box. We have such a box that held the company's Lincoln Capri coupe and also a box for the house trailer the Lincoln pulled.

The first Smitty Toys were made of cast-aluminum with solid rubber tires. Bright metal furniture glides were pressed into an indentation of the rubber tires to look like wheel discs. The letters S-M appeared on the discs. Spoked cast-aluminum wheels were soon adopted.

Smith-Millers were expensive for the 1940s and 1950s. For example, the Mack Bulldog hook and ladder had a list price of $24.95. It was big though, measuring 35-1/2 inches in length. The company's advertising message made no excuse for the high price and said, with positiveness, "Cost More Because They Give More."

With design replication that far outshone its competitors, the Smith-Miller toy has become an outstanding collector item of its era. And, in this case, the quality has proved victorious. Smith-Miller has been revived and is still making expensive, but desirable toys today. Connoisseurs sing the praises of the craftsmanship carried by the names of Smith and Miller and Ironson, whether they are 50 years old or one year old.

Important to emphasize is that the Smith-Miller truck was a strong replica item. It looked like the real truck it was patterned after. There was nothing "fantasy" or "toy-toy" about its design. It was always in proper scale, too.

The original Smitty Toy was a cab-over-engine truck. Although it bore no identification as such, it was a GMC replica. Apparently, Smith-Miller could not get clearance from General Motors to use the GMC name on its toy vehicles. This doesn't stop collectors from giving it a "GMC" designation.

As far as the company's merchandise identification was concerned, it changed from Smitty Toys to Smith-Miller right after World War II. The toy also went to the aluminum cast wheels at this point.

In the four-wheel, light-duty variety, the cab-over-engine Smitty Toys trucks came in six models. They included a flat bed lumber truck, a Heinz 57 stake truck, a shield-sided oil truck, a rack-sided materials truck, an Arden milk truck and a Coca-Cola truck. Tractor-and-trailer combinations were the Bekins moving van, a stake truck and a timber truck. There was also a polished shield-sided body with matching cab.

With the formal change to the Smith-Miller name came a famous new line of Mack Bulldogs. The toy Mack trucks carried on and enhanced two characteristics of the manufacturer ... they were realistic and expensive. Embossed on each side of the hood was the Mack logo script. The Bulldog mascot adorned the radiator of most, but not all of the toys. The early series is referred to as the "L." It was later succeeded by the "B" Series. The latter can be identified by a new flat nose radiator cap and the elimination of the Mack hood script.

As a guide to the basics, I have developed a partial chart of Smith-Miller models. It includes, in order of listing, the model number, description, length, color and original price. There may have been additions to the above, along with advertising variations. The Miller-Ironson product, succeeding Smith-Miller in the final years, came with a redesigned hood and radiator and without Mack identification insignias.

Although it carried the same dimensions as the Smith-Miller Mack, on a technical basis, the Miller-Ironson version can be considered a composite replica. This truck was even more advanced than the Smith-Miller Macks. It has functional left- and right-hand cab doors and a steering wheel mechanism. The wheels also went back to a form of discs with the Miller-Ironsons.

In the final three years of the firm's early history, Smith-Miller toys were merchandised concurrently with Miller-Ironson toys. With the new and redesigned product, there were inventory stocks to be carried over, along with parts and tooling that had to run its course.

As to truck body types, Miller-Ironson apparently made a total of at least six. I'm talking body types, not variations of the original issue with different graphics. The list of six includes a tow truck, lumber truck, hydraulic dump truck, Lift-O-Matic stake truck, semi tractor and trailer, Bekins van and aerial ladder fire truck. There could have been other versions and prototypes, however.

In addition to its half-dozen trucks, Miller-Ironson also made its replica of the Lincoln Capri coupe. The car is 14 inches long overall. It pulled a 26-inch house trailer as a companion piece. The Lincoln a hardtop body shell, which was introduced in 1952 and continued through 1955 on real cars. For toy-toy purposes, the Capri became a convertible with the removal of its hardtop.

I once purchased a Miller-Ironson Lincoln new in the box. My son Bruce and I were traveling east from one coast to another. No true automobile buff crosses the country without stopping in Auburn, Indiana to see the Auburn-Cord-Duesenberg Museum. Around this time, there was also an impending toy auction as well to be conducted by Kruse International, the well-known Auburn-based auctioneers. In pinstripe navy blue suit, Dean Kruse was in uniform on a blistering July day. We felt very "California beach-bummish," but comfortable in the Americana vacation uniform of shorts and sandals.

The 1953 Smith-Miller Number 807 Bekins Van Lines moving truck is 27-1/2 inches long and cost $15.95 when new. It's also based on the Mack Model L.

Our schedule wouldn't allow staying for the auction, but we did the pre-display, in breakneck abandon, and landed on the never-sold Miller-Ironson. It was the Capri pulling the house trailer. The original box for each was there, too. That really "sent" us. We found a friend, stuffed him with the wherewithal, and told him not to stop (bidding) until the ceiling was reached for this type of toy. We moved on, but became absentee bidders. (That's different than an absentee bid.)

You can imagine the suspense surrounding our return trip! Did we have the high bid? We walked into the living room of our friend and asked, "Did we get It?" My attention was so glued on his answer I didn't see the Miller Ironson house trailer and car on the dining room table. He had to point to it. The "find" at the home of Auburn and Cord, the summer atmosphere in Indiana, the suspense and our friend ... all this is enmeshed in our memory of the thrill of that acquisition.

Incidentally, we displayed the boxes for the Lincoln hardtop and house trailer as proudly as we did the toy. What is there about new in the-box that excites collectors? I leave that to a psychologist to figure out.

Smith-Miller also deviated from its truck line when it produced an exceedingly realistic railroad box car that was 33 inches in length. It had sliding doors and the roof lifted off allowing it to be used as a toy storage device. Hard rubber simulated trucks and aluminum construction make it lightweight and manageable. It came in bright orange and freight car red. Today, it finds great favor with train collectors as a decor item.

When I think of Smith-Miller, I am reminded of a veteran collector of the marque. This is Bill Hall of West Hartford, Connecticut. We crossed paths in the toy hobby for over 20 Years. Hall was the first person to start a toy publication, which is now out of existence. He also was the inaugurator of a toy show known as the "Cavalcade of Toys." Bill Hall restored Smith-Millers and reproduced parts of air horns, headlights, Bulldog radiator emblems and rubber tires. He also reproduced advertising circulars. His specialties for Smith-Millers included the repair of bumper ends. Hall, like many of us, always felt that the future of the quality toy is in restoration and, that for that reason, demand will never dry up.

Smitty Toys, Smith-Millers and Miller-Ironsons are hot items. Originals remain, in their desirable state, valuable collectibles. However, the future is in reproduction of parts and restoration.

Regarding why it took me all these years to figure out that cast aluminum toys were destined become hot items, maybe the above answers it. How about toys made of plastics and synthetics? It all depends on quality. If it's there, you better start saving specimens from the garbage can before it's too late!

The green Smith-Miller Tandem Timber Hauler dates from 1953. It included a trailer (not seen here) and cost $16.95 originally. This one has a dual rear wheel modification.

Smith-Miller's P.I.E. semi-tractor is a 27-1/2-inch replica of the 1950 Mack Model L with red tractor and polished aluminum trailer. Originally, it sold for $19.95. This one has been modified with twin dual wheels on rear.

The family that collects together...

By Al Marwick

It is an evening to remember when you can sit opposite Bill and Lillian Gottschalk munching local Maryland apples and discussing, in depth, the inner core of the automobile hobby. Between apple bites, I lay sight and ear to a bevy of motoring history as it is lived by the Gottschalks in theme and lifestyle. Their approach to pleasures, facets and ramifications of the collectible "gas buggy" is a story to be told.

Although it's growing in that direction, husband-wife teams are far from quorum in the total makeup of a Hershey, a Carlisle or a car meet anywhere. I am aware of the old car widow, who is a first cousin to the golf widow. Since Adam and Eve's first day, women have been predestined to be, statistically speaking, kindred with widowhood of some kind.

As a husband and wife duo, the Gottschalks, of Parkton, Maryland, present a unique slant. They double up on each other's related automobile interests. When necessary, they split and go solo, each in their own specialty sphere. Their hobbies find them both into automobiles of the old cars variety. One spouse primarily pursues real cars, while the other goes the toy route.

This emerges as Bill the car collector and Lillian the toy collector. Lillian Gottschalk is a past president of Antique Toy Collectors of America. She is also a lecturer on the subject and stewardess of one of the outstanding vehicular toy collections (in point of balance) perhaps in the world. This is my opinion after 20 years of searches and viewing different collections.

Working in the plastics industry since 1947, Bill was a manufacturer and inventor who vocationally savored the history of the automobile. He carried this involvement into his retirement. Together, with children now grown, Bill and Lillian have made the automobile a lifestyle. As a nomenclature, lifestyle is at its ultimate when you can "do the thing." This interesting aside I find appropriate in describing the Gottschalks.

Bill Gottschalk is the kind of man another man instantly likes. He is a handsome, low key gentleman. He's a former Army Air Corps pilot who used his GI educational benefit to study mechanical engineering at the University of Wisconsin. With his partner in Falcon Plastics of Culver City, California, he went on to make funny faces (a novelty item) pay off in a very successful business endeavor. Remember "Flicko The Clown," whose face fitted over light switches and glowed in the dark? They sold by the thousands back in the early 1950s.

Lillian Gottschalk is a decisive woman of perception and intelligence, who has raised a lawyer-daughter and doctor-son. She has handled herself, with aplomb, in a hobby that was long dominated by males, although the female contingent is now coming on super strong. Gottschalk has written a book on the toy automobile. It is heavily pictorial and has parallel interest for all classifications of toy collecting. However, far from being inundated in the automobile, big and little, Lillian Gottschalk can just as easily explore the subjects of pre-Colombian art and the histories and culture of old Mexico.

Although Bill and Lillian have lived in Maryland since 1965, they met and married in Southern California.

The Gottschalk's residence sits on 41 acres of rolling Maryland countryside. They live in a remodeled barn. Bill once rented it to store his old cars and work on them there. The setting inspired the idea of acquiring the barn and the land. Today it has evolved into no ordinary barn.

Bill and Lillian purchased three other 150-year-old barns. They had them dismantled and trucked them to Parkton, Maryland. With used bricks from old buildings, the combined barns became one huge, atmospheric abode to be decorated with automotive artifacts. The barn's original silo is the anchor for a large second story patio that wraps itself around the cylinder. The old bricks became a base for the exterior facing and provided the courtyard paving.

The bottom floor of the house or barn once held stalls for dairy cows, but is now a showroom and work room for Bill's car collection. An adjacent trophy room contains related automobilia. Seven or eight cars are displayed on the first floor. Upstairs, there are the living quarters. A railed loft, overlooking the living room below, has become a gallery for the cast iron section of Lillian's toy cars and trucks.

To the rear of the kitchen which, incidentally, is a cook's delight, there is a sitting room whose barnboard walls are filled with specimens of antique tin toys. The house was a feature of Maryland's 40th annual "House and Garden Pilgrimage" in 1977. It's a country dwelling representing a myriad of automotive history most attractively worked into its rustic decor.

The toy collection is impressive. For example, one of the rarest of cast iron toy passenger cars seen is a 1931 Reo Royale Victoria coupe. It should not to be confused with Arcade's 1931 Reo Royale two-passenger rumbleseat coupe. In big car nomenclature, Reo Motor Car Company called it the model 8-35. The manufacturer of the toy version of the four-passenger Victoria has never been identified. The specimen is 11 inches long and Lillian Gottschalk owns the only one I have ever seen.

The captivating evolution of the gas buggy in the 20th century is reflected everywhere in the Gottschalk household. Toys, accessories and collectibles from big cars intermingle in the downstairs trophy room with China closets and old showcases. Overall, this environment engulfs the collecting emotions and thrills one to the creativity involved in making a staunch old dairy barn into a residence of comfort and luxury.

For years, Lillian and her husband conducted an antique toy seminar at the annual meeting of the Antique Automobile Club of America (AACA). The seminars have grown to such popularity and proportion as to require the largest room for a workshop at the Philadelphia-based conclave. A show of hands at one AACA toy seminar revealed that about 90 percent of those in the audience owned at least one antique toy automobile. Gottschalk's other lectures on old toys included a program for the Glidden-Pocono tour and many done in conjunction with museum exhibits she has organized in Eastern cities.

At the Hershey and Carlisle shows each autumn, Bill Gottschalk is a quiet and reserved fixture. He considers these two consecutive weeks in Pennsylvania "his time" and the pinnacle of the automobile hobby year. With his German Shepherd "Blitzen" at his side, Bill has enjoyment and serenity written all over his face. He goes about a car meet with an air of calm, while most of his fellow hobbyists are indulging themselves in various degrees of the cardiac caper.

Lillian got into toys in the early 1950s, after Bill decided to get into the automobile hobby and started searching for a full-size taxicab. In a Van Nuys, California antique shop that answered Bill's request for a taxicab, Lillian fell upon the next best thing. It was a Arcade cast iron Yellow Cab toy symbol of the real thing. She bought it for Bill, but kept it for herself. Remember, however, their hobbies overlap. Thus, Lillian was turned on to being a toy collector as her husband launched into full-size cars.

Bill Gottschalk's favorite big car in his collection is, without ostentation, a maroon 1929 Hupmobile coupe with sidemounts. I think it's the story behind the Hupp that has warmed Bill's heart as much as the car. The man he acquired it from had used it on his honeymoon. Then, he drove it all his married life. The Hupmobile had served him well. For Bill, this sentimental old car has won an AACA first at Timonium in Maryland.

Other full-sized cars that Bill Gottschalk possesses range from a 1922 Detroit Electric to a 1927 Series 81 Pierce-Arrow town car to a 1931 Auburn boattail. The list goes on. Bill's favorite toy in Lillian's collection is a French tin toy manufactured by Charles Rossignol. It's a Tracadero bus with fantastic detail and color.

To give you maximum information without over-exercising any flair for saying things my way, I like to revert to quotes. With poignant thought, the following is a series of toy hobby statements by Lillian Gottschalk.

"In my toy seminars, I never advocate purism. I had those leanings once, but scarcity won't allow it now. I have bent with the times. I have classes on restoration, how to remove paint, the whole bit."

"Generally the larger the toy piece the scarcer it is."

"The year 1939 marks the beginning of the end to the pure side of collectible toy iron and tin."

"We live in a different era flow. We live in an era of the plastic kit."

"Toy vehicles are not intrinsically beautiful. They possess little of the grace and detail of a model ship."

"Differing from a model, solidity was the essential quality of a toy in those days and even in these days."

"One of my main interest in old toys is research. I am very proud of the annual reproduced catalogs which are prepared by The Antique Toy Collectors of America."

"I chose toys for good original paint."

"To achieve the best, I upgraded over the years. The new collector doesn't have many opportunities to do this."

"The European toy collector differs from the American in that he cares less about origin and manufacture. He loves the toy and cares little about who made it."

"Which was once sentiment in toys is now value. Third and fourth generation heirs are bringing them out of the attic to realize their value."

"I always learn something from a seminar audience. Recently, for instance, it was a renewed interest in the large pressed steel toys, such as Buddy Ls."

"The favorite toy in my collection? Give me a year to think about that."

"I never answer questions on toy prices."

No column on the Gottschalks would be complete without a quotation from Bill that steers away from the iron and steel, the oil and the grease, the fabric and rubber and verbally lands like this: "There is a camaraderie among auto collectors I have never found elsewhere. They weave a web that ties them together. I have never known an old car collector to be a bore. Every collector seems to make a contribution .... technical knowledge, research information, sometimes and most importantly, humor."

Well, the crisp, Maryland apples got eaten and the time got late. The Gottschalks and myself never knew entertainment such as this, before old automobiles, real ones and play ones, became our passion.

Airflows in miniature

By Al Marwick

My first ride in a motor car was in a Model T center-door sedan in 1924. Memory of the event is more vivid now than what happened to me yesterday ... whatever that was. I was four-years-old. In 1925, I got a ride in an air-cooled Franklin with a split v-windshield. I sat between my auntie and her boy friend Lester Barce. Her perfume and his slicked down hair (with center part) made almost as strong an impression as the Franklin. Time leaped on.

Soon, I was a teenager of 14. It was 1933. Free rides were being given around a simulated test track adjacent to the Chrysler Building at Chicago's Century of Progress Exhibition. For most Chrysler products, it was the year of the "Floating Power" engine mounting system. Neat, uniformed attendants handled the tourist line for free rides in Chrysler products featuring Floating Power. One tried to push me into a Plymouth first, then a Dodge. I would have none of it. A DeSoto Airflow? Almost acceptable, but I waited for the big, new Chrysler Airflow instead. What a car!

When the Airflow pulled to a stop, I managed to slither past a few adults to a position in the front seat, next to the driver. The Chrysler Airflow I pulled away in was a gold, khaki, olive-drab color. Every time I think of an Airflow, my mind automatically paints the color-blend described.

Will the automobile industry ever again know ... within a short decade and less ... such great change as the advancement between a Model T (its last year was 1927) and the ultra-streamlined hulk that was Walter P. Chrysler's Airflow?

We'll get back to the ride in the real Airflow, but meantime, let's review toy Airflows.

The Airflow received significant attention from toy designers and manufacturers. The car was a breakthrough, a design way ahead of its contemporaries. Probably the most outstanding toy specimen of the breed is an American-made toy of pressed steel. It is 17 inches in length overall and quite rare. For a long time it went unidentified as to manufacturer among advanced automotive toy collectors.

When Marco Bossi, of Italy, did his superb pictorial hardcover entitled *Auto Hobby* in the early 1970s, the toy Airflow mentioned above appeared on page 46 as plate 55. It was listed as a Chrysler Airflow, with the collector credit in parenthesis and nothing else. I am told European collectors aren't as academic as we Americans as to a toy's background. They are more of the "let's just enjoy it school," for which I praise them.

Later, somebody started calling it a Cor Cor toy, no doubt with some validity of research. Automotive toy historians are always calling for clippings, pamphlets, flyers, literature, advertising Lear sheets, the tales of former employees and anything else they can get their hands on to embellish the history, and even some of the folklore, of collectible toys. Historical data gives a toy image and interest. It becomes a part of the "nostalgia cocktail."

There were many toy makers who did an Airflow in the 1930s besides Cor Cor. Among them were Kingsbury, Hubley, Wyandotte and so on. The Cor Cor copy was the largest, and probably most realistic, of all the toys made to resemble the exotic Chrysler streamliner. The Cor Cor has bumpers, an exposed spare tire, electric headlights and friction power. It used a much heavier grade of steel than Kingsbury, for example, employed. Colors I have observed the toy in are dark green, maroon and bright red. Mine was red.

This Airflow sedan in steel is painted red.

An Airflow coupe made of sheet metal has a silver body. Black fenders and front and rear bumpers set it off.

An Airflow coupe in medium blue body, with dark blue fenders and front/rear bumpers. Same as the silver car, but has a different grille.

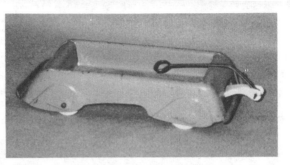

A small "Comet" wagon. This one is light green with no lettering. There's a pink tongue, black tiller, and yellow wheels. Finish may be non-authentic.

An Airflow coupe of slush metal is painted silver gray with white balloon tires. Body details are engraved in the metal.

An Airflow model. The metal four-door sedan is painted off-white with a black top insert. It's highlighted by bright metal trim.

This Shell Airflow tanker is painted chrome yellow with red Shell lettering. Approximately nine inches long, it has fully enclosed rear fenders.

A large coaster wagon with Airflow styling. It is red with white trim and a black tiller. It has small "headlights" in front.

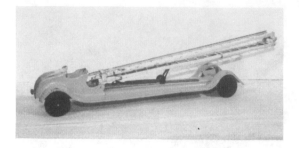

This open cab hook and ladder sports Airflow type styling. It's painted red with a yellow aerial ladder and a silver waterfall grille.

A small coaster wagon with Airflow-like styling is painted red. A silver-painted front waterfall grille adds to its looks.

An Airflow-like toy truck or bus in molded Rubber. It's painted blue with black rubber tires.

A teardrop-shaped (airflow style) trailer painted red. The full-skirted fenders and black rubber tires add to its appearance.

A toy tractor and three-compartment tanker-trailer with "Airflow" styling. The metal toy is painted green. It has white rubber tires.

A small "Comet" coaster wagon with Airflow-like styling. It is painted dark green with black "Comet" lettering.

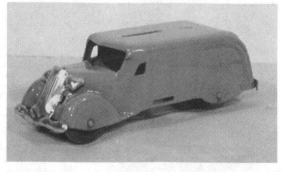

This Airflow sedan is painted red-orange with dark green fenders. A bright metal waterfall grille and front bumper set it off.

This toy truck has Airflow-like styling. Made of sheet metal, it's painted red. It has a bright metal grille, bullet headlights and veed front bumper.

Kingsbury of Keene, New Hampshire, probably made the most Airflow toys. You read the story of Kingsbury earlier in this book. In 1934, when both Chrysler and DeSoto Airflows first appeared, Kingsbury was quick to produce a well-made, thin, pressed-steel replica as a toy. They then followed the big car model changes, from year to year, as the cars went through face-lifted design treatments during a four year span until 1937. Chrysler's major change was softening the bluntness of the waterfall grille with a protruding v-shaped grille, which was popular at the time, and adding a trunk contour to enclose the spare. This gave the rear a bit of a bustle shape and a slight beaver tail appearance.

The Kingsbury toy Airflow is approximately 14 inches long. It was powered by a spring motor as standard equipment. Options, such as a high-grade electric horn, were available on some models. The horn action was entirely automatic. It sounded a "beep, beep" every few feet the toy traveled. There was also an electric lights option. Toys with electric horns or electric lights used a standard flashlight battery. There was also a "radio-equipped" model in which tuneful melodies came bursting forth from a concealed music box. The Kingsbury slogan for their toy line was: "Not just another toy, but a real Chrysler Airflow in miniature."

Hubley Toy Company, of Lancaster, Pennsylvania, is still in business. Hubley made a toy Airflow in cast iron. It came with electric lights and a detachable frame and in different sizes (up to about eight inches). They also did a two-door DeSoto Airflow in eight-inch size. Instead of the horizontally paneled Chrysler Airflow hood louver, the toy DeSoto Airflows treatment overlapped the louvers like a Venetian blind.

Using the toy symbols as a reminder, I now relate memories of my first Airflow ride at the "Worlds Fair" in Chicago. My first impression in the front seat that day, back in June in 1934, was, "Wow, it's as wide as a bus." The solid, heavy feel, the almost perpendicular positioning of the steering wheel in the driver's lap, the stubby waterfall drop off of the hood and the heavy chrome tubing outlining the upholstery bolsters stand out in my memory, even though I haven't been inside an Airflow since then. There's no question that the car was way ahead of its time.

Had Walter Chrysler followed the philosophy of Paul Masson, he would have sold no product before its time. But, the automobile business isn't the wine business. Chrysler tried protruding the grille and adding a little rump in the rear, but it never did get the bulkiness, fatness and tank-like silhouette out of the Airflow. To me, it wasn't an ugly car, just a bulky one. Two years later, Edsel Ford took the streamline theme and introduced the 1936 Lincoln-Zephyr. It had much more esthetic acceptance. I have always been an admirer of prewar Lincoln-Zephyr styling. However, for good old fashioned collector charisma, I'll take an Airflow.

Here is a modern die-cast metal model of the Chrysler Airflow that was sold by The Airflow Club of America as a club commemorative model. It is red and had the club logo on its door. (Courtesy David Askey/*Airflow Newsletter*)

A toy with Airflow styling. Although molded in one piece, it resembles a "fifth-wheel" trailer. It's made of molded rubber and painted blue and yellow.

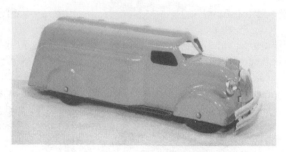

This Airflow tanker is made of sheet metal. It's painted bright red. The four-compartment tanker body has ribs on top. Note the fin on the hood.

This silver, slush metal bus has Airflow type styling. The Greyhound name is embossed on its sides.

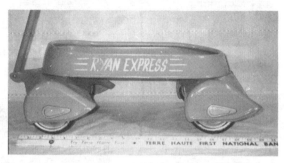

A "Ryan Express" coaster wagon. It has four red "Airflow" style fenders with silver "wing" decorations. The red wagon body has yellow speedlines.

This coaster wagon has four "Airflow" style fenders. The red wagon body is set off by black-finished fenders, tongue and tiller. It has white tires.

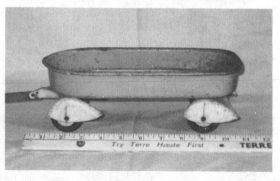

Another coaster wagon with "Airflow" style fenders. This one also has a red wagon body, but yellow finish is on the fenders, tongue and tiller.

An Airflow coupe in red-orange with dark blue fenders. Light blue finish appears on the hood. A spare painted on the rear deck is light and dark blue with an orange center.

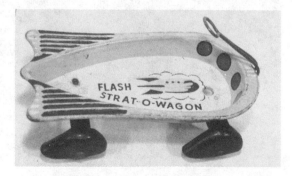

The Flash Strat-O-Wagon has four "Airflow" fenders. The body has red, blue, white and yellow rocket-ship graphics with flat fins extending from the rear.

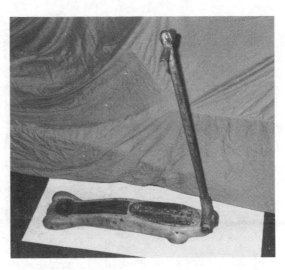

This pedal car is a Chrysler Airflow. It's red with white trim. The ladder rails with wooden ladders and bell make it a fire truck.

One of the most unusual Airflow items is this auto jack. It's painted bright orange-red. The rear section has a fin-like shape.

This metal Airflow sedan is painted all dark green. Fully skirted front/rear fenders stress the streamlined look.

An Airflow pedal car. It's red and cream and it has separate "catwalk" grilles on each side and parking "lamps" on the tops of the front fenders.

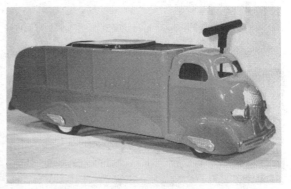

Another Airflow tanker. It's painted medium-dark green with Sinclair Gasoline markings. The three-compartment tank body has no ribs on top.

A kid's ride-on toy styled after the famous Dodge Airflow trucks. There is a black seat on the rear dump box. A black T-handle protrudes from the cab.

Edw. K. Tyron Co., of Philadelphia, cataloged the No.710 Streamlined Pedal Bike in 1938. It has Airflow-like styling. Its wholesale price was $1.60.

An unusual baby buggy with "Airflow" styled chrome-plated fenders. Blue plaid fabric is featured, along with chrome hubcaps and black tires.

Frank Kleptz of Terre Haute, Indiana, maintains a large collection of Chrysler, DeSoto and Dodge Airflow toys. Dodge? That's right ... one toy in the case is a replica of the streamlined Dodge Airflow tank trucks.

Dozens of different types of antique toy Airflows have been manufactured by a long list of toy companies. In addition, there are Airflow pedal cars and modern toys and models of Airflow style. Frank Kleptz has most of them.

Nuts and bolts modeling

By Bob Lemke

If you're the "hands-on" type of enthusiast, into busted knuckles and the nuts and bolts of old car restoration and maintenance, you may not be a fan of model car kit building. Sure, it is building, but somehow plastic and glue just aren't close enough to what you do in the garage or under the shade tree.

So, how about building toy cars the nuts and bolts way? Dig out your Erector set. You remember your Erector set ... two weeks after Christmas, your kid sister flushed all the nuts down the commode and you stuck the rest up in the attic.

It's probably gone, now, though, right? So what, you can go down to Sears and pick up a new one and build all those great cars and trucks you did 15, or 25, or 45 years ago, right?

Maybe. I bought my last Erector set for my little girl for Christmas in 1980. She was a year old then. Of course, I decided I'd break it in for her until she was old enough to use it. The big $75 set with three motors and two transmissions. I ripped into the plan book, ready to find blueprints for Model Ts and open cab fire trucks ... and all I found were R2-D2s and X-wing hyperspace laser blasters.

I guess the Erector set people figure today's young engineers aren't interested in anything as mundane as four-wheeled vehicles.

Now, I'm not imaginative enough to build a touring car from scratch without a plan to work from, so the Erector set went back up to the attic. And I started a search for old Erector set manuals. I haunted toy shows, flea markets, used book stores and antique papers with no luck ... until I found one literally right in my own backyard.

I was wandering the grounds of the Iola '81 old car show on Sunday morning, checking out the swap meet vendors for baseball cards, neat model kits, etc. Then I saw it .... a 1934 Erector set, complete down to every nut and bolt and with the original manual.

Flipping through the manual, I was in "hog heaven." There were fire trucks, stake bed trucks, tankers and all other manner of cars and trucks and all 1930s vintage.

The set's owner must have thought I looked like the only likely candidate, from among 50,000 or so on the lot, that would want to carry a 20-pound metal box full of loose scrap metal under my arm all day. So, he cut his asking price in half and I had my Erector set and original old manual.

The next weekend, after my daughter was in bed, I took out my new toy and began to work on the fire truck shown in the book. I discovered then, that I had a slightly cheaper set than the book called for to build a lot of trucks. Set Number 7 had a real radiator and hood assembly and special axle hangers. I was working with Set Number 4. It was no real problem, though, as I was easily able to make do with the parts on hand. I didn't even have to cannibalize my new set. I wanted to build the old cars and trucks with just the old set.

Besides, the many red-painted panels and brass parts helped make a nifty looking fire truck.

As I was well into my first hour of building, dinking around with all those tiny nuts and bolts, a friend dropped by with a cold 12-pack. He immediately dropped down next to me on the carpet and grabbed a

Here's a fire truck from un old 1934 Erector set. Using the original manual for a starting point, a vintage Erector set can provide endless challenge to the model builder who wants to put together old car/truck toys.

wrench. He also closed the plan book, figuring that, since we didn't have all the right parts anyway, we might as well "wing" it.

We got more creative as the 12-pack got lighter and, by the end of a long night, we had a really "boss" Erector set fire truck. I mean simulated siren, ladders, pumper, hose and all sorts of custom features.

And this was more than a hunk of plastic. It was nearly two feet long and weighed several pounds. It was a solid piece of engineering. And it was fun. You could roll it right at the cat and he couldn't hurt it when he counter-attacked. Even an 18-month old baby, couldn't wreck it when she got her hands on it.

After some photos were taken, it was time to dismantle the truck and start on something new. Like a stake truck ... or a wrecker ... or a speedster.

Winter is fixing to come down hard here and this old Erector set is going to help pass some long quiet evenings. By the time I've gone through all the old car projects in the manual, I should be able to work up a lot more models from scratch.

There's something mighty satisfying about nuts and bolts toys, compared to plastic and bent tin.

Mini-history of Smith-Miller toys

By Neil McElwee

The original Smith-Miller toy company was a California company in business for roughly 10 years until 1955. Most of you know they made a line of toy trucks out of cast aluminum, using wood for decks and sides when appropriate.

In their 10-year history, they made four basic models. All of them are very collectible. They are the Mack Model L, the Cab Over, the Mack Model B and the Miller-Ironson Corporation MIC.

The model type is derived from the appearance of the cab.

Illustrated is a Mack Model L truck cab dating from the mid-1940s. A complete cab has separate headlights standing on pedestals and a bulldog hood ornament or distinct radiator cap. Casting details include a script "Mack" on each side, a grille, vents, and well-defined doors.

The cabs are easily separated from the frame by removing several metal screws, which is nice to know when you're looking at junkers. Wheel detail is excellent, as they are dished and have four broad spokes. The tires are v-treaded. We don't know all of the types of trucks made in this configuration. For those of you who have yet to jump into Smith-Miller collecting, we can tell you the aerial ladder truck is a knockout and not hard to find. The tandem trailer lumber truck is in green and black, and the army truck seems to be common and very nice.

Very different from the Mack Model L is the spiffy Cab Over configuration. We don't know what the designers intended this to look like ... probably just a toy truck. The casting detail includes a futuristic grille with headlights and parking lights integrated into the fenders. Above the grille is a stylized "SM." Like the Mack Model L, the cab can easily be removed from the frame. There are three distinct wheel and tire configurations.

The 1951 Mack Model L Merchandise van is popular.   The 1950 Mack Model L Lyon van.

Trucks made before 1949 had solid rubber tires mounted directly on the axles; embedded in the outsides of these solid tires were steel caps with S-M stamped on them. With the introduction of the 1949 line, the Cab Overs used the same four-spoke wheels found on the Mack Model Ls with the tires being pressed on.

A slight change was made to the wheel casting in 1954. It was made with five spokes. In all cases, the Cab Over tires were molded with a standard street tread. We know of the following cab over models:

Model No.	Type	Model No.	Type
301-W	Wrecker	307-V	Lyon Van
401-W	Wrecker	408-H	Machinery Hauler
302-M	Materials	309-S	Super Cargo
402-M	Materials	409-G	Mobilgas (also Mobiloil)
*303-R/403-R	Rack	310-H	Hi-Way Freighter
304-K	Kraft	410-F	Transcontinental Freight
404-B	Bank	311-E/411-E	Silver streak Express
*305-T/405-T	Triton	312-P/412-P	P.I.E. Semi Truck
306-C	Coca Cola	4X-O	Dump/Tractor
*305-L	Lumber		(Remote-control, steerable)
307-L	Logger	1954-401	Tow Truck
308-V	Lyon Van	1954-402	Dump
		1954-403	Scoop Dump

* Same truck but a change in wheel style. All other trucks are significantly different in other ways.

The Mack Model B is, to our eyes, a very modern-looking truck, yet it was made over 30 years ago in 1954 (and just for one year). No wonder we have had a hard time finding one. The Model B has square fenders with headlights inserted, a rakish air horn overhead and the traditional bulldog hood ornament. Wheels are the cast five-spoke type with tires using a v-tread. The Mack Model Bs we're aware of are:

404	Lumte Truck & optional trailer
405	Silver Streak
406	Bekins Van
407	Searchlight Truck
408	Blue Diamond Dump
409	P.I.E. Semi Truck
410	Aerial Ladder

To come across a Mack Model B tractor pulling all sorts of trailers can easily be imagined. But, if the trailer has wheels other than the five-spoke variety, we wonder if the new truck type is a legitimate baby?

Particularly well-made is the Miller-Ironson Corporation (MIC) Buddy L. This truck cab configuration has operating doors and steering. Made in 1953-1955, it was the last of a grand line. The cab is an Autocar. The headlights stand separately on the fenders. There is a prominent rectangular grille-radiator assembly. On the doors are the MIC decals. We don't know how many types of MIC

The Miller-Ironson Corporation (MIC) truck cab was made in 1953-1955.

trucks were put out. We have seen the following: tow truck, dump truck and stake truck.

We have heard about a tractor pulling a Fruehauf heavy equipment trailer. And we have seen a fire truck, which is a long wheelbase two-axle truck with an extending ladder. This truck's doors are operable and it does steer. It's an outstanding truck. But, it doesn't carry the MIC decal. Instead, it is marked Smith-Miller. Perhaps this was a transition truck.

Collectors of these toys may be interested in my collector's guide #1 titled *Smith-Miller 1944-1955*. The latest revised and combined edition sells for $17 from McElwee's Collector's Guide, 40 Fornof Lane, Pittsburgh, PA 15212. This source also sells guides to postwar Buddy L, Doepke, big Ertl, Ny-Lint and Tonka trucks and gasoline company toys.

Be-Mac Transport Company name is on 1949 GMC semi-truck.

The 1950 Mack Model L material truck is valued by collectors.

Marshall Field & Company 1949 GMC tractor trailer.

The Mack Model B is modern-looking truck, yet it was made only in 1954.

The Smith-Miller logo.

(All text, illustrations and checklists courtesy of Neil McElwee.)

Buddy L "Flivvers"

By Gordon Rice

Henry had a great idea. Henry Ford, that is. He was going to put America on wheels. Henry envisioned a land teaming with motorized carriages to free mankind from the pollution and inconvenience inherent in horse and buggy transportation. Henry knew the needs of the people and planned accordingly. He even let the public choose the color of their vehicle, as long as it was black.

The story of the nickname "flivver" escapes me, but it seems to fit the machine. Every size, shape and description vehicle was based on the Ford Model T chassis.

The first of Buddy L's toy flivvers was introduced in 1924. The number 210 Ford truck was a roadster-topped pickup with operating tailgate and simulated canvas folding top. The entire toy was constructed of heavy gauge pressed steel with cast aluminum wheels. The wheels allowed a concession to color in Buddy L toys. They had red paint on their spokes.

Steering was accomplished via a steering wheel placed in the cab of the toy vehicle, slightly left of center.

The roadster was 12 inches long by 5-5/8 inches wide by 6-3/4 inches tall and weighed approximately three pounds. Two types of flivver pickup trucks were made, with the difference being the type of Buddy L decal affixed to the underside of the pickup frame. A third variation of the flivver pickup was produced in red. It is considered a rarity.

The second flivver introduced in the Buddy L lineup was the number 210-A flivver roadster. The roadster was 11 inches long by 5-5/8 inches wide by seven inches tall. It also weighed-in at three pounds. The flivver roadster had the top of the roadster pickup, but with the sloping rear roadster deck of the flivver coupe. This model was also made with two variations in decals, but none have been reported in any other color than basic black.

The third model to arrive on the flivver scene was the flivver coupe or "doctor's car," number 210-B. This toy was a two-door "high-boy" model with a tall roof line and five windows, not counting the windshield. Specifications were 11 inches by 5-5/8 inches by seven inches and three pounds, the same as the 210-A flivver roadster. Again, two variations of decals were used. Black is the logical choice to request one in, because that's the only color it was made in. It was known as the doctor's car or "Grandma's car" to readers of Walt Disney comics of the 1950s, because Daisy and Donald Duck's Grandma drove one around her farm.

Drastic changes were in store for the next two issues of the Buddy L toy flivvers. The charm of the enclosed vehicle was lost in an attempt to capture an open-air, topless design produced during those days.

Buddy L's number 211 Ford dump cart was 12-1/2 inches long by 5-5/8 inches wide by 4-1/2 inches tall. The height was drastically altered by the lack of a top on the vehicle. The weight remained about three pounds. The flivver dump cart had a short tapered dump box. It raised to a point about half the height of the dump box, at the rear of the vehicle. The design negated the need for a tailgate. The dump operated via a latch at the front of the box. It was located just behind the bench seat. The steering operated in the same manner as all the other flivvers in the Buddy L series. The dump cart was also sold in two decal variations.

The number 211-A Ford dump truck was another open vehicle. It was similar to the previously introduced number 211. The major difference was in the dump box of the truck. The dump box on the 211-A

The third model to arrive on the flivver scene was the flivver coupe or "doctor's car," number 210-B. This toy was a two-door "high-boy" model with a tall roof line and five windows, not counting the windshield.

was of the pickup variety, with a conventional tailgate that could be opened or closed. The dump mechanism was totally different from the 211's, with a lever being used to raise the box by manually changing the position of the lever's handle. The number 211-A flivver dump truck was listed as 11 inches by 5-5/8 inches by 4-1/2 inches. The variation in height, from number 211, is probably only in measurement ... not real height. The weight remained at three pounds. As in past cases, the vehicle was produced in two decal variations. The number 211 and number 211-A dump variations are half-fendered vehicles with fenders over the front wheels only and runningboards reaching to the rear of the eat. This arrangement contrasts with the full-fendered toys produced earlier.

The next four or five vehicles in the flivver series were commercial vehicles. Commerce was just beginning to understand that the motor truck was a big boon to the operation of a successful business.

Number 212 was a Ford 1-ton Express truck measuring 14-1/4 inches long by 5-5/8 inches wide and seven inches tall. It weighed-in at four pounds. The truck was a five-window model (not including windshield) with front fenders and runningboards extending about an inch past the rear of the cab area. The rear wheels were fenderless. The bed or box area was 5-5/8 inches by 7-1/4 inches with an operating tailgate. The sides of the truck bed were flared, with six stake pockets, and the sides of the box had two panels per side designed into them, between the stake pockets.

A possible unnumbered variation of the number 212 truck had red stake sections that were detachable and fit into the stake pockets on the sides of the truck bed. No documentation is available to prove that this is a production version toy.

The number 212-A Ford 1-ton delivery truck was similar to the number 212, but it had a top. This top was supported, over the bed, by six posts placed in the stake pockets. It continued from the front of the windshield to the rear of the truck bed. The tailgate also operated on this model. The size reflected a slight variance, probably attributable to manufacturing tolerances or the method in which the toys were measured. Fourteen inches by 5-5/8 inches by 6-3/4 inches is listed. In all likelihood, it should match the height of the other trucks in the series. Four pounds is given as the weight. Trucks of this type were sometimes referred to as "hucksters," in reference to their business use.

A variation of the number 212 truck was listed as number 212-B and billed as a Ford mail truck. Its size was 14 inches by 5-5/8 inches by seven inches. The weight was four pounds. The shape and description were the same as the Ford delivery truck, except that wire mesh screen sides were installed above the bed sides of the truck. Screened doors were hinged on each side of the rear of the truck, above the tailgate. It is not known if production examples of this toy exist today.

At least one unnumbered 212 variant has been reported. It is a Ford flatbed stake truck measuring 14 inches by 5-5/8 inches by seven inches and weighing-in at 3-1/2 pounds. This truck had an enclosed cab and front fenders and running boards like the other trucks in the 212 series. The flatbed cargo area is reported to have had four stakes inside pockets. Chains connected the stakes to each other near the top. This toy was possibly a factory sample or preproduction test idea. Only one has been discovered.

The Buddy L flivver story ended some 50 years ago. It is possible that other variations were proposed for production, but none have surfaced if they were. The flivver series has been revived and seems to be going strong.

Doepke toys were postwar standouts

By Dennis Schrimpf

The hobby of toy collecting encompasses many areas, one of which is the steel construction toys of the postwar era.

Many different toy companies built construction toys: Tonka, Structo, NyLint, Reuhl, Ertl and others. One company, Doepke, stands above the rest in size, quality and exactness of detail.

The Doepke brothers, Charley and Fred, decided to go into the toy business around 1945. The name of the toy line was "Model Toys." Charley designed and built a wooden mock-up of a Woolridge road-scraper from a catalog photo. A visit with the president of the Woolridge Company secured support and, more importantly, detailed engineering plans of the complete Woolridge line of construction equipment.

The first toy the Doepkes came up with was actually the huge Woolridge off-road dump truck. The roadscraper, when reduced to the 1/16-scale used by the Doepkes, was too delicate. It would have cost too much to produce.

The brothers had a difficult time trying to convince buyers at the annual New York Toy Show that consumers would fork over $15 or more for a quality toy. The store buyers liked the toys, but were convinced no one would purchase them because they were priced relatively high.

In desperation, the brothers hit the road with a car full of Woolridge dump trucks. Sales were slow, but gradually they began to get feedback. Demand for the toy grew slowly, but steadily. When Christmas 1946 had passed, the Model Toy Company had sold some 32,000 toys. They were on their way.

The Doepke toys best known among car toy collectors are a very large and detailed MG-TD and a Jaguar XK120. Fire engine buffs search for American LaFrance ladder and pumper trucks.

The following list of Doepke models was compiled by Neil McElwee, publisher of *"Collector's Guides"* covering many toy trucks:

Doepke Toys Check List

1946-1947

Model Number	Description
No. 2000	Woolridge Earth Hauler (Doepke's first toy)
No. 2001	Barber-Greene Bucket Loader on steel treads
No. 2002	Jaeger Concrete Mixer

1948

No. 2006	Adams Road Grader

1949

No. 2007	Unit Mobile Crane 1950-'53
No. 2008	American LaFrance Aerial Ladder Truck

Model Number	Description
No. 2009	Euclid Earth Hauling Truck
No. 2010	American LaFrance Pumper Truck
No. 2011	Heiliner Earth Scraper
No. 2012	Caterpiller D-6 Bulldozer
No. 2013	Barber Greene Bucket Loader on wheels
No. 2014	American LaFrance Aerial Ladder truck (*)

1954

No. 2015	Clark Airport Tractor and Baggage Trailers
No. 2017	"MT" Automobile - the MG-TD

1955

No. 2018	Jaguar XK120
No. 2023	American LaFrance Searchlight Truck

(*) Note: The number 2013 American LaFrance Aerial Ladder Truck is substantially different from the 2008 American LaFrance Aerial Ladder Truck. The newer one has the bell at middle of side.

On a personal note, the three Doepke construction toys pictured here are the author's. They date from Christmas 1948 and Christmas 1949. Many scale-tons of sand, dirt and gravel were hauled and mixed in these toys. That they still look so good is a credit to the foresight of the Doepke brother's commitment to quality of design, manufacturing and finish.

The Doepke toys best known among car toy collectors are a very large and detailed MG-TD, the American LaFrance ladder truck and pumper truck and this Jaguar XK120.

Three of over 16 Model Toys are the (left to right) Adams motor grader, Jaeger cement mixer and Woolridge earth mover. Dennis Schrimpf received these as Christmas presents in 1948 and 1949 and played very hard with them.

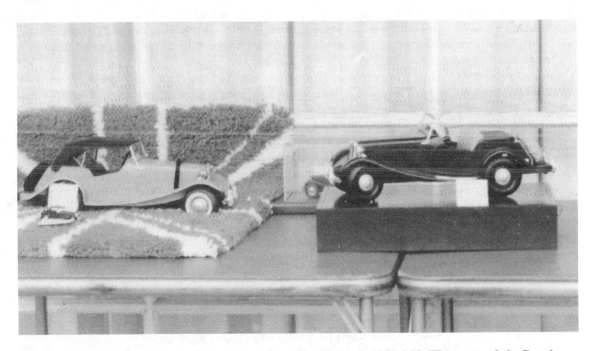

This display at an MG club convention showcased a pair of the early 1950s MG-TDs, one made by Doepke.

Mini-history of Sturditoys

By Neil McElwee

Sturditoys are large-scale pressed steel trucks that were made in the latter 1920s and early 1930s by the Sturdy Corporation of Pawtucket, Rhode Island. They are very similar, in character and quality, to the Keystone Packard trucks that were being made, at the same time, just 50 miles away in Boston.

There are a fair number of Keystone Packards around and much is known about them. Sturditoys are a different story. They are difficult to find and little of a definite nature is generally known about these Rhode Island toys. We don't have any old literature with the official names, nomenclature or numbers. Nor do we know of any collector who has an extensive collection of these trucks. But, we do know of a few trucks here and there.

Illustration number 1 shows a front-quarter view of a simple fixed-box truck with no roof over the cab. We'll call this truck number 1. This illustration serves to highlight the prominent features of the Sturditoy front end. This truck had a distinctive hood and shell design. The hood had the appearance of a ridged house-roof and the radiator shell looked like a gable wall beneath that roof.

Some collectors believe this truck was just a fanciful toy; not a replica. They may be correct. However, around 1925 American LaFrance was making both commercial trucks and fire equipment that were styled much like the Sturditoys of the period. Whatever the case, when you see these toys, you'll know them.

Some Sturditoy trucks were made with headlamps and a license plate. Others weren't. Complete trucks had a Sturditoy decal on the upper face of the radiator shell. For wheels, steel disc hubs and rubber tires were used.

Sturditoy made an Army truck (illustration number 2). We've illustrated one with its fixed bed and canvas cover. Another fixed bed truck was made. This one (illustration number 3) had a roof over the cab.

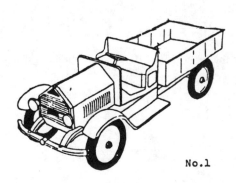

The Fixed Box truck is known as Sturditoy number 1.

Sturditoy modified this truck even more by adding six support posts and a cover over the bed. This truck (illustration number 4) is referred to as the Huckster truck. We haven't seen this truck and therefore didn't illustrate it.

Sturditoy made two dump trucks: a low side dump (illustration number 5) and a high side dump (illustration number 6).

Three emergency vehicles were made. The first was a chemical pumper (illustration number 7). "Number 7" was on this truck's hood originally. A very desirable ambulance (illustration number 8) was made. To go with these two pieces, Sturditoy issued an impressive water tower (illustration number 9). Yes, this truck originally had a "number 9" decal.

The U.S. Army truck is known as Sturditoy number 2.   The two-axle one-compartment tanker by Sturditoy.

Any kind of coal truck today is considered an oddity. One with a side chute takes us back in time. Sturditoy's Coal Company toy (illustration number 10) is a warm reminder of the past.

Two particularly good-looking toys were the wrecker (illustration number 11) and the armored car (illustration number 12). All sorts of wreckers were made over the years, but we haven't encountered many armored cars.

Like Keystone, Sturditoy made a variety of screenside vans. We believe the two-panel screenside was called the U.S. Mail (illustration number 13). We aren't certain. Trucks with three panels and four panels per side have been reported. The Police Patrol and a Railway Express truck were screenside vans, as we understand it (there are no illustrations for these number 14-15-16 toys). Sturditoy also made a traveling store. It was similar to the Buddy L traveling store.

Illustration number 17 shows the two-axle fixed tank truck. Sturditoy made two other tankers. They are the kind of toys you dream about. Both were semis. One tanker was painted red and is known as the oil tanker (illustration number 18). The other tanker semi was painted white and is known as the dairy tanker (illustration number 19).

Likely, there is more to be said about Sturditoy. You may have a truck we don't know of or an angle on this company nobody has heard of. It is about time this excellent, large-scale American toy was better understood and placed in a prominent light.

(Neil McElwee is publisher of *McELWEE'S Collector's Guides*. These publications are dedicated to both postwar and prewar toy trucks, autos and construction vehicles. Contact him at 40 Fornof Lane, Pittsburgh, PA 15212.)

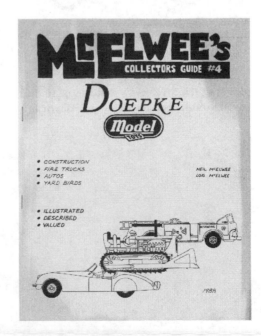

McELWEE's Collector Guide #3   **McELWEE's Collector Guide #4**

This page shows Neil McElwee's sketches of 10 different trucks offered by Sturditoy. The number 8 Ambulance is very desirable, as is the number 9 American LaFrance fire truck. (Drawings and text by Neil McElwee)

Conway Toys little known in hobby

By Neil McElwee

The Conway Company of Skokie, Illinois introduced their beautiful replica of a Packard convertible in 1948.

It was a substantial toy made of heavy plastic and steel. The bumpers, grille, hubcaps, headlight rims and taillight rims were nickel-plated and polished. The toy was made with pneumatic-type tires. For a touch of class, the seats were upholstered.

A hefty clockwork mechanism was used to drive this Packard and a battery powered the electric horn and headlamps. You pressed the steering wheel horn ring to operate the toy's horn. You twisted the steering wheel to turn the lights on and off

The Packard is fairly big, measuring about 12 inches long and five inches wide. Every example we've seen or heard of was made with a yellow body We have literature that indicates Conway continued to wholesale this 1948 Packard as late as 1950. In that year, it was available in a clear acetate display box and the toy retailed for about $5.

Naturally, the question arises: What else did Conway make? Dwight Dollinger, of North Carolina, tells us he has a toy truck, similar to a 1949 Chevy, that was made by Conway.

Relatively small, the toy is a Baby Ruth-Butterfinger candy bar truck. It was made the same general way as the Packard, out of heavy plastic and plated metal. Dollinger believes Conway made a replica of a 1949 Kaiser convertible. The car he has in mind had a plastic body, plated grille and trim, rubber tires and clockworks motor. It was about 10 inches long.

The Conway 1948 Packard convertible is a rare item today.

Gallery of automotive toys

Model Cars

1978 was a good year for dealer promotional models

By Dennis Doty

Dealer promotional models of real cars have been with us for many years. They came into their own in 1949. At least that's when the first *plastic* dealer promotionals were introduced by AMT Corporation.

AMT stood for Aluminum Model Toys. A year earlier, in 1948, the same company had issued its first dealer promotional. It was a Ford made of aluminum. Like the real cars of the 1950s, the promotional models were stand outs in that decade. Two-tone versions were common and, often, there was a wide variety of body types including sedans, hardtops, station wagons and, of course, convertibles.

Collectors of promotional models, such as *Old Cars* research editor Ken Buttolph, existed even back then. Of course, they were in the minority and the little cars often wound up in the hands of small children who treated them roughly. (We admit that Ken is in his second childhood, but he does treat his more than 100 promotional models with the best of care.)

The original intent behind these models was to utilize them as a sales promotion tool. They did a nice job of representing real cars and showing what they looked like in different colors, with varying trims. Children often received a model that looked like the family's real car when dad finally broke down and bought a new one from his friendly neighborhood dealer.

Times have changed though. Just try asking a new-car dealer for a promotional model today! Chances are, he'll want to know what the heck you're talking about. While they still exist, you rarely see promotionals in the office at a car dealership. They must produce most of them for the collector's marketplace.

Collecting dealer promotional models is more popular than ever, especially with the model car fan that doesn't have either the skill or the time to build a model up from a kit. Although models in the current crop of promotionals are not nearly as exciting as those from the past, a few of particular years stand out as those to add to collections before prices zoom. One of those "hot" years is 1978.

That year, eight different cars were produced as factory-assembled dealer promotional models. One was a Cadillac Coupe deVille made by Jo-Han, a firm which then had the longest tenure as a promotional model maker. It had been producing them for 23 years, since 1955.

Cadillac was in its second year of a body design cycle in 1978, so the revisions needed to update the Jo-Han promotional to 1978 design specifications were minor. The grille had more vertical bars than the previous year, the sun roof got a clear-plastic panel and the taillights ran the length of the bumper.

This model came in four colors called Basil Green Metallic, Mediterranean Blue Metallic, Western Saddle Metallic and Carmine Red. Wire wheels and a hood ornament helped to really set it off nicely.

Model Products Corporation (MPC) was in its 13th year of producing promotionals in 1978. It produced the balance of seven models offered that season. Included in the basic Chevrolet line were replicas of the Monza, the Chevette (a second year revision) and the totally-revised-for-1978 Monte Carlo. This trio came in three different metallic colors called Dark Camel, Light Blue and Medium Green.

Models of the 1978 Corvette were available two ways. One was all-Silver. The other was a two-tone (Charcoal and Silver) version of the full-sized "Silver Anniversary" edition, which was a limited-edition package.

For its first year, the revised Monte Carlo was not modeled in a kit, so the promotional model was the only way to obtain a small-scale version. A kit was listed as being available and shown in the 1978 MPC sales catalog, but it was canceled before it was ever released.

The 1978 Corvette promotional models were the big news among collectors, as the 1978 Corvette was news in general. It was the 25th anniversary of the marque. A Corvette was selected to pace the Indy 500 and the limited edition pace car was making headline news nationwide. It was reported to be an "instant collector car" and dealers were selling them for way over sticker prices.

Models of the Chevrolet sports car were available two ways. One was all-Silver. The other was a two-tone (Charcoal and Silver) version of the full-sized "Silver Anniversary" edition, which was another limited-edition package.

The all-Silver Corvette model was available first, but only as part of a dealer assortment that included three of each Chevrolet promotional model ... a dozen in all.

There turned out to be an unusual variation on the all-Silver model. To make it easier to spray a second color of paint on the two-toned "Silver Anniversary" model, MPC ran a lip around the cars. (It is almost impossible to make a paint mask to do a two-tone, unless there is such a cut-off line on the body. Some of the all-Silver models were made with the cut-off line for the two-toned Corvette. These were produced simply to complete a run of dealer assortment packages. As a result, the all-Silver Corvettes with the parting lines are the rarest 1978 promotional models.

Actually, all of the all-Silver 1978 Corvette promotionals are considered rare and those who deal in selling these models ask high prices for them. In reality, over 9,000 of them were produced, so they aren't as rare as some folks want people to believe.

Collectors must also be careful about paying a premium to get an all-Silver Corvette with the paint parting line. The more common (two-toned) Silver Anniversary edition can be carefully re-painted to resemble the all-Silver version with a parting line. If offered an all-Silver with parting line, I suggest that you remove the chassis to see if the interior "locaters" have been tampered with. If they have, it could be a Silver Anniversary edition that was carefully re-painted all-Silver.

The final General Motors promotional for 1978 was the Pontiac Firebird Trans Am. This model is distinctive. While it was a true promotional item, you had to assemble it. It came with a pre-painted body and assembly was very simple, as there were very few parts.

Kit format versions of Firebird promotionals were offered since 1975, so the 1978 version was nothing really new. The colors it came in were Starlight Black and Platinum Metallic. Its box art was very nice, but unfortunately, it didn't really represent the model that was actually made available

MPC also made two Chrysler Corporation promotional models in 1978. They represented the Plymouth Volare and the Dodge Monaco. The Volare came with decals to make it into a Road Runner, but the owner of the model had to apply them. It came in colors of Starlite Blue Metallic and Spitfire Orange. The Dodge Monaco was available in Augusta Green Metallic and Starlite Blue Metallic.

Naturally, the prices of all of these dealer promotionals are on the upswing. Remember, though, the values of these models will never be cheaper than they are right now.

Cadillac was in its second year of a body design cycle in 1978, so the revisions needed to update the Jo-Han promotional to 1978 design specifications were minor.

Included in MPC's basic 1978 Chevrolet line of dealer promotional models were replicas of the Monza, the Chevette (a second year revision) and the totally-revised-for-1978 Monte Carlo.

Some small cars worth weight in gold

By John Marshall

$200 an ounce!

"Worth it's weight in gold" is an often-used phrase, but one that is rarely used in it's literal sense. There are few items to which it can be truly applied. An exception, of course, would be in the area of precious gem stones.

Certainly, one would not expect to find any toy cars in that category, especially something manufactured as recently as the late 1950s. However, at least one exists: the Matchbox model car number 27-A-1 Bedford Low Loader Truck in "factory" two-tone blue. This tiny toy is a gem in it's own right. Although it only weighs slightly over half-an-ounce and cost a mere 49-cents in 1956, Match box collectors will pay hundreds of dollars for it today. The reason is that it's rare. While several thousand of these models were made in green and tan, very few were made in two-tone blue. That fact makes it one of the most sought after Matchbox collectibles.

The value of number 27-A-1 represents quite a large return on investment, but one that is not all uncommon in the field of "small" (Matchbox-size) toy car collecting. However, to look upon this fascinating and rewarding hobby as only an investment is to miss all of the fun and excitement of searching and finding these little gems. Why do adults collect model cars?

There are as many reasons for collecting small model cars as there are collectors. The one most commonly heard is, "My son started collecting them when he was small and I became fascinated along with him." For others, it is nostalgic to possess something they remember owning as a child a decade to a quarter-century (or more) ago.

There are some who love classic or vintage automobiles, but lack the extra $20,000 or so that it takes to buy one. For them, the next best thing is to own a toy replica. Perhaps for others, who were not fortunate as children in leaner times, collecting is a form of fulfilling a childhood desire. Whatever the reason, once one gets hooked on collecting these models. There is no turning back.

Where does one find small models?

Certainly lucky are those who return to their homes, after college or a hitch in the Armed Forces, to find that their room just as it was, including the top box full of little treasures.

For those not that fortunate, there are local toy and hobby shops, antique shops, swap meets, advertisements in model toy publications, garage sales and finally, shows with dealers who trade especially in antique toys for collectors.

Current prices would seem to be the next consideration. Here, even a volume would not cover the subject completely. As with all other collectibles, value is a matter of supply and demand. Naturally, most older and rarer models command very high prices. For instance pre-World War II Dinkys and Tootsietoys, that cost 10-cents originally, easily bring 1,000 times that amount today. Some are worth much more, depending on their condition and rarity.

Easy to find are many Matchbox models made by the Lesney Company. Most every child has owned one, like this 1934 Riley, in the approximately 45 years that they have been manufactured. (Matchbox photo)

Certainly lucky are those who return to their homes, after college or a hitch in the Armed Forces, to find that their room just as it was, including the top box full of Matchbox "Models of Yesteryear." (Matchbox photo)

Sometimes, only a few collectors are fortunate enough to find any of these items at any price, since there are few for sale that have survived 25, 35 or 45 years.

Easier to find, however, and probably the toys that are most familiar to current collectors, are Matchbox models made by the Lesney Company. Most every child has owned one or more of these little gems in the 35 years that they have been manufactured. Although many millions of each model have been made, there are several Matchbox models produced in the late 1950s that are very valuable. Although these originally sold for 39-cents to 49-cents, today they are bringing 50 times that price. Others, like the highly sought after number 7-A Horse Drawn Milk Float are worth more than 150 times their original price.

Even if you have nothing left from the 1940s or the 1950s, do not give up hope yet. There were several toy companies that made model cars right up to the late 1960s. Then because of a plant fire, strike, bankruptcy, etc., they ceased production. Their models were plentiful in the shops at the time they were in production, but as soon as production ceased, the models disappeared and immediately became collectors' items. Some examples of these are Dugu, Rami and Tekno models and the "Classic" series toy vehicles made by Corgi.

The 1970s are getting collectible!

Still not impressed? Let's get into the 1970s. Already, some of the models made by England's Dinky and Corgi, plus all of the models made by the French Dinky branch, are considered obsolete. Some are already worth many times their original prices. A prime example is the Starsky & Hutch Ford Torino.

Sometimes, these types of models can still be found in toy and hobby shops located in small towns that are off the beaten tracks. There they sit, gathering dust on the back shelves. Usually, when one makes such a discovery, the shopkeeper is quite unaware of the fact that his stock is a collectors' item. He or she is only too glad to get rid of it at the original price or even give a discount to move it out.

As in other types of collecting, the cars which seem to become collectors' items are always the very ugly or the very beautiful ones. Ugly toys become wanted because, at the time they were produced, no one wanted them. Production was often stopped prematurely, creating a short run and making the toy scarce. Beautiful toys are naturally desirable, because everyone wants one. This quickly dries up the supply.

Model car collecting can be quite lucrative financially. Often, a collector can realize very many times his investment in a few years. However, to enter this hobby with only the thought of making a profit as an

There are some who would love to buy classic 1938 Lagonda, but lack the disposable income it takes to buy one. For them, the next best thing is to own this Matchbox version. (Matchbox photo)

255

Model car collecting can be financially lucrative. This late 1970s "Models of Yesteryear" 1928 Mercedes SS is appreciating in value. However, to enter the hobby with profit-making in mind is to miss all the fun. (Matchbox photo)

incentive is to miss the great delight to be had in owning and displaying these small gems of engineering. Missing will be the thrill that comes when one finds that long sought-after item needed to complete a set.

Are there many toy car collectors in the USA?

It would be hard to estimate the total number of toy collectors. In the Matchbox Collectors Club alone, there were over 5,000 members when this was written. A model car dealer in Costa Mesa, California claims to have 1,500 collectors on his mailing list. Those who collect these toys represent every profession you could name. The hobby is not limited to men and boys. There are many female collectors, too. The largest collection could certainly be that of a certain university professor who has in excess of 16,000 models.

How should models be stored?

Matchbox-size model cars beg to be displayed, rather than kept in their original boxes, locked away in a cupboard. Any type of display cabinet can be used, but the ideal type is one that has glass shelves, sliding glass doors and a light inside. Displayed in this manner, the models will always be a conversation piece. Unlike a collection of gold or silver coins, which should be kept in a safe deposit box, model cars can be openly displayed with little fear that a burglar will give them more than a second glance.

For readers who have already have the urge to put down this book and go searching attics and old toy chests, lots of luck and happy collecting.

Model hobby is great winter fun

By Dennis Doty

Cold weather in the northern areas of the United States doesn't bring an end to the car shows and swap meets, but it does usually drive them inside. How many people want to rummage through a bunch of rusty parts in a 10-degree blizzard? Indoors, it is nice and dry and perfect for looking for that special model car that will complement your collection. Keep an eye out for some of these goodies if you happen to be touring the classic car auctions in Arizona in January, the Atlantic City swap meet in February or other mid-winter activities.

Many vendors at these meets sell only promotional models. Many collectors of this type of model attend these meets. There are a lot of rare promotional models starting to show up. Here we'll discuss some you should be on the lookout for.

The 1960 Buick promotional isn't a really rare model or one of unusually high value. However, there are two types of them. Buick's trademark for many years were front fender portholes. As I hear it, there were rumors of these being dropped for the 1960 models. While the real cars for 1960 had these standard Buick features, some of the promotional models were released without the portholes. I have seen both hardtop and convertible versions without the portholes.

It's very likely that, when AMT first started molding these models, Buick had decided against the portholes. They then changed their mind. Rather than scrap the models they had already molded, AMT released them and created a special collector's item. The porthole-free models are worth from 50 percent to 100 percent more than their correct counterpart.

Continuing with the 1960 Buick, there was a rarer release than the ones without portholes. This one was made for the dealers only and not sold to the public directly. It is an unusual model of the 1960 Buick chassis. This promo consisted of a chassis complete with exhaust system, engine and brake drums. The brake drums were on one side of the model, with the regular wheels and tires on the

The 50th anniversary plaque with a bubble containing a model of the first, 1911, Chevrolet and the "new" 1962 dealer promotional model.

257

other. The frame details were all painted a different color. Since this was done with paint masks, there was a very high rejection rate.

The engine in the chassis was the same engine that was used in the kit of the 1960 Buick and the chassis model came in its own, special promotional box. It is one of the more unusual promotionals of the 1960s, along with the 1960 Rambler body in white. Unlike the Rambler, though, the Buick chassis is extremely hard to find and worth a good deal of money. However, it is not worth as much as it would have been if they would have included a clear body with it. This promotional is easy to pass up at a meet. When you first look at it, the appearance is like something that has been made up from a kit.

Another unusual item came out in the early 1960s from Chevrolet. It was a special plaque commemorating 50 years of Chevrolet. This plaque was approximately 18 X 23 inches. It consisted of a model of the first 1911 Chevrolet and the latest 1962 Chevrolet promotional model. These came in a modern gold frame and were protected by a large, clear-plastic bubble. It was made so that the 1962 Chevrolet model could be changed to keep the plaque up to date. That 1962 Chevrolet promotional was made by AMT in the United States. It is one of the most sought-after kits ever released. The kit never had a commercial release. It was available only through Chevrolet dealers. The model didn't even have a regular box, though I can't say exactly how they were packaged, as I have never even seen an unassembled kit of this model.

It is also interesting to note that the molds for a prototype of the 1911 Chevrolet model, with a windshield, were made in Germany. (The actual model never came with a windshield). This tooling was probably made of aluminum, rather than steel, as aluminum was cheaper for short production runs. Of course, the aluminum tooling didn't hold up as long, at least back then. The 1911 Chevrolet in the bubble was factory assembled and is a true promotional model, which is very rare.

I obtained a kit. While it is a simple model, it was not easy to build. The plaques with both models are not all that hard to find, but most people who have them want to trade only. For the promotional model collector, this item adds much to your display room.

Promotionals come in all forms. They are models used to promote something else. One of the more interesting is the promotional model of a vintage Global Van Lines moving van from Disneyland. I snapped a picture of the truck at a toy fair in Dearborn, Michigan, but I have little information on this model. Although it is more of a toy, the quality is excellent. So is the detail.

With promotionals like these, it is hard to discern the distinctions between a toy and a model. The two types of automotive miniatures sometimes come so close that it is hard to tell one from the other. I do not know the value of this toy. When I spotted it, I had run out of money and I was afraid the price might have been reasonable, so I did not ask.

Kits of all types and ages are also showing up more than ever before at automotive swap meets. Collector interest in unbuilt kits is very high right now. You can still find bargains in plastic kits. Some of the best buys are kits from Revell's "Highway Pioneers" series. Even though these kits first came out in the early 1950s, they were re-issued several times into the early 1960s. The original kits still sell quite reasonably. They are still a real bargain for kits about 30-35 years old. The rare Highway Pioneer kits (Cord, Duesenberg and most higher number kits) sell for a lot more. While built-up older kits do have collector values (depending on how well they were constructed), they are usually valued at less than an unbuilt kit.

Kits along the lines that we know today didn't really start until 1958, when AMT's three-in-one customizing kits arrived. These were barely more than unassembled promotional models with a few extra custom pieces (louvers, fender skirts, mirrors, etc.). However, they are what actually started the hobby as we know it today.

The first real AMT kits are extremely hard to find today. For some reason, the 1958 Edsel and 1958 Buick hardtop are most commonly seen. The 1958 Ford is hardest to find and the 1958 Chevrolet runs a close second to the Ford. All these models were available in both hardtop and convertible versions. Also available in that first year was a Pontiac, that came in hardtop and convertible kits, and an Imperial convertible kit.

My research indicates that the first yearly kit from Jo-Han appeared a year later, in 1959. The Plymouth Fury, Dodge Custom Royal, Cadillac and Oldsmobile were the only cars available. MPC didn't get into the yearly kit business until 1964, when they made a Corvette coupe (with non-stock wheels).

Some highly collectible model kits from before the 1958 AMT models included a 1955 Cadillac Coupe DeVille and a 1955 Cadillac convertible in a size larger than the normal 1/24th-scale. These were Monogram model kits. The Cadillacs were molded in acetate and tended to warp. In fact, the top of the Coupe DeVille was a separate piece that really warped badly. Good examples are hard to find and bring good money.

Some 1960 Buick models. Up front is the scarce one without portholes. There was an even rarer promotional made for the dealers only and not sold directly to the public. It is a detailed model of the 1960 Buick chassis.

Probably one of the hardest items in the model car field to collect is the styling mock-up. These are usually made of plaster. They are very well-detailed.

In 1956, only the Cadillac convertible was made. The material that it was molded in changed to Styrene plastic. A contest giving away a real 1956 Cadillac was connected to this kit. What ever happened to those good old contests?

Revell issued one of the best detailed kits ever. It was a 1957 Ford Country Squire station wagon. This was a 1957 release in 1/25th-scale. The only thing that would date this kit, if it could be reintroduced today, is its multi-piece body construction. Unfortunately, this kit was converted into a customized 1957 Ford Ranchero, which was available up until some 10 years ago. Revell also issued a 1959 Ford Skyliner convertible with a working retractable top. This was another well-detailed kit. It was available as a re-issue, also until about 10 years ago.

As mentioned above, all built-up kits have collector value, depending on how well they are built. However, an assembled kit is not considered built-up if it was built by the kit manufacturer. At first glance, such factory-assembled models may appear to be regular kits that some modeler assembled. In fact, they are often hard to tell apart.

There is no set rule to telling the difference. You must be careful here. Revell was one of the first companies to offer assembled models for use as in-store displays to help sell kits. Many of the Highway Pioneer models were made for these promotions and even the later (1957) series 1/25th-scale models were made by Revell. These models are all rare and bring a pretty good price when they turn up. The Highway Pioneers have lower values.

Some people call these factory-assembled models promotionals, but they really aren't. They were never intended for individual sale. You will find most companies made these models at one time or another. In fact, they are still sometimes made today. For many years, Monogram Model Company had models built-up for store displays, including assembled versions of its 1/8th-scale models in very nice settings.

Revell even had many of its working Goodyear Blimp models built-up. They made most effective in-store displays. With their revolving signs, they looked just like the real blimp. I am sure this really helped sell the models. You could hardly miss the display. Hubley/Gabriel also made in-store displays of their classic and antique models. These came in their own bubble-packed display and are also worth seeking.

In-store displays are pretty much a thing of the past, but revivals do seem to take place from time to time. You can bet that any such models will be highly collectible items in the future. If you ever see one, ask the store manager if there's a chance you can buy it.

Probably one of the hardest items in the model car field to collect is the styling mock-up. These are usually made of plaster. They are very well-detailed. Collecting them presents a special problem for several reasons. One problem is size. Some of these plaster models are in 1/4th-scale. That makes for one large model! A second problem is that they are made of plaster. One little slip can create lots of damage. A third problem is that these were made for the real car companies and not intended to be collected. How many survived is anyone's guess, but they are collectible. Whatever ones remain are rare and valuable.

Because these items are considered rare, prices are usually in the hundreds of dollars. At various toy shows you see a few of them, Some are for sale, but most are intended for display only. Often, there's a wanted sign asking for leads for more of these models. If you have never seen one of these models, it is hard to imagine how well-detailed they can be. I have even seen examples with interiors, although most have solid windows which are usually painted silver. While this type of model does not turn up at every meet, when you can get your hands on them, they make unique items to add to your collection. If you don't want one, I know a Ford stylist who does.

As mentioned above, a fine line sometimes exists between toys and scale-models. Right now, one of the hot items in toys are modern Smith-Miller trucks. These came out in 1979 when a man named Fred Thompson purchased the Smith-Miller name and parts inventory. He then began producing limited-edition toy trucks that are what he calls "new-issue" Smith-Millers. Thompson took the company from where its early history stopped and went forward from there.

"I do not reproduce original Smith-Miller designs," Thompson told us. "For the past 15 years, I've been making new toys that are continuations of the Smith-Miller line and of the same high-quality as the originals."

Anyone interested in information about these products can contact Fred Thompson/Smith-Miller, 22667 Keswick, West Hills, CA 91304 or call (818) 703-8588.

Another toy field that is coming on strong is the tin toy model car. These cars were turned out by the thousands, mainly by Japanese firms. They do not deserve the once prevalent image of being cheap "Made In Japan" toys. While all tin toy cars are not exciting, when you come across one that is well-detailed and in good condition, you have a treasured piece for your collection.

I advise collectors to get into tin cars carefully. They are highly addictive and the range of models is extremely wide. Just when you think you have it an under control, along comes something you never expected in tin. Don't say I didn't warn you!

This should give you a good idea of some toys and models to look for this winter. You may not find anything I have written about. You may find something few people have ever heard of. The variety of items at an indoor swap meet or toys and models show can stagger the imagination. Just when you think you have the picture pretty well in control, some item will pop up and throw the focus off once again. Of course, that is probably the nicest thing about the model car hobby. Even the experts don't know everything (though sometimes, they pretend that they do). Good hunting!

The Global Van Lines promo from Disneyland featured an antique C-cab style moving van. It is a very well-detailed promotional that bridges the gap between toy vehicle and scale-model.

Car dealer promotional models

By Dennis Doty

What seems to show up most at car meets these days is promotional models. The histories of the manufacturers would take up too much space, so let me just point out some of the more interesting promotional models that have been available through the years.

Car dealer promotional models really came into their own in the 1950s, when plastic promotional models became popular. However, promotional models started out being cast in pot metal and slush-molded.

Molten metal was poured into a mold and, almost immediately, poured out again to make these. This type of promotional model first appeared on the scene way back in 1934. The first was a Studebaker made by National Products Company. The major pot metal promotional models came from National Products, Master Caster and, most notably, from Banthrico (who is still in business today).

One example of a pot metal car is a Rambler Custom convertible of 1951. It was made by National Products. At the time, National Products was owned by Banthrico.

Not many pot metal cars came with interiors, though the few convertibles released did have interiors. Most of the slush-molded bodies were molded in one piece. Details in these models were not up to those of later plastic models, but still pretty good. Things like nameplates are depicted. Because these had basically one-piece bodies, grilles and side trim were usually masked off, as were the bumpers. In this way, the bare metal gave a chrome-like effect.

All metal promotional models are hard to come by and bring a very high dollar. This seems unusual, as most of these were produced in the hundreds of thousands, but you must remember, they were usually considered banks and toys. Kids can be rough with such items. Being made of metal, you would think more would have survived, but if they have, they are hiding well.

AMT started making promotional models back in 1948. AMT stood for Aluminum Model Toys. The first product was an aluminum Ford. AMT changed to plastic a year later, however. One of the more unusual promotional models they made then was a 1951 Packard-Henney ambulance. This was not only unusual for the type of model it was, but because it was also in a larger size (about 1/20th-scale).

Promotionals give you something to look for at model car shows you visit.

Early promotionals were made of acetate plastic and tend to warp.

Car dealer promotional models really came into their own in the 1950s.

The clear 1956 Rambler. This view shows the interior "guts." The detailling here is extremely well done. The size is larger than the 1/25th-scale that is used for the vast majority of promotional models. (Dennis Doty photo)

The 1958 Pontiac had everything gold-plated: body, interior, chassis, bumpers, windows and tires. It isn't one of the more attractive promotional models with those plated tires. However, it is very collectible.

This pot metal 1948 Chevrolet was offered as a sales promotion tool.

The detailing on the Packard was extremely good. Unlike most promotional models of the time, this one came with all chrome trim molded and plated separately from the body. Packard was hot-stamped on the hood and Henney was also hot-stamped low on the body, behind the front wheel, on some of the models. The hood ornament was a very delicate item. To find this model with the ornament intact is rare.

Actually, locating a complete model is exceptionally difficult and prices run very high. The side trim also tended to lose some pieces. Another negative aspect of this model was its tendency to warp. All plastic promotional models of the 1950s to the early 1960s were made of acetate plastic. The brand name was Tenite. It was manufactured by Eastman Kodak. Sooner or later, all of these miniatures wind up getting somewhat warped. There seems to be nothing that can be done about this. The Packard-Henney had no interior features other than a steering wheel. It was powered by a key-wound spring-type motor.

There are several promotional models that were produced by unknown firms. No one, today, seems to know who made them. One of these was a Hudson of about 1948-1949 vintage. It was plastic and done in a large scale. It came in many versions, including one that was half-painted and half clear-plastic. Another mystery model was a 1956 Rambler four-door sedan. The Rambler seemed very unique. The only known version was made of clear-plastic. This model was hard to photograph, since it's clear. It was also divided down the middle by a plastic mirror on the inside of the body. When you looked at one side of the model, you saw the frame through the clear body. When you looked at the other side, you saw the "guts" of the interior. I believe this was called "body in white."

The mirror gave the impression of a complete model on either side ... one a chassis and the other side the "guts." The detailing here was extremely well done and once again, the size is larger than 1/25th-scale (the normal size for promotional models). Details were not lacking and, if this model went out painted and detailed, it would be one of the better promotional models for 1956. I have heard that the model was later updated to a 1957 Rambler. This was a common practice in the promotional model field.

Switching to unusual promotional models from known manufacturers, we have Jo-Han's B.F. Goodrich service truck. The basic cab resembled a 1948 to 1953 Chevrolet Advance-Design pickup, but with quad headlights. It was not intended to be styled after a specific truck though. The model was two-toned in tan and blue. Lettering was hot-stamped on the model and usually holds up well. The wheels were well-detailed for the time and the tires had Goodrich lettering on them, something seldom done in the 1950s.

The model came out in early 1958 and no more than 15,000 were made. That is how many were anticipated after Goodrich placed its order on October 7, 1957. There is always the possibility that the full order was not produced. These truck models were made for B.F. Goodrich tire dealers only. They were not intended for public sale. This makes the special promotional very rare today. They always bring top prices when they show up, which seldom happens.

The service truck was very well-detailed. It had a movable boom. The boom swiveled 360-degrees and could be raised and lowered. The boom came with a chain and hook, which are usually missing. Details molded into the truck bed included a compressor and tank. There was no interior. I don't think they were built to any specific scale, but they look slightly smaller than 1/25th-scale.

Though the model companies didn't plan them, from time to time, a small quantity of regular promotional models would be released for special promotions, usually within automobile companies. These special promotional models would be used at banquets, as awards to long-time employees or dealers who sold their quotas, etc. Sometimes, only hundreds (or possibly not even that many) were turned out.

Special gold-plated models have been around for a long time. One of the rarest promotional models is a gold-plated Tucker. Early plastic was very hard to plate, because it was made of acetate. One of the neatest early plated plastic models was a 1957 Pontiac. It was followed, the next year, by a gold-plated 1958 Bonneville two-door hardtop.

Both of these gold-plated Pontiac models were the work of Jack Stewart, who worked for Pontiac's advertising agency at the time. One of Stewart's jobs to develop Pontiac Motor Division's "General Manager's Award," which went to the top Pontiac salesmen in the nation. Semon "Bunkie" Knudson had just taken over as general manager of Pontiac and was in the midst of revamping the company image. He asked Stewart to come up with a new and inspiring type of award. The answer was the gold-plated scale-models.

As an aside, Jack Stewart also designed a large, fiberglass 1956 Pontiac child's car with light-up head-lights that his children could ride in, and which is worth thousands of dollars now. Other well-known General Manager Awards that he produced included the 1959-1961 Lucite paperweights and a series of paintings including the one of "Fireball" Robert's 1962 Pontiac stock car and another called "Apache Trail" that depicts an imaginary scene of Pontiacs racing through the desert. In 1979, Stewart was called upon to produce another award and did his own painting of a Pontiac Trans Am Pace Car starting the Daytona 500. Stewart has contributed a lot to the automobilia that Pontiac enthusiasts collect today.

On the 1958 Pontiac model, everything was plated gold: the body, interior, chassis, bumpers and even the windows and tires. Unless you are a real nut on plated promotional models, it isn't one of the more attractive models with those plated tires. However, it is very collectible.

A person has to be careful purchasing plated models as collectibles. I have heard of a few cases of bootlegged plated models. These are regular models that have been plated to make them worth more. A plated model can cost up to twice the price of its unplated twin. Plated models are not for everyone.

Collectors tend to either have a series of plated models in their collection or none at all. Like pewter models that look out of place among regular models, the plated replicas really stand out. Some such models were made in very limited quantities. However, since many were special awards and never treated as toys, a good share of those made still exist.

Taxis and police cars are another area of the promotional model market. I do not think that any replica of a taxi or police car made as a regular sales promotion tool. Most were considered toys and were sold in stores. Because they were considered toys, not that many survive today. This makes them rare and valuable.

Taxis and police cars are two items you don't often see at the various meets, even the model car collector meets. However, you never know when one will turn up on a table. A lot of the later promotional models were made only in two-door body styles, so fewer cab and police models were turned out. That didn't eliminate them completely, though. Into the 1960s, Jo-Han was releasing two-door cabs and cop cars.

Some Chevrolet cabs of the 1950s even came with the sign boards and a sign on the back. I have not personally seen that many cab and police models, so can't comment on them in depth. I do know about Jo-Han's 1959 Plymouth taxi and 1962 Dodge Dart police car. Jo-Han had the lettering on these models done by hot-stamping, which is a lot better than decals. Heat-stamping is permanent.

There was at least one promotional police car model. It was done for the television show "Car 54 Where Are You?" I have only seen one of these. I recall that it was a 1961 or 1962 Plymouth. It was made in very limited quantities and is rare, to say the least.

There is another type of promotional model. It's the type where the model itself stays the same and products it promotes keep changing. This is done today by several firms, such as the Winross company. Winross makes promotional trucks in 1/64th-scale for many companies and hobby events. Collecting Winross trucks is very popular.

The Winross models also came in United States Bicentennial models, election-year models and many other variations. The styles of cabs and trailers also vary. These trucks are a story unto themselves, but mentioning them gives you an idea of how much is out there.

Another popular promotional effort is a series of nearly 1/25th-scale panel delivery vans. I have heard these come in over 20 variations, even through the truck is the same. The two I have in my personal collection are from Mills Bakery and Wilson Dairy. These models are banks, with a slot in the top, and not easy to come by. I don't know who the manufacturer was, but I have heard rumors the company did a promotional of their own.

The above items should give you something different to look for at the next model car show you visit. If you would like to follow up on any of these products, you may be interested in publications helpful to collectors. Naturally, Krause Publication's magazines *Toy Shop* and *Toy Collector & Price Guide* are very helpful, as well as Krause's line of toy books an price guides. For information about these write: Krause Publications, Toy Department, 700 East State Street, Iola, WI 54990 or call (715) 445-2214.

Another publication that is available and aimed more specifically at model car collectors is *Model Car Journal*, PO Box 154135, Irving, TX 75015-4135, telephone (214) 790-5346.

The Wilson dairy truck promo. Details were generally on the crude side, except for the grille/headlight assembly. It is a different type of promotional model for sure. (Dennis Doty photo)

National Product's 1951 Rambler Custom convertible was modeled in pot metal. Details in these models were not up to those of later plastic models, but still pretty good. Things like nameplates were depicted.

How AMT makes a model car

By Dennis Doty

Years ago, when Lesney Products Corporation purchased AMT model company and moved its manufacturing arm to Baltimore, Maryland from Troy, Michigan, the creative operation in Warren, Michigan retained an engineering staff, art department and wood shop. I was one of about 30 members of the Michigan Model Car Collectors (MMCC) that took a Saturday tour of the operation. Because the AMT facilities were rather small, it was a huddled, but happy group. The tour guides were Terry Sansom (head of the Warren facility), John Mueller, Jerry Adrian and Tim Rice.

The tour assembled in the reception office, where the MMCC members could look at some assembled AMT models. The group then broke up into four small groups. My group went to the instruction sheet department first. Even though the AMT instruction sheets no longer gave as much information as in the past, they were larger because more symbols were being used so that the kits could be sold worldwide. At the time, our tour was the first to learn that AMT was adding a seventh language (Japanese) to its instruction sheets.

Someone raised the question of how these instructions are translated. The group was told this was a very small problem, since Lesney was a worldwide operation. Instructions are simply sent to each country and translated on home ground to insure that it is done correctly.

The instruction sheet area was also the kit check out area. There, kits were built up to see how easily they could be assembled and if there were any problems that should be corrected. It was pointed out that a popular kit was about to be pulled from the line because there was a problem in assembling the kit. This was brought to AMT's attention through a letter from a builder. AMT just decided to pull it from the line, so the problems could be corrected. This was not an inexpensive proposition, but it was cheaper than tooling a new kit. When the problems were corrected, the kit was re-introduced.

From the instruction sheet and model check out area, our tour group moved to the engineering department. There, all the parts needed to produce a model were drafted to exact scale. The tour got a real surprise, as the engineering drawings shown were for a Datsun 280 Turbo ZX which was a kit that hadn't reached the market yet. It was exciting to see something like that in the earliest phase of the production system.

The next stop was at the art department. While AMT was then planning to go almost exclusively to photographic box art, our group saw some of the renderings that AMT artists were capable of. They were excellent and highly impressive pieces of art. Much more goes into box art than most builders suspect and many steps are involved in producing a finished box to hold the parts of a model car kit.

Here our tour was also shown the early test shots of box art depicting a 1968 Camaro. At that time, the release of the Camaro kit had been delayed over a year. Collectors were concerned it wouldn't come out at all. However, from the looks of the test shots we previewed, we knew that the extra wait was well worth enduring.

From the art department, our group moved to the wood shop. This was a most impressive phase of the tour. We learned that all of the master parts for a model car kit must first be made to 1/10th-scale to facil-

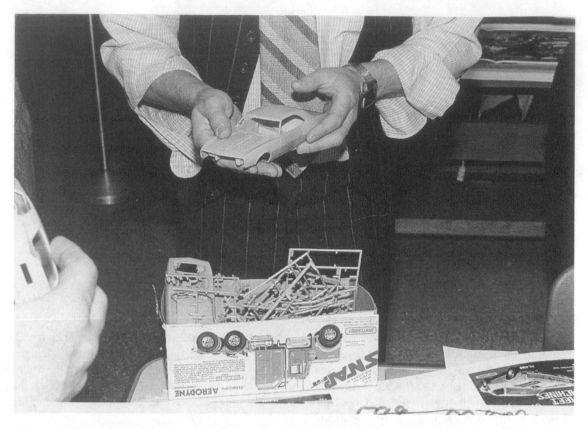

When we took our tour of the AMT/Lesney facility in Warren, Michigan, one of the highlights was the opportunity to see this 1968 Camaro model car kit going through some of the pre-production phases involved in its creative process.

itate the production of patterns. For the most part, the master parts are made of wood, although clay is also be used. How well these hand-carved parts are made determines how authentic the finished kit will be.

Once the wood "masters" are made, resin molds are taken from them. These molds are required to make a 1/10th-scale resin casting. This casting is then used as a pattern to make the tools needed to actually produce the kits. The full process was really a lot more complicated than described, but my summary gives you the basics. It is not a procedure that can be concluded in a few weeks. That is why the time required to produce a kit from conception to finished model is a year or more in most cases.

Someone brought up the interesting point that the wood used to make the patterns is very special type. It is called perfect plank. Each plank costs hundreds of dollars. It takes three planks to make wood patterns for each model and this is another reason that models cost so much today,

The final leg of our tour took the group past an example of the actual tools used to produce kits. These tools can weigh several tons and are expensive. All in all, model car kits are not cheap to produce.

Since the AMT Warren facility was not a production plant producing models during our tour, we did not actually see giant plastic-injection-molding machines or any vacuum-plating facilities. However, even without viewing actual production operations, that AMT tour was a learning experience.

Certainly, in the time since we took this tour, computer-aided design and manufacturing systems have come into greater use in model-car production. Still, we're sure that many basics of the process are unchanged. It is very hard to comprehend all that it takes to produce a model car kit, until you go on a tour such as we did. All of us went away with a new respect for our favorite hobby.

Looking at a kit in the box makes it hard to visualize just how complex the tooling that's required to produce it can be. This is the tool for AMT's "Red Alert" 1972 Chevelle model. It was in to be re-worked. Re-working a tool is an ongoing maintenance process necessary to keep models easy-to-assemble.

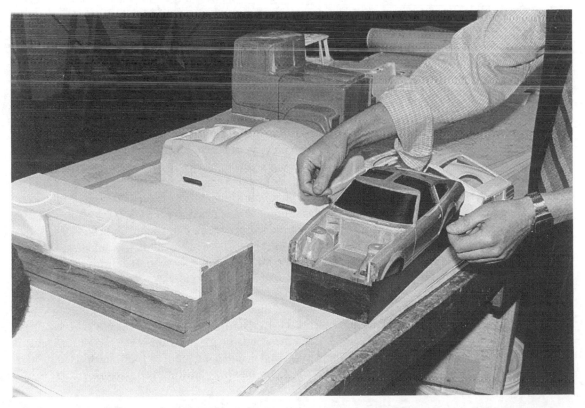

These 1/10-scale wood prototypes for a kit are used to make molds for plastic models. The resulting resin casting is then employed as a pattern to make the tools needed to actually produce kits. (Dennis Doty photos)

Looking at auto miniatures

By Wayne Moyer

Why 1/43-scale?

The hobby of collecting small scale-model cars or, more correctly, automotive miniatures, has become very popular in this country since the mid-1980s. These are not the familiar 1/25-scale plastic kits and car dealer promotional models, but fully-finished models and kits made of die-cast metal, white-metal or resins. They are done in the international collector's scale of 1/43 (seven millimeters equals a foot).

What seems like an odd scale, to Americans, originated in Europe, as did the 1/43-scale models themselves. In Europe, 1/43-scale is the standard for model railroading. Its use was carried into the automotive modeling field.

There are several reasons for the boom, in collecting these models, in recent years. First, the models evolved from children's toys ("a car just like papa's") into superbly-finished, highly-detailed miniatures that were intended solely for adult collectors. Then, the European manufacturers discovered the United States market and began producing models aimed directly at American enthusiasts. Next, several small American and Canadian companies began making high-quality miniatures of American muscle cars, dream cars and special-interest cars. Finally, by the early 1990s, a wide variety of American sedans, NASCAR stock cars and other racing car models was also made available.

Die-cast Models

In order to talk intelligently about 1/43-scale-models, it's necessary to define some terms. *Die-cast* models are cast from zamac, a hard alloy metal. High pressure is used to inject the molten metal into tool-steel molds or dies. The castings are smooth, thin, hard and relatively brittle.

The tool steel dies are very expensive to make, but they will produce hundreds of thousands of copies. That means that die-cast models are, almost always, high-volume items. Prices on them range from a couple of dollars, for a K-Mart toy that's a reasonable facsimile of a real car, to nearly $50 for collectors' die-cast models with separate chrome-plated trim, multi-color paint schemes and hand-applied decals.

The classic toys of our youth, such as Dinky and Matchbox issues, were all die-cast models. Many of the companies that helped start the boom in demand for 1/43-scale die-cast models ... firms like Politoys, Tekno and Marklin ... are now long gone. Other firms, like Solido, Corgi, Dinky and others, are shadows of their former selves.

Several newer companies, such as Brumm, Vitesse, Bang and Best, currently make some very nice models. So do the German firms of Gamma and NZG. Rio, an Italian company, doesn't introduce new models as often as they used to, but has established the standards for other makers to shoot at. The Rio models come with a full frame, complete running gear and detailed engine. They are constructed using a combination of die-cast metal bodies with plastic, injection-molded parts for everything else.

White-metal Models

In contrast to die-cast models, *white-metal* models are produced by a centrifugal casting process. It uses a much softer, bendable alloy metal and hard, vulcanized rubber molds. The cost of making the "master" model is about the same as the cost of making a die-cast master, although the rubber molds run only a fraction of the cost of tool-steel dies. However, they wear out after only a few hundred models are made. They are also more difficult to control accurately. This leads to many rejections during the production process. More importantly, the rubber molds also require a fair amount of hand work for clean up and preparation.

White-metal kits tend to have low-volume production runs, with only 300 to 800 copies being made, although some companies do produce a few thousand kits, by continually making new molds. The low-volume production runs and hand work required to produce them make white-metal kits expensive. Prices run from around $35 to upwards of $75, depending on the complexity of the kit.

Brooklin Models began producing "factory-built" white-metal models in Canada and, later, moved to England. Western Models had already begun making similar miniatures, also in England, at about the same time. Brooklin, whose line now includes 45 models, plus some variations, makes only models of American cars. The company has certainly been a major factor in the growing popularity of 1/43-scale models in this country.

Factory-built Models

Factory-built white-metal models are just that; they are factory-assembled miniatures made from white-metal castings. The quality of finish and the assembly and workmanship are usually very good. You get what you pay for in terms of interior and exterior detail. Brooklin models, for example, usually have the major trim items (wheels, bumpers, grilles and, maybe, stone guards or hood ornaments, chrome plated). However, the side trim, window surrounds, door handles and name badges are cast in relief and painted over. Interiors are typically done in two colors, but multi-color upholstery is not duplicated.

A typical production run for Brooklin amounts to about 4,000 models. The current price for standard models is $65. Brooklin also sells higher-priced, limited-edition variations of its models, often as promotional items. These usually have production runs of 300-500 units.

Western Models includes a number of American cars in its line. These, typically, have much of the chrome trim reproduced. They often have two-tone or tri-tone color paint schemes. Western's prices run about $100 to $125.

U.S. Model Mint and design studios are other manufacturers. Both of these companies are from America. Their products fall between the two extremes (Brooklin and Western) in detail and price.

Handbuilt Models

Handbuilt white-metal models are produced, too. These are done in limited runs of 100 to 350 models. They are usually superbly finished and completely detailed with lots of small, chrome-plated pieces. They often have Bare-Metal Foil applied to their cast-in details. Other enhancements are liberal use of photo-etched chrome trim and multi-color decals for body badges, instrument dials, etc. Prices vary, depending upon just how much hand work is involved in the model, but they typically range from $200 to $300.

Mini-Marque 43 was the first company to produce the high-quality, handbuilt miniatures of American cars. However, a couple of American shops ... American Dream Machines and Motor City USA ... are now producing some very realistic examples of superb quality.

Resin Model Kits

Resin kits and models are cast, from epoxy or polyurethane resins, in very flexible rubber molds. The soft molds and cold pouring techniques allow an amazing amount of detail to be included in a single-piece casting, although the softer molds wear out somewhat rapidly. The best resin kits have very smooth, clean surfaces and require very little clean up on the part of the builder. However, lower quality kits may reveal more "flash" and some bubble holes that need to be filled.

Resin is cheaper than white-metal, so resin kits are usually less expensive than metal ones. They are also easier to build. For some reason, the best resin kits of American cars come from the French manufacturers Starter and Provence Moulage. However, a couple of American companies named Highway Travelers and Pro Line Miniatures make excellent, highly-detailed handbuilt resin models at prices very competitive with their metal counterparts.

Some Classic 1/43rd-scale Issues

Before we look at some recent examples of collectible 1/43-scale models that you can buy directly from dealers, let's check out some of the older classic editions made from five to 15 years ago. These are miniatures that you will have to locate through specialty shops, swap meets, toy shows or other collectors. In many cases, they are worth quite a bit more than their original list prices given below.

Precision Miniatures produced several Mustang kits. They included a 1965 Shelby GT-350 in street trim and a 1966 GT-350/GT-350H kit to build as either the standard GT-350 or Hertz GT-350H. These kits were well-engineered, very nicely cast and easy to build. They originally cost about $29. A limited number of built-up models were sold at $55.

Model fire apparatus collectors were delighted by the die-cast model of a vintage American La France truck made by Conrad. The castings were crisp and clean and included sprockets and chain-drive details in the chassis. A fine red finish was complemented by rub-on "Hastings-on-Hudson" markings for a New York fire company. Plastic ladders and vinyl hoses finished off a very appealing 1/43-scale model.

Eligor (a French firm) did a variety of 1933 and 1934 Ford pickups and vans. They followed these with a die-cast 1958 Chrysler New Yorker convertible. It was offered in a variety of colors. Mine had metallic green finish over a crisp, clean body casting. The molded plastic interior had good seat detail and an adequate dash, but no inner door panels. The basic body lines were good, though a transparent windshield frame helped to make the windshield look too high. The bumpers and wheels were plated, although whitewall tires would have helped their appearance. Most of the trim detail was cast into the body, but painted over. The original price was a very modest $9.95.

Brooklin also issued its number 17 model, a 1952 Studebaker Starlight Coupe, some years back. It combined excellent castings, a flawless black finish and superb workmanship to produce a beautiful model. The bumpers and wheels were very nicely plated, although plating or foil trimming the scuff plates, window surrounds and air vent would have added to the feeling of realism. The Studebaker model compared very well to photos and the wheelbase was exactly 1/43-scale. Overall, Brooklin did an excellent job of capturing the look of this early 1950s trendsetter for the low original price of $32.95.

Mini-Auto Emporium also released a mammoth, finned, 1959 Cadillac Series 62 convertible as its first white-metal model. The castings were excellent and the powder-blue finish on our sample was just as good. It had only a slight trace of orange-peel on the hood. The interior was nicely detailed and finished with a clear windshield. The bumpers and wheels were plated. The "Ca-Doo's" body lines and details matched photos of the real car quite well. The model's dimensions scaled out to 1/41-scale. It was a very fine first effort for Mini-Auto Emporium. All casting and assembly was done by a husband-and-wife team at only about $40 original cost. This model was worth the price.

Those who fondly remember the European-American hybrid cars of the 1950s and 1960s were delighted with EnCo Model's excellent Facel Vega II. This copy of the French-built "Chrysler" featured hand-painted details on the dashboard. Chassis detail was minimal, but hand work on the body ... including all lights and chrome trim around the windows ... was exceptional. The body and finish were flawless, with very clear windows and an interior that included plated parts. Overall, this classic model was a beautifully built, very well detailed model that matched photos of the actual hybrid very nicely. It was scaled to the 1/43rd standard. EnCo Models, of Northants, England, was responsible for this fine miniature.

Today's Collector Models

Now that we've reviewed some of the older 1/43-scale model cars, let's survey some of the latest releases. Many models issued in this category are conceived of as "quick Classics" that become valuable overnight. Therefore, the models do not have to be five, 10 or 15 years old to be collectible.

Vitesse already had a 1956 Ford convertible on the market, but it recently added a neatly molded plastic roof to the model. This turned the Sunliner into a 1956 Fairlane Victoria hardtop. The color of the plastic top is a very good match for the Peacock Blue lower body color. Other authentic-looking colors are available, too.

The fairly thick B-pillars are painted body color and make the model look more like a Fairlane Club Sedan, than a Victoria. However, it would be very easy to cut away the pillar or thin it down and "plate" it with foil to make the model look more like a Victoria. Vitesse replaced the Sunliner badges and decals with Victoria scripts. The top is correct for either the sedan or the standard Victoria hardtp. The Crown Victoria had a wrapover tiara band.

Like the ragtop, the Vitesse hardtop has much more detail than most models in its price range. It features lots of well done chrome trim on the body and inside. The two-tone seats and door panels and highly detailed dashboard are done with decals. Only the side and rear window trim needs to be detailed. As on the convertible, there are no exterior door handles.

From Vitesse comes this 1/43-scale model of the 1956 Ford Victoria.

Brooklin has released this 1953 Oldsmobile Fiesta model in the popular scale.

Motor City USA did an excellent job making the 1950 Ford woodie in miniature.

Western Models' handsome 1/43-scale model of the DeSoto Adventurer.

Great American Dream Machines has brought back Virgil Exner dream car.

Even hot rodders are buying the 1/43-scale models that collectors prefer.

The model's chrome wheels are accurate and the wide whitewalls are very realistic. There's good chassis detail in the metal base plate, too. Body lines and details compare very well to photos and all major dimensions check out to precisely 1/43-scale. It is available from Miniature Cars, 369 Springfield Avenue, PO Box 188, Berkley Heights, N.J. 07922-0188.

Brooklin Models has just released a nicely done, two-tone model of the 1953 Oldsmobile Fiesta. They've done it by casting the rear upper body as a separate part and painting it aqua, while the rest of the body is white. The rear section on my sample was just a little too wide, but this may not be typical. All castings are clean and smooth and the finish is a flawless, high-gloss paint. The windshield frame, bumpers, wheels, lights, hood ornament, hood badge and stone guards are chrome-plated. The taillight lenses have been given a coat of translucent red paint.

The real 1953 Fiesta was loaded with chrome and Brooklin has cast all the remaining trim in relief, but it's painted over. Some time spent applying Bare-Metal foil will really pay off on this model.

A nicely-replicated interior and good upholstery detail on the seats and inner door panels add to this issue. The door panels even have trim moldings and handles. The dashboard details appear to be correct, too, but nothing has been "picked out." However, Brooklin *has* modeled the brake and accelerator pedals. Interior colors are the same as the exterior colors, but are done in a realistic semi-gloss paint. Overall, the body lines compare very well to photos of the real Fiesta and the dimensions are exactly 1/43-scale.

Brooklin has done its homework well and their Fiesta is a superbly made and very attractive collector's item. Brasilia Press, PO Box 2023, Elkhart, IN 46515 is the importer of this model and, upon request, will send you a list of shops that stock it.

Motor City USA is now making a superb 1/43-scale white-metal model of the 1950 Ford Custom Deluxe Station Wagon, as part of its line of handbuilt models. The metal body panels (metal on the real car) have excellent, high-gloss finish in a choice of black, Cambridge Maroon, Casino Cream or Hawthorne Green. However, it is the simulated woodwork that makes these models stand out.

Motor City has cast the simulated birch framework in relief and then hand-painted it with realistic colors. The mahogany panels are replicated with carefully applied decals. Every piece of trim, inside and out, has been reproduced. Most of the trim is made of tiny, chrome-plated pieces. All of the interior woodwork has been reproduced, as was done on the outside. The dashboard has a correctly-painted woodgrain effect. The detailed gauge faces, interior door handles and window cranks are individually plated pieces.

All work on this model is of top quality, with no blemishes of any kind. Motor City USA, 13333 Saticoy, North Hollywood, CA 91605, is the sole source of this very accurate and superbly made model.

The latest addition to Western Model's line of 1/43-scale, white-metal "collector" models is a very nicely done 1959 DeSoto Adventurer convertible. Our sample had a smooth and glossy Pearl White finish, with the side flash reproduced in miniature, using a photo-etched piece of chrome with an Adventurer Gold insert. Photo-etched pieces are also used for the rocker panel moldings and for the gold-tinted grille.

Small parts like the fender trim, door handles and taillights of the DeSoto are separately-plated pieces, while the badges, logos and rear deck lid strips are all reproduced with metallic decals. The complex rear bumper is chrome-plated and has correct gold inserts.

The seats and door panels on the model have a basic beige finish, with realistic walnut two-tone panels, but the Adventurer Gold interior trim of the actual car is not reproduced. The instrument panel is plated and has good detail, but the panel faces need to be picked out. Chassis detail is cast in relief in the base plate.

Western has modeled the DeSoto Adventurer's lines very well and has also included a lot of detail for the price of this model. Major dimensions check out accurately, as well. The Adventurer is, without a doubt, one of the best models seen yet in this line. It's available from Sinclair's Auto Miniatures, PO Box 8403, Erie, PA 16505.

Great American Dream Machines has released its second Chrysler dream car. It is the 1952 Chrysler C-200 convertible, originally seen at the early postwar auto shows. Great American Dream Machines has accurately modeled the differences between this dream car and the 1951 Chrysler K-310 coupe, which they released a model of earlier.

As is typical with this company's models, the large body casting is perfectly smooth and the correct light green and black two-tone finish is flawlessly applied. It has a very high-gloss appearance. Also reproduced, with chrome decals, are the C-200 badges on the front fenders. All other trim is done with separate, chrome-plated pieces. The grille, with all of its engraved detail, is especially nice. The model is also equipped with a beautiful set of photo-etched wire wheels.

Separate inserts are used to reproduce the C-200's two-tone, black-and-green seat upholstery. A crisply-printed decal is used for the instrument faces and all dashboard details. Door handles, inside and out, are scraped to bare, shiny metal, as is the wheel arch trim on all four fenders. The windshield trim and vent window frames need to be "plated" with Bare-Metal Foil.

This model exhibits finish and assembly workmanship as good as you'll find anywhere. Virgil Exner's 1950s Chrysler dream cars set trends for the whole industry and Great American Dream Machines has done full justice to the C-200. This model will be available at specialty shops advertising in such hobby publications as *Old Cars, Toy Shop* and *Toy Collector & Toy Prices*. Buy now, before it goes out of production and prices rise.

Miniature Cars U.S.A. sold this 1954 Pontiac ragtop model.

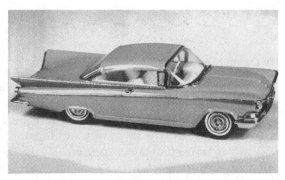

Collector, look for this 1/43-scale 1959 Buick in hardtop and convertible styles

1957 Mercury Turnpike Cruiser is a great find at shows.

1947 Chrysler Town & Country is a collectible diecast model.

The history of historic car models

By Dennis Doty

Back in those good old days, when the model-car hobby was just being born, model kits were vastly different than the kits we know today. A few model-car kits did appear before World War II and some military type kits were actually released during the war. However, it was during the immediate postwar period that the model-car kit market truly began.

This was before the era of plastic model kits. The wood kits (some with a few plastic or die-cast metal parts) required a lot of work to assemble. In a way, it was almost like making a scratch-built model, although a long-time scratch builder will likely argue with that view.

The BMW model was designated number 701. It was molded in white (body) and black and came with plated parts. I liked the decals supplied for the dashboard dials, which made detailing much easier than using paint.

Antique kits are not hot sellers in the collectors' market. Early "Hudson Miniatures" balsa wood kits seldom bring the prices you'd expect. Plastic "Highway Pioneer" and "Li'l Old Timers" sell for peanuts or not at all.

Up to the early 1950s, the only kits being modeled (with very few exceptions) were of "pioneer" type antique cars. How times change! Looking at major model manufacturer's catalogs now, you will see very few kits of cars older than 1960 models. In fact, post-1960 cars are being viewed, by all too many modern plastic kit companies, as the only types of cars the kiddie market warrants. Unfortunately, the manufacturers don't realize that the kiddie market has nearly evaporated, because of the high cost of kits today and the lure of the video game.

Nevertheless, the market for pioneer type antique car models really doesn't seem to be there anymore. With few exceptions, antique car kits are not even hot sellers in the collectors' market. Early "Hudson Miniatures" balsa wood antique car kits seldom bring the prices you'd expect for kits that haven't been produced in almost 30 years. Plastic "Highway Pioneer" and "Li'l Old Timers" sell for peanuts or, in many cases, not at all.

Back in the 1950s, when pioneer antique cars were enjoying popularity, a small company in Manitowoc, Wisconsin released two of the best-detailed antique car kits ever issued. They depicted a 1902 Rambler and, probably, a 1909 Hupmobile. The company was called Kaysun and the models carried the Keepsake trade name. The Rambler was first released in 1954. I don't have an original Keepsake Hupmobile, but guess it was released at this time as well.

The Rambler came with a simply-detailed engine. While the sides of the car were multi-piece, the detailing was truly excellent, especially for 1954. Another interesting feature was the fact that the Rambler was molded in poly-styrene plastic, when acetate plastic was normal for the time. Also, while the 1/24-scale used for these is common for models today, it was unusual in the early 1950s. Most plastic kits of the day were done in 1/32-scale. The kit number for the Rambler was K-10. It sold for 79-cents in 1954. I wonder if there were K-1 to K-9 Keepsake models and what they were? These models were re-issued a number of times, so obtaining one of the releases should not be impossible.

In about 1960, Strombecker model company released these two kits again. These are shown in the 1960 second edition of the *Auto World Catalog*. The Hupmobile was number T1 and the Rambler was number T2. These editions were shown last in the 1962 *Auto World Catalog*.

In 1964, Hawk model company released the two models again. The Rambler was number 634 and the Hupmobile was number 635. The 634/635 models were last shown in the 1966 *Auto World Catalog*.

The final known issuance of the models was their release by Hawk in 1969. They were a bit different this time, however. Hawk offered both models with a display case (an old small Simms showcase) and plated the models in gold. The Rambler was designated number 300 and the Hupmobile was number 301. The *Auto World Catalog* again showed these models in 1969 and 1970, but with the old 1964 prices and numbers. Testor, a maker of kits and model-building supplies, bought Hawk in 1971. It's likely the company still has the tools for these excellent kits.

Miley's is another company that made models. It produced hand-assembled models that had the look of the cast iron toys of the 1930s. These models were not duplicates of any of those interesting old toys, but new designs that looked old. Since they were cast in aluminum, there was no way they could be confused with the originals. This is something that cannot be said for the "reproductions" that are cast in iron. A novice could get burned with these, if he or she didn't know better.

Several designs were available from Miley's. One was a Model T Ford Parcel Post Delivery Van. This model was seven inches long and painted black, with a gold radiator. The headlights were cast to the radiator with the lenses painted white. Red wheels set the color scheme off. The Parcel Post Mail Service graphics were applied via a self stick piece.

While the Miley's models are not from the 1930s, they did have the look of the era. If you like and collect such old toys, these "new-old" models might warrant a place in your collection. They have become collectors' items to a degree. Originally, the Parcel Post Van sold for $27. A Model T Ford Telephone Line Maintenance Truck was also available, along with a Telephone Construction Truck.

One French model company that gave collectors really good variety in the 1980s was the firm of Heller. Because these models were not seen in every K-Mart or Toys 'R Us, a lot of modelers are still unfamiliar with the "goodies" this firm issued. Fortunately, many Heller models were imported into this country by Polk's Modelcraft Hobbies, so they can be found for sale.

Another 1/24th-scale Heller kit modeled the Renault 4CV. This small car from the late 1940s was also very well done. The blue body was molded in one piece. Another color used was gray and there were plated parts, as well.

If you are a fan of European sports cars of the 1930s, Heller's BMW 328 should be near the top of your want list. It was the first 1/24-scale plastic kit of this car and looked quite beautiful. Heller became known for its detailed parts and quality, with as few parts as possible. There were just 95 components in the BMW 328 kit. That usually made assembly easier.

The BMW model was designated number 70l. It was molded in white (body) and black and came with plated parts. I liked the decals supplied for the dashboard dials, which made detailing much easier than using paint. There was one drawback to this 1983 release, which I couldn't understand. The basic body was cast in two pieces. It was easier to manufacture a model-making tool that way, but it meant that the builder had to join the two body parts and fill-in the seam. This was a minor point though, as the kit was well worth that bit of trouble.

Another 1/24-scale Heller kit modeled the Renault 4CV. This small car from the late 1940s was also very well done. The blue body was molded in one piece. Another color used was gray and there were plated parts, as well. The instructions were wordless, but all the parts were carefully numbered on Heller kits. That helped the builders a great deal. Heller also listed paint detail features, which was a great help when you had little reference on the real car. Unlike a 1/43-scale 4CV released a few years earlier by Heller, the 1983 model came with a detailed engine in the rear and an opening trunk up front.

Heller kits did not come cheap, but for your money, you got a well-executed kit of a model-car that wasn't available from other companies. Heller kits are still be produced. I'm not sure that they have an exclusive American importer, as they did years ago. They are definitely available from International Hobby Supply, PO Box 426, Woodland Hills, CA 91365 and are collectors' items.

The Rambler came with a simply-detailed engine. While the sides of the car were multi-piece, the detailing was excellent, especially for 1954. Another interesting feature was the fact that the Rambler was molded in poly-styrene plastic.

Several designs came from Miley's. One was a Model T Ford Parcel Post Van. This model was seven inches long and painted black, with a gold radiator. The headlights were cast to the radiator, with the lenses painted white.

In the 1950s, when pioneer antique cars were enjoying popularity, a small company in Manitowoc, Wisconsin released two of the best-detailed antique car kits ever. They depicted a 1902 Rambler and a 1909 Hupmobile.

Building models from scratch

By Tom LaMarre

Nearly every model car builder reaches a stage where he has assembled practically all of the kits in his field of interest. This is particularly true for collectors of classic, antique and special interest auto models. Every year we see a flood of models of the same cars ... Camaros, Firebirds and Corvettes. Each model manufacturer seems to be turning out the same kits as its competitors. Will we ever see a model kits of a 1950 Buick? What about a 1949 Cadillac, 1933 Pierce-Arrow Silver Arrow or 1940 Packard-Darrin?

Unfortunately, it is unlikely that plastic kit manufacturers will ever produce models of these cars, or similar types, unless they can be convinced that a sufficient market exists. But, there is an alternative for the experienced model maker ... scratch building a model.

Many hobbyists are under the false impression that you have to be an expert like Gerald Wingrove or Manuel Olive to build a decent-looking, scratch-built model. Perhaps we have become spoiled. We're so accustomed to the quality and detail of plastic kits, that we are unwilling to settle for anything less than perfection. What a contrast to the situation in the 1940s, and earlier, when commercially-produced model-car kits did not even exist.

Using simple materials and a lot of improvisation, many modelers nevertheless managed to construct replicas that, while not perfectly proportioned or detailed, were still close approximations of actual autos. And there is no reason why their methods cannot still be used today.

Such was my feeling as I decided to build a model of the 1949 Packard, a car that will probably never show up in kit form on hobby shop shelves. Lacking any artistic ability, I first had to find some good photographs and basic specifications. From this material, plan and profile drawings were worked out, in roughly 1/25-scale, and templates were cut from cardboard.

Outlines of the car were then marked on a 1 x 3-inch length of select white pine with the body profile template. These pieces were then cut out and glued together, forming the basic body of the model.

From this point on, it was a matter of much filing, sanding and filling, until the proper contours were achieved. Doors, windows and fender skirts were etched in with an X-acto knife blade. Finally, the model was ready for sealing and painting. It required five coats of Scalecoat sanding sealer, sanded with number 400 paper between coats, to achieve a smooth surface. Next, it received 15 coats of gold automotive touch-up lacquer, which was wet-sanded between coats. Upon completion the model was rubbed out and waxed. The window area was then painted with brown enamel.

Trim pieces were adapted from various plastic kits. For example, the parking lights were cut from the body of a Monogram 1955 Chevrolet model and used as taillights for the Packard. The bumpers were cut from cardboard, while aluminum tape was used for side trim. Overall, about 100 hours of work went into the Packard model.

The techniques described here can be used to build a model of practically any car. Useful references include the old Fisher Body Craftsmen's Guild contest booklet, which can still be found in many libraries, and the *Model Car, Truck, & Motorcycle Handbook*, authored by Robert H. Schleicher.

Although the end result of a scratch building project may not be in the same league as the work of Cyril Posthumus or Henri Baigent, it nonetheless provides a great sense of satisfaction to transform humble, raw materials into a one-of-a-kind model.

Good photos and basic specifications can be used to make plan and profile drawings in roughly 1/25-scale. Then, templates are cut from cardboard. Packard literature was helpful during the shaping of the 1949 Packard model.

Aluminum tape was used for side chrome strips. The bumpers were cut from cardboard. Overall, about 100 hours of work went into the Packard model. Fifteen coats of gold automotive lacquer finished off the Packard.

Trim pieces were adapted from various plastic model-car kits. For example, the parking lights were cut from the body of a Monogram 1955 Chevrolet model and used as taillights for the Packard.

Although the end result might not be of top professional quality, there is, nonetheless, a great sense of satisfaction in transforming humble raw materials into a one-of-a-kind model.

Die-cast model cars began with an airplane

By Dennis Doty

Considering the current state of the die-cast model car industry in this country, one would never guess the industry was born in the United States. This happened back in 1910, with the introduction of a toy "aeroplane" by the Dowst company.

Dowst, which is best known for its Tootsietoy line, is now owned by Strombecker. It is still producing die-cast toy cars that are worth collecting, but its first die-cast car dates to 1911. It was cast in a lead alloy. Tootsietoy originated the die-cast model car and, eventually, an entire hobby. For more information on Tootsietoys, order the book *Tootsie Toys; World's First Die-cast Models* by Ed Force and James Wieland. It was originally published in the early 1980s by Classic Motorbooks, P.O. Box 1, Osceola, WI 54020 and is listed in their 1994 catalog.

Although Tootsietoy got the ball rolling, it was model cars made by Dinky Toys that really helped bring the hobby to prominence. They began when Tootsietoy switched production to models that collectors had little interest in.

Dinky Toys were products of Meccano Ltd., with the first model-cars being released in 1934. While a number of these early releases were interesting, there is great focus on the cars released in 1940. This series was called number 39 and the models produced were the 39a Packard Super 8 Touring Sedan, 39b Oldsmobile Six Sedan, 39c Lincoln-Zephyr Coupe, 39d Buick "Viceroy" Saloon, 39e Chrysler Royal Sedan and 39f Studebaker State Commander Saloon.

If some of these descriptions sound British, that's because Dinky Toys were produced in England. I believe all these cars were 1939 model-year vehicles.

These models are not easy to come by. They are highly desired, especially by collectors in the United States. The first run of these models was a short one. Production stopped in 1940 and remained closed for the duration of the war. It started again in 1946 and these models were available until 1950.

I consider myself fortunate to have the 39d Buick in my collection. It is not a mint condition model, but it was never played with very hard and the paint chips are very minor. On this model, the headlights were cast separately, with the lenses and grillwork painted silver. My model is painted a dirty tan color, which is hard to describe.

This model was found a couple of years ago in a hobby shop. Taken in on a trade, it was priced at only $10. That is considerably under its normal value. For more information on these cars, look for *The History of British Dinky Toys 1934-1964*, by Cecil Gibson, in used book stores. Also available through the *Classic Motorbooks Catalog* are two newer titles by Tony Stanford: *Dinky Toys; Always Something New 1962-64* and *Dinky Toys: Masterpieces in Miniature 1951-58*.

Even some more modern die-cast model-cars are collectible. This entire story could be devoted to the three different 1/43-scale white-metal models of the 1965 Mustang produced by Precision Miniatures. These were the number PM018 Mustang Convertible with Indy 500 Pace Car Decals; the number PM019 Mustang Fastback and the number PM020 Shelby Mustang GT 350.

Detailing on these three kits was truly excellent, with separate parts for things like door handles, windshield wipers and the side scoop trim. The convertible and the number 019 Fastback also came with extra parts to make them into regular, non Shelby Mustang GTs. These parts included the GT steering wheel,

On the 39d Buick model, the headlights were cast separately, with the lenses and grillwork painted silver. The car is painted a dirty tan color, which is hard to describe. There is great focus on the Dinky Toy cars released in 1940.

The number PM018 Mustang Convertible with Indy 500 Pace Car Decals; the number PM019 Mustang Fastback; and the number PM020 Shelby Mustang GT 350 were made by Precision Miniatures in the early 1980s and are already collectible.

The Mercury model came with wide whitewall tires and fender skirts. The plated parts were very well done. The side chrome trim piece was painted body color.

dash, shifter, console, rear valence and bumper, tail pipes, back-up lights, grille and gas cap! The regular Mustangs came with the stock wheelcovers, while the Shelby version came with mag-style wheels. Both designs were nicely reproduced.

The Shelby model also had the scoop molded to the hood and there were provisions on the hood for locking pins. Like the real Shelby, there was no back seat, though there was a spare tire cover. These kits also came with a number of well-plated parts and instruction sheets that should have gotten the job done. There were photos as well, to help the more inexperienced builder along. However, the photos are did not show, step-by-step, how to build the model. Extensive decal sheets were also provided. They made these kits among the best of the 1/43-scale, white metal models available at the time they were issued.

The models were available from mail-order dealers, a few hobby shops, or direct from Precision Miniatures in Costa Mesa, California. The kits were $29.95 each. For those who didn't like to do their own building or spend time making models, built-up models were available for $50 each.

Brooklin Models, of England, made many nice die-cast models. They included a 1940 Cadillac and the number 15 two-door 1949 Mercury Club Coupe cast in white metal. The Mercury was available only in built-up form and it was equal to anything Brooklin released earlier. The wheelbase checked out, in scale, to about an inch of the real car's wheelbase. The body proportions were right on, too.

The Mercury model came with wide whitewall tires and fender skirts. The plated parts were very well done. The side chrome trim piece was painted body color (which was, and still is, normal for this type of factory-built model). It seemed a little too wide, but not enough to take anything away from the miniature. The paint was a glossy (and also rather thick) cream and off-white combination, with a well-detailed, but hard to see, red interior. The steering wheel was body-colored.

For those into 1/43 scale models of American cars, Brooklin has long been considered one company no enthusiast should overlook. They originally sold in the $40 range. Dealers who handled them included Brasilia Press; Grandpa's Attic; Dale Dannefer; and Automotive Miniatures. Currently, *Toys & Prices* (a book available from Krause Publications) values the 1949 Brooklin Mercury, the 1953 Brooklin Studebaker Indiana State Police Car, the 1954 Brooklin Dodge Indianapolis 500 Pace Car and the Mini-Marque Packard Convertible. Brooklin models were highly collectible right from the start. A complete set would be truly impressive.

There are many other types of die-cast model-cars. *Toys & Prices* lists current collector prices for many die-cast models made by Brooklin, Corgi, Dinky, Hotwheels, Matchbox and Tootsietoys. Krause's magazines *Toy Shop* and *Toy Collector & Price Guide* are also very helpful to collectors of such models. For information about these products write: Krause Publications, Toy Department, 700 East State Street, Iola, WI 54990 or call (715) 445-2214.

Another publication that is available and aimed more specifically at model-car collectors is *Model Car Journal*, PO Box 154135, Irving, TX 75015-4135, telephone (214) 790-5346.

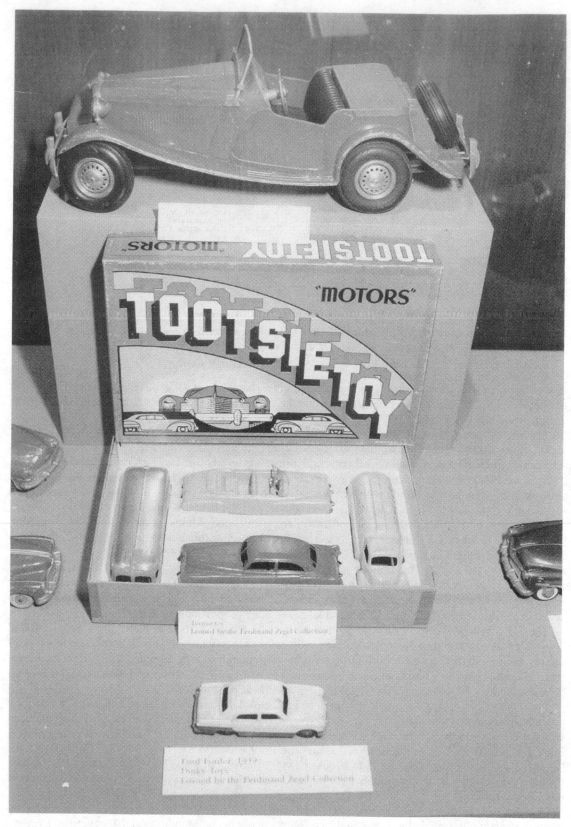

Tootsietoy originated the die-cast model car and, eventually, an entire hobby. For more information on Tootsietoys, try to get a copy of the book *Tootsietoys* by Ed Force and James Wieland.

Young model makers took "Guild Trip"

Researched by John L. Jacobus

Automotive development includes people, as well as technology. Many designers, engineers and executives had their interests and talents nurtured by the Fisher Body Craftsman's Guild.

William A. Fisher, Fisher Body Corporation president, organized the Fisher Body Craftsman's Guild in 1930 and served as its first president. He hoped it could revive the spirit of medieval craft guilds. "Above all, it is the fully trained and competent craftsman who can carry this machine civilization to higher levels of efficiency and service to humankind in the future," Fisher said in a 1934 advertisement for the Fisher Body Craftsman's Guild competition.

A total of $23,000 worth of awards was offered, that season, to boys 12- to 19-years-old who enrolled in the contest. The top prizes were four university scholarships valued at $5,000. Smaller awards were also given.

Until 1937, participants created 1/8-scale, three-dimensional, scratch-built models of coaches, like the one used for the Fisher Body trademark. There were actually two coach designs. The first, called a traveling coach, was simpler. An ornate Napoleonic coach challenged more advanced model-makers.

Until 1937, participants created 1/8-scale, three-dimensional, scratch-built models of coaches, like the one used for the Fisher Body trademark. There were two designs: traveling coach and a more ornate Napoleonic coach.

Dating from 1947 is Stan Parker's regional winner. (General Motors photo)

Through local General Motors automobile dealers, as many as 145,000 youths enrolled in the Fisher Body Craftsman's Guild in some years. The Boy Scouts of America (BSA) also adopted the goals and objectives of the contest for a merit badge. Although the program ended in 1968, BSA handed out 7,000 "Model Design and Building" badges as late as 1981.

It was in 1937 that the contest was expanded to include a classification for 1/12-scale autos. Designs were then limited by size and body style (four-door sedan), but participants still had more room to develop individualized concepts, since the earlier coach designs had been based on a set of standard plans. Still, the coach category lasted until 1947.

During World War II, the contests were suspended. They resumed, basically unchanged, in 1946. After discontinuing the building of coaches the following season, the car category was enlarged, in 1948, to include body styles other than sedans.

In one sense, the competition was a marketing ploy to get the General Motors name into millions of homes. At the same time, however, it tapped America's creative young minds for new ideas. Thousands of youths were also encouraged to work with their hands. Who knows how many young men developed their future vocations?

Perhaps the greatest attraction of the contest was the potential for kids to participate in the prophecy of American automobile design. Via the guild, young craftsmen had a direct pipeline to communicate their ideas to those who fashioned Detroit's latest dream machines.

In 1968, General Motors phased-out the Fisher Body Craftsman's Guild program due to declining interest. However, before it ended, many of America's top dream car makers went through it.

One famous guilds man was Virgil Exner, Jr., who was a national winner in 1946. (Earlier, his father, Virgil Exner, Sr., was a guild judge). General Motors design staff director Chuck Jordon and General Motors stylist Terry Henline (who now works at the GM Advanced Concept Center, in Southern California) both entered the competition. Other General Motors design staff members who participated included S. Denek; P. Tatseos; G. Anderson; Tony Ingolia; R. Menking; Chuck Torner; J. Folden; Ron Hill; Bob Cadaret; and Edward Taylor. Harvey Whitman, of Oldsmobile Engineering and Nissan chief designer Allen Flowers were other guilds men.

Not too long ago, a beautiful display of Fisher Body Craftsman's Guild models designed from 1948 to 1966 was added to the National Museum of American History, in Washington, D.C., as part of the Smithsonian Institution. Another display of models is underway at the Henry Ford Museum in Dearborn, Michigan.

Entry number 2566 in the 1962 Maryland First State competition was submitted by author John Jacobus. It scored 342 points out of a possible 450 or a 76 percent. (Courtesy John Jacobus)

Tony Ingolia took state honors, in 1937, with his Tatra-like car.

This 1950 first place winner was created by Ron Hill. (General Motors photo)

One of the entries, in 1958, was done by Gordon Brown (General Motors photo)

Ron Meyer was another home-state winner, in 1955. (General Motors photo)

A view of the Fisher Body Craftsman Guild competition in the 1960s. This competition in 1964 attracted hundreds of entries, but four years later the guild competition ended. (General Motors photo)

Pricing

Prices for automobilia mentioned or pictured in this book are listed on the following pages. They are in the order that each story appears. The first story appearing is automobile literature, etc.

Estimated values for each item in Good, Very Good and Excellent condition are given. "Excellent" means like-new or restored to like-new condition. "Very Good" items reflect minimal wear and tear or an amateur restoration. Items in "Good" condition are better than average for their age and restorable.

Items in conditions too poor to be restored correctly are not appraised. A uniform system for pricing automobilia items in lesser conditions seems impossible to devise. Toys and license plates, can be restored and, therefore, retain more value when in "poor" condition.

Clothing, literature and photographs, are virtually worthless after a certain amount of wear and tear occurs. This is why we use only three conditions.

This "Automobilia Price Guide" was created in the spring of 1994. The values for the items were determined by asking the advice of dozens of dealers and collectors who specialize in various types of automobilia. Pricing collectible items is always an "inexact science." Therefore, the values presented should always be used only as a guide.

We welcome any information that would help to refine this list and make it more useful to collectors as the years go by. Contact: Old Cars, Books Department, 700 E. State Street, Iola, WI 54990.

Old Softies

AUTOMOBILE LITERATURE

DESCRIPTION	GOOD	VG	EXC.
1911 Locomobile, sales catalog, hard cover	43	72	110
1912 Locomobile, sales catalog, hard cover	43	72	110
1910 Lorraine-Dietrich, sales pamphlet, soft cover	40	65	100
1912 Ford, sales literature	30	50	75
1938 Chilton's Repair Manual	16	26	40
1939 Chilton's Repair Manual	16	26	40
1904 *ALAM* Hand Book of Gasoline Automobiles (original)	63	105	125
1905 *ALAM* Hand Book of Gasoline Automobiles (original)	60	100	150
1906 *ALAM* Hand Book of Gasoline Automobiles (original)	50	82	125
1907 *ALAM* Hand Book of Gasoline Automobiles (original)	40	65	100
1908 *ALAM* Hand Book of Gasoline Automobiles (original)	40	65	100
1909 *ALAM* Hand Book of Gasoline Automobiles (original)	40	65	100
1910 *ALAM* Hand Book of Gasoline Automobiles (original)	33	55	85
1911 *ALAM* Hand Book of Gasoline Automobiles (original)	33	55	85

(NOTE: Several editions of the ALAM Hand Book of Gasoline Automobiles have been reprinted by Floyd Clymer and Dover Press. These are now getting old and have some appeal to collectors, although they are far less valuable than original editions.)

1912 Automobile Board of Trade Hand Book (original)	30	50	75
1913 Automobile Board of Trade Hand Book (original)	30	50	75
1914 *NACC* Hand Book (original)	27	45	70
1915 *NACC* Hand Book (original)	27	45	70
1916 *NACC* Hand Book (original)	27	45	70
1917 *NACC* Hand Book (original)	25	42	65
1918 *NACC* Hand Book (original)	25	42	65
1919 *NACC* Hand Book (original)	23	40	60
1920 *NACC* Hand Book (original)	20	33	50
1921 *NACC* Hand Book (original)	20	33	50
1922 *NACC* Hand Book (original)	20	33	50
1923 *NACC* Hand Book (original)	20	33	50
1924 *NACC* Hand Book (original)	20	33	50
1925 *NACC* Hand Book (original)	20	33	50
1926 *NACC* Hand Book (original)	20	33	50
1927 *NACC* Hand Book (original)	23	40	60
1928 *NACC* Hand Book (original)	25	42	65
1929 *NACC* Hand Book (original)	27	45	70
1906 *MoToR*'s Directory of Motor Cars	14	23	35
1907 *MoToR*'s Directory of Motor Cars	14	23	35
1908 *MoToR*'s Directory of Motor Cars	14	23	35
1909 *MoToR*'s Directory of Motor Cars	14	23	35
1910 *MoToR*'s Directory of Motor Cars	14	23	35
1911 *MoToR*'s Directory of Motor Cars	14	23	35
1912 *MoToR*'s Directory of Motor Cars	14	23	35
1913 *MoToR*'s Directory of Motor Cars	14	23	35
1936 Dodge owner manual, "Maintaining Dodge Dependability"	14	23	35

DESCRIPTION	GOOD	VG	EXC.
1956 Ford Truck, shop manual	14	23	35
1951 Kaiser-Frazer shop manual with 1952-1953 supplement	18	30	45

AUTOMOBILE SALES LITERATURE

1914 Rolls-Royce sales catalog (Percy Northey color photos)	90	130	225
1930 Pierce-Arrow sales catalog, full color (standard version)	60	100	150
1930 Pierce-Arrow, all-line, "jumbo" Sales Catalog, 35 pages, 10-1/4 x 16-3/4 x 30 inches	300	500	750
1954 Kaiser Manhattan, sales catalog, folio edition, 10 color plates	20	33	50
1927 Packard, "jumbo" sales catalog, 23 pages, 10 x 13-1/2 x 28 inches	140	230	350
1928 Packard, "jumbo" sales catalog, 23 pages, 10 x 13-1/2 x 28 inches	165	280	425
1919 Packard, Twin Six, hard cover presentation album, 39 pages, size 8-3/4 x 12 inches	370	620	950
1938 Rolls-Royce, Phantom I, sales catalog, 44 pages, 9-1/2 x 13 inches	90	150	225
1939 Rolls-Royce, Phantom I, sales catalog, 44 pages, 9-1/2 x 13 inches	90	150	225
1970 Cadillac, all-line sales catalog	4	6	10
1928 Bentley Six, 6.5 liter, sales catalog No. 27	350	600	900
1930s Flewitt Coachwork album, Rolls-Royce PI and 20 horsepower	150	245	375
1930s Swallow side car, sales literature	80	130	200
Jaguar SS, sales literature, four separate pieces	390	650	1000

AUTOMOBILE TECHNICAL LITERATURE

1915 Ford reference book	12	20	30
1916 Ford reference book	12	20	30
1917 Ford reference book	12	20	30
1918 Ford reference book	12	20	30
1919 Ford reference book	12	20	30
1920 Ford reference book	10	16	25
1921 Ford reference book	10	16	25
1922 Ford reference book	10	16	25
1923 Ford reference book	10	16	25
1924 Ford reference book	10	16	25
1925 Ford reference book	10	16	25
1926 Ford reference book	10	16	25
1927 Ford reference book	10	16	25
1928 Ford reference book	26	43	65
1929 Ford reference book	26	43	65
1930 Ford reference book	26	43	65
1931 Ford reference book	27	45	70
1932 Ford reference book	16	26	40
1933 Ford reference book	16	26	40
1934 Ford reference book	16	26	40
1915 Chevrolet reference book	20	32	50
1916 Chevrolet reference book	20	32	50
1917 Chevrolet reference book	20	32	50
1918 Chevrolet reference book	20	32	50
1919 Chevrolet reference book	20	32	50
1920 Chevrolet reference book	18	30	45
1921 Chevrolet reference book	18	30	45
1922 Chevrolet reference book	18	30	45
1923 Chevrolet reference book	16	26	40
1924 Chevrolet reference book	16	26	40
1925 Chevrolet reference book	14	23	35

DESCRIPTION	GOOD	VG	EXC.
1926 Chevrolet reference book	14	23	35
1927 Chevrolet reference book	12	20	30
1928 Chevrolet reference book	12	20	30
1929 Chevrolet reference book	12	20	30
1930 Chevrolet reference book	12	20	30
1931 Chevrolet reference book	12	20	30
1932 Chevrolet reference book	14	23	35
1933 Chevrolet reference book	10	16	25
1934 Chevrolet reference book	10	16	25
1978 Mercury Owner Maintenance and Light Repair manual	6	10	15
1968 Corvette, shop manual Supplement ST-34, 100 pages	7	11	17
1963 Corvette, shop manual, ST-21	12	20	30
1934-1941 Chilton's Repair Manuals	16	26	40
1934-1941 MoToR's Repair Manuals	16	26	40
1934-1941 Audel's Repair Manuals	14	23	35
1934-1941 Glenn's Repair Manuals	16	26	40
Pontiac Service Craftsman News, June 1963	1	3	5
1939 DeSoto, sales catalog	22	36	55
1933 Plymouth, sales catalog	20	33	50
1934 Plymouth, sales catalog	20	33	50
1964 Mercury, paint chart	3	5	8
1957 Pontiac, Bonneville, factory publicity photo	4	6	10
1958 Dodge, paint chart, spring colors	3	5	8
1963 GMC truck sales catalog No. TSP63-6-20M, 7000 series fire trucks	1	3	5
Kaiser-Frazer accessories booklet	6	10	15
1933 Plymouth advertisement	1	3	5
1934 Plymouth advertisement, (*Cosmopolitan*)	1	3	5
1934 Plymouth advertisement, "New Series," with Walter P. Chrysler near car in photo	1	3	5
1929 Oakland, master parts catalog	18	30	45
1962 Buick, sales catalog, 16 page booklet	2	6	12
1956 Ford, truck operator's manual	6	9	14
1931-1933 Ditz-Lac paint color chart with color samples and mix formulas	4	6	10

SALES LITERATURE

DESCRIPTION	GOOD	VG	EXC.
1955 Chevrolet sales catalog	12	20	30
1957 Ford Skyliner (retractable) sales folder	6	10	15
1964 Cadillac sales brochure, 24 pages	8	13	20
1964 American Motors, sales folder	3	5	8
1920s Chandler, sales booklet	20	30	45
1932 Chevrolet, sales booklet	20	30	45
1974 Chevrolet Corvette, sales catalog	8	13	20

AUTOMOBILE LITERATURE

DESCRIPTION	GOOD	VG	EXC.
1933 Packard Twelve, sales catalog	600	1000	1500
1934 Packard Twelve, sales catalog	600	1000	1500
(2) Model T Ford, factory publicity photos (original)	25	40	60
1959 Cadillac shop manual	15	25	35
1916 Ford Times, single issue	5	10	15
1936 Packard 12, deluxe sales catalog	115	200	300
1969 American Motors, AMX, color sales catalog	5	8	10
1955 Ford Thunderbird, color sales folder	10	17	25
1931 Ford News, (single issue and supplement)	15	25	35

AUTOMOBILE PHOTOGRAPHS

DESCRIPTION	GOOD	VG	EXC.
1904-1906 and 1908-1912 Vanderbilt Cup race photos, by Spooner & Wells (each)	5	8	12
1901 Panhard, photo of car in New York to Buffalo Race, by J.A. Sietz, Syracuse, N.Y., framed, 8 x 10	4	7	10
1949 Kaiser, factory photo, "camera car"	3	5	8
1866 Dudgeon steam wagon, photograph	4	2	10

AUTOMOBILE SALES CATALOG ART

DESCRIPTION	GOOD	VG	EXC.
1909 Reo sales catalog, one- and two-cylinder cars, 24 pages, 8 x 9-3/4 inches	45	75	110
1913 Renault sales catalog, 54 pages, 9-3/4 x 12-1/2 inches	50	85	125
Circa 1925 Elcar sales catalog, 15 pages, 8 x 10 inches, fours and sixes	15	25	40
1938 Chrysler Imperial (Canadian) 22 pages, 8-1/2 x 11, plastic spiral binding	30	50	75
1912 Rolls-Royce sales catalog	60	100	150
1930 Willys-Knight sales catalog	20	30	45
1920 Cole sales catalog	33	55	85
1926 Packard "Attributes of Packard," eight-page specialty sales catalog, 8-1/2 x 11 inches, color art work	40	65	100

DESCRIPTION	GOOD	VG	EXC.
1926 Packard, "The Packard," auto company magazine	30	50	75
1926 Packard "Passenger Transportation," corporate magazine	30	50	75
Circa 1920s Dodge catalog, with pen- and-ink sketches (possibly by artist Norman Bel Geddes)	25	42	65
1928 Oldsmobile sales catalog, size approximately 7-3/4 x 11-1/2 inches	14	23	35
1929 Oldsmobile, "Details of Construction," sales catalog, approximately 24 pages, size 9-3/4 x 15-1/2 inches, covers F-29 and F-30 models	14	23	35
1930 Oldsmobile, "Details of Construction," sales catalog, approximately 24 pages, size 9-3/4 x 15-1/2 inches, covers F-29 and F-30 models	18	30	45
1919-1920 Cadillac, Open Cars, sales catalog with folio, size 7 x 11 inches sepia-and-ink sketches	80	130	200
1935 Studebaker, President, sales catalog, 16 pages, 10 x 12 inches	20	33	50
1917 Oakland Model 34, sales catalog	25	40	60
1929 Ford Model A, showroom poster, factory issued original	25	40	60
1929 Ford Model A, showroom poster, reproduction by Autographics	60	100	150
1935 Ford V-8 poster, shows the Ford V-8 engine, original	215	360	550
1935 Ford V-8 poster, shows the Ford V-8 engine, reproduction by Banner King	30	50	75

AUTOMOBILE POSTER ART

DESCRIPTION	GOOD	VG	EXC.
1934/1935 Fiat, "Balilla" poster	200	325	500
1935 Fiat, "Manifesto Fiat" poster for Fiat 1500 by C. Riccobaldi	155	260	400
1936 Fiat, "Dipinato Fiat 500" poster, by M. Sironi	175	290	450
Fiat 509, "Centaur" poster, 30 x 25 inches, color	175	290	450
1899 Fiat, "Victoria" poster, 30 x 25 inches	315	525	800
1930 Renault, "Renault 1930," poster. Reinastella model depicted	175	290	450
1925 Renault, "Aviation/Automobile" poster	200	325	500

AUTOMOBILE TRADING CARD SETS

DESCRIPTION	GOOD	VG	EXC.
Circa 1907 Turkey Red, automotive cigarette card set	200	325	500
Circa 1930s Bilderdienst (German), automotive cigarette card set	80	120	200
Mid-1930s John Player & Sons, (Great Britain) automotive cigarette card set with English and American cars	115	200	300
1966 Mobil Oil Company, "Great Days of Motoring" trading cards	30	50	75
1971 Full-Speed, (Dutch) automotive cigarette cards, by Piet Olyslager	30	50	75
1926 Lambert & Butler, Third Series, automotive cigarette card set	115	200	300

AUTOMOBILE FACTORY PHOTOGRAPHS

DESCRIPTION	GOOD	VG	EXC.
1902 Studebaker Electric, press kit with seven photos (9 x 12 inches for newspapers; 8 x 10 inches for period magazines)	40	65	100
1935-1941 Ford/Lincoln/Mercury photos by N.W. Ayer Advertising Agency (each photo)	235	390	600
1948 Tucker photo (Preston Tucker with car by factory)	4	6	10
1963 Studebaker Avanti photo, with designer Raymond Loewy	2	3	5
1937 Nash Ambassador, factory photo with car and baseball player Babe Ruth	2	3	5
1932 Studebaker Commander Regal sedan photo with Laurel and Hardy at Hal Roach Studios	3	4	7
1932 Packard factory photo, phaeton with actress Jean Harlow	3	4	7
1930 Marmon factory photo, Model 78 sedan, car with actress Lupe Velez	1.50	2.50	4
1941 Pontiac factory photo, Pontiac Torpedo sedan with adventurer Lowell Thomas	1.50	2.50	4
1959 Studebaker factory photo, Lark at Miami Beach hotel	1.50	2.50	4
1957 Chevrolet press packet with mislabeled 1956 Corvette photo	14	23	35

DESCRIPTION	GOOD	VG	EXC.
1942 Studebaker "Commander" 8 Deluxe Cruising Sedan retouched factory photo (car depicted is actually a Studebaker President model)	1.50	2.50	4
1925 Wills Sainte Claire factory photo (copied from Manning Brothers original negative)	4	6	10
1948 Austin (English) factory photo	2	3	5
1980 Chevrolet Corvette, factory photo, original print	3	5	8

AUTOMOTIVE POSTCARDS

DESCRIPTION	GOOD	VG	EXC.
1946 Chevrolet postcard, Dealers Supply Company, brown-toned	1	2	3
1958 Chevrolet postcard, Dealers Supply Company, brown-toned	1	2	3
1954 Chevrolet, Corvette, postcard, red-toned	6	10	15
1954 Chevrolet, Corvette, postcard, green-toned	6	10	15
1958 Chevrolet, Corvette, postcard	6	10	15
1959 Chevrolet, Corvette, postcard	30	50	75
1960 Chevrolet, Corvette, postcard	10	16	25
1961 Chevrolet, Corvette, postcard	10	16	25
1962 Chevrolet, Corvette, postcard	14	23	35
1963 Chevrolet, Corvette, postcard	8	13	20
1964 Chevrolet, Corvette, postcard	14	23	35
1965 Chevrolet, Corvette, postcard	6	10	15
1966 Chevrolet, Corvette, postcard	4	6	10
1968 Chevrolet, Corvette, postcard	4	6	10
1969 Chevrolet, Corvette, postcard	4	6	10
1970 Chevrolet, Corvette, postcard	4	6	10
1971 Chevrolet, Corvette, postcard	2	3	5
1972 Chevrolet, Corvette, postcard	2	3	5
1973 Chevrolet, Corvette, postcard	2	3	5
1974 Chevrolet, Corvette, postcard	1	2	3
1975 Chevrolet, Corvette, postcard	1	2	3
1976 Chevrolet, Corvette, postcard	1	2	3
1977 Chevrolet, Corvette, postcard	1	2	3
1978 Chevrolet, Corvette, postcard	1	2	3
1978 Chevrolet, Corvette, Indianapolis 500 Pace Car, postcard (issued by West Coast collector, not by Chevrolet)	.50	1	2
1979 Chevrolet, Corvette, postcard	.50	1	2
1980 Chevrolet, Corvette, postcard	.50	1	2
1981 Chevrolet, Corvette, postcard	.50	1	2
1982 Chevrolet, Corvette, postcard	.50	1	2
1984 Chevrolet, Corvette, postcard	.50	1	2

(NOTE: The 1970 and 1971 Corvette postcards are the same. Two-card sets showing the coupe and the convertible were issued in 1963 and 1964)

DESCRIPTION	GOOD	VG	EXC.
1923 Chevrolet, truck, postcard	6	10	15
1923 Chevrolet, car, postcard	4	6	10
1927 Chevrolet, car, postcard	4	6	10
1928 Chevrolet, car, postcard	4	6	10
1933 Chevrolet, car, postcard, full-color	4	6	10
1937 Chevrolet, cars, postcards, set of 12, full-color	60	100	150
1940 Chevrolet, postcard	3	5	7
1941 Chevrolet, postcard	3	5	7
1942 Chevrolet, postcard	3	5	7
1952 Chevrolet, postcard	3	5	7
1954 Chevrolet, postcard	3	5	7
1955 Chevrolet, postcard	4	6	10
1956 Chevrolet, postcard	4	6	10
1957 Chevrolet, postcard	4	6	10
1958 Chevrolet, postcard	4	6	10
1959 Chevrolet, postcard	4	6	10
1960 Chevrolet, postcard	3	5	7
1961 Chevrolet, postcard	2	3	5
1962 Chevrolet, postcard	2	3	5
1963 Chevrolet, postcard	2	3	5
1964 Chevrolet, postcard	2	3	5
1965 Chevrolet, postcard	1	2	3
1966 Chevrolet, postcard	1	2	3
1967 Chevrolet, postcard	1	2	3
1967 Chevrolet, Camaro, Indianapolis 500 Pace Car, postcard, large	5	8	12
1968 Chevrolet, postcard	1	2	3
1969 Chevrolet, postcard	1	2	3
1967 Chevrolet, Camaro, Indianapolis 500 Pace Car, postcard	4	6	10
1970 Chevrolet, postcard	1	2	3
1971 Chevrolet, postcard	1	2	3
1972 Chevrolet, postcard	.50	1	2
1973 Chevrolet, postcard	.50	1	2
1974 Chevrolet, postcard	.50	1	2
1975 Chevrolet, postcard	.50	1	2
1976 Chevrolet, postcard	.50	1	2
1977 Chevrolet, postcard	.50	1	2
1978 Chevrolet, postcard	.50	1	2
1979 Chevrolet, postcard	.50	1	2
1980 Chevrolet, postcard	.50	1	2
1981 Chevrolet, postcard	.30	.50	1
1982 Chevrolet, postcard	.30	.50	1
1983 Chevrolet, postcard	.30	.50	1
1984 Chevrolet, postcard	.30	.50	1
1985 Chevrolet, postcard	.30	.50	1
1986 Chevrolet, postcard	.30	.50	1
1978 Chevrolet, postcard	.30	.50	1
1988 Chevrolet, postcard	.30	.50	1
1989 Chevrolet, postcard	.30	.50	1
1990 Chevrolet, postcard	.30	.50	1
1991 Chevrolet, postcard	.30	.50	1
1992 Chevrolet, postcard	.30	.50	1
1993 Chevrolet, postcard	.30	.50	1
1994 Chevrolet, postcard	.30	.50	1
Chevrolet, dealership, postcard, Florida dealer, Roger Dean Chevrolet	.50	1	2
Chevrolet, dealer postcard, Kansas City, Missouri dealer, Lane-Goddard Chevrolet	2	3	5
1954 Chevrolet dealer postcard, Baltimore, Maryland dealer, Park Circle Chevrolet, (shows 150 model)	8	13	20
1957 Chevrolet dealer postcard, Wheaton, Maryland dealer, Tom's Chevrolet (shows Bel Airs)	4	6	10

CAR CHRISTMAS CARDS

	GOOD	VG	EXC.
1927 Ford, Model A, "Merry Christmas" greeting card (shows 1928 Ford)	5	8	12
1939 Chevrolet greeting card, "Happy and Prosperous New Year," (shows 1940 Chevrolet Special Deluxe Sport Coupe)	6	10	15
1955 Ford, Christmas card and phonograph record (1956 Ford Victoria hardtop depicted)	6	10	15

AUTOMOTIVE "COMPARISON" ADVERTISEMENTS

	GOOD	VG	EXC.
1970 Ford Pinto, advertisement, "Put a Pinto in your portfolio"	1	2	3
1975 Cadillac, advertisement, (shows a 1930 Cadillac Series 452-A Roadster)	1	2	3
1975 Cadillac, advertisement, (shows a 1931 Cadillac Phaeton)	1	2	3
1975 Cadillac, advertisement, (shows a 1933 Cadillac Model 355 dual-cowl Phaeton)	1	2	3
1975 Cadillac, advertisement, (shows a 1932 Cadillac Model 355 Convertible)	1	2	3
1976 Buick Regal, advertisement, (shows a 1953 Buick Roadmaster)	1	2	3
1977 Buick Riviera, advertisement, (shows a 1963 Buick Riviera)	1	2	3
1969 Lincoln Continental, advertisement, (promotes Wisconsin dealers), shows a 1931 SEP Lincoln advertisement)	1	2	3

(NOTE: The following advertisements all feature cars of two or more eras in the same advertisement)

	GOOD	VG	EXC.
1975 Buick advertisement, from 1/1/75 issue of *Psychology Today*	1	2	3
1976 Buick advertisement, from 10/27/75 issue of *Newsweek*	1	2	3
1976 Buick advertisement, from 10/1/76 issue of *Classic* magazine	1	2	3
1977 Buick advertisement, from 10/76 issue of *Esquire*	1	2	3
1975 Cadillac advertisement, from 12/74 issue of *Fortune*	1	2	3
1975 Cadillac advertisement, from 1/20/75 issue of *Newsweek*	1	2	3
1973 Chrysler advertisement, from 10/1/72 issue of *Fortune*, (showing a 1924 Chrysler sedan)	1	2	3
1973 Chrysler advertisement, from 2/73 issue of *Smithsonian*, (showing a 1941 Chrysler Town & Country "barrelback")	1	2	3
1973 Chrysler advertisement, from 4/73 issue of *Fortune*, (showing a 1946 Chrysler Town & Country Convertible)	1	2	3
1973 Chrysler advertisement, from 3/5/73 issue of *Sports Illustrated*, (showing a 1946 Chrysler Town & Country Convertible)	1	2	3

DESCRIPTION	GOOD	VG	EXC.
1975 Corvette advertisement, from 11/14/74 issue of *Sports Illustrated*	1	2	3
1933 Packard advertisement, from 5/33 issue of *Fortune*, "Buy your car in '33 the way they did in 1903," (has Albert Dorne drawing of 1903 Packard showroom)	1	2	3
1934 Packard advertisement, from 5/34 issue of *Fortune* "Maybe you were that boy"	1	2	3
1937 Packard, advertisement, from 2/13/37 issue of *Saturday Evening Post*	1	2	3
1946 Packard advertisement, from 11/14/46 issue of *Saturday Evening Post*, Clipper Deluxe four-door sedan (shows 1902, 1923 and 1946 Packards)	2	3	5
1953 Nash Ambassador, advertisement, from 8/1/53 issue of *Saturday Evening Post*, "To the boy who wanted a Stutz Bearcat."	2	3	5
1929 Pierce-Arrow advertisement, from 2/29 issue of *House Beautiful* "Reproduced from a painting by Adolph Treidler." (shows older advertising art of 1912 model)	2	3	5
1929 Pierce-Arrow advertisement, from 2/29 issue of *Country Life* "Twenty years ago." (shows older advertising art of 1919 model)	2	3	5
1930 Pierce-Arrow advertisement, from 3/30 issue of *Fortune*, "The Tyranny of Tradition." "(shows the advertising artwork for 1919 car)	2	3	5
1931 Pierce-Arrow advertisement, (with Adolphus Busch)	2	3	5
1931 Pierce-Arrow advertisement, from the 4/31 issue of *Sportsman* magazine (with Stephen Baker)	2	3	5
1931 Pierce-Arrow advertisement, from 4/31 issue of *House Beautiful* (with New York Governor Horace White)	2	3	5
1932 Pierce-Arrow advertisement, (shows 12-cylinder Club Sedan with reproduction of 1908 ad artwork)	2	3	5

(**NOTE:** Pierce-Arrow advertisements showing cars from two different eras also appeared in the following issues of leading magazines: 2/2/29 *Literary Digest*; 3/29 *House Beautiful*; 3/16/29 *Literary Digest*; 4/13/29 *Literary Digest*; 5/11/29 *Literary Digest*; 6/8/29 *Literary Digest*; 8/31/29 *Literary Digest*; 9/14/29 *Literary Digest*; 10/19/29 *Literary Digest*; 11/2/29 *Literary Digest*; 11/29 *House Beautiful*; 3/30 *House Beautiful*; 4/30 *House & Garden*; 5/3/30 *Literary Digest*; 6/7/30 *Literary Digest*; 9/30 *Sportsman*; 9/30 *House Beautiful*; 9/6/30 *Literary Digest*; 10/30 *House Beautiful*; 10/11/30 *Literary Digest*).

AUTOMOTIVE ADVERTISEMENTS, FULL-LINE

DESCRIPTION	GOOD	VG	EXC.
1928 Chevrolet, full-line advertisement	4	6	10
1931 Chevrolet, full-line advertisement	4	6	10
1932 Chevrolet, full-line advertisement	6	10	15
1934 Chevrolet, full-line advertisement	4	6	10
1935 Chevrolet, full-line advertisement	4	6	10
1936 Chevrolet, full-line advertisement	3	5	8
1939 Chevrolet, full-line advertisement	3	5	8
1940 Chevrolet, full-line advertisement	3	5	8
1949 Chevrolet, full-line advertisement	2	3	5
1952 Chevrolet, full-line advertisement	2	3	5
1954 Chevrolet, full-line advertisement	2	3	5
1955 Chevrolet, full-line advertisement	2	3	5
1955 Chevrolet, full-line (station wagons only) ad	2	3	5
1956 Chevrolet, full-line advertisement	2	3	5
1956 Chevrolet, full-line (station wagons only) ad	2	3	5
1957 Chevrolet, full-line advertisement	2	3	5
1957 Chevrolet, full-line (station wagons only) ad	2	3	5
1958 Chevrolet, full-line advertisement	2	3	5
1938 Pontiac, full-line advertisement	3	5	8
1939 Pontiac, full-line advertisement	3	5	8
1940 Pontiac, full-line advertisement	3	5	8
1941 Pontiac, full-line advertisement	3	5	8
1942 Pontiac, full-line advertisement	3	5	8
1948 Pontiac, full-line advertisement	2	3	5
1946 Buick, full-line advertisement	2	3	5
1947 Buick, full-line advertisement	2	3	5
1948 Buick, full-line advertisement	2	3	5
1942 Plymouth full-line advertisement	2	3	5
1953 Plymouth full-line advertisement	2	3	5
1955 Ford full-line (cars) advertisement	2	3	5
1956 Ford, full-line (station wagons only) ad	2	3	5

DESCRIPTION	GOOD	VG	EXC.
1955 Mercury, full-line advertisement	2	3	5
1957 Mercury, full-line advertisement	2	3	5
1949 Oldsmobile, full-line advertisement, "Here they come, the new Futurmatics"	2	3	5

AUTOMOTIVE ADVERTISEMENTS

DESCRIPTION	GOOD	VG	EXC.
1936 Lincoln-Zephyr, small format advertisement, from 2/36 issue of *Fortune*	2	3	5
1936 Lincoln-Zephyr, small format advertisement, from 3/21/36 *Saturday Evening Post*	2	3	5
1936 Lincoln-Zephyr, small format advertisement, from 4/36 issue of *Fortune*	2	3	5
1936 Lincoln-Zephyr, small format advertisement, from 7/36 issue of *Fortune*	2	3	5
1937 Lincoln-Zephyr, small format advertisement, from 10/12/36 issue of *Time*	2	3	5
1937 Lincoln-Zephyr, small format advertisement, from 11/36 issue of *Fortune*	2	3	5
1937 Lincoln-Zephyr, small format advertisement, from the 12/36 issue of *National Geographic*	2	3	5
1937 Lincoln-Zephyr, small format advertisement, from 12/36 issue of *Fortune*	2	3	5
1937 Lincoln-Zephyr, small format advertisement, from the 2/37 issue of *National Geographic*	2	3	5
1937 Lincoln-Zephyr, small format advertisement, from the 3/37 issue of *National Geographic*	2	3	5
1937 Lincoln-Zephyr, small format advertisement, from 4/37 issue of *Esquire*	2	3	5
1937 Lincoln-Zephyr, small format advertisement, from 7/3/37 issue of *Saturday Evening Post*	2	3	5
1937 Lincoln-Zephyr, small format advertisement, from the 8/37 issue of *National Geographic*	2	3	5
1938 Lincoln-Zephyr, small format advertisement, from the 11/20/37 *Saturday Evening Post*	2	3	5
1938 Lincoln-Zephyr, small format advertisement, from 12/18/37 issue of *Collier's*	2	3	5
1938 Lincoln-Zephyr, small format advertisement, from the 1/38 issue of *National Geographic*	2	3	5
1938 Lincoln-Zephyr, small format advertisement, from the 3/38 issue of *National Geographic*	2	3	5
1938 Lincoln-Zephyr, small format advertisement, from 3/38 issue of *Esquire*	2	3	5
1938 Lincoln-Zephyr, small format advertisement, from 3/4/38 issue of *Saturday Evening Post*	2	3	5
1938 Lincoln-Zephyr, small format advertisement, from the 5/38 issue of *National Geographic*	2	3	5
1939 Lincoln-Zephyr, small format advertisement, from 12/10/38 issue of *Saturday Evening Post*	2	3	5
1939 Lincoln-Zephyr, small format advertisement, from 2/39 *National Geographic*	2	3	5
1939 Lincoln-Zephyr, small format advertisement, from 2/18/39 *Saturday Evening Post*	2	3	5
1939 Lincoln-Zephyr, small format advertisement, from 3/39 *Fortune*	2	3	5
1939 Lincoln-Zephyr, small format advertisement, from 3/4/39 issue of *Saturday Evening Post*	2	3	5
1939 Lincoln-Zephyr, small format advertisement, from 4/1/39 issue of *Saturday Evening Post*	2	3	5
1939 Lincoln-Zephyr, small format advertisement, from 5/39 issue of *Fortune*	2	3	5
1939 Lincoln-Zephyr, small format advertisement, from 6/12/39 issue of *Time*	2	3	5
1939 Lincoln-Zephyr, small format advertisement, from 7/15/39 issue of *Saturday Evening Post*	2	3	5
1939 Lincoln-Zephyr, small format advertisement, from 7/15/39 issue of *Time*	2	3	5
1939 Lincoln-Zephyr, small format advertisement, from 8/12/39 issue of *Saturday Evening Post*	2	3	5
1940 Lincoln-Zephyr, small format advertisement, from 10/14/39 issue of *Saturday Evening Post*	2	3	5
1940 Lincoln-Zephyr, small format advertisement, from 11/27/39 issue of *Time*	2	3	5
1940 Lincoln-Zephyr, small format advertisement, from 3/4/40 issue of *Time*	2	3	5
1940 Lincoln-Zephyr, small format advertisement, from 3/30/40 issue of *Saturday Evening Post*	2	3	5
1940 Lincoln-Zephyr, small format advertisement, from 4/27/40 issue of *Saturday Evening Post*	2	3	5
1940 Lincoln-Zephyr, small format advertisement, from 6/10/40 issue of *Time*	2	3	5
1941 Lincoln-Zephyr, small format advertisement, from 9/28/40 issue of *Saturday Evening Post*	2	3	5

DESCRIPTION	GOOD	VG	EXC.
1941 Lincoln-Zephyr, small format advertisement, from 10/12/40 issue of *New Yorker*	2	3	5
1941 Lincoln-Zephyr, small format advertisement, from 10/12/40 issue of *Saturday Evening Post*	2	3	5
1941 Lincoln-Zephyr, small format advertisement, from the 11/40 issue of *National Geographic*	2	3	5
1941 Lincoln-Zephyr, small format advertisement, from 11/11/40 issue of *Life*	2	3	5
1941 Lincoln-Zephyr, small format advertisement, from 12/2/40 issue of *Life*	2	3	5
1941 Lincoln-Zephyr, small format advertisement, from 12/2/40 issue of *Time*	2	3	5
1941 Lincoln-Zephyr, small format advertisement, from 12/40 issue of *Fortune*	2	3	5
1941 Lincoln-Zephyr, small format advertisement, from 12/14/40 issue of *Saturday Evening Post*	2	3	5
1941 Lincoln-Zephyr, small format advertisement, from 12/16/40 issue of *Life*	2	3	5
1941 Lincoln-Zephyr, small format advertisement, from the 1/41 issue of *National Geographic*	2	3	5
1941 Lincoln-Zephyr, small format advertisement, from 1/13/41 issue of *Life*	2	3	5
1941 Lincoln-Zephyr, small format advertisement, from 2/3/41 issue of *Life*	2	3	5
1941 Lincoln-Zephyr, small format advertisement, from 2/22/41 issue of *Saturday Evening Post*	2	3	5
1941 Lincoln-Zephyr, small format advertisement, from 2/24/41 issue of *Life*	2	3	5
1941 Lincoln-Zephyr, small format advertisement, from the 3/41 issue of *National Geographic*	2	3	5
1941 Lincoln-Zephyr, small format advertisement, from the 3/8/41 issue of *Saturday Evening Post*	2	3	5
1941 Lincoln-Zephyr, small format advertisement, from 3/17/41 issue of *Life*	2	3	5
1941 Lincoln-Zephyr, small format advertisement, from 3/22/41 issue of *Saturday Evening Post*	2	3	5
1941 Lincoln-Zephyr, small format advertisement, from 4/7/41 issue of *Life*	2	3	5
1941 Lincoln-Zephyr, small format advertisement, from 4/28/41 issue of *Life*	2	3	5
1941 Lincoln-Zephyr, small format advertisement, from the 5/41 issue of *National Geographic*	2	3	5
1941 Lincoln-Zephyr, small format advertisement, from 5/5/41 issue of *Life*	2	3	5
1941 Lincoln-Zephyr, small format advertisement, from 5/17/41 issue of *Saturday Evening Post*	2	3	5
1941 Lincoln-Zephyr, small format advertisement, from 5/19/41 issue of *Life*	2	3	5
1941 Lincoln-Zephyr, small format advertisement, from 6/16/41 issue of *Life*	2	3	5
1942 Lincoln-Zephyr, small format advertisement, from 9/29/41 *Life*	2	3	5
1942 Lincoln-Zephyr, small format advertisement, from 10/20/41 issue of *Life*	2	3	5
1942 Lincoln-Zephyr, small format advertisement, from 10/25/41 issue of *Saturday Evening Post*	2	3	5
1942 Lincoln-Zephyr, small format advertisement, from 11/10/41 issue of *Life*	2	3	5
1942 Lincoln-Zephyr, small format advertisement, from 11/15/41 issue of *Saturday Evening Post*	2	3	5
1942 Lincoln-Zephyr, small format advertisement, from the 1/42 issue of *National Geographic*	2	3	5
1957 Edsel, advertisement, from 7/22/57 issue of *Life*	1	2	3
1957 Edsel, advertisement, from 8/5/57 issue of *Life*	1	2	3
1957 Edsel, advertisement, from 8/19/57 issue of *Life*	1	2	3
1957 Edsel, advertisement, from 9/2/57 issue of *Life*	1	2	3
1957 Edsel, advertisement, from 9/9/57 issue of *Life*	1	2	3
1957 Edsel, advertisement, from 9/14/57 issue of *Saturday Evening Post*	1	2	3
1957 Edsel, advertisement, from 9/30/57 issue of *Life*	1	2	3
1957 Edsel, advertisement, from 10/5/57 issue of *Saturday Evening Post*	1	2	3
1957 Edsel, advertisement, from the 10/14/57 issue of *Life*	1	2	3
1957 Edsel, advertisement, from 10/19/57 issue of *Saturday Evening Post*	1	2	3

DESCRIPTION	GOOD	VG	EXC.
1957 Edsel, advertisement, from 10/28/57 issue of *Life*	1	2	3
1957 Edsel, advertisement, from 11/2/57 issue of *Saturday Evening Post*	1	2	3
1957 Edsel, advertisement, from 11/11/57 issue of *Life*	1	2	3
1957 Edsel, advertisement, from 11/16/57 of *Saturday Evening Post*	1	2	3
1957 Edsel, advertisement, from 11/25/57 issue of *Life*	1	2	3
1957 Edsel, advertisement, from 11/30/57 issue of *Saturday Evening Post*	1	2	3
1958 Edsel, advertisement, from 4/14/58 issue of *Life*	1	2	3
1958 Edsel, advertisement, from 6/16/58 issue of *Life*	1	2	3
1959 Edsel, advertisement, from 11/29/58 issue of *Saturday Evening Post*	1	2	3
1959 Edsel, advertisement, from 12/22/58 issue of *Life*	1	2	3
1959 Edsel, advertisement, from 1/19/59 issue of *Life*	1	2	3
1959 Edsel, advertisement, from 4/1/59 issue of *Holiday*	1	2	3
(**NOTE**: Edsels in other advertisements of other companies) 1957 Edsel, advertisement, rom 10/12/57 issue of *Saturday Evening Post* (ad of Champion Spark Plugs Company)	1	2	3
1957 Edsel, advertisement, from 12/7/57 issue of *Saturday Evening Post* (ad of Gulf Oil Company)	1	2	3
1958 Edsel, advertisement, from 2/10/58 issue of *Life* (ad of Simonize Wax)	1	2	3
1953 Cadillac, Eldorado, advertisement from 2/24/53 issue of *Look* (AC Spark Plug Company ad)	1	2	3
1953 Cadillac, Eldorado, advertisement from 8/29/53 issue of *Saturday Evening Post* (AC Spark Plug ad)	2	3	5
1953 Cadillac, Eldorado, advertisement from 9/7/53 issue of *Life* (AC Spark Plug Company ad)	1	2	3
1954 Cadillac, Eldorado, advertisement from 8/23/54 issue of *Life*	2	3	5
1955 Cadillac, Eldorado, advertisement from 3/55 issue of *Holiday*	2	3	5
1955 Cadillac, Eldorado, advertisement from 4/55 issue of *Fortune*	2	3	5
1955 Cadillac, Eldorado, advertisement from 5/55 issue of *Holiday*	2	3	5
1955 Cadillac, Eldorado, advertisement from 6/55 issue of *Fortune*	2	3	5
1955 Cadillac, Eldorado, advertisement from 7/55 issue of *Holiday*	2	3	5
1955 Cadillac, Eldorado, advertisement from 8/55 issue of *Fortune*	2	3	5
1956 Cadillac, Eldorado, advertisement from 3/56 issue of *Fortune*	2	3	5
1956 Cadillac, Eldorado, advertisement from 3/56 issue of *Holiday*	2	3	5
1957 Cadillac, Eldorado, advertisement from 11/12/56 issue of *Life*	2	3	5
1958 Cadillac, Eldorado, advertisement from 12/16/57 issue of *Life*	2	3	5
1958 Cadillac, Eldorado, advertisement from 3/58 issue of *Fortune*	2	3	5
1959 Cadillac, Eldorado, advertisement from 10/11/58 issue of *Saturday Evening Post*	2	3	5
1960 Cadillac, Eldorado, advertisement from 2/60 issue of *Holiday*	1	2	3
1963 Cadillac, Eldorado, advertisement from 3/22/63 issue of *Life*	1	2	3
1963 Cadillac, Eldorado, advertisement from 4/63 issue of *Holiday*	1	2	3
1967 Cadillac, Eldorado, advertisement from 11/66 issue of *Holiday*	1	2	3
(**NOTE**: A beginner's collection of early color auto advertisements.)			
1925 Cadillac, advertisement from 3/25 issues of *Harper's, Review of Reviews* and *Century*	3	5	8
1925 Cadillac, advertisement from 4/25 issues of *Harper's, Review of Reviews, Atlantic*	3	5	8
1925 Cadillac, advertisement from 4/25 and 5/25 issues of *Harper's, Review of Reviews*	3	5	8
1925 Cadillac, advertisement from 4/25 and 11/25 issues of *Harper's*	3	5	8

DESCRIPTION	GOOD	VG	EXC.
1933 Cadillac, advertisement from 4/33 and 2/33 issues of *National Geographic*	3	4	7
1933 Cadillac, advertisement from 3/33 issue of *National Geographic*	3	4	7
1933 Cadillac, advertisement from 4/33 issue of *National Geographic*	3	4	7
1933 Cadillac, advertisement from 5/33 issue of *National Geographic*	3	4	7

(**NOTE**: These are the first color car advertisements to appear in *National Geographic*. Buick followed shortly thereafter, as did Dodge.)

1920 Chalmers, advertisement, from the 6/20 issue of *Century*	2	3	5
1925 Diana, advertisement, from the 9/25 issue of *Harper's*	2	3	5
1925 Diana, advertisement, from the 10/25 issue of *Century*	2	3	5
1925 Diana, advertisement, from the 11/25 issue of *Harper's*	2	3	5
1918 Franklin, advertisement	2	3	5
1919 Franklin, advertisement	2	3	5
1920 Franklin, advertisement	2	3	5

(**NOTE**: Franklin color advertisements appeared in various magazines).

1922 Haynes, advertisement from 12/22 issue of *Schribners*	2	3	5
1923 Haynes, advertisement, from 3/23 issue of *Century*	2	3	5
1924 Haynes, advertisement, from 3/24 issue of *Harper's*	2	3	5
1924 Haynes, advertisement, from 4/24 issue of *Harper's*	2	3	5
1918 Jordan, advertisement, from the 2/18 issue of *The World's Work*	3	4	7
1920 Jordan, advertisement, from 4/20 issue of *Century*	3	4	7
1920 Jordan, advertisement, from 6/20 issue of *Century*	3	4	7
1924 Lincoln, advertisement, from 1/24 issue of *Harper's*	2	3	5
1924 Lincoln, advertisement, from 3/24 issue of *Harper's*	2	3	5
1924 Lincoln, advertisement, from 5/24 issue of *Harper's*	2	3	5
1924 Lincoln, advertisement, from 7/24 issue of *Harper's*	2	3	5
1924 Lincoln, advertisement, from 9/24 issue of *Harper's*	2	3	5
1924 Lincoln, advertisement, from 10/24 issue of *Harper's*	2	3	5
1924 Lincoln, advertisement, from 11/24 issue of *Harper's*	2	3	5
1924 Lincoln, advertisement, from 12/24 issue of *Harper's*	2	3	5
1926 Lincoln, advertisement, from 1/26 issue of *Harper's*	2	3	5
1926 Lincoln, advertisement, from 2/26 issue of *Harper's*	2	3	5
1926 Lincoln, advertisement, from 3/26 issue of *Harper's*	2	3	5
1926 Lincoln, advertisement, from 4/26 issue of *Harper's*	2	3	5
1926 Lincoln, advertisement, from 5/26 issue of *Harper's*	2	3	5
1926 Lincoln, advertisement, from 6/26 issue of *Harper's*	2	3	5
1926 Lincoln, advertisement, from 7/26 issue of *Harper's*	2	3	5
1926 Lincoln, advertisement, from 8/26 issue of *Harper's*	2	3	5
1926 Lincoln, advertisement, from 12/26 issue of *Harper's*	2	3	5
1922 Maxwell, advertisement, from 11/22 issue of *Review of Reviews*	2	3	4
1922 Maxwell, advertisement, from 12/22 issue of *Review of Reviews*	2	3	4
1925 Moon, advertisement, from 6/25 issue of *Review of Reviews*	2	3	4
1925 Moon, advertisement, from 4/25 issue of *Harper's*	2	3	4
1925 Moon, advertisement, from 5/25 issue of *Review of Reviews*	2	3	4
1925 Moon, advertisement, from 7/25 issue of *Atlantic*	2	3	4

DESCRIPTION	GOOD	VG	EXC.
1925 Moon, advertisement, from 7/25 issue of *Review of Reviews*	2	3	4
1925 Moon, advertisement, from 8/1/25 issue of *Harper's*	2	3	4
1911 Oldsmobile, advertisement, from 6/17/11 issue of *The Outlook*	3	4	7
1911 Pierce-Arrow, advertisement, from the 9/11 issue of *Everybody's Magazine*	3	4	7
1913 Pierce-Arrow, advertisement, from 10/13 issue of *Century*	4	6	10
1914 Pierce-Arrow, advertisement, from 1/14 issue of *Century*	4	6	10
1915 Pierce-Arrow, advertisement, from 7/14/15 issue of *The Outlook*	4	6	10
1915 Pierce-Arrow, advertisement, from 10/20/15 issue of *The Outlook*	4	6	10
1915 Pierce-Arrow, advertisement, from 1/15 issue of *Century*	4	6	10
1921 Pierce-Arrow, advertisement, from 11/21 issue of *Century*	3	4	7
1927 Pierce-Arrow, advertisement, from 10/27 issue of *Atlantic*	3	4	7
1919 Rauch & Lang Electric, auto advertisement, from 3/19 issue of *Review of Reviews*	3	4	7
1920 Standard, advertisement, from 2/20 issue of *Century*	2	3	5
1921 Standard, advertisement, from 2/21 issue of *Harper's*	2	3	5
1921 Standard, advertisement, from 11/21 issue of *Century*	2	3	5
1919 Studebaker, advertisement, from 6/19 issue of *Review of Reviews*	2	3	5
1913 Stevens-Duryea, advertisement, from 11/13 issue of *Harper's*	1	2	3
1910 Woods Electric, advertisement from 6/18/10 issue of *The Outlook*	2	3	5

CAR MAGAZINES

	GOOD	VG	EXC.
Rod & Custom magazine, May, 1953 issue (Volume 1, Number 1)	14	23	35

AUTOMOTIVE POSTAGE STAMPS

	GOOD	VG	EXC.
1952 United States, postage stamp, 50th anniversary of American Automobile Association	.10	.16	.25
1971 German postage stamps, set of four (4) stamps honoring Berlin-to- Pottsdam Race, Depict Opel rocket car, Auto Union, Mercedes SSK and racing scene	.75	1	2
1988 United States Stamps, Ken Dallison artwork; set of five (5) Classic autos includes 1928 Locomobile, 1929 Pierce-Arrow, 1931 Cord, 1932 Packard and 1935 Duesenberg SJ	.10	.16	.25

Pumps, Plates, Parts

VISIBLE GASOLINE PUMPS

	GOOD	VG	EXC.
Gasoline pump, Fry, early "Mae West" 5-gal. model	1170	1950	3000
Gasoline pump, Fry, early "Mae West" 10-gal. model	1000	1625	2500
Gasoline pump, Hays, early model	600	975	1500
Gasoline pump, Gilbert-Barker, early "lighthouse" model	1300	2500	3500
Gasoline pump, American, "slab-side" model	315	520	800

GASOLINE PUMP GLOBES

	GOOD	VG	EXC.
Gasoline pump globe, No. 218 oval center, Shamrock brand gasoline, glass body	115	195	300
Gasoline pump globe, No. 218 oval center, Zephyr brand gasoline, glass body	115	195	300
Gasoline pump globe, No. 218 oval center, Zephyr brand gasoline, plastic body	70	115	175
Gasoline pump globe, No. 218 oval center, Site brand gasoline, glass body	110	180	225
Gasoline pump globe, No. 218 oval center, Site brand gasoline, plastic body	70	115	175
Gasoline pump globe, Crown Ethyl, Red Crown	315	525	800
Gasoline pump globe, Crown Ethyl, Gold Crown	235	390	600
Gasoline pump globe, Baron brand gasoline, glass body	300	500	750
Gasoline pump globe, Dino Supreme brand gasoline, plastic body	60	100	150

DESCRIPTION	GOOD	VG	EXC.
Gasoline pump globe, Sinclair H.C. brand gasoline, glass body	235	390	600
Gasoline pump globe, Sinclair H.C. brand gasoline, plastic body	70	115	175
Gasoline pump globe, White Rose brand gasoline, "metal body	600	1000	1500
Gasoline pump globe, White Eagle brand gasoline, one-piece	1300	2500	3500
Gasoline pump globe, Mustang brand gasoline, glass body	135	230	350
Gasoline pump globe, Dixcel brand gasoline, metal body	350	585	900

TIRE VALVE CAPS

DESCRIPTION	GOOD	VG	EXC.
Red Crown valve cap (original; set of 4)	6	10	15
Gold Crown valve cap (original; set of 4)	8	13	20

CALIFORNIA LICENSE PLATES

DESCRIPTION	GOOD	VG	EXC.
1908 California license plate, issued by Automobile Club of Southern California	115	195	300
1914 California license plate, all-porcelain	110	180	225
1915 California license plate, black and yellow (hard to find)	80	130	200
1916 California license plate, blue on white	110	180	200
1924 California license plate, white on bright green (only early year plates with six or seven characters)	80	130	200
1927 California license plate (hard to find)	60	100	150
1939 California license plate, "California World's Fair" wording only	20	33	50
1939 California license plate, "California World's Fair" wording with art showing bridge and skyline	20	33	50
1939 California license plate, "Cal '39," (non-World's Fair; rarest plate issued in California in 1939)	27	45	70
1940 California license plate, first round-cornered design	16	26	40
1942 California license plate (rare)	20	33	50
1944 California registration sticker for windshield (rare)	14	23	35
1951 California license plate	4	6	10
1955 California license plate	4	6	10
1956 California license plate (smaller)	4	6	10
1963 California license plate	4	6	10

LICENSE PLATES

DESCRIPTION	GOOD	VG	EXC.
1903 Commonwealth of Massachusetts, license plates; number, plus "Mass. Automobile Register," first year, steel-coated plates with dark blue porcelain	140	230	350
1903 Ontario, Canada license plate; black-and-silver metal numbers and Provincial coat-of-arms	80	130	200
1905 Wisconsin license plate, first issue	140	230	350
1985 District of Columbia special "50th American President Inaugural" license plates	12	20	30

INTERNATIONAL OVALS

Pricing undetermined

BRITISH LICENSE PLATES

DESCRIPTION	GOOD	VG	EXC.
1962 British license plate (LKE prefix)	12	20	30
1967 British license plate (E suffix)	10	18	27
1976 British license plate (P suffix)	6	10	15
1978 British license plate (N suffix)	6	10	15
1933 British license plate	12	20	30
1953 British license plate	10	18	17

LICENSE PLATE TAG TOPPERS

DESCRIPTION	GOOD	VG	EXC.
License plate tag topper, Farm Bureau Mutual Insurance	8	13	20
License plate tag topper, Silvertown Safety League	12	20	30
License plate tag topper, cat	16	26	40
License plate tag topper, Chevrolet dealer	30	50	75
License plate tag topper, State Farm Insurance	8	13	20
License plate tag topper, American Automobile Association (AAA)	6	10	15
License plate tag topper, Griffith Motor Car Company, Carthage, Missouri	16	26	40
License plate tag topper, Brewer Motor Car Company, Manhattan, Kansas	16	26	40
License plate tag topper, Livingood Lincoln-Chrysler-Plymouth	16	26	40
License plate tag topper, auto parts store	8	13	20

(**NOTE**: Plain, tin car dealer tag toppers sell for approximately $30 in top condition and proportionately less in lesser conditions).

ANTIQUE AUTO TURN SIGNALS

DESCRIPTION	GOOD	VG	EXC.
Circa mid-1930s "wig-wag" taillight (accessory type)	60	100	150
1920s Outlook combination stop/taillight (beehive shape; prismatic)	20	45	75
1918 British "aluminum-hand" signaling device	900	1600	2000

MASCOTS AND HOOD ORNAMENTS

DESCRIPTION	GOOD	VG	EXC.
1920 Minerva hood mascot (Athena)	50	80	125
1930s Bugatti Royale hood mascot, designed by Rembrandt Bugatti (white elephant)	160	260	400
1912 Boyce Moto Meter	16	26	40
1932 Chevrolet hood mascot (eagle)	68	114	175
1928 Pontiac hood mascot (Indian)	40	65	100
1929 Pontiac hood mascot (Indian)	40	65	100
1930 Pontiac hood mascot (Indian)	50	80	125
1931 Pontiac hood mascot (Indian)	50	80	125
1932 Pontiac hood mascot (Indian)	50	80	125
1928 Oakland hood mascot (golden eagle)	40	65	100
1929 Oakland hood mascot (golden eagle)	40	65	100
1930 Oakland hood mascot (golden eagle)	40	65	100
1931 Oakland hood mascot (golden eagle)	40	65	100
1934 Ford hood mascot (greyhound)	60	100	150
1935 Ford hood mascot (greyhound)	60	100	150
1936 Ford hood mascot (greyhound)	60	100	150
1936 Ford hood mascot (lazy 8)	295	490	750
1932 Chrysler hood mascot (first use of gazelle mascot)	80	130	200
1949 DeSoto hood mascot (head of Spanish explorer Hernando De-Soto)	50	80	125
1950 DeSoto hood mascot (head of Spanish explorer Hernando De-Soto)	50	80	125
1933 Plymouth hood mascot (first use of Mayflower mascot)	40	65	100
1924 Franklin hood mascot (first use of lion mascot)	50	80	120
1928 Franklin Airman hood mascot ("Spirit of St. Louis")	55	90	140
1929 Gardner hood mascot (griffin)	40	65	100
1928 Kissel hood mascot (eagle)	40	65	100
1928-1929 Pierce-Arrow hood mascot (archer with foot down)	110	180	275
1912-1928 Moon hood ornament (crescent moon)	40	65	100
1929 Packard hood mascot ("Goddess of Speed")	135	230	350
1930 Packard hood mascot ("Adonis")	215	360	550
1938-1940 Packard hood ornament (pelican)	90	150	225
1926-1935 Stutz hood ornament (the Egyptian sun god Ra)	100	165	250
1934-1937 Lincoln hood ornament (greyhound)	100	165	250
1956 Lincoln hood ornament (knight)	50	80	125
1925-1928 Diana hood ornament (goddess)	40	65	100
1927-1930 Cadillac LaSalle hood ornament ("Sieur de LaSalle")	135	230	350
1933-1936 Cadillac hood ornament V-12 and V-16 cars, special order (goddess)	255	425	650
1932 Dodge hood ornament (first use of ram mascot by Dodge)	40	65	100
Lalique hood ornament	315	520	800
Hood ornament, aftermarket novelty type (aero engine)	30	50	75
Hood ornament, aftermarket novelty type (god Mercury running)	31	55	80
Hood ornament, aftermarket novelty type (Minute Man)	30	50	75
Wall plaque, shaped like 1950s style DeSoto hood ornament; this is probably a dealer promotional item	47	81	125
1920s hood ornament, aftermarket novelty type (Pan)	30	50	75
1930-1932 Cadillac LaSalle hood ornament (heron)	135	230	350

HOOD MASCOTS & ORNAMENTS

DESCRIPTION	GOOD	VG	EXC.
1911 Rolls-Royce, hood mascot "Spirit of Ecstasy," by Charles Sykes	60	100	150
1926 Liberty Bell hood mascot, aftermarket fraternal type done for "Odd Fellows"	10	16	25
1909 Goobo, God of Good Luck, hood mascot, aftermarket novelty type created by L.V. Aronson	14	23	35
1915 Lalique crystal glass, hood ornament. First mascot by Rene La-lique	470	780	1200

AUTO RADIATOR SCRIPTS & NAMEPLATES

Description	GOOD	VG	EXC.
Willys-Knight "WK" radiator script	30	50	75
Interstate nickled namescript	25	42	65
Texan nameplate	8	13	20
Empire nameplate	23	40	60
Duesenberg nameplate	26	42	65
Wolverine nameplate (with red insert)	8	13	20
Beggs Six nameplate (porcelain with red glass background)	8	13	20
Diana badge (oval, black background)	8	13	20
Kaiser badge (postwar, chrome buffalo)	12	19	30
Frazer badge (postwar, coat-of-arms)	12	19	30
Bentley "wings" (B with black label)	18	29	45
Bentley "wings" (B with green label)	16	26	40
Bentley "wings" (B with red label)	16	26	40
Bentley "wings" (B with blue label)	16	26	40
Bugatti nameplate	26	42	65
Cadillac script	16	26	40

MISCELLANEOUS COLLECTIBLES

Description	GOOD	VG	EXC.
Minerva screw-on hubcap	14	23	35
Dort screw-on hubcap	8	13	20
Krit screw-on hubcap	6	10	15
Velie screw-on hubcap	6	10	15
Pierce-Arrow screw-on hubcap	16	26	40
Packard screw-on hubcap	16	26	40
Stutz screw-on hubcap	16	26	40
Maxwell screw-on hubcap	6	10	15
Studebaker screw-on hubcap	6	10	15
Ford screw-on hubcap	4	6	10
Essex screw-on hubcap	4	6	10
Dodge screw-on hubcap	4	6	10
Oakland screw-on hubcap	4	6	10
Nash screw-on hubcap	4	6	10
Cadillac screw-on hubcap	16	26	40
1928 Arcade, toy car, Model A Ford	225	325	450
1932 Cor Cor, toy car, Graham "Blue Streak" sedan	470	780	1200
Mid-1930s Auburn Rubber Company, toy car, Auburn Speedster	29	49	75
1950 "Shoe Box" Ford, toy car (plastic model with a battery-powered motor	80	130	200

The Hard Stuff

OLD CAR SHAVING MUGS

Description	GOOD	VG	EXC.
Shaving mug with 1902 Oldsmobile illustration	10	16	25
Shaving mug with 1902 Crestmobile illustration	10	16	25
Shaving mug with 1904 Winton illustration	10	16	25
Shaving mug with 1904 Peerless illustration	10	16	25
Shaving mug with 1906 Royal Tourist illustration	10	16	25
Shaving mug with 1909 Winton truck illustration	10	16	25
Shaving mug with 1910 Peerless illustration	10	16	25
Shaving mug with 1911 Locomobile illustration	10	16	25
Shaving mug with 1913 Haynes illustration	10	16	25
Shaving mug with 1914 Hupmobile illustration	10	16	25
Shaving mug with 1915 Star auto illustration	10	16	25
Shaving mug with 1915 Chevrolet bakery truck illustration	10	16	25
Shaving mug with 1916 Cadillac illustration	10	16	25
Shaving mug with 1917 Chevrolet illustration	10	16	25
Saving mug that belonged to auto body man named "DeRosa;" shows car body being painted	600	1000	1500
Shaving mug that belonged to auto mechanic; shows mechanic working on car	390	650	1000
Shaving mug with name "J.Field"	500	845	1300
Shaving mug depicting old car	10	16	25
Shaving mug showing sedan owned by Mr. Scheid	500	845	1300

DESCRIPTION	GOOD	VG	EXC.
Shaving mug showing touring car owned by Mr. Zahn	500	845	1300
Shaving mug showing an old truck	12	19	30
Shaving mug showing auto engine	8	13	20
Shaving mug showing runabout owned by Mr. Rushworth	600	1000	1500
Shaving mug showing runabout owned by Mr. Young	600	1000	1500
Shaving mug showing old car	12	19	30
Shaving mug showing panel van	12	19	30
Shaving mug showing panel van	12	19	30
Shaving mug showing canopied express truck	14	23	85
Shaving mug showing large touring car owned by Mr. Nostrand	500	800	1200
Shaving mug showing large touring car owned by Mr. Merit	500	800	1200
Shaving mug showing car owned by Mr. Mitterich	500	800	1200
Shaving mug showing car owned by Mr. Quigley	500	800	1200
Shaving mug showing non-auto transportation scene	12	19	30

AUTOMOTIVE COINS & TOKENS

Description	GOOD	VG	EXC.
1910 Parry automobile, token	7	12	18
1892 Columbus Buggy Company token (issued a Columbian Exposition in Chicago, Illinois)	16	26	40
1933 Ford Chicago World's Fair "Century of Progress" souvenir medal honoring "30 Years of Progress" on Ford Motor Company's 30th anniversary (shows 1933 Ford grille on front/V-8 logo on back)	6	10	15
1934 Ford Chicago World's Fair "Century of Progress" souvenir medal (shows V-8 emblems on both sides)	6	10	15
1978 "50th Anniversary of Model A Ford" medallion	4	6	10
1954-1955 General Motors "50 Millionth Car" commemorative medal. Issue dated November 23, 1954. (Pictures the 1955 Chevrolet Bel Air two-door hardtop)	4	6	10
1939 Chevrolet, "Best of '39 Jubilee," commemorative token. Back is stamped "Chevy Showboat, Greenbrier, White Sulfur Springs, West Virginia"	3	5	7
1940 Oldsmobile token. Front of 1940 Oldsmobile on obverse. Says "America's biggest money's worth: 1940 Olds" on reverse. Believed to be scarce.	5	8	12
1935 Pontiac token. Indian head and "silver streaks"	6	10	15
1940 Buick encased silver dollar. Believed very rare.	50	100	150
1941 Buick encased silver dollar. Believed very rare.	50	100	150
1954 General Motors "Motorama" spinner token	2	3	5
1955 General Motors "Motorama" spinner token	2	3	5
1956 General Motors "Motorama" spinner token	2	3	5
1963 Mercury "Silver Anniversary" commemorative medal (heavily chrome-plated	10	16	25
1934 Chrysler Corporation, medal, Airflow: "A Century of Progress in a Decade." (1924 Chrysler on back - 10th anniversary of Chrysler)	4	6	10
1956 Chrysler Corporation, medal "Forward Look." (arrowhead logo on one side; brand names of Chrysler marques listed on other side	6	10	15
Mid-1930s Dodge Truck Division token with sales pitch imprint (believed to be scarce)	8	13	20
1966 AMC, aluminum token, obverse reads "Sensible Spectaculars;" and reverse says "Rambler Extra Value Features Make Your Rambler Dollar a Bigger Dollar." Has car names on one side. Only known AMC promotional medal	2	4	6
Madison Mint .999 fine silver ingot illustrating Stanley Steamer roadster	11	19	30
Auburn-Cord-Duesenberg four token issue (modern commemorative)	10	16	25

OLD CAR WHISKEY DECANTERS

Description	GOOD	VG	EXC.
Garnier bottle, circa-1912 touring car	18	29	45
Decanter, circa-1912 Rolls-Royce Silver Ghost Town Car	18	29	45

DESCRIPTION	GOOD	VG	EXC.
Jewel Tea Company, antique delivery wagon, (1974 issue)	29	49	75
1976 whiskey decanter, ceramic, 1911 Thomas-Flyer (car owned by William Winslow of Galena, IL.) Not Great Race car.	25	42	65
1976 whiskey decanter, ceramic, 1911 Thomas-Flyer (car owned by William Winslow of Galena, IL.) Not Great Race car.	25	42	65
1977 whiskey decanter, ceramic, 1914 Stutz, monocle windshield, (yellow and black)	23	38	58
1977 whiskey decanter, ceramic, 1914 Stutz, monocle windshield, (gray and black)	23	38	58
1977 whiskey decanter, ceramic, 1913 Cadillac	17	32	50
Jim Beam whiskey decanter, Circa mid-1980s, ceramic and plastic, Model A Ford Fire Truck	55	91	140
Jim Beam whiskey decanter, Circa mid-1980s, ceramic and plastic, Model A Ford Ambulance	17	32	50
Jim Beam whiskey decanter, Circa 1980s, ceramic and plastic, 1935 Duesenberg roadster	68	114	175
Jim Beam whiskey decanter, Circa early-1980s, ceramic and plastic, 1917 Mack Fire Truck (first Jim Beam fire truck)	40	65	100

JIM BEAM WHISKEY DECANTERS

DESCRIPTION	GOOD	VG	EXC.
1970 Jim Beam, whiskey decanter, 1911 Marmon Wasp (modeled from Ed McCormick's car)	35	60	90
1970 Jim Beam, whiskey decanter, Mint 400, "World's Greatest Off-Road Race"	31	52	80
1975 Jim Beam, Bobby Unser Indianapolis 500 racing car, Olsenite Eagle	22	36	55
1976 Jim Beam, whiskey decanter, Sports Car Club of America	19	32	50
1972 Jim Beam, whiskey decanter, "Beam on Wheels" series, 1902 Curved Dash Oldsmobile (honored 75th anniversary of Oldsmobile)	27	45	70
1973 Jim Beam, whiskey decanter, "Beam on Wheels," Volkswagen Bug (red)	18	29	45
1973 Jim Beam, whiskey decanter, "Beam on Wheels," Volkswagen Bug (blue)	18	29	45
1974 Jim Beam, whiskey decanter, 1913 Model T Ford runabout (black)	19	32	50
1974 Jim Beam, whiskey decanter, 1913 Model T Ford runabout (green)	19	32	50
1977 Jim Beam, whiskey decanter, AC Spark Plug Company	14	23	35
1978 Jim Beam, whiskey decanter, 1978 Corvette (25th Anniversary of the Chevrolet Corvette)	55	91	140
1978 Jim Beam, whiskey decanter, Mr. Goodwrench	18	29	45
1978 Jim Beam, whiskey decanter, Delco Freedom Battery	9	15	25
1978 Jim Beam, whiskey decanter, 1957 Chevrolet Bel Air	27	45	70
1978 Jim Beam, whiskey decanter, 1903 Ford Model A runabout (red with black trim)	19	32	50
1978 Jim Beam, whiskey decanter, 1903 Ford Model A runabout (black with red)	19	32	50
1981 Jim Beam, whiskey decanter, Ford Model A Fire Chief's car, red	45	75	115
1981 Jim Beam, whiskey decanter, Ford Model A Fire Chief's car, yellow (100 made for Jim Beam salesmen)	60	100	150
1981 Jim Beam, whiskey decanter, Ford Model A Fire Chief's car, black (25 made for Jim Beam sales people who hit their quotas)	90	150	225
1981 Jim Beam, whiskey decanter, Ford Model A four-door phaeton light blue	40	65	100
1981 Jim Beam, whiskey decanter, Ford Model A four-door phaeton, dark blue, Police Car	40	65	100
1981 Jim Beam, whiskey decanter, 1928-1929 Ford Model A pickup	60	98	150
1981 Jim Beam, whiskey decanter, 1930 Ford Model A Police Paddy Wagon	48	82	125
1981 Jim Beam, whiskey decanter, 1934 Duesenberg Model J Town Car (blue body with white top)	90	150	225
1982 Jim Beam, whiskey decanter, 1934 Duesenberg Model J Town Car, commemorates 27th annual Auburn-Cord-Duesenberg Fest in Auburn, Indiana, Labor Day Weekend 1982, (midnight blue body)	100	165	250

AUTOMOTIVE ADVERTISING SIGNS & BADGES

DESCRIPTION	GOOD	VG	EXC.
Mobil red horse sign, 30 x 45 inches, circa late-1930s	315	520	800
White Eagle Oil Company (white glass eagle)	315	520	800
1930s to 1950s Texaco "Fire Chief" small gas pump sign	30	50	75
1950s, AAA, porcelain sign	35	60	90
Teens, AAA, brass radiator badge	20	33	50
1920s, AAA, radiator badge, poured glass or porcelain	30	50	75
1930s, AAA, stamped die-cast badge	9	15	25
1950s, AAA, stick-on decal	4	7	10
1931 Nash Motor Car Company, porcelain dealership sign	390	650	1000
1931 Packard Motor Car Company, porcelain dealership sign	450	780	1200
India Gas sign, porcelain	30	50	75
Humble Gas sign, porcelain	30	50	75
Standard Oil Company sign, porcelain, with Donald Duck, "Knockouts for Winners" sales promotion	120	195	300
1930s Willard Batteries sign	19	32	50
AAA, porcelain sign(s), with state name(s)	48	82	125
Havoline Motor Oil sign (red, white and blue)	48	82	125
Oakland Motor Car Company (became Pontiac), porcelain dealership sign	60	100	150
Chrysler/Plymouth porcelain dealership sign	80	130	200
Pontiac, porcelain dealership sign (round with Indian head)	155	260	400
American Motors, porcelain dealership sign	40	65	100

PARKING METERS

	GOOD	VG	EXC.
1965 parking meter	32	52	80
1930S parking meter	60	98	150
Duncan parking meter, two-hour limit	29	50	75
Double parking meter, 12-hour limit	48	82	125
1950s Duncan model D-2 parking meter (made into lamp)	14	23	35

ANTIQUE CLOTHING

	GOOD	VG	EXC.
Burberry style dust wrapper	14	23	35
Burberry style motorcycle slip-on and pullover	12	19	30
Ulster overcoat	14	23	35
Burberry suit	18	29	45

MUSIC VIDEOS FEATURING OLD CARS

	GOOD	VG	EXC.
"Bad Girls"	6	10	15
"Big Log"	6	10	15
"Brass in the Pocket"	6	10	15
"Church of the Poison Mind"	6	10	15
"Cry, Cry, Cry"	6	10	15
"Cut Loose"	6	10	15
"Gimme All Your Lovin'"	6	10	15
"Hot Girls in Love"	6	10	15
"How Do You Spell Love"	6	10	15
"I'm Still Standing"	6	10	15
"I Want A New Drug"	6	10	15
"I Won't Stand in Your Way"	6	10	15
"My Town"	6	10	15
"New Frontier"	6	10	15
"New Song"	6	10	15
"Our Lips Are Sealed"	6	10	15
"Sexy & 17"	6	10	15
"Sharp Dressed Man"	6	10	15
"Should I Stay or Should I Go"	6	10	15
"Street of Dreams"	6	10	15
"Tender is the Night"	6	10	15
"Thriller"	6	10	15
"Why Me?"	6	10	15
"Wonderin'"	6	10	15
"Uptown Girl"	6	10	15
"You Make My Heart Beat Faster"	6	10	15

STANLEY WANLASS SCULPTURES

	GOOD	VG	EXC.
"Quicksilver"	5700	9500	14,500
"Visions"	5900	9800	15,000
"The Benz Pentennial"	7000	12,000	18,000
"Spirit of the Automobilist"	7000	12,000	18,000
"Five Miles to the Gallon"	7000	12,000	18,000
"The California Kid"	4300	7800	11,000
"Two Thoroughbreds"	10,000	16,000	25,000
"Cool 50"	4300	7800	11,000
"High Gear"	9000	15,000	23,000

Toy Autos

PEDAL CARS *

DESCRIPTION	GOOD	VG	EXC.
Gendron pedal car, Cadillac (standard)	1560	2600	4000
Gendron pedal car, Cadillac (deluxe)	1755	2925	4500
Gendron pedal vehicle, Tri-motor airplane	2340	3900	6000
Citroen juvenile car (electric)	2145	3575	5500
1925 Packard pedal car	2730	4550	7000
Gendron pedal car, Model 153 Packard roadster	1835	3055	4700

(* See story 42 for additional pedal car pricing)

KID AND JUVENILE CARS

	GOOD	VG	EXC.
Shaw cyclecar	585	975	1500
1932 Syco Sales Company Juvenile car	585	975	1500

PEDAL CARS

	GOOD	VG	EXC.
1920s pedal car, Star Auto Racer	290	490	750
1920s pedal car, Dodge Racer	330	555	850
1920s pedal car, Green Auto Racer	330	555	850
1920s pedal car, Speed King Racer	330	555	850
1920s pedal car, Dan Patch "Big Racer"	350	585	900
1923 pedal car, American National Toy Company, Packard	780	1300	2000
1923 pedal car, American National Toy Company, Tandem Drive Packard Touring	3120	5200	8000
1937 pedal car, Gendron Pontiac with silver streaks	1440	2400	3700
1949 pedal car, Murray-Ohio, "James Dean" Mercury	175	295	450
1950s pedal car, Giordini Italian), "Juan Fangio" Grand Prix racer	780	1300	2000
1953 pedal car, Kidillac	290	490	750
1956 child's car, Pontiac fiberglass body, electric lights. Designed by Jack K. Stuart	1440	2400	3700
1957 child's car, Mercury Junior	225	370	575
1964 pedal car, Ford Mustang	265	442	675

KINGSBURY TOY CARS

	GOOD	VG	EXC.
1934 Chrysler Airflow	255	400	650
1935 Chrysler Airflow	255	425	650
1936 Chrysler Airflow	255	425	650
1937 Chrysler Airflow	295	490	750
1928-1932 Kingsbury Classic Series, Cabriolet Coupe	860	1430	2200
1928-1932 Kingsbury Classic Series, Roadster (top down)	780	1300	2000
1928-1932 Kingsbury Classic Series, two-window Brougham	1170	1950	3000
1928-1932 Kingsbury Classic Series, three-window Brougham	1440	2400	3700
1928-1932 Kingsbury Classic Series, Chauffeured Town Car	595	990	1525
1928-1932 Kingsbury Classic Series, Truck	975	1495	2500
1928-1932 Kingsbury Classic Series, Station Wagon	1015	1700	2600
1928-1932 Kingsbury Classic Series, Malcolm Campbell "Blue Bird"	660	1100	1700

EARLY CAST IRON TOY CARS

	GOOD	VG	EXC.
Hubley cast iron Packard, straight 8, hood raises, detailed cast motor, 11 inches long, 1927	7500	12,750	18,000
Carette tin limousine	60	98	150
1950s Thunderbird (Japan)	40	65	100
Kenton cast iron "Spider" horseless carriage	860	1430	2200
Kenton cast iron toy limousine	330	550	850
Harris tiller buggy	250	420	650
1900 Ives & Hubley spring-wind cast iron horseless carriage	1500	2600	4000
1920s German cast iron car	170	290	450

1971 SEARS REPRODUCTIONS OF 1926 CAST IRON TOY CARS

	GOOD	VG	EXC.
"1926" Touring Car (10 inches long, folding top; figurines, bright red with gold stripes and black top and fenders	195	325	500
"1926" Sedan (13 inches long, bright red with gold stripes and black top and fenders	295	490	750
"1926" Model T Ford Coupe 13 inches long, bright red with gold stripes and black top and fenders	195	325	500

BUDDY L TOY TRUCKS

	GOOD	VG	EXC.
Buddy L toy truck, model no. 200, Open Express Truck	895	1495	2300

DESCRIPTION	GOOD	VG	EXC.
Buddy L toy truck, model no. 200A, Closed Express Truck	1015	1700	2600
Buddy L toy truck, model no. 201, Dump Truck (manual)	390	650	1000
Buddy L toy truck, model no. 201A, Dump Truck (hydraulic)	585	975	1500
Buddy L toy truck, model no. 201B, Dump Truck (manual with A-frame hoist)	430	715	1100
Buddy L toy truck, model no. 202A, Sand and Gravel Truck	1290	2150	3300
Buddy L toy truck, model no. 203A, Lumber Truck	1130	1885	2900
Buddy L toy truck, model no. 206, Street Sprinkler	975	1495	2500
Buddy L toy truck, model no. 202, Coal Truck	975	1495	2500
Buddy L toy truck, model no. 206A, Oil Truck	975	1495	2500
Buddy L toy truck, model no. 207, Ice Truck	1130	1885	2900
Buddy L toy truck, model no. 203B, Baggage Truck	1290	2150	3300
Buddy L toy truck, model no. 204, Moving Van	585	975	1500
Buddy L toy truck, model no. 205, Fire truck (chemical)	975	1495	2500
Buddy L toy truck, model no. 205A, Fire truck (pumper)	780	1300	2000
Buddy L toy truck, model no. 205B, Fire truck (aerial Ladder)	505	845	1300
Buddy L toy truck, model no. 205C, Fire truck (insurance patrol)	390	650	1000
Buddy L toy truck, model no. 204A, Railway Express	1015	1700	2600
Buddy L toy bus, model no. 208, Coach Bus	1290	2150	3300
Buddy L toy truck, model no. 209, Auto Wrecker	1290	2150	3300
Buddy L toy truck, model no. 210, Model T Ford Roadster Pickup	505	845	1300
Buddy L toy car, model no. 210A, Model T Ford Roadster	470	780	1200
Buddy L toy car, model no. 210B, Model T Ford Coupe	585	975	1500
Buddy L toy truck, model no. 211, Model T Ford Dump Truck, Scoop Bed	700	1170	1800
Buddy L toy truck, model no. 211A, Model T Ford Dump Truck, Rectangular Sided	628	1040	1600
Buddy L toy truck, model no. 212, Model TT Ford, One-Ton Express Truck	975	1495	2500
Buddy L toy truck, model no. 212A, Model TT Ford, One-Ton Express Huckster	780	1300	2000

SMITH-MILLER/IRONSON TOYS **

	GOOD	VG	EXC.
Smitty toy truck, Heinz 57 Cab-Over-Engine Truck	200	325	500
Smitty toy truck, Arden Milk Cab-Over-Engine Truck	175	290	450
Smitty toy truck, Stake Bed Truck	200	325	500
Smitty toy truck, Polished shield-side body with matching cab	270	455	700
Miller-Ironson, Tow Truck	145	245	375
Miller-Ironson, Lumber Truck	155	260	400
Miller-Ironson, Hydraulic Dump Truck	155	260	400
Miller-Ironson, Lift-O-Matic Stake Truck	390	650	1000
Miller-Ironson, Semi Tractor and Trailer Truck	290	488	750
Miller-Ironson, Bekins Van Lines, Moving Truck	390	650	1000
Miller-Ironson, Fire Engine, Aerial Ladder Truck	390	650	1000
Miller-Ironson, 1954 Lincoln Capri and trailer	375	620	950

(** See Story 51 for additional Smitty and Smith-Miller pricing)

CAST IRON TOY CARS

	GOOD	VG	EXC.
1931 Arcade, "Reo Royale," Victoria Coupe (small)	500	820	1250
1931 Arcade, "Reo Royale," Victoria Coupe (10 inches long, scarce)	3900	6500	10,000

AIRFLOW TOYS AND COLLECTIBLES

	GOOD	VG	EXC.
1934 toy car, Cor Cor, Chrysler Airflow (green)	585	975	1500
1934 toy car, Cor Cor, Chrysler Airflow (maroon)	585	975	1500
1934 toy car, Cor Cor, Chrysler Airflow (bright red)	600	1000	1550
1934 toy car, Kingsbury, Chrysler Airflow, 14 inches long	295	490	750
1935 toy car, Kingsbury, Chrysler Airflow, 14 inches long	255	425	650
1936 toy car, Kingsbury, Chrysler Airflow, 14 inches long	255	425	650

DESCRIPTION	GOOD	VG	EXC.
1937 toy car, Kingsbury, Chrysler Airflow, 14 inches long	295	490	750
Toy car. Airflow four-door sedan. Steel. Painted red. All-white tires. Has bright metal waterfall grille and front bumper. Three air vents on side of hood. No skirted fenders.	165	275	425
Toy car. Airflow four-door sedan. Painted red-orange w/dark green fenders. Both front and rear fenders skirted. Metal. Dark green door/hood seams and silver hood vents painted on body. Bright metal waterfall grille and front bumper. Criss-cross pattern painted on the running boards.	49	82	125
Toy car. Airflow two-door coupe. Red-orange with dark blue fenders. Front and rear fenders full skirted. Light blue hood. Spare tire painted on rear deck lid in light and dark blue. Orange spare tire center.	49	82	125
Toy car. Airflow four-door sedan. Metal. Painted all dark green. Fully skirted front/rear fenders.	40	65	100
Toy car. Airflow two-door coupe. Sheet metal. Silver body. Black fenders and front and rear bumpers. Rear fenders fully enclosed. Bright metal waterfall grille.	60	98	150
Toy car. Airflow two-door coupe. Sheet metal. Medium blue body. Dark blue fenders and front/rear bumpers. Same as above, but different grille. Rear fenders fully enclosed. Bright metal waterfall grille.	70	115	175
Toy Car. Airflow two-door coupe. Slush metal. Painted silver gray. White balloon tires. No skirted fenders. Body details engraved in metal.	65	110	165
Toy car. Airflow two-door coupe. Metal. Painted red. Fully skirted front and rear fenders. Bright metal grille and front bumper. Key hole for key-wind mechanism on left side.	55	90	140
Model car. Airflow. Four-door sedan. Metal. Painted off-white with black top insert. Bright metal waterfall grille, headlights, bumpers and trim. Rear mounted spare tire. Fully skirted rear fender.	585	975	1500
Toy truck or bus. Airflow. Molded rubber. Painted blue. Fully skirted rear wheels. Black rubber tires.	40	65	100
Toy teardrop (airflow) trailer. Metal. Painted red. Full skirted fenders. Black rubber tires.	1050	1755	2700
Toy bus. Airflow styling. Silver. "Greyhound" embossed on sides. Slush metal. Protruding molded headlights and hood ornament. Fully skirted rear fenders. White rubber tires.	30	50	75
Toy tractor and three-compartment tanker-trailer. "Airflow" styling. Metal. Painted green. White rubber tires.	30	50	75
Toy truck. "Airflow" like styling. Sheet metal. Painted red. Bright metal grille, bullet headlights and veed front bumper. Fully enclosed front/rear fenders. Black rubber tires.	30	50	75
Model truck. Shell Airflow tanker. Painted chrome yellow with red Shell lettering. Bright metal grille, wheels, windshield frame and bumpers. Approximately nine inches long. Fully enclosed rear fenders. Black rubber tires. (Modern)	20	33	50
Toy truck. Airflow tanker. Sheet metal. Painted bright red. Four-compartment tanker body with ribs on top. Fin on front of hood. Bright metal waterfall grille, headlights and double-bar front bumper. Fully enclosed front/rear fenders. Black rubber tires.	60	100	150
Toy truck. Airflow tanker. Sheet metal. Painted medium-dark green. Has Sinclair Gasoline markings on sides. Three-compartment tanker body. No ribs on top of tank body. Snub-nose cab. Bright metal front grille, headlights and single-bar, fluted and veed, front bumper. Fully enclosed front/rear fenders. Black rubber tires.	60	100	150
Toy truck. Airflow-like styling. One-piece, but resembles fifth-wheel style house trailer. Molded rubber. Painted mostly medium blue with top of trailer in chrome yellow. Fully enclosed front and rear fenders on "cab" and rear on "trailer." Black rubber tires.	20	33	50
Toy fire truck. Airflow type styling. Hook and ladder with open cab. Painted red with yellow aerial ladder. Silver painted waterfall grille Open fenders. Black rubber tires.	23	40	60
Pedal car. Airflow styling. Late 1930s. Red and cream. Has separate "catwalk" grilles on each side and parking "lamps" on tops of fenders.	1300	2500	3500
Pedal car. Fire truck. Chrysler Airflow. Red w/white trim. Ladder rails with wooden ladders. Bell.	1440	2400	3700
Kid's ride-on toy truck. Dodge Airflow. Seat on rear dump box and T-handle juts out of cab. Metal. Painted bright red. Fully enclosed front and rear fenders with bright metal "wing" ornaments. Has bright metal grille, headlamps and bumper. White wheel discs and black rubber tires.	80	130	200
Small coaster wagon. Airflow-like styling. Metal. Painted red. Silver-painted front waterfall grille. Black rubber tires.	30	50	75
Small "Comet" coaster wagon. Airflow-like styling. Metal. Painted dark green with black "Comet" lettering. Black tiller. Black rubber tires.	350	585	900

DESCRIPTION	GOOD	VG	EXC.
Small "Comet" coaster wagon. Airflow-like styling. Metal. Painted light green with no "Comet" lettering. Pink tongue. Black tiller. Yellow wheels. (Possibly incorrect finish).	390	650	1000
Coaster wagon. Has four "Airflow" style fenders. Red wagon body. Black fenders, tongue, and tiller. White tires.	390	650	1000
Coaster wagon. Has four "Airflow" style fenders. Red wagon body. Yellow fenders, tongue, and tiller. Black tires.	390	650	1000
Coaster wagon. Has four red "Airflow" style fenders with silver "wing" decorations. Red wagon body with yellow speedlines and lettering graphics. Red tongue, and tiller. Silver wheels with black rubber tires.	390	650	1000
Flash Strat-O-Wagon coaster wagon. Has four "Airflow" style fenders. Red wagon body with red, blue, white and yellow rocketship graphics. Body is basically teardrop shaped with flat fins extending from rear. Four streamlined black fenders. Black axles and tiller.	450	780	1200
Large coaster wagon. Airflow styling. Red with white trim. Black tiller. Has small "headlights" in front. Curved-horizontal grille impression. Skirted front and rear fenders. Red spoke wheels and whitewall tires.	450	780	1200
Large coaster wagon. Airflow style. Green with cream trim. Black tiller. Has small "headlights" in front. Waterfall grille. Skirted front/rear fenders. Cream spoke wheels and whitewall tires.	400	600	1000
1938 Edw. K. Tryon Co. (Philadelphia) No. 710 Streamlined Pedal Bike. Has Airflow-like styling. 22 inches long overall. Seat height is 10-1/2 inches. Red and cream. Front wheel eight inches; rear five inches. One-half inch rubber tires. Black rubber pedals. One-piece body. Came six-in-carton to dealers. Weight 10 pounds. Originally cost $1.60 each (wholesale)	450	780	1200
Baby buggy. "Airflow" styled chrome-plated fenders. Blue plaid fabric. Chrome hubcaps. Black rubber tires.	120	195	300
Auto jack. Airflow-like styling. Painted bright orange-red. Rear section has fin-like shape.	43	72	110

ERECTOR SET

DESCRIPTION	GOOD	VG	EXC.
1934 Erector set (with three motors and two transmissions)	32	52	80

SMITTY AND SMITH-MILLER

DESCRIPTION	GOOD	VG	EXC.
Toy truck, Smitty Cab-Over, model 301-W Wrecker	175	292	450
Toy truck, Smitty Cab-Over, model 401-W Wrecker	175	292	450
Toy truck, Smitty Cab-Over, model 302-M Materials	175	292	450
Toy truck, Smitty Cab-Over, model 402-M Materials	175	292	450
Toy truck, Smitty Cab-Over, model *303-R and 403-R Rack	215	360	550
Toy truck, Smitty Cab-Over, model 304-K Kraft	215	360	550
Toy truck, Smitty Cab-Over, model 404-B Bank	215	360	550
Toy truck, Smitty Cab-Over, model *305-T and 405-T Triton	215	360	550
Toy truck, Smitty Cab-Over, model 306-C Coca Cola	195	325	500
Toy truck, Smitty Cab-Over, model *305-L Lumber	155	260	400
Toy truck, Smitty Cab-Over, model 307-L Logger	155	260	400
Toy truck, Smitty Cab-Over, model 308-V Lyon Van	215	360	550
Toy truck, Smitty Cab-Over, model 307-V Lyon Van	215	360	550
Toy truck, Smitty Cab-Over, model 408-H Machinery Hauler	155	260	400
Toy truck, Smitty Cab-Over, model 309-S Super Cargo	165	275	425
Toy truck, Smitty Cab-Over, model 409-G Mobilgas (also Mobiloil)	235	390	600
Toy truck, Smitty Cab-Over, model 310-H Hi-Way Freighter	255	425	650
Toy truck, Smitty Cab-Over, model 410-F Transcontinental Freight	255	425	650
Toy truck, Smitty Cab-Over, model 311-E/411-E Silver streak Express	255	425	650
Toy truck, Smitty Cab-Over, model 312-P and 412-P P.I.E. Semi Truck	290	488	750
Toy truck, Smitty Cab-Over, model 4X-O Dump/Tractor (Remote-control, steerable)	215	360	550
Toy truck, Smitty Cab-Over, model 1954-401 Tow Truck	145	245	375
Toy truck, Smitty Cab-Over, model 1954-402 Dump	155	260	400
Toy truck, Smitty Cab-Over, model 1954-403 Scoop Dump	175	295	450

* Same truck but a change in wheel style. All other trucks are significantly different in other ways.

DESCRIPTION	GOOD	VG	EXC.
Toy truck, Smith-Miller, Mack Model B, model 04 Lumte Truck & optional trailer	390	650	1000
Toy truck, Smith-Miller, Mack Model B, model 05 Silver Streak	470	780	1200

DESCRIPTION	GOOD	VG	EXC.
Toy truck, Smith-Miller, Mack Model B, model 06 Bekins Van	380	650	1000
Toy truck, Smith-Miller, Mack Model B, model 07 Searchlight Truck	470	780	1200
Toy truck, Smith-Miller, Mack Model B, model 08 Blue Diamond Dump	390	650	1000
Toy truck, Smith-Miller, Mack Model B, model 09 P.I.E. Semi Truck	290	488	750
Toy truck, Smith-Miller, Mack Model B, model 10 Aerial Ladder	390	650	1000

BUDDY "L" 1924 MODEL T FORD "FLIVVER"

DESCRIPTION	GOOD	VG	EXC.
Toy truck, Buddy L, 1924 Model T Ford model no. 210 Roadster Pickup, size 12 x 5-5/8 x 6-3/4 inches (canvas top and operating tailgate)	505	845	1300
Toy car, Buddy L, 1924 Model T Ford model no. 210A Roadster, size 11 x 5-5/8 x 7 inches (black, canvas top)	470	780	1200
Toy car, Buddy L, 1924 Model T Ford model no. 210B Doctor's Coupe, size 11 x 5-5/8 x 7 inches (black)	585	975	1500
Toy car, Buddy L, 1924 Model T Ford model no. 210B Doctor's Coupe, size 11 x 5-5/8 x 7 inches (black; same as above with decal variation)	585	975	1500
Toy truck, Buddy L, 1924 Model T Ford model no. 211 Dump Cart, size 12-1/2 x 5-5/8 x 4-1/2 inches	700	1170	1800
Toy truck, Buddy L, 1924 Model T Ford model no. 211 Dump Cart, size 12-1/2 x 5-5/8 x 4-1/2 inches (same as above with decal variation)	700	1170	1800
Toy truck, Buddy L, 1924 Model T Ford model no. 211A Dump Truck, size 11 x 5-5/8 x 4-1/2 inches	625	1040	1600
Toy truck, Buddy L, 1924 Model T Ford model no. 211A Dump Truck, size 11 x 5-5/8 x 4-1/2 inches (same as above with decal variation)	625	1040	1600
Toy truck, Buddy L, 1924 Ford Model TT, 1-Ton, model 212 Express, size 14-1/4 x 5-5/8 x 7 inches	975	1495	2500
Toy truck, Buddy L, 1924 Ford Model TT, 1-Ton, model no. 212A Delivery Truck or Truckster, size 14 x 5-5/8 x 6-3/4 inch	780	1300	2000
Toy truck, Buddy L, 1924 Ford Model TT, 1-Ton, model no. 212B U.S. Mail Truck, size 14 x 5-5/8 x 6-3/4 inch	975	1495	2500
Toy truck, Buddy L, 1924 Ford Model TT, 1-Ton, model no. 212 Stake Bed Truck, size 14 x 5-5/8 x 7 inches.	780	1300	2000

DOEPKE TOY TRUCKS/TRACTORS/CARS

DESCRIPTION	GOOD	VG	EXC.
Toy truck, Doepke, Model no. 2000 Woolridge Earth Hauler (Doepke's first toy)	155	260	400
Toy tractor, Doepke, Model no. 2001 Barber-Greene Bucket Loader on steel treads	200	325	500
Toy truck, Doepke, Model no. 2002 Jaeger Concrete Mixer	255	425	650

1948

Toy tractor, Doepke, Model no. 2006 Adams Road Grader	100	160	250

1949

Toy truck, Doepke, Model no. 2007 Unit Mobile Crane 1950-1953	115	200	300
Toy truck, Doepke, Model no. 2008 American LaFrance Aerial Ladder	165	275	425
Toy truck, Doepke, Model no. 2009 Euclid Earth Hauling Truck	115	200	300
Toy truck, Doepke, Model no. 2010 American LaFrance Pumper Truck	155	260	400
Toy tractor, Doepke, Model no. 2011 Heiliner Earth Scraper	185	310	475
Toy tractor, Doepke, Model no. 2012 Caterpillar D-6 Bulldozer	185	310	475
Toy tractor, Doepke, Model no. 2013 Barber Greene Bucket Loader on wheels	235	390	600
Toy fire truck, Doepke, Model no. 2014 American LaFrance Aerial Ladder truck (*)	175	295	450

1954

Toy tractor, Doepke, Model no. 2015 Clark, Airport Tractor and Baggage Trailers	390	650	1000
Toy car, Doepke, Model no. 2017, "MT" Automobile, MG-TD	200	325	500

1955

Toy car, Doepke, Model no. 2018 Jaguar XK120 Roadster	255	425	650
Toy truck, Doepke, Model no. 2023 American LaFrance Searchlight Truck	585	975	1500

(*) **NOTE:** The no. 2013 American LaFrance Aerial Ladder is substantially different than the no. 2008 American LaFrance Aerial Ladder Truck. The newer one has the bell at middle of side.

STURDITOY TOY TRUCKS

1925 toy truck, Sturditoy, Fire Truck American LaFrance, Open Cab Box Truck	585	975	1500
1920s toy truck, Sturditoy, ARM Truck	780	1300	2000

DESCRIPTION	GOOD	VG	EXC.
1920s toy truck, Sturditoy, Enclosed Cab Fixed Bed Truck	390	650	1000
1920s toy truck, Sturditoy, Huckster	390	650	1000
1920s toy truck, Sturditoy, Low-Side Dump Truck	390	650	1000
1920s toy truck, Sturditoy, High-Side Dump Truck	700	1170	1800
1920s toy fire truck, Sturditoy, Chemical pumper truck	700	1170	1800
1920s toy truck, Sturditoy, Ambulance	700	1170	1800
1920s toy truck, Sturditoy, American LaFrance Water Tower	895	1495	2300
1920s toy truck, Sturditoy, Coal Truck	975	1495	2500
1920s toy truck, Sturditoy, Armored Car	975	1495	2500
1920s toy truck, Sturditoy, Two-panel Screenside U.S. Mail Truck	700	1170	1800
1920s toy truck, Sturditoy, Police Patrol Truck	780	1300	2000
1920s toy truck, Sturditoy, REA Truck	470	780	1200
1920s toy truck, Sturditoy, Two-axle Fixed Tank Truck	505	845	1300
1920s toy truck, Sturditoy, Semi Oil Tanker (red)	1170	1950	3000
1920s toy truck, Sturditoy, Semi Oil Tanker (green, rare)	1550	2600	4000
1920s toy truck, Sturditoy, Dairy Tanker (white)	390	650	1000

CONWAY TOY CARS

1948 toy car, Conway, Packard Convertible (clockwork motor; 12 x 5 inches; cream yellow; battery-powered electric horn and headlights)	70	115	175
1949 toy car, Conway, Kaiser Convertible (plastic body; clockwork motor; 10 inches long)	70	115	175
Toy truck, Conway, Baby Ruth/Butterfinger Candy Truck (plastic and plated metal)	40	65	100

DEALER PROMOTIONAL MODELS

1978 Jo-Han, Cadillac Coupe de Ville (Basil Green Metallic)	10	16	25
1978 Jo-Han, Cadillac Coupe de Ville (Mediterranean Blue Metallic)	10	16	25
1978 Jo-Han, Cadillac Coupe de Ville (Wesstern Saddle Metallic)	10	16	25
1978 Jo-Han, Cadillac Coupe de Ville (Carmine Red)	10	16	25
1978 MPC, Chevrolet Monza	14	23	35
1978 MPC, Chevette	6	10	15
1978 MPC, Chevrolet Monte Carlo	10	16	25

(**NOTE:** The Chevrolet Monza, Chevette and Monte Carlo all came in three different colors, Dark Camel, Light Blue and Medium Green)

1978 MPC, Corvette (all-Silver without "lip" on paint parting line)	56	95	145
1978 MPC, Corvette (all-Silver with "lip" on paint parting line) (Rare)	60	100	150
1978 MPC, Corvette Silver Anniversary (Charcoal and Silver)	20	32	50
1978 MPC, Pontiac Firebird Trans Am (Starlight Black)	15	23	35
1978 MPC, Pontiac Firebird Trans Am (Platinum Metallic)	15	23	35
1978 MPC Plymouth Volare without Road Runner decal option (Starlight Blue Metallic)	12	20	30
1978 MPC Plymouth Volare without Road Runner decal option (Spitfire Orange)	12	20	30
1978 MPC Plymouth Volare with Road Runner decal option (Starlight Blue Metallic)	15	23	35
1978 MPC Plymouth Volare with Road Runner decal option (Spitfire Orange)	15	23	35
1978 MPC Dodge Monaco (Augusta Green Metallic)	12	20	30
1978 MPC Dodge Monaco (Starlight Blue Metallic)	12	20	30

MATCHBOX MODELS

1956 Matchbox, model 27-A-1, Bedford Low Loader Truck (Two-tone)	175	295	450
1950s Matchbox, model 7-A-1, Horsedrawn Milk Float	30	50	75
1970s Starsky & Hutch Ford Torino	35	55	85
1970s Matchbox, "Models of Yesteryear," 1938 Lagonda	10	16	25
1970s Matchbox, "Models of Yesteryear," 1934 Riley	10	16	25
1970s Matchbox, "Models of Yesteryear," 1928 Mercedes	15	23	35

Model Cars

MODEL CARS

AMT 1960 Buick dealer promotional model (with portholes)	60	100	150
AMT 1960 Buick dealer promotional model (without portholes)	60	100	150
AMT 1960 Buick chassis, dealer promotional model (dealer only edition)	155	260	400
AMT 1960 Rambler (see-through body in white)	20	32	50
AMT 1962 Chevrolet dealer promotional model	135	230	350
AMT 1962 Chevrolet dealer promotional model (in bubble with 1911 Chevrolet model)	275	455	700

DESCRIPTION	GOOD	VG	EXC.
AMT 3-in-1 model car kit, 1958 Edsel (first year; most common)	120	195	300
AMT 3-in-1 model car kit, 1958 Buick (first year; most common)	110	180	275
AMT 3-in-1 model car kit, 1958 Ford (first year; hardest to locate)	117	195	300
AMT 3-IN-1 model car kit, 1958 Chevrolet (first year; second hardest to locate)	117	195	300
Jo-Han model car kit, 1959 Plymouth (first Jo-Han models)	78	130	200
Jo-Han model car kit, 1959 Dodge Custom Royal (first Jo-Han models)	78	130	200
Jo-Han model car kit, 1959 Cadillac (first Jo-Han models)	78	130	200
Jo-Han model kit, 1959 Oldsmobile (first Jo-Han models)	78	130	200
MPC model kit, 1964 Corvette (first MPC model)	55	85	130
Monogram dealer promotional model, 1955 Cadillac Coupe de Ville	212	325	500
Monogram dealer promotional model, 1955 Cadillac Convertible	212	325	500
Monogram dealer promotional model, 1956 Cadillac Coupe de Ville	212	325	500
Revell model car kit, 1957 Ford Country Squire Station Wagon (1/25th scale)	92	153	235
Revell model car kit, 1957 Ford Ranchero Sedan-Pickup (1/25th scale)	39	65	100
Revell model car kit, 1959 Ford Skyliner Convertible (1/25th scale)	30	50	75

DEALER PROMOTIONAL MODELS

	GOOD	VG	EXC.
Dealer promotional model, 1934 Studebaker National Products Company	165	275	425
Dealer promotional model, 1951 Rambler, National Products Company/Banthrico, Pot metal	145	245	375
Dealer promotional model, 1951 Packard, Henney ambulance (1/20th scale hot-stamped acetate)	212	325	500
Dealer promotional model, 1956 AMC Rambler, Clear plastic	117	195	300
Dealer promotional model, 1957 AMC Rambler, Clear plastic	155	260	400
Dealer promotional model, 1948-1953 Jo-Han Chevrolet (B.F. Goodrich service truck)	98	165	250
Dealer promotional model, 1957 Pontiac, Bonneville convertible, designed by Jack K. Stuart as PMD General Manager Award	98	165	250
Dealer promotional model, 1958 Pontiac, Bonneville Sport Coupe, designed by Jack K. Stuart as PMD General Manager Award	98	165	250
1959 model car, Jo-Han, Plymouth Police Car	88	145	225
1962 model car, Jo-Han, Dodge Police Car	78	130	200
1961-1962 model car, Jo-Han, Plymouth Police Car "Car 54 Where Are You?"	25	40	50
Mills Bakery 1/25th scale delivery van Wilson Dairy 1/25th scale delivery van	14	23	35
1948 Chevrolet, promotional model (pot metal)	127	212	325

AMT MODELS

	GOOD	VG	EXC.
AMT Datsun 280 Turbo ZX model car kit	6	10	16
AMT 1972 Chevelle "Red Alert" dragster model car kit	18	30	45

DIE-CAST MODEL CARS

	GOOD	VG	EXC.
Die-cast model, Precision Miniatures, 1/43rd scale, 1965 Shelby Mustang GT-350	30	55	80
Die-cast model, Precision Miniatures, 1/43rd scale, 1966 Shelby Mustang GT-350	30	50	75
Die-cast model, Precision Miniatures, 1/43rd scale, 1966 Shelby Mustang GT-350H (Hertz Rent-A-Car)	30	50	75
Die-cast model, Conrad, vintage American LaFrance fire truck, 1/43rd scale	18	30	60
Die-cast model, Eliger (French), 1/43rd scale, 1933 Ford pickup	15	25	35
Die-cast model, Eliger (French), 1/43rd scale, 1934 Ford pickup	15	25	35
Die-cast model, Eliger (French), 1/43rd scale, 1958 Chrysler New Yorker Convertible	30	50	75
Die-cast model, Brooklin, 1/43rd scale, model no. 17, 1952 Studebaker Starlight Coupe	31	52	80
Die-cast model, Mini Auto Emporium, 1/43rd scale, 1959 Cadillac Series 62 convertible	40	65	100
Die-cast model, EnCo Models, 1/43rd scale, Facel Vega	40	65	100
Die-cast model, Vitesse, 1/43rd scale, 1956 Ford Sunliner Convertible	40	65	100
Die-cast model, Vitesse, 1/43rd scale, 1956 Ford Victoria Hardtop	30	55	80

DESCRIPTION	GOOD	VG	EXC.
Die-cast model, Brooklin, 1/43rd scale, 1953 Oldsmobile Fiesta Convertible	60	95	150
Die-cast model, Motor City USA, 1/43rd scale, 1950 Ford Custom DeLuxe	30	55	80
Die-cast model, Western Models, 1/43rd scale, 1959 DeSoto Adventurer convertible	30	55	80
Die-cast model, Great American Dream Machines, 1/43rd scale, 1952 Chrysler C-200 dream car	30	55	80

EARLY MODEL CARS

	GOOD	VG	EXC.
Model car kit, Hudson Miniatures, balsa wood	13	22	35
Model car kit, Revell "Highway Pioneers" 1/32nd scale, plastic	7	10	15
1954 Model car kit, Keepsake, kit no. K-10, "1902 Rambler," 1/32nd scale	13	22	35
1954 Model car kit, Keepsake, kit no. K-11, "1909 Hupmobile," 1/32nd scale	13	22	35
1960-1962 Model car kit, Strombecker, kit no. T-2, "1902 Rambler" (reissue of Keepsake K-10)	10	15	25
1960-1962 Model car kit, Strombecker, kit no. T-1, "1909 Hupmobile" (reissue of Keepsake K-10)	10	15	25
1960-1962 Model car kit, Strombecker, kit no. T-2, "1902 Rambler" (reissue of Keepsake K-10)	10	15	25
1960-1962 Model car kit, Strombecker, kit no. T-1, "1909 Hupmobile" (reissue of Keepsake K-10)	10	15	25
1964 Model car kit, Hawk, kit no. 634, "1902 Rambler" (reissue of Keepsake and Strombecker kits)	10	15	25
1964 Model car kit, Hawk, kit no. 635, "1909 Hupmobile" (reissue of Keepsake and Strombecker kits)	10	15	25
1969 Model car kit, Hawk, kit no. 300, "1902 Rambler" (reissue of Keepsake and Strombecker kits; gold-plated; includes display case)	7	10	15
1969 Model car kit, Hawk, kit no. 301, "1909 Hupmobile" (reissue of Keepsake and Strombecker kits; gold-plated; includes display case)	7	10	15
Model car, Miley's, Model T Ford Parcel Post Van. Seven inches long. Black with red wheels. Parcel post graphics. (Cast aluminum model; reproduction of 1930s cast iron toy)	25	40	50
Model truck, Miley's, Model T Ford Parcel Post Van. Seven inches long. Black with red wheels. Parcel post graphics. (Cast aluminum model; reproduction of 1930s cast iron toy)	25	40	50
Model truck, Miley's, Model T Telephone Line Maintenance Truck. Seven inches long. (Cast aluminum model; reproduction of 1930s cast iron toy)	25	40	50
Model truck, Miley's, Model T Telephone Construction Truck. Seven inches long. (Cast aluminum model; reproduction of 1930s cast iron toy)	25	40	50

SCRATCH-BUILT MODELS

Prices inestimable

DIE-CAST MODEL

	GOOD	VG	EXC.
Model car, Dinky, model no. 39a, Packard Super 8 Touring Sedan	75	115	150
Model car, Dinky, model no. 39b, Oldsmobile Six Sedan	65	100	130
Model car, Dinky, model no. 39c, Lincoln-Zephyr Coupe	80	120	160
Model car, Dinky, model no. 39d, Buick "Viceroy" Saloon	70	110	140
Model car, Dinky, model no. 39e, Chrysler Royal Sedan	70	110	140
Model car, Dinky, model no. 39f, Studebaker State Commander Sedan	65	100	130
Model car, Precision Miniatures, model no. PM018 1965 Mustang Convertible with Indianapolis 500 Pace Car decals	85	130	175
Model car, Precision Miniatures, model no. PM019 1965 Mustang Fastback	75	115	150
Model car, Brooklin, 1940 Cadillac	35	50	75
Model car, Brooklin, 1949 Mercury Club Coupe	25	45	65
Model car, Brooklin, 1953 Studebaker, Indiana State Police Car	30	50	80
Model car, Brooklin, 1954 Dodge Indianapolis 500 Pace Car	40	65	100
Model car, Mini-Marque 43, Packard Convertible	40	65	100

FISHER CRAFTSMAN GUILD MODELS

Prices inestimable

Acknowledgements

Special thanks go to the following automobilia price analysts: Rich Adams; Terry V. Boyce; Ken Buttolph; Roger Case; Dennis Doty; Arthur Evans; Tom Hammel; Stan Hurd; Eric von Klinger; John Koutre; Mark Larson; Skip Marketti; Bill McBride; Bonnie Miller; Bruce Perry (Yellow Dog Garage); Greg Plonski; Jan Prasher; Joseph F. Russell; Ray Schirmer; William D. Siuru, Jr.; Ed Tilley; Michael J. Welch; William A. Winslow and George R. Zaninovich.

Additional thanks for photographic aids go to Vicki Cwick of the Sears Archives; Chrysler Airflow collector Frank Kleptz; and the Smithsonian Institution.

Sources

The following are sources to contact for additional information about different types of automobilia:

AUTO ADS

Bill McBride
McBride Auto Ads
585 Prospect Avenue
West Hartford, CT 06105

Bruce Perry
Yellow Dog Garage
10 Bank Street
Bradford, Pennsylvania 16701

BOOKS

Ed Tilley
PO Box 4233
Cary, NC 27519
(Also promotional models)

COLLECTIBLES
(General)

Jay Katelle
Jay Katelle Collectibles
3721 Farwell
Amarillo, TX 79109

Joseph F. Russell
Distinctive Early Motoring Collectibles
455 Ollie Street
Cottage Grove, WI 53527-9622

William Winslow
PO Box 330
Galena, IL 61036-0389

DECANTERS

Rich Adams
355 Highway 41
Caledonia, WI 53108

International Association of Jim Beam
Bottle and Specialty Clubs
2015 Burlington Avenue
Kenanee, IL 61443

LITERATURE

Applegate & Applegate
Box 1
Annville, PA 17003

Stan Hurd
W3008 Palmer Road
Rio, WI 53960

MODEL CARS

Jerry Byrne
3613 Russett Lane
Northbrook, IL 60062

Dennis Doty
Model Car Journal
1109 Mohawk Drive
Irving, TX 75061

John Marshall
8573 LaBaya Avenue
Fountain View, CA 92708

TOYS

Micheal J. Welch
Trucks & Stuff
3700 Route 6 RR2
Eastham, MA 02642

George R. Zaninovich
28562 S. Monterenia Drive
San Pedro, CA 90732

TRADING CARDS

Greg Plonski
93 Beaver Drive
Kings Park, NY 11754-2209

Harry A. Victor
1408-18th Avenue
San Francisco, CA 94122